CAMBRIDGE TEXTS IN THE
HISTORY OF PHILOSOPHY

IMMANUEL KANT
*Observations on the Feeling of the Beautiful and
Sublime and Other Writings*

T0381766

CAMBRIDGE TEXTS IN THE HISTORY OF PHILOSOPHY

Series editors

KARL AMERIKS
Professor of Philosophy, University of Notre Dame

DESMOND M. CLARKE

Emeritus Professor of Philosophy, University College Cork

The main objective of Cambridge Texts in the History of Philosophy is to expand the range, variety, and quality of texts in the history of philosophy which are available in English. The series includes texts by familiar names (such as Descartes and Kant) and also by less well-known authors. Wherever possible, texts are published in complete and unabridged form, and translations are specially commissioned for the series. Each volume contains a critical introduction together with a guide to further reading and any necessary glossaries and textual apparatus. The volumes are designed for student use at undergraduate and postgraduate level, and will be of interest not only to students of philosophy but also to a wider audience of readers in the history of science, the history of theology, and the history of ideas.

For a list of titles published in the series, please see end of book.

IMMANUEL KANT

Observations on the Feeling of the Beautiful and Sublime and Other Writings

EDITED BY

PATRICK FRIERSON
Whitman College

PAUL GUYER
University of Pennsylvania

WITH AN INTRODUCTION BY

PATRICK FRIERSON

CAMBRIDGE
UNIVERSITY PRESS

CAMBRIDGE
UNIVERSITY PRESS

University Printing House, Cambridge CB2 8BS, United Kingdom

Cambridge University Press is part of the University of Cambridge.

It furthers the University's mission by disseminating knowledge in the pursuit of education, learning and research at the highest international levels of excellence.

www.cambridge.org
Information on this title: www.cambridge.org/9780521711135

© Cambridge University Press 2011

First published 2011

A catalogue record for this publication is available from the British Library

ISBN 978-0-521-71113-5 Paperback

Contents

Introduction

Kant in the 1760s

On April 22, 1764, Immanuel Kant turned 40 years old, reaching what would turn out to be the midpoint of his life. From his humble beginnings as the son of a father who was a harness maker and a mother who was a devoted Pietist, Kant had risen through school to graduate in philosophy from the University of Königsberg; and 1764 marked the year in which Kant was first offered a professorship, the highest honor of his academic guild. By the end of his life, forty years later, Kant had become the most influential philosopher in Europe. This influence was due primarily to a series of *Critiques*, the first of which – Kant's *Critique of Pure Reason* – was not published until 1781, when Kant was already 56 years old. In the wake of that "all-crushing" book, Kant developed a philosophical system to make sense of our understanding of the world and moral obligations, an a priori system within which pure reason held sway.

But in 1764 Kant was not offered a professorship in metaphysics or logic, but in rhetoric and poetry. In this year he published a short book – *Observations on the Feeling of the Beautiful and the Sublime* – and an essay ("Maladies"), both written in a playful and entertaining style that one would expect from a teacher of rhetoric. He also published an elegant though more analytical *Inquiry Concerning the Distinctness of the Principles of Natural Theology and Morality*, conceived as a potential "Prize Essay" for the Berlin Academy. These works take up the study of the world "more with the eye of an observer than of the philosopher"

(2:207).[1] They show a Kant who is younger, more empirical, more playful, and more romantic than the Kant who would emerge over the next several decades. In fact, starting with the Russian occupation of Königsberg in 1758, Kant attended regular dinner parties, and his elegance and wit earned him the title "the life of the party."[2] Kant had friends from a wide variety of social classes and regularly attended dinners and parties with military officers, bankers, merchants, noblemen and noblewomen. During this period he even warns his young student Herder "not [to] brood so much over his books, but rather follow his own example."[3]

Nonetheless, Kant did not *wholly* give up brooding over books. In the 1760s he was immersed in the latest philosophical developments in Germany and beyond. He was intensely engaged in debates between religious Pietist followers of Augustus Crusius and rationalist "Wolffians" (heirs of Leibniz). He was sympathetic with a growing movement of *Popularphilosophie* that sought a less abstract and more applicable philosophy, a movement exemplified by Christian Thomasius, who advocated philosophy conducted in "an easy manner, comprehensible to all rational persons of whatever station or sex."[4] British philosophers were also increasingly important: David Hume's *Enquiry Concerning Human Understanding* was first translated into German in 1755; Francis Hutcheson's *A System of Moral Philosophy* in 1756; and Edmund Burke's *Philosophical Enquiry into the Origin of Our Ideas of the Sublime and the Beautiful* was made popular through a review written by Moses Mendelssohn in 1758. Kant personally knew a translator of Locke's works, and one of his closest friends in Königsberg was an English merchant who kept Kant up to date on the latest gossip about British philosophers. Of these, Hume was to have the most lasting influence on Kant. In his *Prolegomena* (1783), Kant writes, "the remembrance of David Hume was the very thing that many

---

[1] Throughout, references to Kant's works are to the Academy Edition volume and page number. These page numbers are available in the margins of the present volume (and in the margins of *The Cambridge Edition of the Works of Immanuel Kant*, from which many of the selections in this volume are taken). Consistent with this overall practice, throughout this introduction I cite *Remarks* in accordance with the Academy Edition pagination. Marie Rischmüller's 1991 edition of *Remarks* is a preferable scholarly source but is not as widely available as the Academy Edition. The translation of *Remarks* in this volume includes both Academy Edition and Rischmüller pagination.
[2] Quoted in John H. Zammito, *Kant, Herder, and the Birth of Anthropology*, University of Chicago Press, 2002, pp. 85–6.
[3] Quoted in Manfred Kuehn, *Kant*, Cambridge University Press, 2001, p. 116.
[4] Quoted in Zammito, *Kant, Herder*, p. 9, translation revised.

years ago first interrupted my *dogmatic slumber* and gave a completely different direction to my researches in the field of speculative philosophy" (4:260). With respect to moral philosophy, Hutcheson and Shaftesbury had a significant influence on Kant (see *Inquiry* 2:300). And British *philosophy* was not all that Kant was reading. His notes contain references to British novels by Fielding and Richardson, Alexander Pope's poetry, and the English *Spectator*, a daily magazine written in England by Joseph Addison and Richard Steele during the years 1711–12.

More important than these British influences, however, was the French philosopher Jean-Jacques Rousseau. Rousseau's novel *Julie* was published in 1761 and both *Emile* (a book tracing the moral and intellectual development of a boy from childhood to adulthood) and *The Social Contract* (laying out Rousseau's political philosophy) were published in 1762. Kant certainly read these works by the time he published *Observations* (see 2:247). But when Kant writes his *Remarks* in 1764–5, we find his most sustained and explicit engagement with Rousseau. He refers explicitly to Rousseau or his works (especially *Emile*) over twenty times, and infuses his discussions of human nature with Rousseauian themes and insights. In these *Remarks*, Kant also explains the profound effect Rousseau had upon his conception of himself as a philosopher:

> I myself am a researcher by inclination. I feel the entire thirst for cognition and the eager restlessness to proceed further in it, as well as the satisfaction at every acquisition. There was a time when I believed this alone could constitute the honor of mankind, and I despised the rabble who knows nothing. *Rousseau* has set me right. This blinding prejudice vanishes, I learn to honor human beings, and I would feel by far less useful than the common laborer if I did not believe that this consideration could impart a value to all others in order to establish the rights of humanity. (20:44; see, too, *Herder Lectures* 27:39)

In addition to reading and socializing, Kant spent much of his time during the 1760s teaching. Although he was not a "Professor," Kant was a "Magister" at the University of Königberg; he was permitted to teach university courses, but received no salary from the university. Kant collected fees from students, and so his income depended wholly upon the frequency and popularity of his lectures. As a result, he devoted extensive time to preparing lectures. He taught between sixteen and twenty-four hours a week, in courses ranging from physical geography and ethics to mathematics and metaphysics. Kant was an excellent lecturer. Herder, Kant's student during these years, writes: "Jest, wit, and caprice were at his command – but always at the right time so that everyone laughed. His public lecture was like an entertaining conversation. He spoke about his author, thought on his own, and often beyond the author . . . I never noticed the smallest trace of arrogance."[5] Kant's teaching was not merely a way of earning money. In his "Announcement" – a sort of advertisement for courses, printed at Kant's expense – Kant articulates a vision for teaching, in which pupils first exercise their judgment and only gradually "learn to philosophize" (2:306). Heavily influenced by *Popularphilosophie*, Kant first and foremost promises to teach each student "something which he can understand, on account of its easiness; . . . and . . . something which he can use, because of the frequency with which it can be given application to life" (2:309–10). Kant offered his students the world-wisdom (*Weltweisheit*)[6] necessary for becoming a good world citizen in such a way that "elegance and appreciation of the beautiful in nature and literature were more important . . . than dry book knowledge."[7]

The Kant of the 1760s, in his breadth of reading, his style of teaching, and his published work, was well suited for a professorship in rhetoric. But Kant turned down this position, waiting six more years before finally being awarded the professorship in logic and metaphysics that he held for the rest of his life and that enabled him to found the "Critical Philosophy" for which he is now famous. We cannot be certain why Kant held out for a professorship in metaphysics and logic when the position in rhetoric and poetry was offered, but it clearly reflects his ambivalence, even during this period of elegance and appreciation for literary pursuits, about his own proper role as a philosopher. This ambivalence appears most strikingly in Kant's teaching throughout this period. On the one hand, his emphasis on practical world-wisdom led him to develop a new course in physical geography (see "Announcement"), to which he eventually added pragmatic anthropology. On the other hand, Kant taught traditional philosophical disciplines such as logic or metaphysics in a

---

[5] See Kuehn, *Kant*, pp. 129–30.
[6] On the term *Weltweisheit*, see Zammito, *Kant, Herder*, pp. 18–23.
[7] Kuehn, *Kant*, p. 133.

rationalist way, while seeking even in these courses to instill independent philosophical thinking. Kant's publications show a similar ambivalence, including both rigorous philosophical treatises in metaphysics, physics, and logic,[8] and popular works, such as *Observations*. Kant would later identify the age of 40 as the earliest age at which one might establish a "character" (7:294), a fixed way of living in the world. The writings in this volume show that by age 40, Kant had not yet established the character that would eventually define him. Instead, these are years of Kant's greatest philosophical vacillation and ambiguity, but they are the years out of which his character would be born.

The texts

The texts collected in the present volume hint at what Kant might have become had he embraced the more elegant and popular style of philosophizing that clearly attracted him during the 1760s. *Observations* is a text written "more with the eye of an observer than of a philosopher" (2:207). Kant's "Essay on the Maladies of the Head," like *Observations*, is light-hearted and elegant, aimed for the general audience of the *Königsberg Scholarly and Political Newspaper* in which it was published. The "Announcement" and lecture notes from Kant's course in moral philosophy show the manifestation of this popular emphasis in his teaching, and *Inquiry*, while more rigorous than *Observations*, shows a similar concern. Finally, the *Remarks* and *Notes* help to show both the directions in which Kant's popular philosophy was taking him and his own struggle from this popular emphasis towards what would eventually become his identity as a Critical philosopher.

Observations on the Feeling of the Beautiful and the Sublime represents the pinnacle of Kant's popular writing.[9] While all of the writings collected in this volume were written by Kant during a period in which he aimed at popularity and accessibility, *Observations on the Beautiful and Sublime* is

---

[8] See, for example, the works collected in *The Cambridge Edition of the Works of Immanuel Kant: Theoretical Philosophy 1755–1770* (translated and edited by David Walford in collaboration with Ralf Meerbote), Cambridge University Press, 1992.

[9] This paragraph and the next borrow from Paul Guyer's introduction to this work from *The Cambridge Edition of the Works of Immanuel Kant: Anthropology, History, Pedagogy*, Cambridge University Press, 2009.

the most polished. Kant starts with a general discussion of the distinction between feelings for the sublime and for the beautiful. To anyone familiar with either Edmund Burke's *A Philosophical Enquiry into the Origin of Our Ideas of the Sublime and Beautiful* or Kant's own later treatment of the beautiful and sublime in the *Critique of the Power of Judgment*, it will be clear why Kant entitled his book *Observations* rather than *Philosophical Enquiry*. Kant's observation that "the sublime *touches*, the beautiful *charms*," or his distinction between "the terrifying sublime, . . . the noble, and . . . the magnificent" hardly measure up to the standards of a worked-out aesthetic *theory*. But Kant *uses* these distinctions between the beautiful and the sublime to offer up a set of observations about human nature that fits well into the tradition of empirical reflections on human nature that includes such works as Hume's "Of National Character."

Observations has four parts. The short first section uses examples to distinguish the beautiful from the sublime. The second applies this distinction to human beings, both in general and with respect to different "temperaments" or personalities. In this second section, Kant develops his account of "true virtue" as "the feeling of the beauty and the dignity of human nature" (2:216). The third section focuses on differences between the sexes, emphasizing that although "each sex will unite both" beauty and sublimity, "the fair sex . . . [is] characterized by the mark of the *beautiful*" while men "could lay claim to the designation of the *noble sex*" (2:228). The fourth and final section distinguishes between different "national characters" in terms of beauty and sublimity, claiming, for example, that "the *Italians* and the *French* . . . most distinguish themselves in the feeling of the *beautiful*, but the *Germans*, the *English*, and the *Spaniards* . . . in the feeling of the *sublime*" (2:243). This is also the section (see more below) in which Kant includes reprehensible generalizations about non-European races.

During the period in which he worked on his *Observations*, Kant wrote his *Inquiry Concerning the Distinctness of the Principles of Natural Theology and Morality* in response to a contest announced in June of 1761 by the Berlin Academy, asking whether

> the metaphysical truths in general, and the first principles of *theologiae naturalis* and morality in particular, admit of distinct proofs to the same degree as geometrical truths; and if they are not capable of such proofs, one wishes to know what the genuine nature of their

certainty is, in what degree the said certainty can be brought, and whether this degree is sufficient for complete conviction.[10]

Kant did not win the prize (that honor went to Moses Mendelssohn), but his entry was judged to be "extremely close to winning."[11] *Inquiry* shows both the range of influences on Kant's thinking and the direction of Kant's thought at this time. The issue at stake in the Berlin Academy's question was of fundamental importance in the eighteenth century, both on the Continent and in Britain. In Germany, Wolffian rationalist moral philosophy proposed an affirmative answer to the Academy's question. In Britain, the debate between moral rationalists such as Samuel Clarke and sentimentalists such as Francis Hutcheson and David Hume was raging fiercely. In his essay, Kant does not – as Mendelssohn did – come down solidly on Wolff's side. With respect to morals, for example, he affirms the "formal ground of obligation" (2:299) of Wolff's perfectionist and rationalist ethical theory, while also claiming that Hutcheson's "moral feeling" provides "a starting point" for working out the "material principles of obligation" (2:300). In the end, *Inquiry* does not resolve the fundamental issue between rationalists and sentimentalists, but it does show the struggle that reappears in Kant's attempt to balance principles and feeling in *Observations*.

Kant's unpublished reflections during this period, many of which are found in *Remarks in the Observations*, show the evolution of this struggle towards the rationalist moral theory that will eventually be formulated in *Groundwork*. In 1764, when Kant published his *Observations on the Beautiful and the Sublime*, he had his own copy of this work published with interleaved blank pages. During 1764–5 Kant used this copy to write down an unedited, unpolished record of his emerging thoughts in aesthetics, ethics, anthropology, and even metaphysics, physics, and cosmology. Kant seems to have intended to publish some *Remarks* in some form (see, e.g., 20:116), but as a whole they are fragmented and unorganized. One fortunate result of this is that one sometimes gets striking insight into the way in which Kant thinks through multiple issues at once (see 20:178–79 for an example of the range of material that can be collected on a single page). What is more, *Remarks* records Kant's *evolving* thought, not only in shifts from earlier to later remarks, but in

---

[10] Walford, *Theoretical Philosophy*, p. lxii.   [11] Ibid., p. lxiii.

frequent places where he writes and then crosses out something or where he inserts later notes in the midst of earlier ones. (One of the most striking examples of this is Kant's struggle at 20:162 to find the right terminology for what will eventually become the distinction between categorical and hypothetical imperatives.) Overall, these *Remarks* are sufficiently rich to reward study not only for the detailed positions worked out in them but also because they show Kant's movement from the popular *Observations* to a more systematic philosophy. Moreover, these notes reflect the most developed record available of Kant's engagement with the writings of Jean-Jacques Rousseau, and they include some of Kant's most extensive reflections on the relationship between men and women.

While *Observations* and *Inquiry* were meant for a wider scholarly public and *Remarks* was a set of purely personal reflections, the Herder lecture notes reflect Kant's semipublic working-out of moral philosophy in the context of his classroom teaching. As Kant explains in his "Announcement," his course in moral philosophy was based on a textbook by the rationalist Alexander Baumgarten, but Kant supplemented this textbook with his own observations, drawn largely from Hutcheson and others. It provides a structured context for Kant to offer remarks on a variety of topics in moral philosophy, from piety and religious tolerance to friendship, sexual ethics, and lying. Johann Gottlieb Herder (1744–1803), the transcriber of these lecture notes, studied medicine in Königsberg between 1762 and 1764. During this time, he was an admirer of Kant and one of his best students, but precisely because Herder was such an original thinker during this time, his notes are not entirely reliable. He revised these notes at home and thus may have introduced ideas of his own that vary from Kant's own teachings. Nonetheless, this text provides a glimpse of Kant's teaching and covers topics discussed in *Remarks* and elsewhere. The notes also provide more details about topics on which Kant only briefly touches in other works of this period, especially the proper role of God in moral philosophy.[12]

In addition to these major works, this volume also contains several shorter texts. "Thoughts on the Occasion of Mr. Johann Friedrich von Funk's Untimely Death" (1760) is a letter that Kant wrote to the mother of

---

[12] This paragraph borrows from J. B. Schneewind's "Introduction" to Herder's lecture notes from *The Cambridge Edition of the Words of Immanuel Kant: Lectures on Ethics*, Cambridge University Press, 1997.

one of his students. It shows Kant applying his philosophical reflection in one of the most intimate and difficult of situations, comforting a mother in the death of her son. Kant's "Essay on the Maladies of the Head" (1764), written for publication in the *Königsberg Scholarly and Political Newspaper*, is in part a response to the increasing popularity of a Polish religious fanatic who had recently appeared outside of Königsberg. Kant uses this occasion to develop a general but popularly accessible taxonomy of mental illness and an apologia for life in the state of nature. Kant's "Announcement" is one of many short pamphlets printed at his own expense to drum up students for his classes. Finally, several Notes and Fragments from the 1760s show the continuing development of Kant's reflections, especially in ethics and anthropology.

Kant's early ethics

The ethics that Kant developed throughout the 1760s is not identical to the moral theory developed twenty years later, but it will prove helpful to look first at that more famous moral theory before turning back to Kant's early ethics. In the moral theory laid out in *Groundwork of the Metaphysics of Morals* (1785), Kant defends the notion of a "categorical imperative" according to which one must "act only in accordance with that maxim through which you can at the same time will that it become a universal law" (4:421) or "act so that you use humanity . . . always at the same time as an end, never merely as a means" (4:429). Kant develops this categorical imperative in the context of "a pure moral philosophy, completely cleansed of everything that may be only empirical" (4:389), and insists in *Groundwork* that to carry out "an action from duty is to put aside entirely the influence of inclination" (4:400). When under moral laws, we are not compelled to act by contingent inclinations, and thus "we take ourselves as free" (4:450). The moral theory that Kant developed in the 1780s thus has an a priori foundation, precludes inclination from a determining influence in morality, and emphasizes freedom and autonomy.

This Kantian morality has had a profound impact. J. B. Schneewind has called the ethics of *Groundwork* "one of the two or three most important contributions that moral philosophers have made to our culture."[13] Even

---

[13] J. B. Schneewind, "Why Study Kant's Ethics?," in *Groundwork for the Metaphysics of Morals*, ed. Allen Wood, New Haven, CT: Yale University Press, 2002, p. 83.

if Kant's emphasis on a priori moralizing is primarily of interest to moral philosophers – where it continues to be of substantial interest – this emphasis brought with it a conception of morality that freed morality from dependence upon religious revelation and hedonistic calculation and thereby opened up a new sense of the inestimable dignity of human beings. The notion that human beings are and ought to be *autonomous* – Kant's term for the self-governance involved in all moral action – is not merely an important philosophical option in ethics, it has impacted more down-to-earth discussions in such areas as medical ethics, human rights, and contemporary political theory.

But the ethical theory of Kant's *Groundwork* has never been without detractors. The range of criticism of this work is broad, but for the purposes of introducing Kant's early ethics, two criticisms of his *Groundwork* are particularly apt. First, *Groundwork*'s rationalism quickly came under fire as insufficiently attentive to the fullness of human nature, and in particular, to the importance of social feelings. Schiller, a romantic critic of Kant who saw his own aesthetic philosophy as following through on the spirit if not the letter of Kant, sought to combine *Groundwork*'s emphasis on the dignity of humanity and of morality with an attention to beauty and grace and thereby to attend more adequately to the *entirety* of the human condition. Second, and relatedly, the morality of *Groundwork* was criticized – most famously by Hegel – as an "empty formalism" incapable of generating concrete ethical duties. Since these early criticisms, Kant's ethics has continued to be criticized for being overly rationalist and abstract. And Kant and his followers continued to respond to these objections.[14]

In many respects, however, Kant's ethical reflections in 1762–63 are closer to those of critics such as Schiller and Hegel than to those of *Groundwork*. In his *Inquiry*, Kant takes up the question of how much "distinctness and certainty" morality is capable of. There he raises "obligation" as a key ethical concept and aims for "fundamental principles" and moral certainty (2:298). Kant insists, as in his later ethics, that the "principle chosen must, if it is to be a rule and ground of obligation, command the action as being immediately necessary and not conditional

---

[14] For Kant's most focused response to Schiller, see *Religion within the Boundaries of Mere Reason* (6:23n).

upon some end" (2:298). But *Inquiry* shares with later critics a concern with empty formalism. Kant insists that the "supreme rule of all obligation must be absolutely indemonstrable" because "in the absence of material first principles, nothing flowed from the first formal principles" (2:299). Moreover, these necessary material principles of morals are tied, in *Inquiry*, to *feeling*: "The faculty of experiencing the good is...an unanalyzable feeling of the good" (2:299; see too 27:16). Kant ends with both an injunction – "The ultimate fundamental concepts of obligation need to be determined more reliably" – and a clue as to how he will fulfill that injunction: "Hutcheson and others have, under the name of moral feeling, provided us with a starting point from which to develop some excellent observations" (2:300).

Unsurprisingly, then, *Observations on the Feeling of the Beautiful and Sublime* explicitly ties morality to "feeling." Moreover, this feeling is not the purely abstract feeling of respect for the moral law on which Kant focuses in *Groundwork*, but a feeling for both beauty and dignity (2:217). Unlike the narrow focus of *Groundwork*, *Observations* discusses ethics in the context of human nature, and in particular of "feeling of the finer sort" (2:208). Kant uses this fine feeling for the beautiful and sublime to discuss "moral qualities," among which "true virtue alone is sublime," though other moral qualities can be "beautiful" (2:215).

For this early Kant, there are four basic motivations for human actions: self-interest, the love of honor, "goodhearted drives" such as sympathy and complaisance, and action in accordance with "principles" (2:227). Kant hardly discusses self-interest in the context of morality, since it has little place in establishing moral worth. In itself, the love of honor is a mere "simulacrum of virtue" and "not in the least virtuous" (2:218), though it "is most excellent" as "an accompanying drive" (2:227; cf. 27:44). Sympathy and complaisance are "beautiful and lovable" moral qualities, but not true virtue. True virtue "can only be grafted upon principles, and it will become the more sublime and noble the more general they are" (2:217; cf. 27:14, 46). Only such *principled* virtue counts as "genuine virtue" (2:218), though sympathy and complaisance are "adopted virtues" insofar as they "have a great similarity to the true virtues" and, when properly subordinated to principles, contribute to "the noble attitude that is the beauty of virtue" (2:217). Even principled virtue, moreover, is a kind of feeling. In the closest he comes to invoking a categorical imperative in his early ethics, Kant claims that true virtue "is the *feeling of the beauty and the dignity of human nature*," which grounds "universal affection" and "universal respect" for human beings (2:217).

Many key elements of the moral philosophy of *Groundwork* are already present here. As in *Groundwork*, virtue takes place "only when one subordinates one's own particular inclination" to principles (2:217). And Kant's insistence that neither sympathy nor complaisance constitute "true virtue" anticipates his infamous claim in *Groundwork* that actions based on "an inner satisfaction in spreading joy around them" have "no true moral worth" (4:398). Kant's descriptions of the nature of moral principles in *Observations* even anticipate his later formulations of the categorical imperative. The most sublime virtue is based on general principles (2:217), a claim echoed later in Kant's "universal law" formulation of the categorical imperative. And the feeling for the dignity of human nature that manifests itself in a universal respect anticipates the formula of humanity, which is based on the fact that "humanity . . . is that which alone has dignity" (4:435).

But *Observations* also differs from *Groundwork* in many of its central points: the ethics of *Observations* is *not* a priori; feeling and inclination *do* play a role in grounding ethics; and freedom is not a central concept. The empirical nature of ethics is clear not only because Kant discusses ethics in the context of "observations" about human beings, but also in the account's overall structure, where virtue is defined in terms of moral qualities that human beings in fact find sublime. Like British moral philosophers such as Hume and Smith, Kant analyzes moral responses that people *actually* have. This empirical dimension becomes clear in Kant's discussion of the sexes, where a difference in the moral qualities that each sex finds appealing in the other dictates a different set of moral demands for each (2:228).[15] The empirical nature of ethics in *Observations* also finds expression in Kant's failure to distinguish between explaining the content of ethical principles and accounting for their motivational force, between what he would later call pure moral philosophy and moral anthropology (4:388; 6:217). One result of pulling those two disciplines together is that feeling is more prominent in the ethics of *Observations*

---

[15] I thank Brian Cutter for bringing to my attention the implications of Kant's account of the differences between the sexes for assessing the empirical nature of Kant's method in this early work. I discuss Kant's account of women in more detail below.

than in *Groundwork*.[16] True virtue is not only identified in terms of the moral quality that is *felt* to be the most sublime in human nature, but is itself a "feeling" or an "inclination" (2:217). And other, less general feelings (like sympathy) play a necessary but subordinate role in "the noble attitude that is the beauty of virtue" (2:217).

Even the similarities between *Observations* and *Groundwork* are not as similar as they initially appear. The emphasis on principle is belied by the fact that the principles "are not . . . rules, but the consciousness of a feeling" (2:217). And while *Observations* agrees with *Groundwork* that sympathy and complaisance are not equivalent to true virtue, *Groundwork* adds that they are "on the same footing with other inclinations" (4:398), while *Observations* describes these feelings as different in kind from and *closer* to true virtue than other merely selfish inclinations (2:218–19). Even "true virtue," in *Observations*, comes in *degrees*: it is "more sublime" the "more general it is" (2:217). Unlike the all-or-none account of virtue in *Groundwork*, *Observations* allows for different types and degrees of moral "worth." And Kant's insistence in *Observations* that true virtue involves both respect *and love* for both the dignity *and beauty* of human nature goes beyond *Groundwork*'s exclusive focus on respect. Finally, the emphasis on abstract principle that *Groundwork* highlights as the essence of morality comes under suspicion in *Observations* (2:227). While important elements in Kant's early ethics are continuous with his *Groundwork*, the overall thrust of *Observations* treats human nature as fundamental to ethics in a way that privileges feeling and gives equal weight to the beauty and the dignity of human beings. In many respects, this more balanced conception of ethical life fits better with critics of Kant's later ethical thought than with the picture that many have found in *Groundwork*.

Given the differences between *Groundwork* and his early ethics, it is clear *that* Kant's ethical thought underwent change. The *Remarks*, a set of private notes written shortly after *Observations*, offers important insights into *how* that change took place. Naturally, many remarks are

---

[16] Feeling is not absent from Kant's mature moral philosophy (see e.g. 4:401–2, 5:73–89). But the role of feeling in *Observations* is significantly different from its role in Kant's later moral philosophy. Morally relevant feelings in *Observations* are not limited to respect for the dignity of human nature, but also include love for what is beautiful. Moreover, feelings of sympathy and complaisance, while not strictly moral, still have distinctively moral worth (2:215, 218) and are thereby fundamentally different from self-interested or honor-seeking inclinations. And feeling in *Observations* is at least a potential *basis* for moral content, not merely a motivator of moral action.

consistent with *Observations* and *Inquiry*. Kant makes extensive use of the notion of moral feeling (see 20:26, 85, 135, 168), and *Remarks* is, like *Observations*, focused on specifically *human* ethics (see 20:22, 24, 46–48, 153; see too 27:13, 45, 62). But Kant also used these unpublished remarks to experiment with different ways of thinking through the implications of his ethical reflections, and one can already find the beginnings of his later moral theory in these experiments. Perhaps most importantly, in *Remarks* Kant begins to explicitly *contrast* moral obligation with the aesthetic categories of beauty and nobility (see 20:119, 127) and to emphasize a conception of obligation in terms of universality and necessity (20:117, 146, 173).

One key theme that permeates both *Observations* and *Remarks* and that becomes central to *Groundwork* is Kant's abhorrence of consequentialism. This shows up briefly in *Observations* (see 2:226–27) and even more explicitly in the *Inquiry* (2:298), but it is a consistent theme in *Remarks* (e.g., 20:65, 118, 138, 146, 155–56, and 168). As Kant experiments with different approaches in *Remarks*, he never entertains the possibility of ethics as merely a means to happiness (either personal or societal).[17] Moreover, *Remarks* gives important clues regarding motivations for Kant's later emphasis on the idea of a will as "good in itself" (20:150). Kant worries that "everything passes by us in a river," laments "changeable taste," and asks, "Where do I find fixed points of nature that the human being can never disarrange, and that can give him signs as to which bank he must head for?" (20:46). Kant aims for a "certainty in moral judgments . . . [that] is just as great as with logic" (20:49), in sharp contrast to his emphasis on the indemonstrability of ethics in *Inquiry* and the Herder lecture notes (2:298–99; 27:5, 16). The concern with certainty and stability helps Kant to see the importance of a good will that is "absolute perfection, whether something is effected by it or not" (20:148). And this fits with Kant thinking of "the objective necessity of actions" themselves as "either conditional or categorical" (20:156),[18]

---

[17] This is not to say that moral virtue will not be conducive to well-being, but only that such well-being is not a criterion of it (cf. 20:150). For a fuller discussion of Kant's (shifting) anti-consequentialism in the 1760s, see Patrick Frierson, "Two Kinds of Universality in Kant's Early Ethics," in *Critical Guidebook to Kant's* Observations *and* Remarks, ed. Susan Meld Shell and Richard Velkley, Cambridge University Press, forthcoming.

[18] Elsewhere, Kant moves even closer to the language of *Groundwork*. In one telling remark, he first writes, "The necessity of an action as means to a possible end is *problematic*, [as a means] to an actual end it is a necessity of *prudence*, the categorical necessity is *moral*" (20:168). Struggling to

with only the latter constituting true obligation. *Remarks* thus provides the rudiments of Kant's eventual argument that a will that is good without qualification must act in accordance with a categorical imperative (*Groundwork* 4:402–03). Kant even gives the example of a lie as an action the permissibility of which is hard to settle in terms of "conditional" goodness, but easy to settle in terms of judging what is "categorically good" (20:156), an example that he uses to the same purpose in *Groundwork* (4:402–03).

A second key theme that shows the transition towards *Groundwork* lies in the universal nature of morality. In *Observations*, Kant insists that one's conduct is more sublime (and thus more virtuous) the more general its principles (2:217). But whereas *Observations* primarily conceived of this universality in terms of the "application" of "benevolence" to all human beings (2:221), *Remarks* begins to conceive of universality in terms of avoiding "contradiction" when one supposes "the same action in others" (20:156; see too 20:67, 145–46, 161). In seeing the universality involved in having a good will in terms of whether that will would "invalidate itself if . . . taken universally" (20:67), Kant leaves behind the vague generality of *Observations* and moves considerably closer to the rigorous a priori Formula of Universal Law[19] that he articulates in *Groundwork*. Moreover, Kant's interest in universality forces him, in *Remarks*, to follow up on a concern raised in *Observations* in a way that begins to lead him away from moral feeling as a basis for ethics. In *Observations*, Kant noted that "as soon as feeling is raised to its proper universality, it is sublime, but also colder" (2:216). He reiterates that concern in *Remarks* (20:22, 25, 173; see too 27:64–67), but begins to resist grouping moral feeling in the same category with other feelings, and ascribes to it a "kind of joy . . . entirely different" from other pleasures (20:145). Kant even suggests that the "feeling" could be a kind of intellect: "Moral position. Either through instinct, sympathy or pity. *Or through intellect*" (20:169, emphasis added; see too 27:42).

A third key theme introduced in *Remarks* is the importance of human *freedom*. In *Observations*, the word "choice" (*Willkühr*) does not even

---

find the right terminology, he then adds "hypothetical" to refer to the necessity of the problematic end, but then crosses it out and adds "conditional" instead.

[19] "I ought never to act except in such a way that I could also will that my maxim should become a universal law" (*Groundwork* 4:402).

occur, and "freedom" plays no significant role.[20] In *Remarks*, by contrast, Kant goes so far as to call freedom the "topmost principium of all virtue" (20:31), and Kant's account of freedom anticipates at least two keys roles that it plays in his later philosophy. First, Kant conceives of morality as fundamentally a matter of acting freely. Moral feeling is defined as a "feeling of pleasure . . . with respect to . . . ourselves as an active *principium* of good and evil through freedom" (20:145) or a "feeling of the perfection of the [free] will" (20:136). Anticipating his later "Formula of Autonomy," [21] Kant explains that "the greatest perfection" is "to subordinate everything to the free faculty of choice" (20:144), and he identifies perfection of the will with being "in accordance with the laws of freedom" (20:136). Moral perfection is complete freedom, both in that only by being morally perfect can one be truly free and in that what it is to be morally perfect is to follow the laws of freedom. Second, Kant connects freedom to the dignity of human nature, such that what one respects when one respects another is precisely their freedom of choice. As he explains, "The human being has his own inclinations, and in virtue of his power of choice he has a hint from nature to arrange his actions in accordance with these. Now, there can be nothing more horrendous than that the action of a human being shall stand under the will of another" (20:88; see too 20:66–67, 93). Not only is such subordination "horrible," but it involves "a contradiction that at the same time indicates its injustice" (20:93; see too 20:66). The logical certainty Kant sought in morality was found in the contradiction implied by treating another person as a thing. As Kant later argues in articulating the Formula of Humanity,[22] human beings have dignity because they have freedom.

A fourth important theme in *Remarks*, one that gets no attention in *Observations* and very little in *Inquiry*, is the relationship between ethics and religion. In both *Remarks* and the Herder lecture notes, Kant struggles with the role of God in determining the content of morality (see 20:68, 136; 27:9–10), the issue of whether religion is needed as a supplementary motive for good actions (see 20:12, 16–19, 57, 104; 27:11, 18, 75), the problem of how to deal with what, in the *Religion*, Kant would later

---

[20] The closest it comes is that the melancholic temperament, which is the temperament best suited to virtue, "breathes freedom in a noble breast" and has a "fervor for freedom" (2:221).

[21] "The idea of the will of every rational being as a will giving universal law" (*Groundwork* 4:429).

[22] "So act that you use humanity, whether in your own person or that of another, always at the same time as an end, never merely as a means" (*Groundwork* 4:429).

call "radical evil" in human nature (see 20:15, 25; 27:16) and the issue of religious tolerance (see especially 27:73–8). In these texts, Kant increasingly rejects any theological voluntarism that would base the content of morality on God's arbitrary will, but also seems to see an important role for religion in providing motivational support for morals, especially for those corrupted by the luxuries of the civil condition. Moreover, Kant's concern with developing a specifically *moral* religion strikingly anticipates the rationalist moral theology developed in his later *Critiques*: "The cognition of God is either *speculative*, and this is uncertain and liable to dangerous errors, or moral through faith, and this conceives of no other qualities in God except those that aim at morality" (20:57).

Already in *Remarks*, Kant sees that morality involves categorical necessity and even that this necessity comes from a universal principle tied to human freedom rather than from the arbitrary will of God. He has the rudiments of his most famous formulations of the categorical imperative, though he does not articulate how universality, human dignity, and freedom fit together into a single overarching moral principle. Moreover, he has not yet seen the extent to which this moral theory will depend upon a transcendental idealism that makes room for a radical, nonanthropological conception of freedom (though see 20:181). And his ethics is still fundamentally a *human* ethics (20:22–23, 41, 45, 47; see too 27:13, 45, 62), far from the ethics of *Groundwork* that "does not hold only for human beings, as if other rational beings did not have to heed it" (4:389).

Observations and the origin of Kantian anthropology

When Kant wrote his *Groundwork*, he insisted on a strict distinction between pure "moral philosophy" and any empirical study of human beings. But even as Kant insisted upon this distinction, he added that moral philosophy "still requires a judgment sharpened by experience" (4:389) and "moral anthropology" is a needed "counterpart of a metaphysics of morals" (6:217). What is more, Kant developed an important course in "Anthropology" that he taught every year from its inception in 1772 until his retirement from teaching. For Kant, "anthropology" was a broad concept, used for the study of human beings as a whole. Thus it included what we would currently group under all of the human sciences: psychology, sociology, anthropology in the narrow sense, and even certain aspects of biology and economics. But Kant's anthropology emphasized a "pragmatic point of view," a focus on popularly accessible insights into human beings that could be put to practical use.

In his own life, Kant's interest in anthropology was not merely peripheral. His *Anthropology from a Pragmatic Point of View*, one of the last two books that he published before his death, was, like *Observations*, one of his most popular works when it was published. This published work grew out of Kant's long-standing commitment to teaching anthropology. In a letter about this anthropology course, Kant explains that moral anthropology not only supplements pure moral philosophy, but is also an essential and "entertaining" part of cultivating world-wisdom through learning "everything that pertains to the practical" (10:145–46). In the same letter, he gives clues as to the origin of his anthropology, describing anthropology alongside "Physical Geography," a course Kant had taught since 1756. The *Announcement of... Lectures for the Winter Semester, 1765–1766* describes this physical geography course and shows the origin of the pragmatic concerns that would develop into Kant's anthropology. He explains the need for "an entertaining and easy compendium of the things which might prepare [students] and serve them for the exercise of practical reason" (2:312), much as he will later refer to his anthropology as "entertaining and never dry" (10:146). The *motive* for developing a course in anthropology is thus well formed during the 1760s, and from this seed an anthropology grew that eventually became central in Kant's teaching and that supplemented his a priori philosophizing.

Like its motive, the content for Kant's eventual anthropology is also present during the 1760s. Much of this content is in Kant's lectures on metaphysics,[23] a substantial portion of which focuses on "empirical psychology." This psychology largely structures the first part of Kant's published *Anthropology* and the bulk of his early lectures on anthropology. But in both, the material drawn from Kant's empirical psychology gives way, in the concluding portion of the book (and the lectures), to extended discussions of the "character" of human beings, both in general and in their diversity. The transitions to this discussion of character often highlight the importance of character for Kant's overall understanding of

---

[23] Selections from these lectures are available in *The Cambridge Edition of the Works of Immanuel Kant: Lectures on Metaphysics* (edited and translated by Karl Ameriks and Steve Naragon), Cambridge University Press, 1997.

human beings, and Kant seems to have devoted more and more attention to character over time. But the lectures on empirical psychology include little to nothing regarding human character. To find the early seeds of *this* aspect of Kant's anthropology, one must turn to *Observations* and *Remarks*.

In similar fashion to the division of sections in *Observations*, Kant's discussion of character in *Anthropology* begins with an account of human character in general, an account that includes his treatment of different temperaments; then the book turns to a discussion of the character of the sexes, then to an account of the character of the nations. Both the specific content and the general tone of these sections are strikingly similar to those in *Observations*. In some cases, the published *Anthropology* directly contradicts the earlier *Observations*, most strikingly in a reversal in Kant's assessments of different temperaments of human beings.[24] When it does not contradict *Observations*, Kant's later published *Anthropology* often shows substantial development from or elaboration of points that are found in primitive form in these earlier works; for example, the sublimity of action in accordance with principle that Kant highlights in *Observations* (2:217) develops into a theory of "character as a way of thinking" in *Anthropology* (7:292). And Kant adds, in *Anthropology*, a crucial discussion of "the character of the species," in which he lays out "the sum total of pragmatic anthropology, in respect to the vocation of the human being" as a whole species (7:324). Elsewhere, the freshness and excitement of Kant's early work results in a richer and better developed treatment of topics that are discussed only briefly in Kant's later *Anthropology*. Kant's account of the character of the sexes in *Observations*, for example, says little about nature's end in establishing womankind, but says much more *to* women about the sorts of excellences that are distinctive for women as such. And the discussions of the nature of luxury and simplicity in *Remarks* far outstrip the *Anthropology*'s very compressed account of the impact of luxury on the faculty of feeling (7:249–50).

---

[24] In *Observations*, Kant clearly favors the melancholic temperament (2:219) and sees the apathetic phlegmatic as virtually unworthy of consideration (2:224). In *Anthropology*, by contrast, the melancholic temperament has a more negative characterization (7:288), while the phlegmatic is a "fortunate temperament" that "will . . . proceed from principles and not from instinct" and that "takes the place of wisdom" (7:290). In Kant's later work, the apathetic phlegmatic temperament becomes a natural approximation to Kant's increasingly apathetic moral ideal rather than a boring tangent with respect to aesthetic qualities.

More important than these differences in detail, however, is the central difference between the systematic place of anthropology in these early writings and in Kant's later philosophy. By the time he publishes *Anthropology*, Kant has made it clear that empirical anthropology is systematically (even if not pedagogically) secondary to the a priori epistemology and moral philosophy developed in his *Critiques* of pure and practical reason. But the anthropological insights of *Observations* and *Remarks* are not insulated from the rest of Kant's philosophical project in this way. And that opens a different sort of relationship between anthropology and philosophy. As already noted, the moral project of *Observations* is largely an anthropological project, explaining what is beautiful and sublime in human nature. *Remarks* makes even clearer Kant's emphasis on *human* ethics (see e.g. 20:22–23, 41, 47), and even human *freedom* is discussed in these early works as a property discernible in human beings through careful empirical anthropology, more like the role it plays in Rousseau than in Kant's eventual Critical philosophy (see, e.g., 20:55–56, 91–93). All of this suggests that however conceptually independent Kant's later moral philosophy is from anthropology, such anthropology lies at the origin of his *thinking* about that morality and even its connection to freedom.

Different nations and races

Central to Kantian anthropology is taxonomy, wherein Kant aims for a "completeness of the headings under which this or that observed human quality of practical relevance can be subsumed" (7:121). Even in his *Critiques*, Kant is a perennial taxonomist, seeking to "exhaustively exhibit the functions of unity in judgment" (A69/B94) in the first *Critique* and classifying all moral theories prior to his own into one of four different categories of heteronomy in the second. *Observations* is similarly taxonomic, beginning with distinctions between different sorts of pleasure, moving to distinguish motives for human behavior to isolate true virtue, and including a classic eighteenth-century taxonomy of human temperaments.

Generally, Kant's taxonomic schemes are treated with bemused indifference. But Kant's desire to characterize individuals by reference to clear categories looks more dangerous from our twenty-first-century perspective when this categorization falls along lines of sex and race. Kant is not bashful about dividing the world in terms of a fundamental "contrast between the sexes" (2:228), various different "national characters" (2:243), and even "different human races" (2:429–43), and insists that "difference[s of aesthetic and moral feelings] in sex, age, education and government, race and climate is to be noted" (20:50). In *Observations*, these differences involve classifying types of beauty and sublimity in humans, but because "the characters of mind of the peoples are most evident in that in them which is moral," Kant considers "their different feeling in regard to the sublime and beautiful from this point of view" (2:245).

Kant's account of "national characters" reads almost like a travel guide, unsurprisingly, since one of his goals during this period is "to make a more certain knowledge of believable travel accounts and to make this into a legitimate course of study."[25] Just as good travel guides describe differences between behaviors and expectations of different peoples, so Kant aims to "make good the lack of *experience*" of his young students (2:212) through characterizing different people with whom they may interact. Thus Kant's reflections during this period focus on different European nations: "the *Italians* and *French* . . . most distinguish themselves in the feeling of the *beautiful*, but the *Germans*, the *English*, and the *Spaniards* . . . are most distinguished . . . in the feeling of the *sublime*" (2:243; see too 27:41).

Kant does not limit his observations to differences between European nations, however, and his discussion of non-European peoples contains some truly horrific mischaracterizations. Regarding Asians, Kant seems to have a level of respect, comparing different Asian peoples with European ones, such that "Arabs are as it were the Spaniards of the Orient . . . Persians are the Frenchmen of Asia . . . [and] the Japanese can be regarded as it were as the Englishmen of this part of the world" (2:252). North American natives are viewed by Kant with ambivalent esteem; they have "little feeling for the beautiful in the moral sense" but "demonstrate a sublime character of mind" (2:253). When Kant turns to "the *Negroes* of Africa," his descriptions are truly reprehensible: "*Negroes* . . . have by

---

[25] Holly Wilson, *Kant's Pragmatic Anthropology: Its Origin, Meaning, and Critical Significance*, Albany, NY: SUNY Press, 2006, p. 9.

nature no feeling that rises above the ridiculous" and "not a single one has ever been found who has accomplished something great" (2:253). In a particularly infamous remark, Kant dismisses the opinion of a "Negro carpenter" by saying, "There might be something here worth considering, except for the fact that this scoundrel was completely black from head to foot, a distinct proof that what he said was stupid" (2:224–25). In these comments, especially about Black Africans, Kant reflects the worst prejudices of his time and even enlists the support of philosophers such as David Hume (see 2:253). Moreover, unlike Kant's later published essays on race, which focus almost exclusively on the physical, this early discussion provides a context for the sorts of moral and intellectual characterizations of other races now so closely tied to racism.

Fortunately, *Observations* is also unlike Kant's later published essays on race in that it avoids or at least mitigates racial and ethnic essentialism. In a crucial footnote to the title of this section, Kant explains,

> [N]o nation is lacking in casts of mind which unite the foremost predominant qualities of this kind. For this reason the criticism that might occasionally be cast on a people can offend no one, as it is like a ball that one can always hit to his neighbor. (2:243n)

Later, he reiterates,

> It is hardly necessary for me to repeat my previous apology here. In each people the finest portion contains praiseworthy characters of all sorts, and whoever is affected by one or another criticism will, if he is fine enough, understand it to his advantage, which lies in leaving everyone else to his fate but making an exception of himself. (2:245n)

Kant does not, at least in this work, see the different characters of nations as deterministic for the possibilities of individuals, and he encourages readers to read negative characterizations of their nation as exhortations to moral strength rather than as signs of inherent inferiority.

Unfortunately, Kant's negative characterizations of non-European races in *Observations* presage the more essentialist racial theory that he develops thirteen years later in "On the Different Human Races" (1775) and lend support to suggestions that this race theory implies a principled basis for the inferiority of other races. It is beyond the scope of this introduction to provide an overview of those texts, but even in *Observations* itself, Kant seems to exclude Negroes from his crucial "apology," in which he insisted that "no nation is lacking" in finer qualities, not only by taking blackness as a universal sign of stupidity but also by describing the inferiority of Negroes to whites as an "essential difference between these two human kinds" (2:253). Seeds of Kant's later theory of race, within which racial characteristics are heritable and relatively fixed, are regrettably already found in *Observations*.

Women

Kant devotes a substantial section of *Observations* – Section 3 – to "the contrast between the two sexes" (2:228). Similar discussions persist throughout his lectures on anthropology and culminate in his discussion of the "character of the sexes" in *Anthropology* (1798). These discussions also provide background for Kant's claims about women's political status (see 6:314–15, 8:295) and the importance of marriage (6:278f). Some comments in *Observations* are perfect sound bites of Kantian misogyny: "A woman who has a head full of Greek . . . might as well have a beard" (2:229). Others seem to be models of egalitarianism: "the fair sex has just as much understanding as the male" (2:229). In fact, the attitude towards women in *Observations* is more subtle than these sound bites suggest; this attitude *both* feeds into more misogynistic positions in Kant's later work *and* anticipates feminist critiques of and alternatives to Enlightenment philosophies such as the later Kant's.

The core of Kant's account of the sexes is that women are primarily characterized by the beautiful, while men are primarily characterized by the sublime. However,

> it is not to be understood that woman is lacking noble [sublime] qualities or that the male sex must entirely forego beauties; rather one expects that each sex will unite both, but in such a way that in a woman all other merits should only be united so as to emphasize the character of the **beautiful**, which is the proper point of reference, while by contrast among the male qualities the **sublime** should clearly stand out as the criterion of his kind. (2:228)

This distinction is both descriptive – women *are* generally more characterized by the beautiful and men by the sublime – and normative: "To this [distinction] must refer all judgments of these two sexes, those of praise as well as those of blame" (2:228).

Unless one keeps both descriptive and normative dimensions of Kant's distinction in mind, Kant's account might seem to preclude virtue in women. Kant says both "It is difficult for me to believe that the fair sex is capable of principles" (2:232; see too 27:49) and "true virtue can only be grafted upon principles" (2:217). This might require, as Jean Rumsey claims, that "women . . . are in Kant's view less than . . . full moral agents."[26] But such attention to the merely descriptive aspect of Kant's distinction misses Kant's insistence in *Observations* that women *are* capable of virtue, but "The virtue of the woman is a **beautiful virtue**" (2:231; see too 27:49–50). Following through on his sexual distinction, Kant insists that women are capable of distinctively feminine virtue. And whereas the principles of which women are not capable "are also extremely rare among the male sex" (2:232), the "love [of] what is good" that serves as the foundation of beautiful virtue is grounded in "goodly and benevolent sentiments" that "providence has implanted . . . in [women's] bosom" (2:232). The impossibility of fulfilling *male* virtue is actually a moral advantage: whereas few men will attain sublime virtue, women are well equipped for beautiful virtue.

Kant's account of beautiful virtue thus invites developing a Kantian feminist (or feminine) ethics. Ever since Carol Gilligan's *In a Different Voice*, many feminist moral philosophers have explored more "feminine" approaches to ethics.[27] Such approaches often emphasize, with the Kant of *Observations*, the importance of "broaden[ing] one's] entire moral feeling . . . and not, to be sure, through moral rules, but rather through individual judgment of the conduct that she sees around her" (2:230). This Kantian ethic of "beautiful virtue," which Kant (like Carol Gilligan and Nell Noddings) sees as a more feminine alternative to the principle-based rationalist ethics of "noble virtue," could be seen as an important

---

[26] Jean Rumsey, "Re-Visions of Agency in Kant's Moral Theory," in *Feminist Interpretations of Immanuel Kant*, ed. Robin May Schott, University Park, PA: Pennsylvania State University Press, 1997, p. 131.

[27] The literature exploring the ethics of care is vast. For one popular example, see Nell Noddings' *Caring: A Feminine Approach to Ethics and Moral Education*, Berkeley/Los Angeles: University of California Press, 1989.

historical precursor to recent ethics of care and, more broadly, to virtue ethics.[28]

Unfortunately, when Kant describes the sexes later in his *Anthropology*, all hope is gone of a feminine Kantian virtue ethics of the sort suggested by *Observations*. Although feelings and sensitive judgments about particulars play some role in the moral philosophy that Kant articulates starting in his *Groundwork*, that moral philosophy shifts to emphasize rational choice to the point that the "beautiful virtue" of *Observations* is merely a sham. So even when Kant admits a distinctive "feminine virtue" in *Anthropology* (7:307), the use of the term "virtue" rings hollow when such virtue falls far short of the "good will" that is the only thing "good without limitation" (4:393). This later Kantian ethics might have suggested another sort of Kantian femin*ist* (but now *not* femin*ine*) ethics, one within which differences between the sexes are seen *not* to be essential, where both women and men are equally capable of rising to the high standards of the categorical imperative. Were it not for his strong insistence that "What is most important is that the man become more perfect as a man and the woman as a woman" (2:241–42), one might even read Kant's admonition regarding nations as applying to sexes as well: "In each people the finest portion contains praiseworthy characters of all sorts, and whoever is affected by one or another criticism will . . . understand it to his [or her] advantage, which lies in . . . making an exception of [one]self" (2:245n). Unfortunately, Kant's anthropological claims about the differences between the sexes change little between *Observations* and *Anthropology*, despite the shifts in his moral philosophy. As a result, in Kant's later moral philosophy the noble ideal of a perfect rational man governed by principles is the *only* unconditionally good will, but women's nature precludes them from such a will.

---

[28] Moreover, Kant's emphasis on feeling in *Observations* fits into his ambivalence about rationality during this period and anticipates feminist critiques of overemphasis on rationality. And Kant's observational approach to knowledge, evidenced in *Observations* and "Maladies" as well as in his teaching during this period, emphasizes knowing human beings in all of their diversity. Kant's focus on human beings with a particular eye to sentiments is precisely what many find to be missing from Kant's later (and, some argue, more masculine) ethics, and it is precisely what Kant describes as women's "philosophical wisdom," "the content of the great science of woman, [which] is the human being" and "sentiment" (2:230). In this early work, moreover, both Kant's anthropology and his ethics are fluid, such that "each sex will unite both" beauty and nobility, and feminine traits are incorporated into Kant's account of true (masculine) virtue.

Kant's "observations" about sexual differences are not written in a personal vacuum, and they are not observations of a disinterested philosopher. During the 1760s Kant struggled with the issue of marriage, and one finds a personal pathos throughout these writings. Kant in *Observations* longs for a woman with whom to make a "united pair" that would "as it were constitute a single moral person" (2:242), a woman who could both "refine" (2:229) and "ennoble" him (2:242), and, most of all, a female *friend* who could unite beauty and nobility of soul and who "can never be valued enough" (2:235). While Kant longs for this ideal woman, though, he also recognizes a *danger* in his ideal. In a partly autobiographical passage, he contrasts crude sexual inclination with "extremely refined taste," which prevents excessive lust but often at the cost of happiness since such refined taste "commonly fails to attain the great final aim of nature" and results in "brooding." Such brooding ends in one of two bad outcomes: "postponement and . . . renunciation of the marital bond or . . . sullen regret of a choice that . . . does not fulfill the great expectations that had been raised" (2:239). Within a few years, Kant will have fallen into the first of these tragic outcomes. Although he will later quip, "When I needed a woman, I couldn't feed one; when I could feed one, I didn't need one any more,"[29] the analysis in *Observations* seems a more likely explanation for Kant's lifelong bachelorhood.

Kant's *Remarks* brings further reflection on the "fair sex." As in *Observations*, *Remarks* emphasizes sexual differences and reiterates that "women have feminine virtues" (20:56). In reading Rousseau, Kant associates women with a Rousseauian ideal "state of simplicity" (20:64), suggests that "before one asks about the virtue of women, one must first ask whether they need such a thing" (20:64), and argues that women "are much less capable of virtue; but they have that which can make it dispensable" (20:98). Here one finds anticipations of Kant's eventual negative characterization of women as incapable of true virtue, but at this stage Kant's interest in Rousseau leads him to see "virtue" as merely a compensation for the loss of innocence that comes with leaving the state of nature. Women are closer to the state of nature (20:50); their inability to be virtuous is a perfection rather than a flaw (see 20:184–85).

Kant's investigation of women shifts in *Remarks* in two important ways. First, Kant focuses more on relationships between sexes, especially

[29] Quoted in Zammito, *Kant, Herder*, p. 121.

in marriage (see, e.g., 20:6–7, 23, 50, 53, 68–69, 83, 95, 120, 131–33, 177). (In this context, Kant also emphasizes the importance of womanly domesticity; see e.g. 20:64–65, 132, 185.) Second, Kant recasts his earlier reflections on women's beauty in terms of an "art of appearing [or illusion, *Schein*]" (20:61, 69, 121, 140).[30] The two shifts are connected. Marriage protects women from being "degraded to the man's power of choice" (20:95), but the art of illusion is needed to trick men into marriage (20:69–70, 177). Illusion is nature's compensation for women's weakness (20:176); through illusion, women "dominate" (20:121) men, who "surrender . . . and let themselves be easily deceived" (20:176). For women, illusion is the key to security and happiness. Even for men, "this art . . . constitutes our entire happiness. Through this the deceived husband is happy" (20:61). Problems come only when "appearance [illusion] . . . ceases in marriage," for then the man "finds less agreeableness than [he] had expected" (20:70; cf. 140).

As in *Observations*, Kant's reflections on women reflect a deeply personal struggle about marriage. Kant associates "true marriage in its perfection" with "perfect happiness" (20:153) and ponders what he would look for "if I should choose a wife" (20:84, 179). He idealizes a "unity . . . tied to equality" that "depends on two forming a whole together in a natural way" (20:73) and insists that "man and woman constitute a moral whole" (20:62; cf. 27:50). But as a whole, *Remarks* shows Kant moving away from marriage as a serious possibility for himself, for three primary reasons. First, Kant is skeptical about whether the illusion that makes marriage beautiful can be sustained: "The ideal of beauty may very well be preserved in hope but not in possession" (20:123). Second, he increasingly sees a gap between his longing for passionate affection and the coldness he receives from women, a gap based not merely on the fact that "one demands [the] illusion [of] . . . women . . . [that they have] no inclination for lustful intimacy at all" (20:136), but also on a real difference between the vulnerabilities of men and women to emotional agitation: "Men are much more in love than women" (20:69; see too 20:75, 100, 167), for "The man is . . . weaker [than the woman] with respect to inclination" (20:137). Finally, Kant sees his era as particularly ill-suited for marriage. He only half-jokingly remarks, "the time of the debaucheries of men

---

[30] Importantly for Kant, "illusion" is not the same as "deceit," and illusion is not necessarily morally blameworthy. For more on the difference between illusion and deceit, see *Anthropology* 7:149–53.

has ended and that of women has begun" (20:86). More seriously, he complains that at "the highest peak of fashionable taste . . . a reasonable man looks like a dolt or pedant . . . and the finer part of society play the role of courtiers" (20:107). In the end, almost in response to his claim in *Observations* that "friendship . . . in a woman can never be valued enough" (2:235), Kant claims, "Friendship is always reciprocal . . . and since the wife never desires the man's well-being as much as the latter desires hers, marriage is only closely related to the most perfect friendship. In the state of opulence, marriages must cease to become friendships." (20:174). Shaking himself free of its throes, Kant now sees the "love of women" not as something "so totally charming" (2:235) but as "the ultimate weakness of the wise" (20:97).

In the 1760s Kant's attitudes towards women are articulated in the greatest detail and change the most. His view throughout this period is that the sexes are and ought to be different, that "equality" between men and women is found in a unity within which women are beautiful and men noble. In *Observations*, Kant's discussion of women is gallant, praising them for their distinctive virtues; and his attitude towards unity with women there is fundamentally positive. But over the course of *Remarks*, Kant's attitude changes. He focuses attention on marriage and emphasizes woman's distinctive trait as proficiency in illusion, a proficiency that inevitably disappoints. As Kant moves further from marriage in his personal life, so he also dislocates women further and further from the ideal of (masculine) virtue that comes to be identified with the good will as such. *Remarks* thus anticipates Kant's eventual treatment of women in *Anthropology* as mere tools by which Nature promotes the twin ends of "preservation of the species" and "cultivation of society and its refinement" (7:305).

Conclusion

Observations on the Feeling of the Beautiful and Sublime, along with the other writings assembled in this volume, contains many of the seeds of views that Kant eventually develops in the *Critique of Pure Reason* and *Groundwork of the Metaphysics of Morals*. The seeds of the first *Critique* are clearest in *Remarks*, such as when he describes "metaphysics" as "a science of the limits of human reason" (20:181; see too *Inquiry* passim). The seeds of the *Groundwork* can be found in his striving for certainty and universality in morals, his developing insistence that moral requirements be unconditional, and the gradual increase in the importance of freedom in his moral remarks. But these works also present a quite different Kant from the austere rationalist associated with his mature philosophy. The very style of these works is that of an "observer" and "inquirer," a Kant of remarks and notes, of gallantry and elegance. With respect to morals, Kant here emphasizes feeling and beauty alongside principles and categorical demands. These writings show Kant with interests far outside of pure philosophy. And this empirical–anthropological interest is neither separate from nor secondary to Kant's concerns with morals, freedom, and even metaphysics.

Chronology

1764	Declines Professorship of Poetry
	Observations on the Feeling of the Beautiful and Sublime
	"Essay on the Maladies of the Head"
	Inquiry Concerning the Distinctness of the Principles of Natural Theology and Morality
1765	"Announcement of the Program of Lectures for the Winter Semester, 1765–1766"
1766	*Dreams of a Spirit-Seer Elucidated by Dreams of Metaphysics*
1770	Appointed Professor of Logic and Metaphysics at the University of Königsberg
1775	"Of the Different Human Races"
1781	*Critique of Pure Reason* (first edition)
1785	*Groundwork of the Metaphysics of Morals*
1788	*Critique of Practical Reason*
1790	*Critique of Judgment* (first edition)
1793	*Religion within the Boundaries of Mere Reason*
1797	*Metaphysics of Morals*
1798	*Anthropology from a Pragmatic Point of View*
1804	Kant dies on February 12

Further reading

Very little has been written about Kant's *Observations on the Feeling of the Beautiful and Sublime.* The forthcoming *Critical Guidebook to Kant's Observations and Remarks* (ed. Susan Meld Shell and Richard Velkley, Cambridge University Press) will represent the first sustained engagement with the *Observations* by Kant scholars working in English. Prior to this volume, the only article in English devoted exclusively to the *Observations* is Susan Shell's "Kant as Propagator: Reflections on *Observations on the Feeling of the Beautiful and Sublime*" (*Eighteenth-Century Studies* 35 [2002]: 455–68), which is a very good introduction to the work as a whole. Paul Schilpp's *Kant's Pre-Critical Ethics* (Evanston, IL: Northwestern University Press, 1938) contains a substantial section on *Observations* (pp. 45–62). Willi Goetschel, *Constituting Critique: Kant's Writing as Critical Praxis,* trans. Eric Schwab (Durham, NC: Duke University Press, 1994) also contains a section on *Observations* (pp. 58–78), and John Zammito's *Kant, Herder, and the Birth of Anthropology* (University of Chicago Press, 2002) discusses the work (pp. 104–13). Joseph Schmucker's *Die Ursprünge der Ethik Kants in seinen vorkritischen Schriften und Reflexionen* (Meisenheim: Anton Hain, 1961) also discusses the *Observations.*

Kant's *Remarks* have received more attention than the *Observations* themselves, particularly with reference to Kant's engagement with Rousseau. Richard Velkley's *Freedom and the End of Reason* (University of Chicago Press, 1989) has an extensive chapter (chapter 3, pp. 61–88) focusing on Rousseau in the *Remarks.* Susan Shell's *The Embodiment of Reason: Kant on Spirit, Generation, and Community* (University of Chicago Press, 1996) and John Zammito's *Kant, Herder, and the Birth of Anthropology* both engage with the *Remarks,* especially but not exclusively in

xxxviii

connection with Rousseau's influence on Kant. Schilpp, in *Kant's Pre-Critical Ethics* (pp. 63–74), and Schmucker, in *Die Ursprünge der Ethick Kants*, also emphasize the *Remarks*.

Other writings in this volume have received little attention. Schilpp discusses *Inquiry* in *Kant's Pre-Critical Ethics* and Dieter Henrich discusses the role of Hutcheson in the work, in "Hutcheson und Kant," *Kant-Studien* 49 (1957/8): 49–69 (translated as "Hutcheson and Kant," in *Kant's Moral and Legal Philosophy*, ed. Karl Ameriks and Otfried Höffe, Cambridge University Press, 2009). Holly Wilson – in *Kant's Pragmatic Anthropology: Its Origin, Meaning, and Critical Significance* (Albany, NY: SUNY Press, 2006) – extensively discusses the *Announcement* in connection with Kant's approach to pedagogy. "Maladies" is discussed in Shell's *Embodiment of Reason* (especially pp. 268–69), Patrick Frierson's "Kant on Mental Disorder" (*Journal of the History of Psychiatry* 20 [2009]: 267–310), and, in connection with "The Philosopher's Medicine of the Body," in Mary Gregor's *Kant's Latin Writings* (New York: Peter Lang, 1993).

With respect to Kant's life and work in the 1760s more generally, the best sources are Manfred Kuehn's *Kant: A Biography* (Cambridge University Press, 2001); John Zammito's *Kant, Herder, and the Birth of Anthropology* (University of Chicago Press, 2002); and the "Introduction" to David Walford (ed.), *The Cambridge Edition of the Works of Immanuel Kant: Theoretical Philosophy 1755–1770* (Cambridge University Press, 1992). Kant's theoretical philosophy during this period is collected in that work and has also been discussed by Shell in *Embodiment of Reason* and in her *Kant and the Limits of Autonomy* (Cambridge, MA: Harvard University Press, 2009), and by Alison Laywine in *Kant's Early Metaphysics and the Origins of the Critical Philosophy* (Atascadaro, CA: Ridgeview, 1993), among others.

The classic texts on Kant's early ethics are Schilpp's *Kant's Pre-Critical Ethics* and – in German – Joseph Schmucker's *Die Ursprünge der Ethik Kants in seinen vorkritischen Schriften und Reflexionen* (Meisenheim: Anton Hain, 1961) and Dieter Henrich's "Über Kants früheste Ethik" (*Kant-Studien* 54 [1963]: 404–31). Other important works that discuss Kant's early ethics include previously mentioned works by Shell, Zammito, and Henrich. Kant's later texts in ethics are translated and collected in *The Cambridge Edition of the Works of Immanuel Kant: Practical Philosophy* (Cambridge University Press, 1999), and valuable further material relevant to ethics can be found in *The Cambridge Edition of the Works of*

Immanuel Kant: Religion and Rational Theology (Cambridge University Press, 2001). For discussions of Kant's later ethics, see Christine Korsgaard's *Creating the Kingdom of Ends* (Cambridge University Press, 1996) and Allen Wood's *Kant's Ethical Thought* (Cambridge University Press, 1999).

Like Kant's ethics, Kant's anthropology is primarily discussed with reference to Kant's *Anthropology from a Pragmatic Point of View* published in 1798, and recently translated as part of *The Cambridge Edition of the Works of Immanuel Kant: Anthropology, History, Pedagogy* (Cambridge University Press, 2008). (*Anthropology* is also available in a separate volume edited by Robert Louden [2006] as part of the series Cambridge Texts in the History of Philosophy.) Recently, attention has also been paid to Kant's lectures on anthropology (a translation of selections from these lectures is forthcoming as part of *The Cambridge Edition of the Works of Immanuel Kant*). Recent work on Kant's anthropology includes Patrick Frierson, *Freedom and Anthropology in Kant's Moral Philosophy* (Cambridge University Press, 2003); Brian Jacobs and Patrick Kain (eds.), *Essays on Kant's Anthropology* (Cambridge University Press, 2003); Robert Louden, *Kant's Impure Ethics* (Oxford University Press, 2000); G. Felicitas Munzel, *Kant's Conception of Moral Character: The "Critical" Link of Morality, Anthropology, and Reflective Judgment* (University of Chicago Press, 1999); Wilson, *Kant's Pragmatic Anthropology*; and Wood, *Kant's Ethical Thought*. With the exception of the forthcoming *Critical Guidebook*, however, there has been virtually no discussion of the anthropological dimensions of Kant's *Observations* and *Remarks*. Even discussions of the origins of Kant's anthropology generally center around either Kant's early lectures on physical geography or his lectures in empirical psychology (for an overview of these debates, see Wilson's *Kant's Pragmatic Anthropology*, pp. 7–26).

For the development of Kant's racial theory beyond the *Observations*, see the essays on race in *The Cambridge Edition of the Works of Immanuel Kant: Anthropology, History, Pedagogy*. For recent discussions of Kant's theory of race, see Pauline Kleingeld, "Kant's Second Thoughts on Race," *Philosophical Quarterly* 57 (2007): 573–92; R. Bernasconi, "Who Invented the Concept of Race? Kant's Role in the Enlightenment Construction of Race," in R. Bernasconi (ed.), *Race* (Oxford: Blackwell, 2001), pp. 11–36; T. McCarthy, "On the Way to a World Republic? Kant on Race and Development," in L. Waas (ed.), *Politik, Moral und*

Religion – Gegensätze und Ergänzungen: Festschrift zum 65. Geburtstag von Karl Graf Ballestrem (Berlin: Duncker und Humblot, 2004), pp. 223–43; E. C. Eze, *Achieving our Humanity: The Idea of the Postracial Future* (New York: Routledge, 2001); and T. E. Hill Jr. and B. Boxill, "Kant and Race," in B. Boxill (ed.), *Race and Racism* (Oxford University Press, 2001), pp. 448–71. With the exception of Kleingeld, most authors treat Kant's views on race as relatively static, and most focus on Kant's later writings on race rather than on the earlier and less essentialist account in the *Observations*.

Those interested in Kant's views on sex and gender beyond the *Observations* and *Remarks* should see Kant's discussion of women in his *Anthropology* (see especially 7:303–11) and *Metaphysics of Morals* (6:277–80, 314–15). A collection of critical essays on Kant's views of women, along with a detailed bibliography, can be found in Robin May Schott (ed.), *Feminist Interpretations of Immanuel Kant* (University Park: Pennsylvania State University Press, 1997). Both Shell (in *Embodiment of Reason*) and Zammito (in *Kant, Herder, and the Birth of Anthropology*) include substantial discussion of Kant's views on women in the context of their discussions of Kant in the 1760s. Other good discussions of Kant on women (with further references) are Pauline Kleingeld's "The Problematic Status of Gender-Neutral Language in the History of Philosophy: The Case of Kant," in *Philosophical Forum* 25 (1993): 134–50, and Louden's *Kant's Impure Ethics*, pp. 82–87. A good discussion of the role of women in Europe during the time that Kant wrote the *Observations* can be found in Joan Landes, *Women and the Public Sphere in the Age of the French Revolution* (Ithaca, NY: Cornell University Press, 1989).

Note on the texts

For all the texts collected in this volume, footnotes marked with letters are Kant's own. Numbered footnotes from the translator indicate textual variants, translations of material left untranslated in the text, the original German, Latin, or French of translated terms, or explanatory notes. Bold type is used for cases in which words appear in spaced type (*Sperrdruck*) in the original German. Italics is used for cases in which words in the German appear in roman type.

"Thoughts on the Occasion of Mr. Johann Friedrich von Funk's Untimely Death" (Gedanken bei dem Ableben des Herrns Johann Friedrich von Funk) was initially written in June of 1760 as a letter of consolation to the mother of one of Kant's students. Later that year, Kant had copies of the letter published by J. F. Driest in Königsberg and they were distributed among his acquaintances. The present translation is based on the version of Kant's letter found in the Academy Edition, volume 2, pp. 37–44. The translation of "Thoughts on the Occasion of Mr. Johann Friedrich von Funk's Untimely Death" was undertaken by Margot Wielgus, Nelli Haase, Patrick Frierson, and Paul Guyer. To the best of our knowledge, this is the first English translation of this work.

Observations on the Feeling of the Beautiful and Sublime was first published by Kanter in 1764. It was followed by a second edition, also published by Kanter, in 1766, and by a third edition, published in Riga by Friedrich Hartknoch, in 1771, which exists in three different versions, marked by three different vignettes on the title page. (Hartknoch would subsequently publish the *Critique of Pure Reason*.) In Kant's lifetime, there were three more editions, in 1797 (Graz), 1797–98 (Königsberg and Leipzig), and 1799 (Halle), in none of which Kant seems to have had a hand. The second and third editions introduce more errors than corrections, and it is not clear whether Kant was personally involved in their production. The editor of the *Observations* in the Academy Edition, Paul Menzer, therefore chose to base his text on the first edition, and it is Menzer's text that is translated here. The translation of *Beobachtungen über das Gefühl des Schönen und Erhabenen* was undertaken by Paul Guyer. This translation also appears in *The Cambridge Edition of the Works of Immanuel Kant: Anthropology, History, and Education*, pp. 18–62.

The *Remarks in* Observations on the Feeling of the Beautiful and Sublime (Bemerkungen in den *Beobachtungen über das Gefühl des Schönen und Erhabenen*) are a series of notes that Kant wrote in his own interleaved copy of the first edition of the *Observations* in 1764–65. These notes were transcribed by Gerhard Lehmann in volume 20 of the Academy Edition (published in 1942), pp. 1–102, and in a much better version by Marie Rischmüller in *Bemerkungen in den "Beobachtungen über das Gefühl des Schönen und Erhabenen." Kant-Forschungen*, vol. III. (Hamburg: Felix Meiner Verlag, 1991). The translation in the present edition is based on Rischmüller's edition, but page numbers in both the Rischmüller edition (noted with an R) and in volume 20 of the Academy Edition are provided. In addition, where there are significant differences between the editions, these are noted in footnotes. In these handwritten *Remarks*, Kant often crossed out portions of remarks and sometimes added extra material later. In this translation, material that Kant crossed out is indicated by a struck-through font. Material that he added later is indicated with triangular brackets. The translators' insertions are noted with square brackets. A selection of these notes has been included in *The Cambridge Edition of the Works of Immanuel Kant: Notes and Fragments*, edited by Paul Guyer (Cambridge University Press, 2005), pp. 1–24. However, while the translators of the present edition consulted that previous version, the translation of the *Remarks* in this volume is new. This is the first published English translation of these *Remarks* in their entirety. The first draft of this translation was made by Thomas Hilgers, with the help of the selection previously translated by Paul Guyer in *Notes and Fragments* and an earlier complete draft by Patrick Frierson and Matthew Cooley. It was then substantially revised by Uygar Abacı and Michael Nance in consultation with Hilgers. An independent draft by Robert R. Clewis was also helpful, especially for a number of the Latin passages. The final draft of the translation by Hilgers, Abacı, and Nance was edited by Guyer.

Kant's "Essay on the Maladies of the Head" (*Versuch über die Krankheiten des Kopfes*) was published in five installments in the *Königsbergische Gelehrte und Politische Zeitungen* (Königsberg Learned and Political Newspaper), edited by Kant's friend and former student, Johann Georg Hamann. The essay was initially published anonymously, but can be reliably ascribed to Kant based on one of the earliest biographies of Kant, by his former student, Ludwig Ernst Borowski.[1] The translation of "Versuch über die Krankheiten des Kopfes" is based on the presentation of the work in Academy Edition 2:257–71 and was undertaken by Holly Wilson. This translation also appears in *The Cambridge Edition of the Works of Immanuel Kant: Anthropology, History, and Education*, pp. 63–77. For this edition, some footnotes and endnotes have been removed or simplified.

The *Inquiry Concerning the Distinctness of the Principles of Natural Theology and Morality* was written for a competition organized by the Prussian Royal Academy in 1763. Although Kant did not win that competition, his essay way published along with the winning essay (by Moses Mendelssohn) by the Academy in 1764. The present translation is based on the presentation of the work in Academy Edition 2:273–301 and was undertaken by David Walford. This translation also appears in *The Cambridge Edition of the Works of Immanuel Kant: Theoretical Philosophy 1755–1770*, pp. 243–75. In the present volume, footnotes and endnotes have been removed or simplified, and the translation has been slightly changed to better accord with the standards of Cambridge Texts in the History of Philosophy. In particular, the German term *Mensch* (and its cognates), previously translated as "man," is now translated as "human," "human being," or "person," depending on the context.

M. Immanuel Kant's Announcement of the Program of his Lectures for the Winter Semester, 1765–1766 was originally published in 1756. As its title suggests, it was one essay of a short series published in order to announce

---

[1] *Darstellung des Lebens und Charakters Immanuel Kants* (1804), reprinted in *Immanuel Kant. Sein Leben in Darstellungen von Zeitgenossen. Die Biographien von L. E. Borowski, R. B. Jachmann und A. Ch. Wasianski*, edited by Felix Groß (Darmstadt, 1974), pp. 1–115, here p. 31.

Kant's forthcoming lectures and to attract students. The present translation is based on the presentation of the work in Academy Edition 2:303–13 and was undertaken by David Walford. This translation also appears in *The Cambridge Edition of the Works of Immanuel Kant: Theoretical Philosophy 1755–1770*, pp. 287–300. For the present volume, footnotes and endnotes have been removed or simplified, and the translation has been slightly changed to better accord with the standards of Cambridge Texts in the History of Philosophy.

Herder's Notes from Kant's Lectures on Ethics is an abridged translation of the notes that Herder wrote and collected during his years as Kant's student. The present translation is based on the edition of these notes included in volume 27 of the Academy Edition and was undertaken by Peter Heath. This abridged translation also appears in *The Cambridge Edition of the Works of Immanuel Kant: Lectures on Ethics*.

The section "**Notes and Fragments**" is based on Kant's handwritten notes, found in the margins and interleaved blank sheets of textbooks used for his courses and in a variety of unbound papers that survived his death. These notes and fragments are collected in the Academy Edition of Kant's works, volumes 14 through 19. The notes collected in the present volume were all written prior to 1770, broadly during the time of the *Observations*, and are from Kant's notes in anthropology (Academy Edition, volume 15) and moral philosophy (Academy Edition, volume 19). Notes are arranged by the volume in which they appear in the Academy Edition, and each is ascribed a number based on the number given it in the Academy Edition. The dating of the notes is often uncertain, but for each note, its likely date of composition is included immediately following the note number. (In cases where there is uncertainty about the date, a different possible date range is provided.) The selections in this volume are taken from the translations in *The Cambridge Edition of the Works of Immanuel Kant: Notes and Fragments*. For this volume, footnotes and endnotes have been removed or simplified.

Thoughts on the Occasion of
Mr. Johann Friedrich von Funk's Untimely Death

Thoughts on the Occasion of
Mr. Johann Friedrich von Funk's Untimely Death

Highborn wife of the cavalry captain, [2:39]
Gracious Lady!

If people living amidst the turmoil of their practical affairs and diversions were occasionally to mix in serious moments of instructive contemplation, to which they are called by the daily display of the vanity of our intentions regarding the fate of their fellow citizens: thereby their pleasures would perhaps be less intoxicating, but their position would take up a calm serenity of the soul, by which accidents are no longer unexpected, and even the gentle melancholy, this tender feeling with which a noble heart swells up if it considers in solitary stillness the contemptibleness of that which, with us, commonly ranks as great and important, would contain more true happiness than the violent merriment of the flippant and the loud laughing of fools.

But thus the greatest crowd of human beings mixes very eagerly in the throng of those who, on the bridge that Providence has built over a piece of the abyss of eternity and that we call **life**, run after certain bubbles and do not trouble to take caution for the planks, who allow one after another to sink beside each other into the depths whose extent is infinity and by which they themselves, in the midst of their impetuous course, are eventually engulfed. In the portrayal of human life, a certain ancient poet brings forth a stirring breath by describing the newly born human being. The child, he says, at once fills the air with sad whimpers,

3

as befits someone who must enter into a world where so many hardships await him. Only in the sequence of years does this human being connect with the art of making himself miserable the art of hiding it from himself with a blanket that he throws on the sad elements of life, and cultivate a

[2:40] flippant carelessness about the amount of ill that surrounds him and as it were inexorably finally drives him back to a much more painful feeling. Although he dreads death most of all ills, he still seems to pay very little attention to the example of it among his fellow citizens, unless closer ties particularly wake his heedfulness. At a time when a raging war opens the bolts of the dark abyss, so as to allow all affliction to break forth over the human race, one sees very well how the common sight of hardship and death instills a cold-natured indifference into those who have been threatened by both, so that they have little heed for the fate of their brothers. Only when in the quiet stillness of civic life, out of the circle of those who either closely concern us or whom we love, who had as many or more promising hopes as we have, and who have been attached to their intentions and plans with the same zeal as we are, only when these, I say, according to the decision of God, who omnipotently rules over all, are taken in the midst of the course of their endeavors; when death in peaceful stillness nears the sickbed of the infirm; when this giant, before which nature shudders, reaches the sickbed with slow steps, to embrace him in iron arms; only then is the feeling of those who otherwise dampen it with diversions truly awakened. A melancholy feeling speaks out of the interior of the heart that which in an assembly of Romans was once heard with so much applause because it is so in accordance with our common perception: **I am a human being, and what befalls human beings can also happen to me.** The friend or relative says to himself: I find myself in the turmoil of business and in the throng of life's duties, and my friend just recently also found himself in the same, I enjoy my life quietly and without worry, but who knows for how long? I amuse myself with my friends and seek him among these same friends,

> Yet he is held fast in that cheerless place
> By him who lets nothing remain [to us]
> In eternity's powerful arms.
> — Haller[1]

[1] Albert von Haller (1708–77), from his "Uncompleted Poem on Eternity" (1736), lines 14–16. This translation is taken from the complete translation of this poem by Arnulf Zweig in *Philosophical*

4

These serious thoughts arise in me because of the early death of your dignified son, gracious woman, which you now so rightly mourn. As one of his former teachers, I feel this loss with grievous sympathy, although I [2:41] can, surely, hardly express the extent of the sadness that must affect those who were linked with **this hopeful young man** through closer bonds. Your grace will allow me to add to these few lines, through which I strive to express the respect that I have entertained for my former pupil, some thoughts that arise in me in my current state of mind.

Every person forms his own plan of his destiny in this world. Skills that he wants to gain, honor and leisure in the future that he expects from them, lasting happiness in married life, and a long line of joys or of ventures constitute the images of the magic lantern that he ingeniously draws and plays in vivid succession in his imagination; death, which puts an end to this shadow play, appears only in the dark distance and is made obscure and unrecognizable by the light that is shed over the more pleasant places. During these reveries our true fate leads us along completely different ways. The lot that will really be granted to us seldom looks similar to what we promised ourselves, in every step that we take we find ourselves deceived in our anticipation; nevertheless the imagination goes about its business and does not tire of drawing up new plans, until death, which still seems to be far away, suddenly brings the whole game to an end. If the person is brought back by understanding from this world of fables, of which he is himself creator through imagination and in which he so gladly resides, to that which providence has truly designed for him, he is thereby put into confusion by a wondrous contradiction that he encounters there and which brings his plans entirely to naught, by presenting to his comprehension insoluble riddles. Budding merits of hopeful youth often fade prematurely under the weight of serious illnesses, and an unwelcome death strikes down the entire plan of hope on which one had counted. The man of skill, of merit, of wealth is not always the one to whom providence has set the farthest end to his life in order fully to enjoy the fruits of all of these. The friendships that are most fond, the marriages that promise the most happiness, are often mercilessly torn by premature death; meanwhile poverty and misery together pull a [2:42] long thread on the dress of the Fates and many only appear to torment

---

Forum 33.3 (2002): 304–11. The addition of "to us" is from the original version of Haller's poem. Kant misremembers "Der nichts zu uns zurücke läßt" as "Der nichts zurücke läßt."

themselves or others by living so long. In this apparent contradiction, the supreme ruler nevertheless distributes his fortune to each with a wise hand. He conceals the end of our destiny in this world in inscrutable darkness, makes us busy with drives, consoled by hope, and, by the happy ignorance of the future, [keeps us] just as constantly thinking of aims and plans when they will soon all come to an end as if we stood at their beginning:

> That each may fill the circle mark'd by Heav'n.
> – Pope[2]

Among these considerations the wise (although how seldom one such is found!) directs attention primarily to his great destiny beyond the grave. He does not lose sight of obligation, which is imposed by his position, which Providence has designed for him. Rational in his plans, but without obstinacy; confident of the fulfillment of his hope, but without impatience; modest in wishes, without dictating; trusting, without insisting; he is eager in the performance of his duties but ready in the midst of all these endeavors to follow the order of the Most High with a Christian resignation if it is pleasing to Him to call him away from the stage where he has been placed, in the middle of all these endeavors. We always find the ways of Providence wise and worthy of worship in those parts where we can understand it to some extent; should they not be more so, where we cannot understand? A premature death of those for whom we had much flattering hope gives us fright; but how often this can be, rather, the greatest grace of heaven! Wasn't the misfortune of many a person primarily in the delay of death, which was much too belated to make an end at the right time, after the most laudable performances of life?

The **hopeful youth** dies, and how much do we believe to be lost through such an early loss? Only in the book of destiny does it perhaps read differently. Seductions that have already arisen from afar in order to dash a not yet well-established virtue, afflictions and tribulations, which the future threatened, this blissfully happy one, whom an early death led [2:43] away in a blessed hour, has escaped all of these; meanwhile friends and relatives, not knowing the future, mourn the loss of those years that they themselves imagine would have someday crowned the life of this family member with glory. Before I close these few lines, I want to draw a small

---

[2] Alexander Pope (1688–1744), from his *Essay on Man* (1733–4), I.i.85.

sketch of the life and character **of the blessedly deceased**. That which I cite is known to me by the communication of his trusted tutor, who mourns him fondly, and from my own acquaintance with him. Yet how many are the good characteristics that are nobler the less they strive to fall openly on the eyes and that are known only to him who sees into the core of the heart!

Herr **Johann Friedrich von Funk** was born on the 4th of October, 1738 into a distinguished noble family in Kurland. From childhood, he never enjoyed full health. He was brought up with great care, showed much diligence in study, and had a heart that was created by nature to be formed to noble qualities. On the 15th of June, 1759, he came, with his younger brother, to this academy under the guidance of their private tutor. He submitted himself with all willingness to the exams of the then dean and brought honor to his diligence and the instruction of his tutor. He attended the lectures of the counselor of the consistory and Professor Teske, who is at the present time Rectoris Magnifici of the university, and likewise attended the lectures of Doctor of Jurisprudence Funck and my own, with an exemplary sedulousness. He lived withdrawn and quietly, through which he still also retained the little strength of his body, which was inclined to emaciation, until near the end of February of this year when he was gradually so weakened that neither the nursing and care that were given him nor the diligence of an adept doctor could any longer preserve him; so weakened that on the 4th of May this year, after he had prepared himself for an uplifting end with the fortitude and ardent devotion of a Christian, with the attendance of his trusted pastor he gently and blessedly passed away and was fittingly buried at the cathedral here.

He was of gentle and calm character, affable and modest toward everyone, kind and inclined toward universal benevolence, zealously solicitous in order to cultivate himself properly to the advantage of his house and his fatherland. He had never grieved anyone except through his death. [2:44] He was eager to have unfeigned piety. He would have become an upright citizen of the world, except that the decree of the Most High willed that he should become one in heaven. His life is a fragment that leaves us much to have wished for, of which we have been deprived by early death.

He would deserve to be represented as an exemplar to those who want to honorably leave behind the years of their upbringing and youth, if emulating a silent service appeals to those of fickle mind as much as the falsely shimmering qualities of those whose conceit pursues only an illusion of virtue without minding the essence of it. He is much mourned by those to whom he belonged, by his friends and everyone who knew him.

These, **gracious lady**, are the traits of the character of your formerly in life rightly so **beloved son**, which, so poorly they may be drawn, nevertheless renew the melancholy that you feel far too much over his loss. But these very bemourned qualities are those that bring no small solace; for only to those who carelessly place the most important of all intentions out of sight can it make no matter in which condition their family is consigned into eternity. I strain myself with the effort to set forth to **your grace** the extensive reasons for solace in this grief. The humble renunciation of our own wishes, when it pleases the wisest Providence to make a different decision, and the Christian longing for the one blessed goal which others before us have reached, are capable of calming of the heart more than all reasons of a dry and feeble eloquence.

I have the honor with the greatest respect to be,

Highborn Lady,
Gracious wife of the captain of cavalry,

Your Grace's

Königsberg,   Most obedient servant
The 6th of June, 1760.   I. Kant.

Observations on the Feeling of the Beautiful and Sublime

[2:205]

Observations
on the Feeling
of the Beautiful and Sublime

By M. Immanuel Kant

Königsberg, by Johann Jakob Kanter, 1764

[first edition]

First Section

On the distinct objects
of the feeling for the sublime and
the beautiful

The different sentiments of gratification or vexation rest not so much on the constitution of the external things that arouse them as on the feeling, intrinsic to every person, of being touched by them with pleasure or displeasure. Hence arise the joys for some people in what is disgusting to others, the passion of a lover that is often a mystery to everyone else, or even the lively repugnance that one person feels[1] in that which is completely indifferent to another. The field for observations of these peculiarities of human nature is very extensive and still conceals a rich lode for discoveries that are as charming as they are instructive. For now I will cast my glance only on several places that seem especially to stand out in this region, and even on these more with the eye of an observer than of the philosopher.

Since a human being finds himself happy only insofar as he satisfies an inclination, the feeling that makes him capable of enjoying a great gratification without requiring exceptional talents is certainly no small matter. Stout persons, whose most inspired author is their cook, and whose works of fine taste are to be found in their cellar, get just as lively a joy from vulgarities and a crude joke as that of which persons of nobler sentiment are so proud. A comfortable man, who likes having books read [2:208] aloud to him because that helps him fall asleep; the merchant to whom all gratifications seem ridiculous except for that which a clever man enjoys when he calculates his business profits; he who loves the opposite sex only insofar as he counts it among the things that are to be enjoyed; the lover of the hunt, whether he hunts fleas, like Domitian,[2] or wild beasts, like A——: all of these have a feeling which makes them capable of enjoying gratification after their fashion, without their having to envy others or even being able to form any concept of others; but for now I do not direct

---

[1] *empfindet*
[2] Domitian was Emperor of Rome from 81 to 96 CE. According to Suetonius, "[a]t the beginning of his reign he used to spend hours in seclusion every day, doing nothing but catch[ing] flies and stab[bing] them with a keenly sharpened stylus"; *The Lives of the Caesars*, trans. J. C. Rolfe, rev. edn London: Loeb Classical Library, 1930, Book VIII, vol. II, p. 345.

any attention to this. There is still a feeling of a finer sort, thus named either because one can enjoy it longer without surfeit and exhaustion, or because it presupposes, so to speak, a susceptibility of the soul which at the same time makes it fit for virtuous impulses, or because it is a sign of talents and excellences of the intellect; while by contrast the former can occur in complete thoughtlessness. It is this feeling one aspect of which I will consider. Yet I exclude here the inclination which is attached to lofty intellectual insights, and the charm of which a **Kepler** was capable when, as **Bayle** reports, he would not have sold one of his discoveries for a princedom.[3] This sentiment is altogether too fine to belong in the present project, which will touch only upon the sensuous feeling of which more common souls are also capable.

The finer feeling that we will now consider is preeminently of two kinds: the feeling of the **sublime** and of the **beautiful**.[4] Being touched by either is agreeable, but in very different ways. The sight of a mountain whose snow-covered peaks arise above the clouds, the description of a raging storm, or the depiction of the kingdom of hell by **Milton** arouses satisfaction, but with dread;[5] by contrast, the prospect of meadows strewn

---

[3] Pierre Bayle says of Kepler, "[w]e may place him among those authors, who have said, that they valued a production of a mind above a kingdom"; "Kepler," in *The Dictionary Historical and Critical of Mr. Peter Bayle*, trans. Pierre Des Maizeaux, 2nd edn, London: 1736, vol. III, pp. 659–60. The article on Kepler is not included in the modern volume of selections from Bayle edited by Richard Popkin (Indianapolis and Cambridge: Hackett, 1991).

[4] The sublime, and the contrast between the beautiful and the sublime, were a constant theme in European letters after the republication of the ancient treatise *Peri hypsous*, falsely attributed to the rhetorician Dionysius Cassius Longinus (*c*. 213–73 CE), translated into English as early as 1652, and, famously, into French by Nicolas Boileau-Despréaux (*Traité du sublime*, Paris: 1674). The most famous work of the eighteenth century on the beautiful and the sublime was by Edmund Burke (*A Philosophical Enquiry into the Origin of our Ideas of the Sublime and the Beautiful*, London: 1757; 2nd edn, 1759). Burke's book became known in Germany via the 1758 review by Moses Mendelssohn, "Philosophische Untersuchung des Ursprungs unserer Ideen vom Erhabenen und Schönen," *Bibliothek der schönen Wissenschaften* 3.2. Kant would cite Burke several times in the *Critique of the Power of Judgment*, notably in the General Remark following § 29 (Academy Edition 5:277).

[5] Virtually all of Book I of *Paradise Lost* offers a graphic description of the imagined terrors of hell. Some sample lines are:

> The dismal situation waste and wild,
> A dungeon horrible, on all sides round
> As one great furnace flamed, yet from those flames
> No light, but rather darkness visible
> Served only to discover sights of woe,
> Regions of sorrow, doleful shades, where peace
> And rest can never dwell, hope never comes
> That comes to all; but torture without end

with flowers, of valleys with winding brooks, covered with grazing herds, the description of Elysium,[6] or **Homer's** depiction of the girdle of Venus[7]

> Still urges, and a fiery deluge, fed
> With ever-burning sulphur unconsumed:
> Such place eternal justice had prepared
> For those rebellious, here their prison ordained
> In utter darkness, and their portion set
> As far removed from God and light of heaven
> As from the centre thrice to the utmost pole.
> (*Paradise Lost*, Book I, lines 60–74;
> *John Milton*, ed. Stephen Orgel and
> Jonathan Goldberg, Oxford University
> Press, 1991, p. 357)

[6] Presumably Kant has in mind the description of Elysium that Virgil gives in the *Aeneid*, Book VI, beginning at line 853:

> His duty to the goddess done, they came
> To places of delight, to green park land,
> Where souls take ease amid the Blessed Groves.
> Wider expanses of high air endow
> Each vista with a wealth of light
>
> . . .
>
> Within a fragrant laurel grove, where Po
> Sprang up and took his course to the world above,
> The broad stream flowing on amid the forest.
> This was the company of those who suffered
> Wounds in battle for their country; those
> Who in their lives were holy men and chaste
> Or worthy of Phoebus in prophetic song;
> Or those who better life, by finding out
> New truths and skills;
>
> . . .
>
> "None of us
> Has one fixed home. We walk in shady groves
> And bed on riverbanks and occupy
> Green meadows fresh with streams . . . "
> (Virgil, *The Aeneid*, trans. Robert Fitzgerald,
> New York: Random House, 1981, Book VI,
> lines 853–903, pp. 182–3)

[7] Hera requested Aphrodite to help her reconcile the feuding Greeks and Trojans:

> "But if words of mine could lure them back to love,
> back to bed, to lock in each other's arms once more
>
> . . .
>
> they would call me their honored, loving friend forever."
>
> Aphrodite, smiling her everlasting smile, replied,
> "Impossible—worse, it's *wrong* to deny your warm request,
> since you are the one who lies in the arms of mighty Zeus."
>
> With that she loosed from her breasts the breastband,
> pierced and alluring, with every kind of enchantment
> woven through it . . . There is the heat of Love,

15

also occasion an agreeable sentiment, but one that is joyful and smiling. For the former to make its impression on us in its proper strength, we must have a **feeling** of the **sublime**, and in order properly to enjoy the latter we must have a **feeling** for the **beautiful**. Lofty oaks and lonely shadows in sacred groves are **sublime**, flowerbeds, low hedges, and trees trimmed into figures are **beautiful**. The night is **sublime**, the

[2:209] day is **beautiful**. Casts of mind that possess a feeling for the sublime are gradually drawn into lofty sentiments, of friendship, of contempt for the world, of eternity, by the quiet calm of a summer evening, when the flickering light of the stars breaks through the umber shadows of the night and the lonely moon rises into view. The brilliant day inspires busy fervor and a feeling of[8] gaiety. The sublime **touches**, the beautiful **charms**. The mien of the human being who finds himself in the full feeling of the sublime is serious, sometimes even rigid and astonished. By contrast, the lively sentiment of the beautiful announces itself through shining cheerfulness in the eyes, through traces of a smile, and often through audible mirth. The sublime is in turn of different sorts. The feeling of it is sometimes accompanied with some dread or even melancholy, in some cases merely with quiet admiration and in yet others with a beauty spread over a sublime prospect. I will call the first the **terrifying sublime**, the second the **noble**, and the third the **magnificent**. Deep solitude is sublime, but in a terrifying way.[a,9] For this reason great and extensive

---

[2:209] [a] I will only provide an example of the noble dread which the description of a total solitude can inspire, and to this end I will extract several passages from **Carazan's dream** in the *Bremen Magazine*, Volume IV, page 539. The more his riches had grown, the more did this miserly rich man bar his heart to compassion and the love of others. Meanwhile, as the love of humankind grew cold in him, the diligence of his prayers and religious devotions increased. After this confession, he goes on to recount: One evening, as I did my sums by my lamp and calculated the profit of

> the pulsing rush of Longing, the lover's whisper,
> irresistable—magic to make the sanest man go mad.
> And thrusting it into Hera's outstretched hands,
> she breathed her name in a throbbing, rising voice:
> "Here now, take this band, put it between your breasts—
> ravishing openwork, and the world lies in its weaving!"
> (Homer, *The Iliad*, trans. Robert Fagles, New York:
> Viking, 1990, Book XIV, lines 251–66, pp. 376–77).

[8] In the second and third editions: for.

[9] The example comes from the *Bremisches Magazin zur Ausbreitung der Wissenschaften und Künste und Tugend. Von einigen Liebhabern derselben aus den englischen Monatschriften gesammelt und herausgegeben* (Bremen Magazine for the Propagation of the Sciences and the Arts and Virtue. Collected and edited from the English monthlies by some lovers of the former) 4 (1761): 539.

wastes, such as the immense deserts of Schamo in Tartary, have always [5:210] given us occasion to people them with fearsome shades, goblins, and ghosts.

The sublime must always be large, the beautiful can also be small. The sublime must be simple, the beautiful can be decorated and ornamented. A great height is just as sublime as a great depth, but the latter is accompanied with the sensation[10] of shuddering, the former with that of admiration; hence the latter sentiment can be terrifyingly sublime and the former noble. The sight of an Egyptian pyramid is far more moving, as **Hasselquist** reports,[11] than one can imagine from any description, but its construction is simple and noble. St. Peter's in Rome is magnificent. Since on its frame, which is grand and simple, beauty, e.g., gold, mosaics, etc., are spread in such a way that it is still the sentiment of the sublime which has the most effect, the object is called magnificent.[12] An arsenal must be noble and simple, a residential castle magnificent, and a pleasure palace beautiful and decorated.[13]

---

my business, I was overcome by sleep. In this condition I saw the angel of death come upon me like a whirlwind, and he struck me, before I could plead against the terrible blow. I was petrified as I became aware that my fate had been cast for eternity, and that to all the good I had done, nothing could be added, and from all the evil that I had done, nothing could be subtracted. I was led before the throne of he who dwells in the third heaven. The brilliance that flamed before me spoke to me thus: Carazan, your divine service is rejected. You have closed your heart to the love of humankind, and held on to your treasures with an iron hand. You have lived only for yourself, and hence in the future you shall also live alone and excluded from all communion with the entirety of creation for all eternity. In this moment I was ripped away by an invisible force and driven through the shining edifice of creation. I quickly left innumerable worlds behind me. As I approached the most extreme limit of nature, I noticed that the shadows of the boundless void sank [2:210] into the abyss before me. A fearful realm of eternal silence, solitude and darkness! Unspeakable dread overcame me at this sight. I gradually lost the last stars from view, and finally the last glimmer of light was extinguished in the most extreme darkness. The mortal terrors of despair increased with every moment, just as every moment my distance from the last inhabited world increased. I reflected with unbearable anguish in my heart that if ten thousand thousand years were to carry me further beyond the boundaries of everything created, I would still see forward into the immeasurable abyss of darkness without help or hope of return. – In this bewilderment I stretched my hands out to actual objects with such vehemence that I was thereby awakened. And now I have been instructed to esteem human beings; for even the least of them, whom in the pride of my good fortune I had turned from my door, would have been far more welcome to me in that terrifying desert than all the treasures of Golconda.

[10] *Empfindung*
[11] D. Friedrich Hasselquist, *Reise nach Palästina in den Jahren 1749–1762* (Journey to Palestine in the Years 1749–1762), Rostock: 1762, pp. 82–94.
[12] Kant refers to both the pyramids and St. Peter's in the course of his explication of the mathematical sublime in the *Critique of the Power of Judgment*, § 26, Academy Edition 5:252.
[13] This sentence anticipates Kant's later account of dependent judgments of beauty; see *Critique of the Power of Judgment*, § 16, Academy Edition 5:230.

A long duration is sublime. If it is of time past, it is noble; if it is projected forth into an unforeseeable future, then there is something terrifying in it. An edifice from the most distant antiquity is worthy of honor. **Haller's** description of the future eternity inspires a mild horror, and of the past, a transfixed admiration.[14]

Second Section

On the qualities of the sublime and the beautiful in human beings in general

Understanding is sublime, wit is beautiful. Boldness is sublime and grand, cunning is petty, but beautiful. Caution, said **Cromwell**, is a virtue for mayors.[15] Truthfulness and honesty is simple and noble, jocularity and pleasing flattery is fine and beautiful. Civility is the beauty of virtue. An unselfish urge to serve is noble, refinement (*politesse*) and courtliness are beautiful. Sublime qualities inspire esteem, but beautiful ones inspire love. People whose feelings run primarily to the beautiful seek out their honest, steady, and serious friends only in case of need; for ordinary company, however, they choose jocular, clever, and courtly companions. One esteems many a person too highly to be able to love him. He inspires admiration, but he is too far above us for us to dare to come close to him with the familiarity of love.

Those in whom both feelings are united will find that they are more powerfully moved by the sublime than by the beautiful, but that without variation or accompaniment by the latter the former is tiring and cannot be enjoyed as long.[b] The lofty sentiments to which conversation in a well-chosen company is sometimes elevated must intermittently dissolve

[b] The sentiments of the sublime stretch the powers of the soul more forcefully and therefore tire more quickly. One will read a pastoral longer at one sitting than Milton's *Paradise Lost* and la Bruyère longer than Young. It even seems to me to be a failing of the latter as a moral poet that he holds forth too uniformly in a sublime tone; for the strength of the impression can only be refreshed by interspersing gentler passages. In the case of the beautiful nothing is more tiring than laborious art that thereby betrays itself. The effort to charm becomes painful and is felt to be wearisome.

[14] Albrecht von Haller, *Über die Ewigkeit* (1736).
[15] Kant attributes this statement to Oliver Cromwell, Lord Protector of Great Britain.

into a cheerful joke, and laughing joys should make a beautiful contrast with moved, serious countenances, allowing for an unforced alternation between both sorts of sentiment. **Friendship** has primarily the character of the sublime, but **sexual love** that of the beautiful. Yet tenderness and deep esteem give the latter a certain dignity and sublimity, while flighty jocularity and intimacy elevate the coloration of the beautiful in this sentiment. In my opinion, **tragedy** is distinguished from **comedy** primarily in the fact that in the former it is the feeling for the **sublime** while in the latter it is the feeling for the **beautiful** that is touched. In the former there is displayed magnanimous sacrifice for the well-being of another, bold resolve in the face of danger, and proven fidelity. There love is melancholic, tender, and full of esteem; the misfortune of others stirs sympathetic sentiments in the bosom of the onlooker and allows his magnanimous heart to beat for the need of others. He is gently moved and feels the dignity of his own nature. Comedy, in contrast, represents intrigues, marvelous entanglements and clever people who know how to wriggle out of them, fools who let themselves be deceived, jests and ridiculous characters. Here love is not so grave, it is merry and intimate. Yet as in other cases, here too the noble can be united with the beautiful to a certain degree.

[2:212]

Even the vices and moral failings often carry with them some of the traits of the sublime or the beautiful, at least as they appear to our sensory feeling, without having been examined by reason. The wrath of someone fearsome is sublime, like the wrath of Achilles in the *Iliad*.[16] In general, the hero of **Homer** is **terrifyingly sublime**, that of **Virgil**, by contrast, **noble**. Open, brazen revenge for a great offense has something grand in it, and however impermissible it might be, yet in the telling it nevertheless touches us with dread and satisfaction. When Shah Nadir was attacked at night in his tent by some conspirators, as Hanaway reports, after he had already received several wounds and was defending himself in despair, he yelled **Mercy! I will pardon you all.** One of the conspirators answered, as he raised his saber high: **You have shown no mercy and**

---

[16] Achilles hated Agamemnon for having taken the girl Briseis from him, and refused to join in the fight against Troy for the recovery of Helen, when, after all, Agamemnon already had Briseis. Agamemnon sent embassadors with gifts to recruit Achilles, but Achilles replied, "I hate that man like very Gates of Death, / who says one thing but hides another in his heart." Homer, *The Iliad*, Book IX, lines 378–79 (Fagles, p. 262).

deserve none.[17] Resolute audacity in a rogue is extremely dangerous, yet it touches us in the telling, and even when he is dragged to a shameful death yet he enobles himself to a certain degree when he faces it spitefully and with contempt. On the other side, a cunningly conceived scheme, even when it amounts to a piece of knavery, has something about it that is fine and worth a laugh. A wanton inclination (*coquetterie*) in a refined sense, namely an effort to fascinate and to charm, is perhaps blameworthy in an otherwise decorous person, yet it is still beautiful and is commonly preferred to the honorable, serious demeanor.

[2:213]

The figure[18] of persons who please through their outward appearance[19] touches now upon one sort of feeling, now upon the other. A grand stature earns regard[20] and respect, a small one more intimacy. Even brownish color and black eyes are more closely related to the sublime, blue eyes and blonde color to the beautiful. A somewhat greater age is associated more with the qualities of the sublime, youth, however, with those of the beautiful. It is similar with difference in station, and in all of those relations mentioned here even the costumes must match this distinction in feeling. Grand, sizable persons must observe simplicity or at most splendor in their dress, while small ones can be decorated and adorned. Darker colors and uniformity in costume are fitting for age, while youth radiates through brighter clothing with lively contrasts. Among the stations of similar fortune and rank, the cleric must display the greatest simplicity, the statesman the greatest splendor. The paramour can adorn himself as he pleases.

Even in external circumstances of fortune there is something that, at least in the folly of humankind, matches these sentiments. People commonly find themselves inclined to respect birth and title. Wealth, even without merit, is honored even by the disinterested, presumably because they associate with the representation of it projects for great actions that could be carried out by its means. This respect is even sometimes extended to many a rich scoundrel, who will never undertake such actions and has no conception of the noble feeling that can alone make riches estimable. What magnifies the evil of poverty is contempt,

---

[17] Jonas Hanaway, *Herrn Jonas Hanaways zuverlässige Beschreibung. Nebst einer unpartheyischen Histoire des grossen Eroberers Nadir Kuli oder Kuli Chams* (Mr. Jonas Hanaway's reliable description. Together with an impartial history of the great Conquerer Nadir Kuli or Kuli Chams), Hamburg and Leipzig, 1754, Part II, p. 396.
[18] *Gestalt*   [19] *Ansehen*   [20] *Ansehen*

which cannot be entirely overcome even by merits, at least not before common eyes, unless rank and title deceive this coarse feeling and to some extent work to its advantage.

In human nature there are never to be found praiseworthy qualities that do not at the same time degenerate through endless gradations into the most extreme imperfection. The quality of the **terrifying sublime**, if it becomes entirely unnatural, is **adventurous**.[c] Unnatural things, [2:214] in so far as the sublime is thereby intended, even if little or none of it is actually found, are **grotesqueries**. He who loves and believes the adventurous is a **fantast**, while the inclination to grotesqueries makes for a **crank**. On the other side, the feeling of the beautiful degenerates if the noble is entirely lacking from it, and one calls it **ridiculous**. A male with this quality, if he is young, is called a **dandy**, and if he is middle-aged, a **fop**. Since the sublime is most necessary for the greater age, an **old fop** is the most contemptible creature in nature, just as a young crank is the most repulsive and insufferable. Jokes and cheerfulness go with the feeling of the beautiful. Nevertheless a good deal of understanding can show through, and to this extent they can be more or less related to the sublime. He in whose cheerfulness this admixture cannot be noticed **babbles**. He who babbles constantly is **silly**. One readily notices that even clever people occasionally babble, and that it requires not a little intelligence[21] to call the understanding away from its post for a brief time without anything thereby going awry. He whose speeches or actions neither entertain nor move is **boring**. The bore who nevertheless tries to do both is **tasteless**. The tasteless person, if he is conceited, is a **fool**.[d]

I will make this curious catalog of human frailties somewhat more comprehensible through examples, for he who lacks Hogarth's burin must use description to make up for what the drawing lacks in expression.[22] Boldly

---

[c] In so far as sublimity or beauty exceed the known average, one tends to call them **fictitious**.

[d] One quickly notices that this honorable company divides itself into two compartments, the cranks and the fops. A learned crank is politely called a **pedant**. If he adopts the obstinate mien of wisdom, like the **dunces** of olden and recent times, then the cap with bells becomes him well. The class of fops is more often encountered in high society. It is perhaps better than the former. At their expense one has much to gain and much to laugh at. In this caricature one makes a wry face at the other and knocks his empty head on the head of his brother.

[21] *Geist*

[22] William Hogarth (1697–1764), British painter and engraver, artist of such famous series as *The Rake's Progress* and author of *The Analysis of Beauty: Written with a view of fixing the fluctuating Ideas of Taste* (London: J. Reeves, 1753).

undertaking danger for our own rights, for those of the fatherland, or for those of our friends is sublime. The crusades and ancient knighthood were **adventurous**; duels, a miserable remnant of the latter out of a perverted conception of honor, are **grotesqueries**. Melancholy withdrawal from the tumult of the world out of a legitimate weariness is **noble**. The solitary devotion of the ancient hermits was **adventurous**. Cloisters and graves of that sort for the entombment of living saints are **grotesqueries**. Subduing one's passions by means of principles is **sublime**. Castigation, vows, and other such monkish virtues are **grotesqueries**. Holy bones, holy wood, and all that sort of rubbish, the holy stools of the Great Lama of Tibet not excluded, are **grotesqueries**. Among the works of wit and fine feeling, the epic poems of Virgil and Klopstock are among the **noble**, those of Homer and Milton among the **adventurous**. The *Metamorphoses* of Ovid are **grotesqueries**, the fairy tales of French lunacy are the most wretched grotesqueries that have ever been hatched. Anacreontic poems commonly come very close to the **ridiculous**.

[2:215]

The works of the understanding and acuity, to the extent that their objects also contain something for feeling, likewise take some part in the differences under consideration. The mathematical representation of the immeasurable magnitude of the universe, metaphysical considerations of eternity, of providence, of the immortality of our soul contain a certain sublimity and dignity. Yet philosophy[23] is also distorted by many empty subtleties, and the semblance of thoroughness does not prevent the four syllogistic figures from deserving to be counted as scholastic grotesqueries.

Among moral[24] qualities, true virtue alone is sublime. There are nevertheless good moral[25] qualities that are lovable and beautiful and, to the extent that they harmonize with virtue, may also be regarded as noble, even though they cannot genuinely be counted as part of the virtuous disposition. Judgment about this is delicate and involved. One certainly cannot call that frame of mind virtuous that is a source of actions of the sort to which virtue would also lead but on grounds that only contingently agree with it, and which thus given its nature can also often conflict with the universal rules of virtue. A certain tenderheartedness that is easily led into a warm feeling of **sympathy** is beautiful and lovable, for it indicates a kindly participation in the fate of other people, to which principles of

---

[23] *die Weltweisheit*   [24] *moralischen*   [25] *sittlichen*

virtue likewise lead. But this kindly passion is nevertheless weak and is [2:216] always blind. For suppose that this sentiment moves you to help someone in need with your expenditure, but you are indebted to someone else and by this means you make it impossible for yourself to fulfill the strict duty of justice; then obviously the action cannot arise from any virtuous resolution, for that could not possibly entice you into sacrificing a higher obligation to this blind enchantment. If, by contrast, general affection towards humankind has become your principle, to which you always subject your actions, then your love towards the one in need remains, but it is now, from a higher standpoint, placed in its proper relationship to your duty as a whole. The universal affection is a ground for participating in his ill-fortune, but at the same time it is also a ground of justice, in accordance with whose precept you must now forbear this action. Now as soon as this feeling is raised to its proper universality, it is sublime, but also colder. For it is not possible that our bosom should swell with tenderness on behalf of every human being and swim in melancholy for everyone else's need, otherwise the virtuous person, like Heraclitus constantly melting into sympathetic tears,[26] with all this good-heartedness would nevertheless become nothing more than a tenderhearted idler.[e]

The second sort of kindly feeling which is to be sure beautiful and lovable but still not the foundation of a genuine virtue is **complaisance:**[27] an inclination to make ourselves agreeable to others through friendliness, through acquiescence to their demands, and through conformity of our conduct to their dispositions. This ground for a charming complaisance is beautiful, and the malleability of such a heart is kindly. Yet it is so far from

---

[e] On closer consideration, one finds that however lovable the quality of sympathy may be, yet it does not have in itself the dignity of virtue. A suffering child, an unhappy though upright woman may fill our heart with this melancholy, while at the same time we may coldly receive the news of a great battle in which, as may readily be realized, a considerable part of humankind must innocently suffer dreadful evils. Many a prince who has averted his countenance from melancholy for a single unfortunate person has at the same time given the order for war, often from a vain motive. There is here no proportion in the effect at all, so how can one say that the general love of humankind is the cause?

[26] Heraclitus of Ephesus, fl. *c.* 500–480 BCE. "The legend of the 'weeping philosopher' is late and based on a combination of a Platonic joke, Heraclitus' theory of flux, and a misunderstanding of Theophrastus' word 'melancholia,' which originally meant 'impulsiveness'"; Michael C. Stokes, "Heraclitus of Ephesus," in Paul Edwards, ed., *The Encyclopedia of Philosophy*, New York: Macmillan, 1967, vol. III, pp. 477–81, at p. 477. For the standard work on Heraclitus, see Charles H. Kahn, *The Art and Thought of Heraclitus: An Edition of the Fragments with Translation and Commentary*, Cambridge University Press, 1979.

[27] Kant's text has a period here.

[2:217]   being a virtue that unless higher principles set bounds for it and weaken it, all sorts of vices may spring from it. For without even considering that this complaisance towards those with whom we associate is often an injustice to those who find themselves outside of this little circle, such a man, if one takes this impulse alone, can have all sorts of vices, not because of immediate inclination but because he gladly lives to please. From affectionate complaisance he will be a liar, an idler, a drunkard, etc., for he does not act in accordance with the rules for good conduct in general, but rather in accordance with an inclination that is beautiful in itself but which in so far as it is without self-control and without principles becomes ridiculous.

Thus true virtue can only be grafted upon principles, and it will become the more sublime and noble the more general they are. These principles are not speculative rules, but the consciousness of a feeling that lives in every human breast and that extends much further than to the special grounds of sympathy and complaisance. I believe that I can bring all this together if I say that it is the **feeling of the beauty and the dignity of human nature.**[28] The first is a ground of universal affection, the second of universal respect, and if this feeling had the greatest perfection in any human heart then this human being would certainly love and value even himself, but only in so far as he is one among all to whom his widespread and noble feeling extends itself. Only when one subordinates one's own particular inclination to such an enlarged one can our kindly drives be proportionately applied and bring about the noble attitude that is the beauty of virtue.

In recognition of the weakness of human nature and the little power that the universal moral feeling exercises over most hearts, providence has placed such helpful drives in us as supplements for virtue, which move some to beautiful actions even without principles while at the same time being able to give others, who are ruled by these principles, a greater impetus and a stronger impulse thereto. Sympathy and complaisance are grounds for beautiful actions that would perhaps all be suffocated by the preponderance of a cruder self-interest, but as we have seen they

---

[28] The argument that virtue depends on principles rather than feeling anticipates Kant's mature moral philosophy; the present reference to the special dignity of human nature should be compared to Kant's statement in the *Groundwork for the Metaphysics of Morals*, § 2, Academy Edition 4:435.

are not immediate grounds of virtue, although since they are ennobled
by their kinship with it they also bear its name. Hence I can call them
adopted virtues, but that which rest on principles **genuine virtue**.　　[2:218]
The former are beautiful and charming, the latter alone is sublime and
worthy of honor. One calls a mind in which the former sentiments rule
a **good heart** and people of that sort **good-hearted**; but one rightly
ascribes a **noble heart** to one who is virtuous from principles, calling
him alone a **righteous** person. These adopted virtues nevertheless have
a great similarity to the true virtues, since they contain the feeling of an
immediate pleasure in kindly and benevolent actions. The good-hearted
person will without any ulterior aim and from immediate complaisance
conduct himself peaceably and courteously with you and feel sincere
compassion for the need of another.

Yet since this moral sympathy is nevertheless not enough to drive
indolent human nature to actions for the common weal,[29] providence has
further placed in us a certain feeling which is fine and moves us, or which
can also balance cruder self-interest and vulgar sensuality. This is the
feeling for honor and its consequence, **shame**. The opinion that others
may have of our value and their judgment of our actions is a motivation
of great weight, which can coax us into many sacrifices, and what a
good part of humanity would have done neither out of an immediately
arising emotion of good-heartedness nor out of principles happens often
enough merely for the sake of outer appearance, out of a delusion that
is very useful although in itself very facile, as if the judgment of others
determined the worth of ourselves and our actions. What happens from
this impulse is not in the least virtuous, for which reason everyone who
wants to be taken for virtuous takes good care to conceal the motivation
of lust for honor. This inclination is also not nearly so closely related as
good-heartedness is to genuine virtue, since it is not moved immediately
by the beauty of actions, but by their demeanor in the eyes of others. Since
the feeling for honor is nevertheless still fine, I can call the similarity to
virtue that is thereby occasioned the **simulacrum of virtue**.

If we compare the casts of mind of human beings in so far as one of
these three species of feeling dominates in them and determines their
moral character, we find that each of them stands in closer kinship with

---

[29] *gemeinnützig*

[2:219] one of the temperaments as they are usually divided,[30] yet in such a way that a greater lack of moral feeling would be the share of the phlegmatic. Not as if the chief criterion in the character of these different casts of mind came down to the features at issue; for in this treatise we are not considering the cruder feelings, e.g., that of self-interest, of vulgar sensuality, etc., at all, even though these sorts of inclinations are what are primarily considered in the customary division; but rather since the finer moral sentiments here mentioned are more compatible with one or the other of these temperaments and for the most part are actually so united.

An inward feeling for the beauty and dignity of human nature and a self-composure and strength of mind to relate all of one's actions to this as a general ground is serious and not readily associated with a fickle wantonness nor with the inconstancy of a frivolous person. It even approaches melancholy, a gentle and noble sentiment, to the extent that it is grounded in that dread which a restricted soul feels if, full of a great project, it sees the dangers that it has to withstand and has before its eyes the difficult but great triumph of self-overcoming. Genuine virtue from principles therefore has something about it that seems to agree most with the **melancholic** frame of mind in a moderate sense.

Good-heartedness, a beauty and fine susceptibility of the heart to be moved with sympathy or benevolence in individual cases as occasion demands, is very much subject to the change of circumstances; and since the movement of the soul does not rest upon a general principle, it readily takes on different shapes as the objects display one aspect or another. And since this inclination comes down to the beautiful, it appears to be most naturally united with that cast of mind that one calls **sanguine**, which is fickle and given to amusements. In this temperament we shall have to seek the well-loved qualities that we called adopted virtues.

The feeling for honor is usually already taken as a mark of the **choleric** complexion, and we can thereby take the occasion to seek out the moral [2:220] consequences of this fine feeling, which for the most part are aimed only at show, for the depiction of such a character.

A person is never without all traces of finer sentiment, but a greater lack of the latter, which is comparatively called a lack of feeling, is found

---

[30] Kant continued to discuss the moral significance of the traditional doctrine of the four temperaments in his anthropology lectures, beginning with his earliest lectures in 1772–73 (see *Anthropologie Collins*, Academy Edition 25:219–26) and continuing through his published handbook *Anthropology from a Pragmatic Point of View* (1798), Part II, Academy Edition 7:288–91.

in the character of the **phlegmatic**, whom one also deprives even of the cruder incentives, such as lust for money, etc., which, however, together with other sister inclinations, we can even leave to him, because they do not belong in this plan at all.

Let us now more closely consider the sentiments of the sublime and the beautiful, especially in so far as they are moral, under the assumed division of the temperaments.

He whose feeling tends towards the **melancholic** is so called not because, robbed of the joys of life, he worries himself into blackest dejection,[31] but because his sentiments, if they were to be increased above a certain degree or to take a false direction through some causes, would more readily result in that than in some other condition. He has above all a **feeling for the sublime**. Even beauty, for which he also has a sentiment, may not merely charm him, but must rather move him by at the same time inspiring him with admiration. The enjoyment of gratification is in his case more serious, but not on that account any lesser. All emotions of the sublime are more enchanting than the deceptive charms of the beautiful. His well-being will be contentment rather than jollity. He is steadfast. For that reason he subordinates his sentiments to principles. They are the less subject to inconstancy and alteration the more general is this principle to which they are subordinated, and thus the more extensive is the elevated feeling under which the lower ones are comprehended. All particular grounds of inclinations are subjected to many exceptions and alterations in so far as they are not derived from such a high ground. The cheerful and friendly Alceste[32] says: I love and treasure my wife, because she is beautiful, flattering, and clever. But what if, when she becomes disfigured with illness, sullen with age, and, once the first enchantment has disappeared, no longer seems more clever than any other to you? If the ground is no longer there, what can become of the inclination? By contrast, take the benevolent and steady Adraste, who thinks to himself: I will treat this person lovingly and with respect, because she is my wife. This disposition is noble and generous. However the contingent charms [2:221] may change, she is nevertheless always still his wife. The noble ground endures and is not so subject to the inconstancy of external things. Such

[31] *Schwermut*
[32] Kant here seems to be referring to characters from Molière, where Alceste appears in the *Misanthrope* and Adraste in *Le Sicilien ou l'amour peintre*. He is not quoting from the plays, but is interpreting Molière's characters.

is the quality of principles in comparison to emotions, which well up only on particular occasions, and thus is the man of principles by contrast to one who is occasionally overcome by a good-hearted and lovable motivation. But what if the secret language of his heart speaks thus: I must come to the help of this human being, for he suffers; not that he is my friend or companion, or that I hold him capable of sometime repaying my beneficence with gratitude. There is now no time for ratiocination and stopping at questions: He is a human being, and whatever affects human beings also affects me.[33] Then his conduct is based on the highest ground of benevolence in human nature and is extremely sublime, on account of its inalterability as well as the universality of its application.

I continue with my comments. The person of a melancholic frame of mind troubles himself little about how others judge, what they hold to be good or true, and in that regard he relies solely on his own insight. Since his motivations take on the nature of principles, he is not easily brought to other conceptions; his steadfastness thus sometimes degenerates into obstinacy. He looks on changes in fashion with indifference and on their luster with contempt. Friendship is sublime and hence he has a feeling for it. He can perhaps lose an inconstant friend, but the latter does not lose him equally quickly. Even the memory of an extinguished friendship is still worthy of honor for him. Talkativeness is beautiful, thoughtful taciturnity sublime. He is a good guardian of his own secrets and those of others. Truthfulness is sublime, and he hates lies or dissemblance. He has a lofty feeling for the dignity of human nature. He esteems himself and holds a human being to be a creature who deserves respect. He does not tolerate abject submissiveness and breathes freedom in a noble breast. All shackles, from the golden ones worn at court to the heavy irons of the galley-slave, are abominable to him. He is a strict judge of himself and others and is not seldom weary of himself as well as of the world.

In the degenerate form of this character, seriousness inclines to dejection,[34] piety to zealotry, the fervor for freedom to enthusiasm. Insult and injustice kindle vengefulness in him. He is then very much to be feared. He defies danger and has contempt for death. In case of perversion of his feeling and lack of a cheerful reason he succumbs

[2:222]

---

[33] Here Kant alludes to the speech by Chremes in the Act i, scene i of Terence's *Self-Tormentor*, "I am a human being; I am interested in everything human"; *The Complete Roman Drama*, ed. George E. Duckworth, New York: Random House, 1942, vol. ii, p. 199.
[34] *Schwermut*

to the **adventurous**:[35] inspirations, apparitions, temptations. If the understanding is even weaker, he hits upon **grotesqueries**:[36] portentous dreams, presentiments, and wondrous omens. He is in danger of becoming a **fantast** or a **crank**.

The person of a **sanguine** frame of mind has a dominant **feeling for the beautiful**. His joys are therefore laughing and lively. When he is not jolly, he is discontent and he has little acquaintance with contented silence. Variety is beautiful, and he loves change. He seeks joy in himself and around himself, amuses others, and is good company. He has much moral sympathy. The joyfulness of others is gratifying to him, and their suffering makes him soft-hearted. His moral feeling is beautiful, yet without principles, and is always immediately dependent upon the impressions that objects make on him at the moment. He is a friend of all human beings, or, what is really the same, never really a friend, although he is certainly good-hearted and benevolent. He does not dissemble. Today he will entertain you with his friendliness and good sorts, tomorrow, when you are ill or misfortunate, he will feel genuine and unfeigned compassion, but he will quietly slip away until the circumstances have changed. He must never be a judge. The laws are commonly too strict for him, and he lets himself be bribed by tears. He is a bad saint, never entirely good and never entirely evil. He is often dissolute and wicked, more from complaisance than from inclination. He is liberal and generous, but a poor payer of his debts, since he has much sentiment for goodness but little for justice. Nobody has as good an opinion of his own heart as he does. If you do not esteem him, you must still love him. In the greater deterioration of his character, he descends to the **ridiculous**, he is dawdling and childish. If age does not diminish his liveliness or bring him more understanding, then he is in danger of becoming an old fop.

He whom one means by the **choleric** constitution of mind has a dominant feeling for that sort of the sublime which one can call the **magnificent**. It is really only the gloss of sublimity and a strikingly contrasting coloration, which hides the inner content of the thing or the [2:223] person, who is perhaps only bad and common, and which deceives and moves through its appearance.[37] Just as an edifice makes just as noble an impression by means of a stucco coating that represents carved stones, as if it were really made from that, and tacked-on cornices and pilasters give

---

35 The original text has a period here. 36 The original text has a period here. 37 *Schein*

the idea of solidity although they have little bearing and support nothing, in the same way do alloyed virtues, tinsel of wisdom, and painted merit also glisten.

The choleric person considers his own value and the value of his things and actions on the basis of the propriety or the appearance[38] with which it strikes the eye. With regard to the inner quality and the motivations that the object itself contains, he is cold, neither warmed by true benevolence nor moved by respect.[f] His conduct is artificial. He must know how to adopt all sorts of standpoints in order to judge his propriety from the various attitudes of the onlookers; for he asks little about what he is, but only about what he seems. For this reason he must be well acquainted with the effect on the general taste and the many impressions which his conduct will have outside of him. Since in this sly attention he always needs cold blood and must not let himself be blinded by love, compassion, and sympathy, he will also avoid many follies and vexations to which a sanguine person succumbs, who is enchanted by his immediate sentiment. For this reason he commonly appears to be more intelligent than he actually is. His benevolence is politeness, his respect ceremony, his love is concocted flattery. When he adopts the attitude of a lover or a friend he is always full of himself, and is never either the one or the other. He seeks to shine through fashions, but since everything with him is artificial and made up, he is stiff and awkward in them. He acts in accordance with principles much more than the sanguine person does, who is moved only by the impressions of the occasion; but these are not principles of virtue, but of honor, and he has no feeling for the beauty or the value of actions, but only for the judgment that the world might make about them. Since his conduct, as long as one does not look to the source from which

[2:224] it stems, is otherwise almost as useful as virtue itself, he earns the same esteem as the virtuous person in vulgar eyes, but before more refined ones he carefully conceals himself, because he knows well that the discovery of the secret incentive of lust for honor would cost him respect. He is thus much given to dissemblance, hypocritical in religion, a flatterer in society, and in matters of political party he is fickle as circumstances suggest. He is gladly a slave of the great in order to be a tyrant over the lesser. *Naïvete,*

---

[f] Although he also holds himself to be happy only in so far as he suspects that he is taken to be so by others.

[38] *Schein*

this noble or beautiful simplicity, which bears the seal of nature and not of art, is entirely alien to him. Hence if his taste degenerates his luster becomes **strident**, i.e., it swaggers repulsively. Then he belongs as much because of his style as because of his decoration to the galimatia,[39,40] (the exaggerated), a kind of grotesquerie, which in relation to the magnificent is the same as the adventurous or cranky is to the serious sublime. In cases of insults he falls back upon duels or lawsuits, and in civil relationships on ancestry, precedence, and title. As long as he is only vain, i.e., seeks honor and strives to be pleasing to the eye, then he can still be tolerated, but when he is conceited even in the complete absence of real merits and talents, then he is that which he would least gladly be taken for, namely a fool.

Since in the **phlegmatic** mixture there are ordinarily no ingredients of the sublime or the beautiful in any particularly noticeable degree, this quality of mind does not belong in the context of our considerations.

Of whichever sort these finer sentiments that we have thus far treated might be, whether sublime or beautiful, they have in common the fate of always seeming perverse and absurd in the judgment of those who have no feeling attuned to them. A person of calm and self-interested industry does not even have, so to speak, the organs to be sensitive to the noble feature in a poem or in an heroic virtue; he would rather read a Robinson than a Grandison[41] and holds Cato[42] to be an obstinate fool. Likewise, that seems ridiculous to persons of a somewhat more serious cast of mind

---

[39] This strange word, much the same in English as in German, is, according to the *Oxford English Dictionary*, of "unknown origin." It means "confused language, meaningless talk, nonsense," and is found in a 1653 translation of Rabelais as well as in the *Spectator*, number 275 (January 15, 1711/12), where Addison fancifully describes an imaginary "dissection of a beau's head, and of a coquette's heart." The skull of the former "was filled with a kind of spungy substance, which the French anatomists call galimatias, and the English, nonsense"; *The Spectator*, ed. A. Chalmers, Boston, MA: Little, Brown, 1869, vol. IV, p. 223.

[40] *Gallimathias*

[41] Here Kant refers to Daniel Defoe's *Robinson Crusoe* (1719) and to Sir Charles Grandison in Samuel Richardson's novel of the same name (1754), "a gentleman of high character and fine appearance" who has rendered great services to others rather than simply seeking his own survival.

[42] Marcus Porcius Cato Uticensis, or Cato the Younger (95–46 BCE), Roman senator and statesman, was an opponent of Julius Caesar's imperial ambitions. "It is said of Cato that even from his infancy, in his speech, his countenance, and all his childish pastimes, he discovered an inflexible temper, unmoved by any passion, and firm in everything"; Plutarch, *The Lives of the Noble Grecians and Romans*, trans. John Dryden, rev. Arthur Hugh Clough, New York: Modern Library, n.d., p. 918. Cato achieved immortality when he committed suicide in order to stir the Romans of Utica to resistance against Caesar. "And a little after, the people of Utica flocked thither, crying out with one voice, he was their benefactor and their saviour, the only free and only undefeated man" (p. 959). Kant also refers to Cato in considering whether there are any circumstances in which

which is charming to others, and the fluttering naïvete of a pastoral affair is to them tasteless and childish. And even if the mind is not entirely without a concordant finer feeling, yet the degrees of the susceptibility to [2:225] the latter are very variable, and one sees that one person finds something noble and appropriate which comes across to another as grand, to be sure, but adventurous. The opportunities that present themselves in the case of nonmoral matters to detect something of the feeling of another can give us occasion also to infer with reasonable probability his sentiment with regard to the higher qualities of mind and even those of the heart. He who is bored with beautiful music arouses a strong suspicion that the beauties of a style of writing and the fine enchantments of love will have little power over him.

There is a certain spirit of trivialities (*esprit des bagatelles*), which indicates a sort of fine feeling, but which aims at precisely the opposite of the sublime:[43] having a taste for something because it is very *artificial* and labored, verses that can be read forwards and backwards, riddles, watches in finger rings, flea chains, etc.; a taste for everything that is measured and painfully **orderly**, although without any utility, e.g., books that stand neatly arranged in long rows in the bookcase, and an empty head that looks upon them and rejoices, rooms that are adorned like optical cabinets and are everywhere washed clean combined with an inhospitable and morose host who occupies them;[44] a taste for everything that is **rare**, however little intrinsic value it may otherwise have;[45] the lamp of Epictetus,[46] a glove of King Charles the Twelfth;[47] in a certain way coin-collecting also belongs here.[48] Such persons are very much under the suspicion that they will be grubs and cranks in the sciences, but in ethics will be without feeling for that which is beautiful or noble in a free way.

---

suicide is not a violation of duty to ourselves; see *Moralphilosophie Collins*, Academy Edition 27:370–71.

[43] The original text has a period here.   [44] The original text has a period here.

[45] The original text has a period here.

[46] The Stoic philosopher Epictetus (*c.* 50–130 CE), was famed for his "great sweetness, as well as personal simplicity" and "lived in a house with a rush mat, a simple pallet, and an earthenware lamp (after the iron one was stolen)"; Philip P. Hallie, "Epictetus," in Edwards, ed., *Encyclopedia of Philosophy*, vol. III, p. 1.

[47] Here Kant refers to Charles XII of Sweden (1682–1718, reigned 1697–1718), under whom Sweden reached the height of its power, but whose death during the Northern War and Sweden's ensuing defeat in 1721 cost the nation the rank of a great European power that it had held since the role of Gustavus Adolphus in the Thirty Years' War. Voltaire published a biography of Charles XII.

[48] The colon and semicolons in this sentence replace periods in the original.

To be sure, we do one another an injustice when we dismiss one who does not see the value or the beauty of what moves or charms us by saying that he does not **understand** it. In this case it is not so much a matter of what the **understanding** sees but of what the feeling is sensitive to. Nevertheless the capacities of the soul have such a great interconnection that one can often infer from the appearance of the sentiment to the talents of the insight. For to him who has many excellences of understanding these talents would be apportioned in vain if he did not at the same time have a strong sentiment for the truly noble or beautiful, which must be the incentive for applying those gifts of mind well and regularly.[g]

It is indeed customary to call **useful** only that which can satisfy our   [2:226]
cruder sentiment, what can provide us with a surplus for eating and drinking, display in clothing and furniture, and lavishness in entertaining, although I do not see why everything that is craved with my most lively feeling should not be reckoned among the useful things. Nevertheless, taking everything on this footing, he who is ruled by **self-interest** is a person with whom one must never argue concerning the finer taste. In this consideration a hen is better than a parrot, a cook pot more useful than a porcelain service, all the sharp heads in the world are not worth as much as a peasant, and the effort to discover the distance of the fixed stars can be left aside until people have agreed on the most advantageous way to drive the plow. But what folly it is to get involved in such a dispute, where it is impossible to arrive at concordant sentiments because the feeling is not at all concordant! Nevertheless, even a person of the crudest and most vulgar sentiment will be able to perceive that the charms and attractions of life which seem to be the most dispensable attract our greatest care, and that we would have few incentives left for such manifold efforts if they were to be excluded. At the same time, practically no one is so crude not to be sensitive that a moral action is all the more moving, at least to another, the further it is from self-interest and the more those nobler impulses stand out in it.

---

[g] One also sees that a certain fineness of feeling counts toward a person's merit. That someone can   [2:226]
have a good meal of meat and cakes and nevertheless sleep incomparably well is interpreted as a sign of a good stomach, but not as a merit. By contrast, he who sacrifices a part of his mealtime to listening to music or who can be absorbed in a pleasant diversion by a painting or happily reads some witty stories, even if they be only poetic trivialities, nevertheless has in everyone's eyes the standing of a more refined person, of whom one has a more advantageous and favorable opinion.

If I observe alternately the noble and the weak sides of human beings, I reprove myself that I am not able to adopt that standpoint from which these contrasts can nevertheless exhibit the great portrait of human nature in its entirety in a moving form. For I gladly grant that so far as it belongs to the project of great nature as a whole, these grotesque attitudes cannot lend it other than a noble expression, although one is far too short-sighted to see them in this connection. Nevertheless, to cast even a weak glance on this, I believe that I can note the following. There are very **few** people who conduct themselves in accordance with **principles**, which is on the whole good, since it is so easy to err with these principles, and then the ensuing disadvantage extends all the further, the more general the principle is and the more steadfast the person who has set it before himself is. Those who act out of **good-hearted drives** are far more **numerous**, which is most excellent, although it cannot be reckoned to individuals as a special personal merit; for these virtuous instincts are occasionally lacking, but on average they accomplish the great aim of nature just as well as the other instincts that so regularly move the animal world. Those always who have their dear self before them as the sole focal point of their efforts and who attempt to make everything turn on the great axis of **self-interest** are the **most common**, and nothing can be more advantageous than this, for these are the most industrious, orderly, and prudent people; they give demeanor and solidity to the whole, for even without aiming at it they serve the common good, supply the necessary requisites, and provide the foundations over which finer souls can spread beauty and harmony. Finally, the **love of honor** is distributed among **all** human hearts, although in unequal measure, which must give the whole a beauty that charms to the point of admiration. For although the lust for honor is a foolish delusion if it becomes the rule to which one subordinates the other inclinations, yet as an accompanying drive it is most excellent. For while on the great stage each prosecutes his actions in accordance with his dominant inclinations, at the same time he is moved by a hidden incentive to adopt in his thoughts a standpoint outside himself in order to judge the propriety of his conduct, how it appears and strikes the eye of the observer. In this way the different groups unite themselves in a painting of magnificent expression, where in the midst of great variety unity shines forth, and the whole of moral nature displays beauty and dignity.

Third Section

On the difference between the sublime and the beautiful in the contrast between the two sexes[49]

He who first conceived of woman under the name of the fair[50] sex perhaps meant to say something flattering, but hit it better than he may himself have believed. For without taking into consideration that her figure is in general finer, her features more tender and gentle, her mien in the expression of friendliness, humor, and affability more meaningful and engaging than is the case with the male sex, and without forgetting as well what must be discounted as the secret power of enchantment by which she makes our passion inclined to a judgment that is favorable for her, above all there lies in the character of the mind of this sex features peculiar to it which clearly distinguish it from ours and which are chiefly responsible for her being characterized by the mark of the **beautiful**. On the other hand, we could lay claim to the designation of the **noble sex**, if it were not also required of a noble cast of mind to decline honorific titles and to bestow rather than receive them. Here it is not to be understood that woman is lacking noble qualities or that the male sex must entirely forego beauties; rather one expects that each sex will unite both, but in such a way that in a woman all other merits should only be united so as to emphasize the character of the **beautiful**, which is the proper point of reference, while by contrast among the male qualities the **sublime** should clearly stand out as the criterion of his kind. To this must refer all judgments of these two genders, those of praise as well as those of blame. All education and instruction must keep this before it, and likewise all effort to promote the ethical perfection of the one or the other, unless one would make unrecognizable the charming difference that nature sought to establish between the two human genders. For it is here not enough to represent that one has human beings before one: one must also not forget that these human beings are not all of the same sort.

---

49 Differences between the sexes would remain a constant theme in Kant's anthropology, from his first lectures in 1772–73 (*Anthropologie Collins*, 25:234–38) to his final handbook (*Anthropology from a Pragmatic Point of View*, Academy Edition 7:303–10).
50 *schönen*

[2:229]   Women have a stronger innate feeling for everything that is beautiful, decorative, and adorned. Even in childhood they are glad to be dressed up and are pleased when they are adorned. They are cleanly and very delicate with respect to everything that causes disgust. They love a joke and can be entertained with trivialities as long as they are cheerful and laughing. They have something demure about them very early, they know how to display a fine propriety and to be self-possessed; and this at an age when our well-brought-up male youth is still unruly, awkward, and embarrassed. They have many sympathetic sentiments, good-heartedness and compassion, they prefer the beautiful to the useful, and gladly transform excess in their support into parsimony in order to support expenditure on luster and adornment. They are very sensitive to the least offense, and are exceedingly quick to notice the least lack of attention and respect toward themselves. In short, they contain the chief ground for the contrast between the beautiful and the noble qualities in human nature, and even refine the male sex.

I hope I will be spared the enumeration of the male qualities to the extent that they are parallel with the former, and that it will be sufficient to consider both only in their contrast. The fair[51] sex has just as much understanding as the male, only it is a **beautiful understanding**, while ours should be a **deeper understanding**, which is an expression that means the same thing as the sublime.

For the beauty of all actions it is requisite above all that they display facility and that they seem to be accomplished without painful effort; by contrast, efforts and difficulties that have been overcome arouse admiration and belong to the sublime. Deep reflection and a long drawn out consideration are noble, but are grave and not well suited for a person in whom the unconstrained charms should indicate nothing other than a beautiful nature. Laborious learning or painful grubbing, even if a woman could get very far with them, destroy the merits that are proper to her sex, and on account of their rarity may well make her into an object of a cold admiration, but at the same time they will weaken the charms by means of which she exercises her great power over the opposite sex. A woman who has a head full of Greek, like Mme. **Dacier**,[52] or who conducts thorough

---

[51] *schöne*
[52] Anna Dacier, née Lefèvre (1654–1720), wife of the philologist André Dacier, translated *The Iliad* and *The Odyssey*, as well as other classics in both Greek and Latin, into French.

disputations about mechanics, like the Marquise du **Châtelet**,[53] might [2:230] as well also wear a beard; for that might perhaps better express the mien of depth for which they strive. The beautiful understanding chooses for its objects everything that is closely related to the finer feeling, and leaves abstract speculation or knowledge, which is useful but dry, to the industrious, thorough, and deep understanding. The woman will accordingly not learn geometry; she will know only so much about the principle of sufficient reason or the monads as is necessary in order to detect the salt in satirical poems which the insipid grubs of our sex have fabricated. The beauties can leave Descartes' vortices[54] rotating forever without worrying about them, even if the suave **Fontenelle** wanted to join them under the planets,[55] and the attraction of their charms loses nothing of its power even if they know nothing of what **Algarotti**[56] has taken the trouble to lay out for their advantage about the attractive powers of crude matter according to Newton. In history they will not fill their heads with battles nor in geography with fortresses, for it suits them just as little to reek of gunpowder as it suits men to reek of musk.

It seems to be malicious cunning on the part of men that they have wanted to mislead the fair sex into this perverted taste. For well aware of their weakness with respect to the natural charms of the latter, and that a single sly glance can throw them into more confusion than the most difficult question in school, as soon as the woman has given way

---

53 Gabrielle Émilie Le Tonnelier de Breteuil, marquise du Châtelet-Lomont (1706–49), a mathematician and physicist, and Voltaire's companion at Cirey for the last fifteen years of her life. Kant alludes to the debate over living forces between her and Cartesians such as Jean-Jacques d'Ortous de Mairan (1678–1771), who wrote a "Lettre a Madame du Châtelet sur la question des forces vives" (Letter to Madame du Châtelet on the question of living forces) (Paris, 1741), in his earliest work, *Thoughts on the True Evaluation of Living Forces* (1747), § 33, Academy Edition 1:45.

54 In his famous theory of vortices, Descartes claimed that "all the bodies in the universe are composed of one and the same matter, which is divisible into indefinitely many parts, and is in fact divided into a large number of parts which move in different directions and have a sort of circular motion"; *The Principles of Philosophy* (1644), Part III, § 46; in the French edition, he added that he would use the word *vortices* "to refer to all matter which revolves in this way around each of the centers." See *The Philosophical Writings of Descartes*, trans. John Cottingham, Robert Stoothoff, and Dugald Murdoch, Cambridge University Press, 1985, vol. I, pp. 256–57.

55 Bernard le Bovier de Fontenelle (1657–1757), a popularizer of the new science, wrote *Entretiens sur la pluralité des mondes* (Dialogue on the plurality of the worlds) (Paris, 1686), presented as a conversation among women on astronomy.

56 Francesco, Conte Algarotti (1712–64), an Italian who spent some years at the court of Frederick the Great, wrote *Newtonianismo per le Dame* (1736), translated into all the major European languages (including English in 1737 and French in 1741), as well as a well-known essay on opera (1755).

to this taste they see themselves in a decided superiority and are at an advantage, which it would otherwise be difficult for them to have, of helping the vanity of the weak with generous indulgence. The content of the great science of woman is rather the human being, and, among human beings, the man. Her philosophical wisdom is not reasoning but sentiment. In the opportunity that one would give them to educate their beautiful nature, one must always keep this relation before his eyes. One will seek to broaden her entire moral feeling and not her memory, and not, to be sure, through universal rules, but rather through individual judgment about the conduct that she sees about her. The examples that one borrows from other times in order to understand the influence that [2:231] the fair[57] sex has had in the affairs of the world, the various relationships in which it has stood to the male sex in other ages or foreign lands, the character of both so far as it can be illuminated by all this, and the variable taste in gratifications constitute her entire history and geography. It is a fine thing[58] to make looking at a map that represents either the entire globe or the most important parts of the world agreeable to a woman. This is done by depicting it to her only with the aim of illustrating the different characters of the peoples that dwell there, the differences in their taste and ethical feeling, especially with regard to the effects that these have on the relationships between the sexes, together with some easy explanations from the differences in regions, their freedom or slavery. It matters little whether or not they know the particular divisions of these countries, their industries, power, and rulers. Likewise they do not need to know more of the cosmos than is necessary to make the view of the heavens on a beautiful evening moving for them, if they have somehow understood that there are to be found still more worlds and in them still more beautiful creatures. Feeling for paintings of expression and for music, not in so far as it expresses art but rather in so far as it expresses sentiment, all of this refines or elevates the taste of this sex and always has some connection with ethical emotions. Never a cold and speculative instruction, always sentiments and indeed those that remain as close as possible to the relationships of their sex. This education[59] is so rare because it requires talents, experience, and a heart full of feeling, and

---

[57] *schöne*   [58] *Es ist schön*   [59] *Unterweisung*

38

a woman can do very well without anything else, as indeed she usually educates[60] herself quite well on her own even without this.

The virtue of the woman is a **beautiful virtue**.[h] That of the male sex ought to be a **noble virtue**. Women will avoid evil not because it is unjust but because it is ugly, and for them virtuous actions mean those that are ethically beautiful. Nothing of ought, nothing of must, nothing of obligation. To a woman anything by way of orders and sullen compulsion is insufferable. They do something only because they love to, and the [2:232] art lies in making sure that they love only what is good. It is difficult for me to believe that the fair sex is capable of principles, and I hope not to give offense by this, for these are also extremely rare among the male sex. In place of these, however, providence has implanted goodly and benevolent sentiments in their bosom, a fine feeling for propriety and a complaisant soul. But do not demand sacrifices and magnanimous self-compulsion. A man should never tell his wife if he risks part of his fortune for the sake of a friend. Why should he fetter her cheerful talkativeness by burdening her mind with an important secret that he alone is obliged to keep? Even many of her weaknesses are so to speak **beautiful faults**. Injury or misfortune move her tender soul to sadness. A man must never weep other than magnanimous tears. Any that he sheds in pain or over reversals of fortune make him contemptible. The **vanity** for which one so frequently reproaches the fair sex, if it is indeed a fault in her, is only a beautiful fault. For even leaving aside that the men who so gladly flatter woman would do badly if she were not inclined to take it well, she actually enlivens her charms by it. This inclination is an impulse to make herself agreeable and to show her good demeanor, to let her cheerful wit play, also to glisten with the changing inventions of her dress, and to elevate her beauty. In this there is nothing that is at all injurious to others, but rather, if it is done with good taste, there is so much refinement that it would be quite inappropriate to scold it with peevish criticism. A woman who is too inconstant and deceptive in this is called a **silly woman**;[61] yet this expression does not have as harsh

----

[h] Above, p. 25 (2:218), this was in a strict judgment designated as adopted virtue; here, where on account of the character of the sex it deserves a favorable justification, it is called in general a beautiful virtue.

[60] *ausbildet*   [61] *Närrin*

a sense as it does when applied with a change of the final syllable[62] to a man, so that, indeed, if one understands the other, it can sometimes even indicate an intimate flattery. If vanity is a fault that in a woman is well deserving of forgiveness, nevertheless **conceitedness** in them is not only blameworthy, as in humans in general, but entirely disfigures the character of their sex. For this quality is exceedingly stupid and ugly and entirely opposed to engaging, modest charm. Such a person is then in a [2:233] slippery position. She would let herself be judged sharply and without any indulgence; for whoever insists on haughtiness invites everyone around her to reproach her. Every discovery of even the least fault is a true joy to everyone, and the expression **silly woman** here loses its mitigated sense. One must always distinguish between vanity and conceitedness. The former seeks approbation and to a certain degree honors those on whose account the effort is made; the second already believes itself to be in complete possession of that approbation, and making no effort to acquire it, it also wins none.

If some ingredients of vanity do not at all disfigure a woman in the eyes of the male sex, still the more visible they are, the more they divide the fair sex from each other. They then judge each other quite sharply, because the charms of one seem to obscure those of the other, and those who still make strong pretensions to conquest are actually rarely friends with each other in the true sense.

Nothing is so opposed to the beautiful as the disgusting, just as nothing sinks more deeply beneath the sublime than the ridiculous. Thus a man can be sensitive to no insult more than that of being called a **fool**, and a woman to none more than being called **disgusting**. The English *Spectator* holds that no reproach can be more upsetting to a man than when he is held to be a liar, and none more bitter to a woman than being held to be unchaste.[63] I will leave this for what it is worth in so far as it is judged with the strictness of morality. Only here the question is not what intrinsically deserves the greatest reproach, but rather what is actually felt[64] as the harshest one. And here I ask every reader whether, if in thought he places

---

[62] i.e., *Narr*, a fool
[63] *The Spectator*, number 6 (Wednesday, March 7, 1710/11): "When modesty ceases to be the chief ornament of one sex, and integrity of the other, society is upon a wrong basis, and we shall be ever after without rules to guide our judgment in what is really becoming and ornamental" (by Richard Steele); *The Spectator*, ed. A. Chalmers, vol. I, p. 131.
[64] *empfunden*

himself in this position, he must not agree with my opinion. The maiden Ninon Lenclos[65] made not the least claims to the honor of chastity, and nevertheless she would have been implacably offended if one of her lovers had gone so far in his judgment; and one knows the dreadful fate of Monaldeschi[66] on account of such an expression in the case of a princess who hardly wanted to represent herself as a Lucretia.[67] It is intolerable that one should not be able to commit evil even if one wants to, because then even its omission would always be only a very ambiguous virtue.

To distance oneself as far as possible from this sort of disgustingness [2:234] takes *purity*, which is indeed becoming for every person, and which in the case of the fair sex is of the first rank among the virtues and can hardly be taken too far by it, although in the case of a man it can sometimes be exaggerated and then becomes ridiculous.

The sense of shame is a secrecy of nature aimed at setting bounds to a most intractable inclination, and which, in so far as it has the call of nature on its side, always seems compatible with good, moral qualities, even if it is excessive. It is accordingly most necessary as a supplement to principles; for there is no case in which inclination so readily becomes a sophist cooking up complaisant principles as here. At the same time, it also serves to draw a secretive curtain before even the most appropriate and necessary ends of nature, so that too familiar an acquaintance with them will not occasion disgust or at least indifference with respect to the final aims of a drive on to which the finest and liveliest inclinations of human nature are grafted. This quality is especially proper to the fair sex and very appropriate for it. It is also a coarse and contemptible rudeness to put the delicate modesty of the fair sex to embarrassment or annoyance by that sort of vulgar jokes that are called **obscenities**. However, since no matter how far one might try to go around this secret,

---

[65] Ninon de Lenclos (1616–1705), a lover of many including La Rochefoucauld, left the young Voltaire a bequest to buy books.

[66] Marchese Giovanni Monaldeschi (d. 1657), equerry for Queen Cristina of Sweden, was assassinated at her orders after she had abdicated the Swedish throne and was living in France.

[67] Lucretia, traditionally the wife of Tarquinius Collatinus, one of the founders of the Roman republic and consul in 509 BCE, was violated by Sextus, son of Tarquinius Superbus; after telling her husband, she took her own life. This incident resulted in a popular rising led by Junius Brutus, also traditionally regarded as a consul in 509 BCE, and the expulsion of the Tarquins. The legend of Lucretia was a favorite in later literature, such as Shakespeare's 1594 poem "The Rape of Lucrece," and also in painting.

the sexual inclination is still in the end the ground of all other charms, and a woman, as a woman, is always the agreeable object of a well-mannered entertainment, it can perhaps thus be explained why otherwise refined men occasionally allow themselves the liberty of letting some fine allusions shine through the little mischief in their jokes, which leads one to call them **loose** or **waggish**, and which, since they are neither accompanied by invasive glances nor intended to injure respect, makes them believe themselves to be justified in calling the person who receives them with an indignant or standoffish mien a **stickler for honorableness**. I mention this only because it commonly is regarded as a somewhat bold feature in refined society,[68] and because in fact much wit has all along been squandered upon it; but as far as strict moral judgment is concerned, it does not belong here, since in the sentiment of the beautiful I have to observe and explain only the appearances.

[2:235]   The noble qualities of this sex, which nevertheless, as we have already noted, must never make the feeling of the beautiful unrecognizable, announce themselves by nothing more clearly and surely than by the **modesty** of a kind of noble simplicity and naïvete in great excellences. From this shines forth a calm benevolence and respect toward others, combined at the same time with a certain **noble trust** in oneself and an appropriate self-esteem, which is always to be found in a sublime cast of mind. In so far as this fine mixture is both engaging in virtue of its charms and moving in virtue of respect, it secures all other shining qualities against the mischief of censure and mockery. Persons of this cast of mind also have a heart for friendship, which in a woman can never be valued enough, because it is so rare and at the same time must be so totally charming.

Since our aim is to judge of sentiments, it cannot be disagreeable to bring under concepts, so far as possible, the variety of the impression that the figure and facial features of the fair sex makes upon the masculine. This whole enchantment is at bottom spread over the sexual drive. Nature pursues its great aim, and all refinements that are associated with it, however remote from it they seem to be, are only veils, and in the end derive their charm from the very same source. A healthy and **coarse taste** that always remains close to this drive, is little troubled by the charms of

---

[68] *vom schönen Umgange*

demeanor, of the facial features, of the eyes, etc., in a woman, and as it is really concerned only with sex, often it sees the delicacy of others as empty flirtation.

If this taste is not exactly fine, still it is not on that account to be despised. For the greatest part of humanity follows by its means the great order of nature in a very simple and certain manner.[i] By this means most marriages are brought about, and indeed among the most industrious part of humanity, and because the man does not have his [2:236] head full of enchanting miens, languishing glances, noble demeanor, etc., and also understands nothing of these, he is thus all the more attentive to domestic virtues, thrift, etc., and to the dowry. As far as the somewhat finer taste is concerned, on account of which it might be necessary to make a distinction among the external charms of the woman, this is directed either to that which is **moral** in the figure and the expression of the face or to the **immoral**. With respect to the latter sort of agreeable qualities, a woman is called **pretty:**[69] a well-proportioned build, regular features, a lovely contrast between the colors of eyes and face: all beauties that also please in a bouquet of flowers and earn a cold approbation. The face itself says nothing, although it may be pretty, and does not speak to the heart. As for the expression of the features, the eyes and the mien that are moral, this pertains either to the feeling of the sublime or of the beautiful. A woman in whom the agreeable qualities that become her sex are salient, especially the moral expression of the sublime, is called **beautiful** in the proper sense; one whose moral design, so far as it makes itself known in the mien or facial features, announces the qualities of the beautiful, is **agreeable**, and if she is that to a higher degree, **charming**. The former lets a glimmer of a beautiful understanding shine through modest glances beneath a mien of composure and a noble demeanor, and as in her face she portrays a tender feeling and a benevolent heart, she overpowers both the inclination and the esteem of a male heart. The latter displays cheer and wit in laughing eyes, a bit of fine mischief, coquetry in her jokes, and

---

[i] As all things in the world also have their bad side, the only thing that is to be regretted about this taste is that it degenerates into dissoluteness more readily than any other. For although the fire that one person has ignited can be extinguished by another, there are not enough difficulties that could restrict an intractable inclination.

[69] In the original text there is a period here.

a roguish coyness. She charms, while the former moves, and the feeling of love of which she is capable and which she inspires in others is fickle but beautiful, while the sentiment of the former is tender, combined with respect, and constant. I will not get too involved with detailed dissections of this sort; for in such cases the author always seems to portray his own inclination. I will still mention, however, that the taste that many ladies have for a healthy but pale color can be understood here. For the latter commonly accompanies a cast of mind of more inward feeling and tender sentiment, which belongs to the quality of the sublime, while the red and blooming color indicates less of the former, yet more of the joyful and cheerful cast of mind; but it is more suitable to vanity to move and enchain than to charm and attract. By contrast, persons without any moral feeling and without an expression that indicates sentiments can be very pretty, yet they will neither move nor charm, unless it be that **coarse taste** that we have mentioned, which occasionally becomes somewhat more refined and then also chooses after its fashion. It is bad that pretty creatures of that sort easily succumb to the fault of **conceitedness** because of the awareness of the beautiful figure that the mirror shows them, and from a lack of finer sentiments; for they then make everyone cold to them, except for the flatterer, who is after ulterior motives and fashions intrigues.

[2:237]

Through these concepts one can perhaps understand something of the very different effect that the figure of one and the same woman has on the taste of men. I do not mention that which in this impression is too closely related to the sexual drive and which may agree with the particularly **voluptuary** illusion with which the sentiment of everyone is clothed, because it lies outside the sphere of finer taste; and it is perhaps correct, as M. de Buffon suspects, that that figure which makes the first impression at the time when this drive is still new and beginning to develop remains the archetype to which in future times all feminine forms[70] must more or less conform, which can arouse the fantastic longing by means of which a somewhat crude inclination is made to choose among the different objects of a sex.[71] As far as a somewhat finer taste

---

[70] *Bildungen*

[71] "Every nation has ideas of beauty peculiar to itself; and every individual has his own notions and taste concerning that quality. These peculiarities probably originate from the first agreeable

is concerned, I maintain that the sort of beauty that we have called the **pretty figure** is judged fairly uniformly by all men, and that opinions about it are not so various as is commonly held. The **Circassian** and **Georgian** maidens have always been considered to be extremely pretty by all Europeans travelling through their lands. The **Turks**, the **Arabs**, and the **Persians** must be of very much the same taste, for they are very eager to beautify their populations with such fine blood, and one also notes that the Persian race has actually succeeded in this. The merchants of **Hindustan** likewise do not fail to extract great profit from a wicked trade in such beautiful creatures, by supplying them to the sweet-toothed [2:238] rich men of their country, and one sees that as divergent as the caprice of taste in these different regions of the world may be, that which is held to be especially **pretty** in one of them is also taken to be such in all the others. But where what is moral in the features is mixed into the judgment on the fine figure, there the taste of different men is always very different, in accordance with the difference in their ethical feeling itself as well as with the different significance that the expression of the face may have in every fancy. One finds that those forms[72] that on first glance do not have a marked effect because they are not pretty in any decided way usually are far more engaging and seem to grow in beauty as soon as they begin to please on closer acquaintance, while in contrast the beautiful appearance that announces itself all at once is subsequently perceived more coldly, presumably because moral charms, when they become visible, are more arresting, also because they become effective only on the occasion of moral sentiments and as it were let themselves be discovered, each discovery of a new charm, however, giving rise to a suspicion of even more; whereas all the agreeable qualities that do not at all conceal themselves can do nothing more after they have exercised their entire effect all at the beginning than to cool off the enamored curiosity and gradually bring it to indifference.

Among these observations, the following remark naturally suggests itself. The entirely simple and crude feeling in the sexual inclinations

impressions we receive of certain objects; and therefore depend more upon chance and habit than upon difference of constitution"; Georges Louis Leclerc, Comte de Buffon, *Natural History, General and Particular*, trans. William Smellie, ed. William Wood, 20 vols., London: 1812, vol. III, p. 203.

72 *Bildungen*

leads, to be sure, quite directly to the great end of nature, and in satisfying its demands it is suited to make the person himself happy without detour; but because of its great generality, it readily degenerates into debauchery and dissoluteness. On the other side, an extremely refined taste certainly serves to remove the wildness from an impetuous inclination and, by limiting it to only a very few objects, to make it modest and decorous; but it commonly fails to attain the great final aim of nature, and since it demands or expects more than the latter commonly accomplishes, it very rarely makes the person of such delicate sentiment happy. The first cast of mind becomes uncouth, because it applies to all the members of a sex, the second brooding, because it really applies to none, but is rather occupied only with an object that the enamored inclination creates in thought and adorns with all the noble and beautiful qualities that nature rarely unites in one person and even more rarely offers to one who can treasure her and who would perhaps be worthy of such a possession. Hence arises the postponement and finally the complete renunciation of the marital bond, or, what is perhaps equally bad, a sullen regret of a choice that has already been made, which does not fulfill the great expectations that had been raised; for it is not uncommon for Aesop's cock to find a pearl when a common barley corn would have suited him better.

[2:239]

Here we can remark in general that, as charming as the impressions of tender feeling may be, nevertheless we have cause to be cautious in the refinement of it, unless we want to bring upon ourselves much discontent and a source of evils through excessive sensitivity. I would recommend to nobler souls that they refine their feeling as much as they can with regard to those qualities that pertain to themselves or those actions that they themselves perform, but that with regard to what they enjoy or expect from others they should preserve their taste in its simplicity: if only I understood how it is possible to bring this off. But if they were to succeed, then they would make others happy and also be happy themselves. It should never be lost sight of that, in whatever form it might be, one should not make very great claims on the happinesses of life and the perfection of human beings; for he who always expects only something average has the advantage that the outcome will seldom disappoint his hopes, although sometimes unsuspected perfections will also surprise him.

In the end, age, the great ravager of beauty, threatens all of these charms, and in the natural order of things the sublime and noble qualities must gradually take the place of the beautiful ones in order to make a person worthy of ever greater respect as she ceases to be attractive. In my opinion, the entire perfection of the fair sex in the bloom of years should consist in the beautiful simplicity that has been heightened by a refined feeling for everything that is charming and noble. Gradually, as the claims to charms diminish, the reading of books and the expansion [2:240] in insight could, unnoticed, fill with Muses the place vacated by the Graces, and the husband should be the first teacher. Nevertheless, when finally the old age that is so terrible to all women arrives, she still belongs to the fair sex, and that sex disfigures itself if in a sort of despair over holding on to this character longer it gives way to a morose and sullen mood.

A person of years, who joins society with a modest and friendly essence,[73] who is talkative in a cheerful and reasonable way, who favors with propriety the enjoyments of youth of which she no longer takes part, and who, with concern for everything, displays contentment and satisfaction in the joy that surrounds her, is always still a more refined person than a man of the same age and is perhaps even more lovable than a maiden, though in a different sense. To be sure, the platonic love asserted by an ancient philosopher when he said of the object of his inclination: **The Graces reside in her wrinkles, and my soul seems to hover about my lips when I kiss her withered mouth,** may be somewhat too mystical; yet such claims must then be relinquished. An old man who acts infatuated is a fop, and the similar pretensions of the other sex are then disgusting. It is never the fault of nature if we do not appear with a good demeanor, but is rather due to the fact that we would pervert her.

In order not to lose sight of my text, I will here add several considerations on the influence that one sex can have in beautifying or ennobling of the feeling of the other. The woman has a preeminent feeling for the **beautiful**, so far as it pertains to **herself**, but for the **noble** in so far as it is found in the **male sex**. The man, on the contrary, has a decided feeling for the **noble** that belongs to **his** qualities, but for the **beautiful** in so far as it is to be found in the **woman**. From this it must follow that the ends of nature are aimed more at **ennobling** the man and **beautifying** the woman by means of the sexual inclination. A woman is little embarrassed by the fact that she does not possess certain lofty insights, that she is

[73] *Wesen*

[2:241] fearful and not up to important business, etc.; she is beautiful and engaging, and that is enough. By contrast, she demands all of these qualities in the man, and the sublimity of her soul is revealed only by the fact that she knows how to treasure these noble qualities in so far as they are to be found in him. How else would it be possible for so many grotesque male faces, although they may have merits, to be able to acquire such polite and fine wives! The man, in contrast, is far more delicate with regard to the beautiful charms of the woman. By her fine figure, her cheerful naïvete and her charming friendliness he is more than adequately compensated for the lack of book-learning and for other lacks that he must make good by his own talents. Vanity and fashion may well give these natural drives a false direction, and make out of many a man a **sweet gentleman**, but out of the woman a **pedant** or an **Amazon**, yet nature still always seeks to return to its proper order. From this one can judge what powerful influences the sexual inclination could have in ennobling especially the masculine sex if, in place of many dry lessons, the moral feeling of woman were developed in good time to make her sensitive to what belongs to the dignity and the sublime qualities of the opposite sex, and thereby prepared to regard the ridiculous fops with contempt and to yield to no other qualities than to merits. It is also certain that the power of her charms would thereby gain overall; for it is apparent that their enchantment is often effective only on nobler souls, while the others are not fine enough to be sensitive to them. Thus when he was advised to let the **Thessalians** hear his beautiful songs, the poet **Simonides** said: **These louts are too dumb to be beguiled by a man such as me.**[74] It has always been regarded as an effect of intercourse with the fair sex that male manners become gentler, their conduct more refined and polished, and their demeanor more elegant; but this is only an incidental

[2:242] advantage.[j] What is most important is that the man become more perfect

---

[j] This advantage is itself very much diminished by the observation that has been made that those men who have become involved too early and too frequently in those parties to which the woman has given the tone commonly become somewhat ridiculous, and are boring or even contemptible [2:242] in male society, because they have lost the taste for an entertainment that is certainly cheerful, but must also have real content, that is humorous but must also be useful because of serious conversations.

[74] Simonides (*c.* 556–468 BCE), lyric and elegaic poet, particularly famous for his encomia and dirges during the period of the Peloponnesian wars. The authenticity of many apothegms attributed to him is dubious. See M. Boas, *De Epigrammatis Simonideis* (1905).

as a man and the woman as a woman, i.e., that the incentives of the sexual inclination operate in accordance with nature to make the one more noble and to beautify the qualities of the other. If things come to the extreme, the man, confident of his merits, can say: **Even if you do not love me I will force you to esteem me**, and the woman, secure in the power of her charms, will answer: **Even if you do not inwardly esteem us, we will still force you to love us**. In the absence of such principles one sees men adopt feminine qualities, in order to please, and woman sometimes (although much more rarely) work up a masculine demeanor, in order to inspire esteem; but whatever one does contrary to the favor of nature one always does very badly.

In marital life the united pair should as it were constitute a single moral person,[75] which is animated and ruled by the understanding of the man and the taste of the wife. For not only can one trust the former more for insight grounded in experience, but the latter more for freedom and correctness in sentiment; yet further, the more sublime a cast of mind is, the more inclined it also is to place the greatest goal of its efforts in the satisfaction of a beloved object, and on the other side the more beautiful it is, the more does it seek to respond to this effort with complaisance. In such a relationship a struggle for precedence is ridiculous, and where it does occur it is the most certain mark of a crude or unequally matched taste. If it comes down to talk of the right of the superior, then the thing is already extremely debased; for where the entire bond is really built only on inclination, there it is already half torn apart as soon as the ought begins to be heard. The presumption of the woman in this harsh tone is extremely ugly and that of the man in the highest degree ignoble and contemptible. However, the wise order of things brings it about that all these niceties and delicacies of sentiment have their full strength only in the beginning, but subsequently are gradually dulled by familiarity and domestic concerns and then degenerate into familiar love, where finally the great art consists in preserving sufficient remnants of [2:243] the former so that indifference and surfeit do not defeat the entire value of the enjoyment on account of which and which alone it was worth having entered into such a bond.

---

[75] Kant would later argue for the equality of man and woman within marriage, at least with regard to economic rights as well as sexual rights, in *The Metaphysics of Morals*, Doctrine of Right, §§ 24–26, Academy Edition 6:277–80.

Fourth Section

On national characters^k in so far as they rest upon the different feeling of the sublime and the beautiful[76]

Among the peoples of our part of the world the **Italians** and the **French** are, in my opinion, those who most distinguish themselves in the feeling of the **beautiful**, but the **Germans**, the **English**, and the **Spaniards** those who are most distinguished from all others in the feeling of the **sublime**. **Holland** can be regarded as the land where this finer taste is fairly unnoticeable. The beautiful itself is either enchanting and touching, or laughing and charming. The former has something of the sublime in it, and in this feeling the mind is thoughtful and enraptured, while in the feeling of the second kind it is smiling and joyful. The first sort of beautiful feeling seems especially appropriate to the Italians, the second sort to the French. In the national character that has in it the expression of the sublime, this is either of the terrifying kind, which inclines a bit to the adventurous, or it is a feeling for the noble, or for the magnificent. I think I have grounds sufficient to attribute the first kind of feeling to the [2:244] Spaniard, the second to the Englishman, and the third to the German. The feeling for the magnificent is not by its nature original, like the other kinds of taste, and although a spirit of imitation can be associated with any other feeling, yet it is more characteristic of that for the glittering sublime, since this is really a mixed feeling out of that for the beautiful and

---

^k My intention is not at all to portray the characters of the peoples in detail; rather I will only outline some features that express the feeling of the sublime and the beautiful in them. One can readily guess that only a tolerable level of accuracy can be demanded in such a depiction, that its prototypes stand out in the large crowds of those who make claim to a finer feeling, and that no nation is lacking in casts of mind which unite the foremost predominant qualities of this kind. For this reason the criticism that might occasionally be cast on a people can offend no one, as it is like a ball that one can always hit to his neighbor. I will not investigate here whether these national differences are contingent and depend upon the times and the type of government, or whether they are connected with a certain necessity with the climate.

[76] Discussion of national characters was a standard part of Kant's lectures on anthropology. Beginning with his first lectures in 1772–73, we find sections on the "Taste of Different Nations" as well as "On National Character" (*Anthropologie Collins*, Academy Edition 25:201–04, 232–34); his handbook *Anthropology from a Pragmatic Point of View* includes the section "On the Character of Nations"; Part II, Section C, Academy Edition 7:311–20.

that for the noble, where each, considered by itself, is colder, and hence the mind is free enough in the connection of them to attend to examples, and also has need for their incentive. The German will accordingly have less feeling in regard to the beautiful than the Frenchman, and less of that pertaining to the sublime than the Englishman, but his feeling will be more suited for the cases where both are to appear as combined, just as he will also luckily avoid the errors into which an excessive strength of either of these kinds of feeling alone could fall.

I touch only fleetingly the arts and the sciences the selection of which can confirm the taste of the nations that we have imputed to them. The Italian genius has distinguished itself especially in music, painting, sculpture, and architecture. There is an equally fine taste for all of these fine[77] arts in France, although here their beauty is less touching. The taste with regard to poetic or rhetorical perfection runs more to the beautiful in France, in England more to the sublime. In France, fine jests, comedy, laughing satire, enamored dalliance, and the light and naturally flowing manner of writing are original;[78] in England, by contrast, thoughts with deep content, tragedy, epic poetry, and in general the heavy gold of wit, which under the French hammer can be beaten into thin little leaves of great surface area. In Germany, wit still glimmers very much through a screen. Formerly it was strident; by means of examples and the understanding of the nation, however, it has become rather more charming and nobler, but the former with less naïvete and the latter with a less bold thrust than in the peoples mentioned. The taste of the Dutch nation for a painstaking order and decorousness that leads to worry and embarrassment also leaves little feeling for the unaffected and free movements of genius, the beauty of which would only be disfigured by the anxious avoidance of errors. Nothing can be more opposed to all the arts and sciences than an adventurous taste, since this distorts nature, which is the prototype of everything beautiful and noble. Thus the Spanish nation has also demonstrated little feeling for the fine arts and sciences.

[2:245]

The characters of mind of the peoples are most evident in that in them which is moral; for this reason we will next consider their different

---

[77] *schöne*

[78] In the original there is a period here, and the remainder of this sentence is printed as if it were a new sentence, but it lacks a verb.

feeling in regard to the sublime and the beautiful from this point of view.[1] The **Spaniard** is serious, taciturn, and truthful. There are few more honest merchants in the world than the Spanish. He has a proud soul and more feeling for great than for beautiful actions. Since in his mixture there is little to be found of generous and tender benevolence, he is often hard and also even cruel. The *Auto da Fe* endures not so much because of superstition as because of the adventurous inclination of the nation, which is moved by a venerable and terrifying rite, in which one sees **San Benito**, painted with figures of the devil, consigned to the flames that have been ignited by a raging piety.[79] One cannot say that the Spaniard is haughtier or more amorous than anyone from another people, yet he is both in an adventurous way that is rare and unusual. To leave the plow standing and walk up and down the field with a long sword and cape until the stranger who is passing by has gone, or in a bullfight, where for once the beauties of the land are seen unveiled, to announce himself to his mistress with a special greeting and then in order to wage a dangerous fight with a wild animal to honor her, these are unusual and strange actions, which greatly diverge from what is natural.

The **Italian** seems to have a feeling which mixes that of a Spaniard and that of a Frenchman: more feeling for the beautiful than the former and more for the sublime than the latter. In this way, I think, the other features of his moral character can be explained.

[2:246] The **Frenchman** has a dominant feeling for the morally beautiful. He is refined, courteous, and complaisant. He becomes intimate very quickly, is humorous and free in conversation, and the expression of a **man** or a **lady of good manners** has a meaning that is comprehensible only to one who has acquired the refined feeling of a Frenchman. Even his sublime sentiments, of which he has not a few, are subordinated to the feeling of the beautiful and acquire their strength only through accord with the latter. He very much likes to be witty, and will without

---

[1] It is hardly necessary for me to repeat my previous apology here. In each people the finest portion contains praiseworthy characters of all sorts, and whoever is affected by one or another criticism will, if he is fine enough, understand it to his advantage, which lies in leaving everyone else to his fate but making an exception of himself.

[79] According to Goldthwait, "The San Benito was a scapular, a loose, sleeveless monastic garment introduced by St. Benedict. That worn by confessed heretics was yellow and was decorated with flames and figures of devils." Immanuel Kant, *Observations on the Feeling of the Beautiful and the Sublime*, trans. John Goldthwait, Berkeley: University of California Press, 1960.

reservation sacrifice something of the truth for the sake of a witticism. By contrast, where he cannot be witty,[m] he displays just as thorough an insight as someone from any other people, e.g., in mathematics and in the other dry or profound arts and sciences. A *bon mot* does not have the same fleeting value with him as elsewhere; it is eagerly spread about and preserved in books, as if it were the most important occurrence. He is a peaceful citizen and avenges himself against the oppressions of the tax collectors by satires or remonstrations to the courts, which, after they have in accordance with their intention given the fathers of the people a beautiful patriotic aspect, accomplish nothing further than being crowned with a glorious rebuke and praised in ingenious laudatory poems. The object to which the merits and national capabilities of this people are most devoted is woman.[n] Not as if she were loved or esteemed here more than elsewhere, but rather because she provides the best opportunity for [2:247] displaying in their best light the favorite talents of wit, cleverness, and good manners; incidentally a vain person of either sex always loves only himself or herself, while the other is only his or her plaything. Now since the French do not at all lack noble qualities, but these can only be animated through the sentiment of the beautiful, the fair sex could here be able to have a more powerful influence in awakening and arousing the noblest actions of the male sex than anywhere else in the world, if one were intent on favoring this direction of the national spirit a little. It is a pity that the lilies do not spin.

The fault which is closest to this national character is the ridiculous or, in a more polite expression, the lighthearted. Important things are treated

---

[m] In metaphysics, morals, and religious doctrines one cannot be too careful with the writings of this nation. They are commonly dominated by much beautiful dazzle, which cannot stand up to a cold examination. The Frenchman loves to be bold in his pronouncements; yet to attain the truth, one must not be bold, but careful. In history he loves anecdotes which leave nothing more to be wished except that they were true.

[n] In France, the woman gives all society and all intercourse their tone. Now it is not to be denied that society without the fair sex is rather tasteless and boring; only if the lady should give it the beautiful tone, the man on his part should give it the noble tone. Otherwise intercourse becomes just as boring, although for the opposite reason: because nothing is so disgusting as pure sweetness. In the French taste it is not: Is the gentleman at home? but rather: Is Madame at home? Madame is at her toilette, Madame has the vapors (a kind of beautiful crankiness); in short, all conversations and all amusements occupy themselves with Madame and for Madame. However, [2:247] the woman is not the more honored by all of this. A person who flirts is always without the feeling of true respect as well as of tender love. I would certainly not want, indeed who knows how much, to have said what **Rousseau** so impudently asserted: **that a woman never becomes anything more than a big child.** Yet the acute Swiss wrote this in France, and presumably, as such a great defender of the fair sex, felt indignant that it was not treated there with more real respect.

like jokes, and trivialities serve for serious occupation. Even in advanced age the Frenchman still sings amorous songs, and is still as gallant as he can be towards the woman. In these remarks I have great authorities from this very same people on my side, and retreat behind a Montesquieu and d'Alembert in order to secure myself from any concerned indignation.

The **Englishman** is at the beginning of every acquaintance cold and indifferent toward a stranger. He has little inclination toward small niceties; by contrast, as soon as he is a friend he is ready to perform great services. In society, he makes little effort to be witty, or to display a refined demeanor, but he is understanding and resolute. He is a poor imitator, does not much ask how others judge, and simply follows his own taste. In relation to the woman he does not have the French refinement, but shows more respect to her and perhaps takes this too far, as in the marital state he commonly concedes an unrestricted authority to his wife. He is steadfast, sometimes to the point of being stiff-necked, bold, and resolute, often to the point of audacity, and acts according to principles, commonly to the point of being headstrong. He easily becomes an eccentric, not out of vanity, but because he troubles himself little about others and does not readily do violence to his own taste out of complaisance or imitation; for this reason he is rarely as much beloved as the Frenchman, but, once he is known, he is commonly more highly esteemed.

[2:248]

The **German** has a feeling that is a mixture of that of an Englishman and that of a Frenchman, but seems to come closer to the former, and the greater similarity with the latter is merely artificial and imitative. He has a happy mixture in the feeling of the sublime as well as the beautiful; and if he is not equal to an Englishman in the former or to the Frenchman in the latter, he surpasses them both in so far as he combines them. He displays more complaisance in intercourse than the former, and even if he does not bring quite as much agreeable liveliness and wit to society as the Frenchman, yet he displays there more moderation and understanding. In love, as in all other sorts of taste, he is also rather methodical, and since he combines the beautiful with the noble, he is in the sentiment of both sufficiently cool to occupy his head with considerations of demeanor, of splendor, and of appearance.[80] Hence family, title, and rank are matters of great importance to him in civic relationships as well as in love. Far more than the previous ones he asks how **people might judge him,**

---

[80] *des Aussehens*

and if there is something in his character that could arouse the wish for a major improvement, it is this weakness, in accordance with which he does not dare to be original, although he has all the talents for that, and that he is too concerned with the opinion of others, which deprives the moral qualities of all bearing, making them fickle and falsely contrived.

The **Dutchman** is of an orderly and industrious cast of mind, and since he looks only to what is useful, he has little feeling for what in a finer understanding is beautiful or sublime. For him a great man means the same as a rich man, by a friend he understands his business correspondents, and a visit that brings him no profit is very boring for him. He makes a contrast to both the Frenchman and the Englishman and is to a certain extent a very phlegmatic German. [2:249]

If we try to apply the sketch of these thoughts to a particular case, in order to assess, e.g., the feeling of honor, the following national differences are revealed. The sentiment for honor is in the Frenchman **vanity**, in the Spaniard **haughtiness**, in the Englishman **pride**, in the German **pomp**, and in the Dutchman **conceitedness**. At first glance these expressions seem to mean the same thing, but in the richness of our German language they mark very noticeable differences. **Vanity** strives for approval, is fickle and changeable, but its outward conduct is **courteous**. The **haughty person** is full of falsely imagined great merits and does not much seek the approval of others; his conduct is stiff and **pompous**. **Pride** is really only a greater consciousness of one's own value, which can often be quite correct (on account of which it is also sometimes called a noble pride; but I can never ascribe a noble haughtiness to someone, since the latter always indicates an incorrect and exaggerated self-appraisal); the conduct of the proud person toward others is **indifferent** and cold. The **vainglorious** person is a proud one who is at the same time vain.° The approval, however, which he seeks from others, consists in testimonies of honor. Hence he likes to glitter with titles, ancestry, and pageantry. The German is particularly infected by this weakness. The words "gracious," "most gracious," "high-born," and "well-born" and more of that sort of bombast make his speech stiff and awkward and very much hinder the beautiful simplicity that other peoples can give to their style of writing. The conduct of a vainglorious person in social intercourse is **ceremony**.

° It is not necessary for a vainglorious person also to be haughty, i.e., to have an exaggerated, false conception of his merits; he may perhaps not appraise himself as worth more than he is, but only has a false taste in manifesting his value outwardly.

The **conceited** person is a haughty person who expresses distinct marks of the contempt of others in his conduct. In behavior he is **coarse**. This miserable quality is the most distant from the finer taste, because it is obviously stupid; for challenging everyone around one to hatred and biting mockery through open contempt is certainly not the means for satisfying the feeling for honor.

[2:250]   In love the German and the English have a fairly good stomach, somewhat fine in sentiment, but more of a healthy and **robust taste**. In this point the Italian is **brooding**, the Spaniard **fantastic**, the Frenchman **dainty**.

The religion of our part of the world is not the matter of an arbitrary taste, but is of honorable origin. Hence only the excesses in it and that in it which properly belongs to human beings can yield signs of the different national qualities. I classify these excesses under the following headings: **credulity, superstition, fanaticism**, and **indifferentism**.[81] The ignorant part of every nation is for the most part **credulous**, although it has no noticeable finer feeling. Persuasion depends simply upon hearsay and merely apparent authority, without any sort of finer feeling containing the incentive for it. One must seek the examples of whole peoples of this kind in the north. The credulous person, if he is of adventuresome taste, becomes **superstitious**. This taste is even in itself a ground for believing something more readily,[p] and of two people, one of whom is infected by this feeling but the other of whom is of a cool and moderate cast of mind, the former, even if he actually has more understanding, is nevertheless more readily seduced by his dominant inclination into believing something unnatural than the latter, who is saved from this excess not by his insight but by his common and phlegmatic feeling. The person who is superstitious in religion gladly places between himself and the supreme object of veneration certain powerful and astonishing

---

[p] It has also been noted that the English, though such a clever people, can nevertheless readily be ensnared at first into believing something wondrous and absurd by a brazen announcement, of which there are many examples. Yet a bold cast of mind, prepared by diverse experiences, in which many strange things have nevertheless been found to be true, quickly breaks through the trivial reservations by means of which a weaker and more distrustful head is quickly stopped and so sometimes saved from error without any merit of its own.

[81] For each of these, Kant has provided both a Germanic and a Latinate word, both of which can be translated by the same (Latinate) word in English. Thus he writes: "*Leichtgläubigkeit* (Credulität), *Aberglaube* (Superstition), *Schwärmerei* (Fanaticism), *und Gleichgültigkeit* (Indifferentism)."

human beings, so to speak giants of holiness, whom nature obeys and whose imploring voices open or close the iron gates of Tartarus, who, while they touch the heavens with their heads, still have their feet on the [2:251] earth beneath. In **Spain**, accordingly, the instruction of sound reason will have great obstacles to overcome, not because it must drive away ignorance there, but rather because it is opposed by an odd taste, to which what is natural is vulgar, and which never believes itself to have a sublime sentiment if its object is not adventurous. **Fanaticism** is so to speak a pious brazenness and is occasioned by a certain pride and an altogether too great confidence in oneself to come closer to the heavenly natures and to elevate itself by an astonishing flight above the usual and prescribed order. The fanatic talks only of immediate inspiration and of the contemplative life, while the superstitious person makes vows before pictures of great wonder-working saints and places his trust in the imaginary and inimitable merits of other persons of his own nature. Even the excesses, as we have noted above, bear signs of the national sentiment, and thus at least in earlier times fanaticism[q] was mostly to be encountered in Germany and England and is as it were an unnatural outgrowth of the noble feeling that belongs to the character of these peoples, and it is in general nowhere near as harmful as the superstitious inclination, even though it is violent at the beginning, since the inflammation of a fanatical spirit gradually cools off and in accordance with its nature must finally attain to an orderly moderation, while superstition stealthily roots itself deeper into a quiet and passive quality of mind and entirely robs the shackled person of the confidence of ever freeing himself from a harmful delusion. Finally, a vain and frivolous person is always without stronger feeling for the sublime, and his religion is without emotion, for the most part only a matter of fashion, which he conducts with decorum and remains cold. This is practical **indifferentism**, to which the **French** national spirit seems to be most inclined, from which it is only a step [2:252] to sacrilegious mockery and which fundamentally, when one looks to its inner worth, is little better than a complete denial.

---

[q] Fanaticism must always be distinguished from **enthusiasm**. The former believes itself to feel an immediate and extraordinary communion with a higher nature, the latter signifies the state of the mind which is inflamed beyond the appropriate degree by some principle, whether it be by the maxim of patriotic virtue, or of friendship, or of religion, without involving the illusion of a supernatural community.

If we now take a quick look through the other parts of the world, we find the **Arab** to be the noblest human being in the Orient, although with a feeling that very much degenerates into the adventurous. He is hospitable, generous, and truthful; but his tale and history and in general his sentiment always has something marvelous woven into it. His inflamed power of imagination presents things to him in unnatural and distorted images, and even the spread of his religion was a great adventure. If the Arabs are as it were the Spaniards of the Orient, then the **Persians** are the Frenchmen of Asia. They are good poets, courtly, and of rather fine taste. They are not such strict observers of Islam and allow their cast of mind, inclined to gaiety, a rather mild interpretation of the Koran. The **Japanese** can be regarded as it were as the Englishmen of this part of the world, although hardly in any other attribute than their steadfastness, which degenerates into the most extreme stiff-neckedness, their courage and their contempt of death. Otherwise they demonstrate few marks of a finer feeling. The **Indians** have a dominant taste for grotesqueries of the kind that comes down to the adventurous. Their religion consists of grotesqueries. Images of idols of enormous shape, the priceless tooth of the mighty ape Hanuman, the unnatural atonements of the Fakirs (heathen mendicant monks), etc., are in this taste. The voluntary sacrifice of the wives in the very same pyre that consumes the corpse of her husband is a repulsive adventure. What ridiculous grotesqueries do the verbose and studied compliments of the **Chinese** not contain: even their paintings are grotesque and represent marvelous and unnatural shapes, the likes of which are nowhere to be found in the world. They also have venerable grotesqueries, for the reason that they are of ancient usage,[r] and no people in the world has more of them than this one.

[2:253]   The **Negroes** of Africa have by nature no feeling that rises above the ridiculous. Mr. **Hume** challenges anyone to adduce a single example where a Negro has demonstrated talents, and asserts that among the hundreds of thousands of blacks who have been transported elsewhere from their countries, although very many of them have been set free, nevertheless not a single one has ever been found who has accomplished something great in art or science or shown any other praiseworthy quality,

---

[r] In Peking, when there is an eclipse of the sun or moon, they still carry on the ceremony of driving away with a great noise the dragon that would devour these heavenly bodies, and they preserve a miserable custom from the most ancient times of ignorance, even though one is now better informed.

while among the whites there are always those who rise up from the lowest rabble and through extraordinary gifts earn respect in the world.[82] So essential is the difference between these two human kinds, and it seems to be just as great with regard to the capacities of mind as it is with respect to color. The religion of fetishes which is widespread among them is perhaps a sort of idolatry, which sinks so deeply into the ridiculous as ever seems to be possible for human nature. A bird's feather, a cow's horn, a shell, or any other common thing, as soon as it is consecrated with some words, is an object of veneration and of invocation in swearing oaths. The blacks are very vain, but in the Negro's way, and so talkative that they must be driven apart from each other by blows.

Among all the **savages** there is no people which demonstrates such a sublime character of mind as that of **North America**. They have a strong feeling for honor, and as in hunt of it they will seek wild adventures hundreds of miles away, they are also extremely careful to avoid the least injury to it where their ever so harsh enemy, after he has captured them, tries to force a cowardly sigh from them by dreadful tortures. The Canadian savage is moreover truthful and honest. The friendship he establishes is just as adventurous and enthusiastic as anything reported from the oldest and most fabulous times. He is extremely proud, sensitive to the complete worth of freedom, and even in education tolerates no encounter that would make him feel a lowly subjugation. **Lycurgus** probably gave laws to such savages, and if a law-giver were to arise among the six nations, one would see a Spartan republic arise in the new world; just as the undertaking of the Argonauts is little different from the military expeditions of these Indians, and **Jason** has nothing

---

[82] In the essay "Of National Characters," Hume wrote:

> I am apt to suspect the Negroes to be naturally inferior to the Whites. There scarcely ever was a civilized nation of that complexion, nor even any individual, eminent either in action or speculation. No ingenious manufactures amongst them, no arts, no sciences. On the other hand, the most rude and barbarous of the Whites, such as the ancient Germans, the present Tartars, have still something eminent about them, in their valour, form of government, or some other particular. Such a uniform and constant difference could not happen, in so many countries and ages, if nature had not made an original distinction between these breeds of men. Not to mention our colonies, there are Negro slaves dispersed all over Europe, of whom none ever discovered any symptoms of ingenuity; though low people, without education, will start up among us, and distinguish themselves in every profession. In Jamaica, indeed, they talk of one Negro as a man of parts and learning; but it is likely he is admired for slender accomplishments, like a parrot who speaks a few words plainly. (David Hume, *Essays Moral, Political and Literary*, Oxford University Press, 1963, p. 213n.)

[2:254]   over **Attakakullakulla** except the honor of a Greek name.[83] All of these savages have little feeling for the beautiful in the moral sense, and the generous forgiveness of an insult, which is at the same time noble and beautiful, is as a virtue completely unknown among the savages, but is always looked upon with contempt as a miserable cowardice. Courage is the greatest merit of the savage and revenge his sweetest bliss. The other natives of this part of the world show few traces of a character of mind which would be disposed to finer sentiments, and an exceptional lack of feeling constitutes the mark of these kinds of human beings.

If we consider the relationship between the sexes in these parts of the world, we find that the **European** has alone found the secret of decorating the sensuous charm of a powerful inclination with so many flowers and interweaving it with so much that is moral that he has not merely very much elevated its agreeableness overall but has also made it very proper. The inhabitant of the **Orient** is of a very false taste in this point. Since he has no conception of the morally beautiful that can be combined with this drive, he also loses even the value of the sensuous gratification, and his harem is a constant source of unrest for him. He falls into all sorts of amorous grotesqueries, among which the imaginary jewel is one of the foremost, which he tries to secure above all others, whose entire value consists only in one's smashing it, and of which one in our part of the world generally raises much malicious doubt, and for the preservation of which he makes use of very improper and often disgusting means. Hence a woman there is always in prison, whether she be a maiden or have a barbaric, inept, and always suspicious husband. In the lands of the **blacks** can one expect anything better than what is generally found there, namely the female sex in the deepest slavery? A pusillanimous person is always a strict master over the weaker, just as with us that man is always a tyrant in the kitchen who outside of his house hardly dares to walk up to anyone. Indeed, Father Labat reports that a Negro carpenter, whom he reproached for haughty treatment of his wives, replied: **You whites**

---

[83] In Greek mythology, Jason was the leader of the Argonauts, who sought the Golden Fleece; the chief source is Apollonius Rhodius (third-century BCE) of Alexandria, author of the *Argonautica*, the great epic of the Alexandrian period. Attakullaculla was a Cherokee chieftain who was brought to England in 1730 by Sir Alexander Cuming, and who later was a leader and peacemaker who saved the life of an English captain. See "Attakullaculla," *Handbook of American Indians North of Mexico*, Smithsonian Institution, Bureau of American Ethnology, bulletin 30 (Washington, 1907), Part I, p. 115. (Goldthwait, trans., *Observations*)

are real fools, for first you concede so much to your wives, and then you complain when they drive you crazy.[84] There might be something here worth considering, except for the fact that this scoundrel [2:255] was completely black from head to foot, a distinct proof that what he said was stupid. Among all the savages there are none among whom the female sex stands in greater real regard than those of **Canada**. In this perhaps they even surpass our civilized part of the world. Not as if they pay the women their humble respects; that would be mere compliments. No, they actually get to command. They meet and take council about the most important affairs of the nation, about war and peace. They send their delegates to the male council, and commonly it is their vote that decides. But they pay dearly enough for this preference. They have all the domestic concerns on their shoulders and share all of the hardships with the men.

If finally we cast a few glances at history, we see the taste of human beings, like a Proteus, constantly take on changeable shapes. The ancient times of the Greeks and Romans displayed clear marks of a genuine feeling for the beautiful as well as the sublime in poetry, sculpture, architecture, legislation, and even in morals. The regime of the Roman emperors altered the noble as well as the beautiful simplicity into the magnificent and then into the false brilliance of which what survives of their oratory, poetry, and even the history of their morals can still instruct us. Gradually even this remnant of the finer taste was extinguished with the complete decay of the state. The barbarians, after they had on their part established their power, introduced a certain perverted taste that is called the Gothic, and which ends up in grotesquerie. One saw grotesqueries not only in architecture, but also in the sciences and in the other practices. The degenerated feeling, once led on by false art, adopted any unnatural[85] form other than the ancient simplicity of nature, and was either exaggerated or ridiculous. The highest flight that human genius took in order to ascend to the sublime consisted in adventures. One saw spiritual and worldly adventurers and often a repulsive and monstrous sort of bastard of both. Monks with the missal in one hand and the battle flag in the

---

[84] Jean Baptiste Labat (1663–1738), *Voyage du père Labat aux îles de l'Amérique* (Haye, 1724), vol. II, p. 54.

[85] Ernst Cassirer's edition substitutes "unnatural" here (*Immanuel Kants Werke*, Berlin: Bruno Cassirer, 1922, vol. II, p. 299), as does the *Werkausgabe* by Wilhelm Weischedel. Only "unnatural" makes a plausible contrast with the "ancient simplicity of nature" to which Kant compares it.

other, followed by whole armies of deceived victims in order to let their bones be buried under other regions of the sky and in a more sacred ground, consecrated warriors, sanctified by solemn oaths to violence and misdeeds, subsequently a strange sort of heroic fantasts, who called themselves knights and sought out adventures, tournaments, duels, and romantic actions. During this period religion together with the sciences and morals was distorted by wretched grotesqueries, and one notes that taste does not readily degenerate in one area without exhibiting distinct signs of its corruption in everything else that pertains to the finer feeling. The monastic vows made out of a great number of useful people numerous societies of industrious idlers, whose brooding way of life made them fit for concocting thousands of scholastic grotesqueries, which went thence out into the larger world and spread their kind about. Finally, after the human genius had happily lifted itself out of an almost complete destruction by a kind of palingenesis, we see in our own times the proper taste for the beautiful and noble blossom in the arts and sciences as well as with regard to the moral, and there is nothing more to be wished than that the false brilliance, which so readily deceives, should not distance us unnoticed from noble simplicity, but especially that the as yet undiscovered secret of education should be torn away from the ancient delusion in order early to raise the moral feeling in the breast of every young citizen of the world into an active sentiment, so that all delicacy should not merely amount to the fleeting and idle gratification of judging with more or less taste that which goes on outside of us.

Remarks in the *Observations on the Feeling of the Beautiful and Sublime*

Remarks in the *Observations on the Feeling of the Beautiful and Sublime*

[1] On the reverse of the cover, opposite 2:205[1]

Men's art of appearing foolish and women's art of appearing clever

A human being can employ two kinds of beneficial emotions on another, respect and love, the former by means of the sublime, the latter by means of the beautiful. A woman unites both. ~~Never is a~~ This composite sentiment is the greatest impression that can ever befall the human heart. But only two faint sentiments can be equally strong. Should one of the two be strong, then the other must be weak. Now, let one ask oneself which of the two one may want to weaken. Principles are of the greatest sublimity. For example, self-esteem demands sacrifice. E.g. a man can be ugly, but not a witty woman.

The *Coquette* oversteps the feminine, the rough *Pedant* the masculine

A *prude* is too masculine and a *petit maitre*[2] too feminine.

---

[1] Throughout, the subheadings are added by the translators, based on notations added in Marie Rischmüller's edition of the *Remarks*. These subheadings indicate where Kant's remarks were found relative to the copy of the *Observations* in which they were written. This first set of remarks, for instance, was written on the back of the cover of the *Observations*. The page numbers beginning with a volume number (such as "2:205") correspond to the page numbers in the *Observations* in the Academy Edition. Page numbers without a volume number (such as "opposite page one," below) refer to the page number in the first edition of the *Observations*.

[2] In his *The Age of Louis XIV* of 1751, Voltaire explains the origin of the term "petit-maitre," which literally means "little master": during the civil war in France against the Mazarin (a puppet governor established by Anne of Austria), Voltaire explains,

It is ridiculous that a man wants to make a young woman fall in love through understanding and great merits.

The diversity of minds[3] like that of faces. Characters

Parallels between feeling and capacity

A more tender	A finer taste
more dull	coarser

<Sympathy with the natural misfortune of others is not necessary, but [sympathy] with the injustice suffered by others is.>

[20:4]   The feeling I am dealing with[4] is so constituted that I do not need to be taught (to ratiocinate)[5] in order to feel it.

[R8] The finer feeling is that wherein the ideal, <not the chimerical,> contains <the noblest ground> of agreeableness.

Voltaire [has] known and I hope <Why women are embarrassed among each other>

Dolce piccante   the pleasantly bitter[6]

Bold <The audacious gulp *Alexander* took from the chalice was sublime though rash>[7]

The War ended and began several times; there was not a man who did not frequently change sides . . . The Duke of Neaufort's secret party at the beginning of the regency had been known as that of *"the importants"*: Condé's was known as the *"party of the petit-maîtres,"* because they wished to become masters of the state. The only traces left today of all these troubles are the names of *petit-maîtres*, applied nowadays to conceited and ill-bred youths, and of *frondeurs*, used to designate the critics of the government. (Voltaire, *The Age of Louix XIV*, trans. Martyn P. Pollack, New York: Dutton, Everyman's Library, 1969, pp. 36–37)

The term *petit maitre* will be left untranslated throughout the *Remarks*.

3 Here we follow Rischmüller's "Gmüther" rather than the Academy Edition's "Weiber" (women).

4 The German here is "Das Gefühl wovon ich handle," which could also be translated as "The feeling from which I act."

5 *vernünfteln*

6 "The pleasantly bitter" (*das angenehm Herbe*) is Kant's German translation of the Italian *dolce piccante*. Kant's marginal note in his personal copy of Baumgarten's *Metaphysica*, at the end of Baumgarten's section (§ 658) on various sources of pleasure, reads, "dolce picqvante" (15:43). David Hume, in his essay "On Tragedy," notes that "Jealousy and absence in love compose the *dolce peccante* of the Italians, which they suppose so essential to all pleasure" (David Hume, *Essays: Moral, Political, and Literary*, ed. Eugene Millar, Indianapolis: Liberty Fund, 1987, p. 101).

7 Kant alludes here to a story told by Plutarch in *The Age of Alexander*:

Alexander was sick, and Philip . . . seeing how critical his case was, but relying on his own well-known friendship for him, resolved to try the last efforts of his art, and rather hazard his own credit and life than suffer him to perish for want of physics, which he confidently administered to him, encouraging him to take it boldly, if he desired a speedy recovery . . . At this very time, Parmenio wrote to Alexander from

The splendor of the rainbow of the setting sun
Cato's death.[8] Sacrifice <Our current constitution makes it so that
women can also live without men, which spoils everything>
strange and peculiar
The powerful one is kind. *Jonathan Wild*.[9]
The brave youth. Temple at *Ephesus*[10]

the camp, bidding him have a care of Philip, as one who was bribed by Darius to kill
him, with great sums of money and a promise of his daughter in marriage. When he
had perused the letter, he put it under his pillow . . . and when Philip came in with
the potion, he took it with great cheerfulness and assurance, giving him meantime
the letter to read. This was a spectacle well worth being present at, to see Alexander
take the draught and Philip read the letter at the same time. (*Plutarch's Lives, vol.* II,
ed. Arthur Hugh Clough, New York: Modern Library, 2001, p. 153)

In his *Émile*, Jean-Jacques Rousseau writes that, when he was discussing Alexander's story at a
country estate,

the greater number [of people present] blamed the temerity of Alexander; some,
after the governor's example, admired his firmness and his courage – which made
me understand that none of those present saw wherein lay the true beauty of this
story: "As for me," I said to them, "it seems that if there is the least courage, the least
firmness, in Alexander's action, it is foolhardy" . . . [What is so fair in the action] is
that Alexander believed in virtue; it is that he staked his head, his own life on that
belief; it is that his great soul was made for believing in it. Oh, what a fair profession
of faith was the swallowing of that medicine! No, never did a mortal make so sublime
a one. If there is some modern Alexander, let him be showed to me by like deeds.
(*Émile*, trans. Allan Bloom, New York: Basic Books, 1979, p. 111)

[8] For the death of Marcus Portius Cato the Younger (95–46 BC), see Plutarch, *Cato the Younger*.
With Caesar's victory at Thapsus, Cato saw the defeat of the free republic, and took his own
life. In antiquity, Cato's suicide was seen by many, especially by the Stoics, to be a sign of great
character. In the eighteenth century his death was regarded as an heroic example of an instance in
which suicide is justifiable, as in Joseph Addison's 1713 tragedy *Cato* (currently available in *Cato:
A Tragedy and Selected Essays*, ed. Christine Dunn Henderson et al., Indianapolis Liberty Fund,
2004) as well as Johann Christoph Gottsched's 1732 *Der sterbende Cato*. See also Rousseau's *Émile*:
"If there is nothing moral in the heart of man, what is the source of these transports of admiration
for heroic actions, these raptures of love for great soul? What relation does this enthusiasm for
virtue have to our private interest? Why would I want to be Cato, who disembowels himself,
rather than Caesar triumphant?" (*Émile*, trans. Bloom, p. 287).

[9] Kant alludes here to Henry Fielding's *The Life of Mr. Jonathan Wilde the Great*, published in
London in 1743, available as Henry Fielding, *The Life of the Late Mr. Jonathan Wild The Great*,
ed. Hugh Amory, Oxford University Press, 1997. This work appeared in German in 1759 as
Lebensgeschichte des Herrn Jonathan Wild des Grossen. Fielding uses the occasion of a fictional
biography of the real-life gangster and criminal Jonathan Wild to satirize contemporary politics,
drawing an important distinction between "greatness," which "consists in bringing all manner
of mischief to mankind" and is the province of conquerors, criminals, and prime ministers; and
"goodness," the kindly virtues that often go unnoticed in the world.

[10] In *Jonathan Wild*, after the main character is killed by hanging, the author, reflecting on the glory
of the "great" (see note 9 above), remarks, "Such names will be always sure of living to Posterity,
and of enjoying that Fame, which they so gloriously and eagerly coveted; for, according to our
great Dramatic Poet: '– Fame / Not more survives from good than evil Deeds, / Th'aspring
Youth that fir'd th'Ephesian Dome, / Outlives in Fame the pious Fool who rais'd it'" (p. 165).

[20:5]   Women are strong[11] because they are weak <their courage>
Menfolk will loosen up after *vapeurs* and hysterical coincidences.[12]
Hat under the arms[13]
Self-revenge is sublime. Certain vices are sublime. Assassination is cowardly and base. Many do not even have the courage for great vices.
Love and respect
Sexual love always presupposes lustful love, either in sensation or memory.
This lustful love is also either coarse or refined.
[R9] Affectionate love has a great mixture of respect, etc.
A woman does not reveal herself easily, which is why she does not drink. Since she is weak, she is clever.
In marriage unity not uniformity.
Affectionate love is also different from marital love[14]

Title page
[2] Obverse, upper margin

– *Quod petis in te est nec te quasi-*   on moral rebirth
veris extra[15]   *Persius*[16]   What satisfies a true or imagined
                                          need is useful

mihi bonum[17]

The reference to the "great poet" is to Colley Cibber, an eighteenth-century writer who attempted to improve upon Shakespeare. These lines are from the end of Cibber's version of *Richard III*. The "youth" is Herostratus, who burned down the temple of Diana in 356 BC.

[11] Here we follow Rischmüller's "stark" as opposed to the Academy Edition's "stärker."

[12] "Vapeurs" were a spasmodic-neurotic complaint fashionable among French women in the eighteenth century. Kant calls them a "kind of beautiful crankiness" in the *Observations* (see 2:246).

[13] Abbé Jean Terrasson (1670–1750) was a French author. In his *Anthropology*, Kant uses Terrasson as an example of a distracted person worthy of being laughed at: "Terrasson entering solemnly with his night cap instead of his wig on his head and his hat under his arm, full of the quarrel concerning the superiority of the ancients and the moderns with respect to the sciences" (*Anthropology from a Pragmatic Point of View*, ed. Robert Louden, Cambridge University Press, 2006, p. 164, Academy Edition 7:264). Reinhard Brandt locates the anecdote in Johann Christoph Gottsched, ed., *Des Abbts Terrassons Philosophie, nach ihrem allgemeinen Einflusse, auf alle Gegenstände des Geistes und der Sitten*, Leipzig, 1756, pp. 45–46.

[14] Due to damage of the margin, an unreadable line of Kant's remarks follows.

[15] Latin for "What you desire is in you; do not look for yourself outside [of yourself]."

[16] Persius, *Satires* i, v. 7.   [17] Latin for "Good for me."

Title page, under "Observations"

> The first part of science is zetetic,
> the other dogmatic.[18]

The desires that are necessary for a human being through his nature are natural desires. [20:6]

The human being who has no other desires, and none in a higher degree, than are necessary through the natural ones, is called the human being of nature and his ~~satisfaction~~ capacity to be satisfied by little is the sufficiency of nature.[19]

The amount of cognitions and other perfection[s] required for the satisfaction of nature is the simplicity of nature. The human being in [R10] whom one encounters the simplicity as well as the sufficiency of nature is the human being of nature.

One who has learned to desire more than what is necessary through nature is opulent.

Under "Beautiful and Sublime"

The needs of the human being of nature are ~~the bare necessities~~ make [breaks off]

One reason why the representations of death do not have the effect that they could is that, as industrious beings, by nature we properly should not think about it at all.

[3] Reverse of title page

Gaiety is wanton, annoying and disruptive, but the soul at peace is benevolent and kind.

Wit belongs to the dispensable things; a man who takes this to be the main thing in a woman is just like he who spends his fortune to buy monkeys and parrots.

---

[18] The Academy Edition has this sentence following the paragraph that begins "The human being who has no other desires" at 20:6 below. See footnote 19.

[19] In the Academy Edition, the sentence reading "The first part of science is zetetic, the other dogmatic" appears after this paragraph. See footnote 18.

[20:7] One of the reasons why the dissipation of the female sex in unmarried circumstances is more reprehensible consists in the fact that if men in these circumstances have led a dissipated life, they have not simultaneously thereby prepared for unfaithfulness in marriage, for their concupiscence has indeed increased, yet their capacity has decreased. By contrast, in a woman the capacity is unlimited; if now concupiscence increases, then it can be held back by nothing. Therefore, it is presumed of unchaste women that they will be unfaithful wives, but not of men of the same kind.

Every purpose of science is either *eruditiv* (memory) or *speculation* (reason);[20] both must result in making human beings more prudent (cleverer, wiser) in the world, which is generally suitable to human nature, and therefore more sufficient

[R11] A tender love for women has the quality of developing other moral qualities, but a lustful one suppresses them.

<The taste that is moral makes one regard science that does not improve as base.>

The sensitive soul at peace is the greatest perfection in speech, in poetry, [and in] society, but it cannot always be so; rather, it is the ultimate goal, even in marriages. Young people indeed have much sentiment, but little taste; the enthusiastic or excited style ruins taste. Taste perverted through novels and gallant flirtations. The healthy, pampered, spoiled taste.

A reasonable but not clever man [is] not cunning, a clever but not wise man. higher manners

[20:8] A woman has a fine taste in the choice of that which can affect the sentiments of men, and a man has a dull [taste]. Hence he pleases best when he thinks least of pleasing. In contrast, a woman has a ~~dull~~ healthy taste for that which is concerned with her own sentiments.

Sheet inserted after the title page
[4] Obverse

Bearded women, unbearded men. Valiant domestic.

---

[20] *Eruditiv* (related to erudition) and *speculation* (speculation) are Latin terms, left untranslated here. The Academy Edition has *speculative*, where Rischmüller has *speculation*.

The honor of a man consists in the valuation of his self, of a woman in the judgment of others. A man marries according to his judgment, a woman not against the judgment of the parents. A woman opposes injustice with tears, a man with anger.[21]

Richardson ~~goes so far~~ at times puts a judgment of Seneca in a woman's mouth and adds to it "as my brother says." If she were married it would say "as my husband tells me."[22]

Men become sweet towards women if the women become masculine. Insult to women in the habit of flattering them. [R12] Softness roots out virtue more than wantonness, the dignity of a housewife.

Vanity in women makes it so that they are only happy in the glitter outside the house.

The courage of a woman consists in the patient bearing of ill fortune for the sake of her honor or love. Of a man, in the eagerness to drive it away defiantly.

Omphale forced Hercules to spin.[23]   [20:9]

Because so many foolish needs make us soft, the mere unrefined moral drive cannot give us enough powers; therefore, something fantastic must come in addition.

Whence the stoic says: My friend is sick, what does it matter to me? There is no human being who does not feel the heavy yoke of opinion, and no one does away with it.

What is chimerical in friendship in our state and fantastic in the ancient. *Aristotle*[24]

---

[21] Here we follow Rischmüller.

[22] Samuel Richardson (1689–1761) was an English writer whose epistolary novels include *Pamela, or Virtue Rewarded* (1740) and *Clarissa Harlowe* (1747–48). Kant may have been familiar with Richardon's work from the 1757 *Sammlung der gemeinnützigen Lehren, Warnungen und moralischen Anmerkungen aus den Werken des Herrn Samuel Richardson*, ed. C. F. Weisse, 1757.

[23] Ovid's *Heroides* records in detail the way in which Hercules was enslaved to Queen Omphala of Lydia, who dressed him in woman's clothes and made him do woman's work, such as spinning. See Ovid, *Heroides*, trans. Harold Isbell, New York: Penguin Classics, 1990, pp. 78–83. Also see *Emile*: "The same Hercules who believed he raped the fifty daughters of Thespitius was nevertheless constrained to weave while he was with Omphale" (p. 361).

[24] For Aristotle's account of friendship, see his *Nicomachean Ethics*, Book VIII.

Cervantes would have done better if, instead of ridiculing the fantastic and romanic[25] passion, he had directed it better. Novels make noble women fantastic and common ones foolish.[26]

noble men also fantastic, common ones lazy[27]

Rousseau's book serves to improve on the ancients

According to the simplicity of nature, a woman cannot do much good without the mediation of a man. In a state of inequality and wealth, she can immediately

Moral *luxury*. In sentiments that are without effect.

[20:10] The inner distress about the inability to help or about the sacrifice in case one helps, as well as the cowardice that [R13] makes us believe that others suffer a lot even though they could easily endure it, brings about sympathy with others. Incidentally, this is a great antidote against selfishness. These drives are altogether very cold in the natural human being.

Natural elevations are degradations below one's rank, for example to raise oneself to the rank of a craftsman.

Relative evaluation is unnecessary, but in the state of inequality and injustice it is good to set oneself against the pompous magnates with a certain pride, or at least indifference, in order to be equal with respect to lower ones.

One must with a certain breadth

[5] Reverse, opposite page 1 of the *Observations*, at 2:207

Although being tall does not make a man great, bodily size still coincides with the judgment about the moral

It is easier to educate a nobleman than a [common] human being. He is a despiser of the common rabble, for so he must in every case call the industrious and oppressed, in order for one to believe that he has been

---

[25] The German term here is *"romanisch."* This term could refer to ancient Romans. It can also be translated as "novelistic" in the sense that something "romanisch" occurs in or is related to novels (*Romane*). One should note that the word "romanisch" is very similar to the word "romantisch", the latter being best translated by the English word "romantic". Thus, it is possible that Kant intended to refer to romantic passions here and simply misspelled the word "romantisch."

[26] Cervantes' *Don Quixote*, written between 1605 and 1615, appeared in German in 1753 under the title *Des berühmten Ritters Don Quixotte von Mancha lustige und sinnreiche Geschichte.*

[27] The Academy Edition has this line as part of the preceding sentence.

created to nourish them. The scholars in China let their nails grow on the left hand.[28]

Among all ranks,[29] none is more useless than [that of] the scholar as long as it is in the [state of] natural simplicity; and none more needed than the same in a condition of oppression through superstition or violence

Deliberations belong to small and beautiful casts of mind. A woman has affects as great as a man, but they are more thoughtful, specifically when it comes to respectability, the man is inconsiderate. The *Chinese* and *Indians* have affects just as great as the Europeans, but they are calmer. [20:11] A woman is vengeful

The rising sun is just as splendid as the setting one, but the [R14] sight of the former touches on the beautiful, the latter on the tragic and sublime. That which a woman does in marriage leads much more to natural happiness than that which the man does, at least in our civilized state.

Because so many unnatural desires are found in the civilized condition, the occasion for virtue also sometimes arises, and since so much luxury is found in enjoyment and knowledge, science arises. In the natural state, one can be good without virtue and reasonable without science.

Whether a human being would have it better in a simple state is now difficult to see, 1. because he has lost his feeling for simple pleasures. 2. because he commonly believes that the corruptions that exist in the civilized state also exist in the state of simplicity. [20:12]

[6] Page 1 of the *Observations*, upper margin, at 2:207

Happiness without taste is based on simplicity and modesty of inclination, happiness with taste is based on the sensitive soul at peace; therefore one also must be able to be happy without society. Amusements, no needs. Rest after work is agreeable. One must not chase after gratification at all.

---

[28] Kant made note of this custom in his lectures on physical geography: "The scholars (in China) never trim the nails on their left hand, so as to indicate their profession" (9:378). The original source of it is unknown.
[29] *Stände*

Lower margin

One must distinguish "he is in accordance with the taste of others" from "he has taste in ~~regard~~ the judgment about others." Women know very well how to evaluate in accordance with the taste of others, and therefore easily know the minds of others and have good taste to satisfy them, but they have a bad taste in other persons, which is good. For this reason, they also all marry the richest.

[R15]

[7] Page 2 of the *Observations*, marginal notes, next to lines 15–18, at 2:208

Tenderness and fondness of sensation
    Taste chooses in trifles

Sheet inserted after page 2 of the *Observations*
[8] Obverse

Logical egoism <skillfulness in taking standpoints.>
    Common duties do not need the hope of another life as their motivation, though greater sacrifice and self-denial surely have an inner beauty, but our feeling of pleasure about this can never be so strong in itself that it outweighs the annoyance of inconvenience unless the representation of a future state, in which moral beauty persists and happiness is increased by finding oneself even more capable of [moral] actions, comes to its assistance.
    All pleasures are either bodily or ideal.
    Concerning the latter [breaks off]
[20:13]   A woman is offended or oppressed ~~by injustice~~ <by crudeness> where no justification but only threat can help. She helps herself to her touching weapons of tears, melancholic reluctance and complaints, yet still endures the ill before she gives way to injustice. See here the courage of women. A man is indignant that one might be so bold as to insult him; he answers violence with violence, ~~threatens~~, frightens, and makes the offender feel the consequences of injustice. See here the courage of a man. It ~~are~~ is not necessary that a man be indignant at the ills of delusion; he can despise

them in a masculine way. Yet he will be infuriated about these ills as true insults if they befall a woman.

[R16] A woman can use the most extreme weapons of her scorn – the scolding of counterreproaches – against a woman, but never against a man, except by means of the threats against another man.

When ~~men~~ women squabble or fight, men laugh about it, but not vice versa.

Duels have – primarily for the sake of women – a ground in nature.

In the current state, a man can use no other means against injustice than a woman, namely not according to the order of nature, but [according to] the civil ~~society~~ constitution by means of the authority. [20:14]

Rousseau. Proceeds synthetically and starts from the natural human being, I proceed analytically and start from the civilized[30] one.

The country life delights everyone, especially the shepherd's life, and yet boredom will consume the civilized one therein.

[9] Reverse, opposite page 3, at 2: 208

The heart of the human being may be constituted as it will, the question here is only whether the state of nature or the ~~moral~~ civilized one develops more actual sin and readiness thereto. Moral ill can be so subdued that merely a lack of greater purity shows itself in actions, but never positive vice in a noticeable degree (whoever is not so saintly is for that reason not vicious); on the contrary, this can develop so far that it becomes detestable. The simple human being has little temptation to become vicious. Opulence alone accounts for the great temptation and the culture of moral sentiments and understanding will ~~apparently~~ never hold it back if the taste for opulence is already great. [20:15]

Piety is the <means of> *complementi*[31] of moral *Bonitaet*[32] towards holiness. In the *relation* of one human being to another that is not [R17] the question. We cannot naturally be holy and we lost this through original sin, although we certainly can be morally good.

Is it not enough for us that ~~we~~ a human being never lies, even though he has a secret inclination, which, were it brought under the conditions that develop it, would [make him] lie?

---

[30] *Gesitteten*   [31] Latin for "complements."   [32] Latin for "goodness."

Do we ask whether a human being undertakes his actions of honesty, fidelity, etc. out of consideration for divine obligation, if he only does them, even though these actions are condemnable before God in so far as they do not arise thereby[?]

In order to prove that the human being is corrupt by nature one appeals to the civilized state. One should appeal to the natural one.

Actions of justice are those whose neglect will naturally make another hate us; actions of love those whose neglect will provide ~~the reason~~ others **no reason for love** towards us.

[10] Page 3 of the *Observations*
On the margin, next to lines 13 and 14, at 2:207

Utility, blooms[33]

Lower margin

[20:16] Because the ~~basic talents~~ basic qualities of women lead them to study man and to easily create a deception for his inclinations, they are made to govern and actually govern in all nations that have taste.

Sheet inserted after page 4 of the *Observations*
[11] Obverse, at 2:208

There is a most perfect (*moral*) world in accordance with the order of nature, and according to this we ask, in the same way, a supernatural [breaks off]

[R18] The virtuous one looks upon the rank of others with indifference, although if he refers it to himself, he looks at it with contempt.

One can either restrict one's opulent inclinations or, by keeping them, invent remedies against their insults. To the latter belong science and contempt for life on account of the imminence of death, and solace of the future [breaks off]

Boredom is a kind of longing for an ideal gratification.

---

[33] This line only appears in Rischmüller. The German word "Blüthen" (blooms), or rather "Blüten," can also be translated as "forgery."

The Holy Scripture has more effect on improvement if supernatural powers accompany it. Good moral education has more if everything should happen only in accordance with the order of nature.

I admit that through the latter we can produce no holiness, which is [20:17] justifying, but we can produce a moral *Bonitaet coram foro humano*,[34] and this is even conducive to the former.

Just as little as one can say that nature has implanted in us an immediate inclination for acquisition (miserly greediness), so little can one say it has given us an immediate drive for honor. In general opulence, both develop and both ~~just as~~ are useful. But from this it can only be concluded that just as nature produces calluses during hard work, it also creates remedies for itself in its injuries.

The difference in rank implies that, as little as one puts oneself in the place of a work horse in order to imagine its wretched food, so little does one put oneself in the place of the miserable one in order to grasp misery.

[12] Reverse, opposite page 5, at 2:208

The precepts for the happy life can be twofold: 1. That one shall show how, after all the inclinations of honor [and] of opulence are already acquired, one acquires one's ends, and at the same time representations, which [R19] can prevent the sorrow that originates thereby, of the future life, of the nullity of this life, etc. 2. Or that one attempts to bring these inclinations themselves to moderation.

The Stoics' mistake [is] that through virtue they only searched for a counterweight to the pains of opulence. *Antisthenes's* school attempted to eradicate opulence itself.[35]

The Stoics' doctrine of anger out of contempt for others.

The current *moralists* presuppose much as ill and want to teach to overcome it, and presuppose much temptation to evil and prescribe motivations to overcome it. The *Rousseau*ian method teaches to hold the former for no ill and, thus, the latter for no temptation.

---

[34] Latin for "Goodness before a human court."

[35] Antisthenes (440–*c.* 370), who became one of Socrates' most ardent followers, is regarded as the founder of the Cynics. He believed that man's happiness lay in cultivating virtue for its own sake.

[20:18]   There is no one more moderate in enjoyment than a miser. The miserly greediness arises from a desire for many enjoyments, to which there is no actual but a chimerical inclination in the miser, since he regards them to be great goods from hearsay, even though he himself is moderate. This is the boldest miserliness. The cowardly miserliness.

The threat of eternal punishment cannot be the immediate ground of morally good actions, although it may well be a strong counterweight to the temptations to evil so that the immediate sensation of *morality* is not outweighed.

There is no immediate inclination at all to <morally> evil actions, but certainly an immediate one to good actions.

[13] Page 5
Upper margin, at 2:208

This ideal feeling sees life in dead nature or imagines seeing it. Trees drink the neighboring brook. The zephyr whispers to the loved one. Clouds cry on a melancholic day. Cliffs threaten like giants. Solitude is yet inhabited by dreamy shadows and the deathly silence of graves.

[R20]
fantastic   From there come the images and
                                                  the spirit rich in imagery.[36]

Right margin, next to lines 12 and 13

ideal ~~therefore beautiful~~

Next to lines 18–24

[20:19]   Philosophical eyes are microscopic. Their vision is exact but limited ~~and is therefore~~ and its intention is truth. The sensual vision is bold and supports enthusiastic dissipation, which is stirring, yet only to be encountered in the imagination.*

---

[36] In the Academy Edition, the last three remarks ("Solitude...," "fantastic," and "From...") follow one another, so that they could be translated as "Solitude is yet inhabited by dreamy shadows and the deathly silence of graves [by] fantastic [ones]. From there come the images and the spirit rich in imagery."

Lower margin

Beautiful and sublime are not the same. The latter swells the heart and makes the attention fixed and tense. Therefore, it exhausts. The former lets the soul melt in a soft sensation, and, in that it relaxes the nerves, it ~~lets~~ puts the feeling into a gentler emotion, which, however, where it goes too far, transforms into weariness, surfeit and disgust.

[14] Page 6
Marginal notes, next to line 2

bold

At the margin, next to lines 24–27

*The majority of men are primarily effeminate or common and thus even worse to associate with than women.

Lower margin

Whence does it come that our parties[37] without women are quite tasteless, since they were not so with the Greeks, nor with the [R21] Romans. At that time one spoke of virtue [and] of the fatherland; now this is an empty *matter*,[38] into whose place, at best, false *devotion* can step. Among nothing but men, jokes have no proper life and also become uncivilized. We are soft and effeminate and must be among women.[39]

Sheet inserted after page 6
[15] Obverse, at 2:209

The good-natured and the well-civilized human being are very much to be distinguished. The first does not need the representation of higher beings in order to control perverse drives, for they are natural and good.[40]

---

37 The German word "Gesellschaften" (parties) could also be translated as "societies" or "companies."
38 The German term here is "Materie."
39 In the Academy Edition, this paragraph appears at 20:21–22. See footnote 44.
40 Kant may have meant here to call the good-natured humans "natural" and "good."

If he thinks thereof he says that maybe he truly is in another life.[41] One must be good and expect the rest. The second is 1. only civilized 2. well civilized. In the former case he has many fantastical joys that, in order to remain good, he must oppose with a representation which never can become intuiting. The second one is a civilized human being, who, if he is extended [in] his morality beyond the simplicity of nature, extends it to the object that he only wishes and believes.

This natural morality must also be the touchstone of all religion. For if it is uncertain whether people in the other religion can become blessed and whether the torments in this world cannot help them toward happiness in the future one, then it is certain that I would not have to persecute them. This latter would not however be the case if the natural sentiment were not sufficient for all execution of duty in this life.

[20:20]   When the *Portuguese* discovered *Celebes* the inhabitants understood the nullity of their religion, but sent to Malacca for *Don ~~Rug~~ Perero* as well as to *Achin* for the queen. [They] received two kinds of priests, etc.[42]

Every coward lies, but not vice versa. That which makes weak produces lies. The ridiculous lust for honor and shame the most.

Shame and prudishness[43] are to be distinguished. The former is a betrayal of a secret through the natural movement of the blood. The latter is a [R22] means of concealing a secret for the sake of vanity, the same in sexual arousal.

It is far more dangerous to be in war with free and profit-seeking people than with the subjects of a monarch. Utility that vanity has hereof.

[20:21]   I will speak of everything where there are only rarely exceptions. For according to the rule of prudence, that which happens so rarely that one

---

[41] In translating this sentence, we changed the German word "ist" ("is") to the German word "in" ("in"), assuming that an error must have occurred here in Kant's remarks. Without this assumption, the sentence does not make any sense and literally translates as: "If he thinks thereof he says maybe he truly is is another life."

[42] The island of Celebes, or Malacca, where the pagan king, proselytized by both Christian and Muslim missionaries, converted to Islam, because the priests expected by the Portuguese arrived later than did the Muslims sent from Achin (in Sumatra). Kant was an avid reader of numerous travelogs, and it is therefore difficult to know from what travelog he draws this reference. A possible source could be the classic geographical-historical work *Allgemeine Historie der Reisen zu Wasser und zu Lande; oder Sammlung aller Reisebeschreibungen (A General History of Travels by Water and Land)*, in the chapter describing the island of Celebes (see vol. XI (1753), especially p. 493).

[43] *Schamhaftigkeit*

thereof can regard it as a ~~f~~ stroke of luck never happens, and ~~in accordance with~~ that is universal according to the rule of prudence where some cases of the contrary cannot be sought according to any rule. I speak of taste, I thus take my own judgments ~~in accordance with the~~ in such a way that they are (*aesthetically*) universally true according to the rule of taste, even though it properly ~~logically~~ – according to the rule of measured reason (*logic*al) – holds only for some of them.[44]

[16] Obverse, opposite page 7, at 2:209

A heart extended through sensibility prepares itself for longing and will   [20:22]
finally be worn out [by] the sensations of all things of life; therefore it sighs
for something which is outside its own circle, and as true as devotion is
in itself it is just as fantastic with respect to most human beings, because
they themselves are chimerical, and that they demonstrate their love
[and] uprightness only with respect to God and are cold with respect to
the former, yet dissemble with respect to the latter, comes from the fact
that one can more easily deceive oneself concerning the former than the
latter.

Because one can form a concept of higher moral qualities, sacrifice for
the common best, everlasting devotion, fulfillment of marital intentions
without lust, immediate inclination to science without honor, one imagines all these to be appropriate to the **condition of a human being** and
finds the state one sees corrupted. But such desires are fantastical and
arise from precisely the same sources as universal corruption. Exactly
these flaws will no longer be regarded as blameworthy with respect to
human beings once the remaining corruption is eliminated

[R23]

Whole *nations* can provide the example of a human being as such. One
never finds great virtues where they are not also combined with great
excesses, as with the English. Canadian savages. What is the cause. The
French are more decent and all sublimity of virtue is also missing

The position of humanity within the order of created beings.

---

44 In the Academy Edition, the paragraph beginning "Whence does it come" (R20–21) appears here.
See footnote 39.

[17] Page 8
At the margin, next to line 7, at 2:210

Beautiful, cute[45]

Sheet inserted after page 8
[18] Obverse, at 2:210

[20:23] All devotion that is natural has a use only if it is the result of a good *morality*. The same goes for natural devotion that is related to a book. For this reason the spiritual teachers correctly say that it is good for nothing if it is not effected through the spirit of God, in which case it is an intuition, otherwise it is very prone to self-deception.

The reason why marriages are so cold-minded is this: because both members have such great external, chimerical connection to dignity [and] daintiness; and if each member so strongly depends on opinion, he becomes indifferent towards the opinion of the other. From this arises disdain, finally hate. In relation to this, romanic[46] love is only the quality of a hero.[47] *Coquette.*

Those who make a doctrine of piety out of the doctrine of virtue make a whole out of the part, for piety is only one kind of virtue.

It now often seems to us more and more that the human race has almost no value if it does not contain great artists and scholars; hence,
[20:24] the country people [and] farmers appear to be nothing to themselves and to be something only as the means for the support of the former. The injustice of this judgment [R24] already shows that it is false. For one feels that if one has extended one's inclinations – one may do whatever one wishes to do – life amounts to nothing and that the extension of these inclinations is therefore harmful.

There is a great difference between overcoming one's inclinations and eradicating them, that is, ~~se~~ bringing it about that one loses them; this is also different from restraining ~~one's~~ inclinations, that is, making it that someone never has them. The former is necessary for old people, the latter for young ones

---

[45] The German here is "schön niedlich," which could also be translated as "quite cute."
[46] *romanisch*; see footnote 25
[47] This sentence is ambiguous in German. It could also be translated as "Therefore, in relation to romanic love, it [marriage] is only the quality of a hero."

There is a great difference between being a good human being and being a good rational being. Being perfect as the latter has no other limits except for finitude, being perfect as the former has many limits.

[19] Reverse, opposite page 9, at 2:210

It takes a very great art to prevent lying in children. For since they are far too wanton and far too weak to tolerate negative responses or punishments, they have very strong incitements to lie that older people never have. Especially since they can do nothing for themselves, as older people can, but everything depends on how they represent something according to the inclination that they notice in others. One must therefore only punish them for what they cannot deny, and not grant them something on the basis of excuses.

If one wants to ~~approve~~ form morality one must above all not introduce any motivations that would not render the action morally good, e.g. punishments, rewards. Therefore, one must also depict the lie [as] immediately ugly, and, as it also is in fact, never subordinate it to any other rule of morality, for example duty towards others.

(One has no duties towards oneself, but one has *absolute* duties, that is,   [20:25] an action is good in and for itself. It is also absurd that, in our morality, we should *depend* on ourselves.)

In *medicine* one says that the doctor is the servant of nature: just the same is valid in morality. Only hold off the external ill, [and] nature will take the best course.

[R25] If the doctor said that nature in itself is corrupted, by what means would he improve it. Likewise the *moralist*

The human being does not take part in the luck or misfortune of others before he himself feels content. Thus, bring it about that he is content with little, and you will make kind human beings.[48] Otherwise, it is in vain.

The universal love of humankind has something high and noble in it, but in a human being it is chimerical. If one aims for it one gets used to deceiving oneself with longings and idle wishes. As long as one is so much dependent on things, one cannot participate in the happiness of others

---

[48] The Academy Edition has a semicolon here.

[20] Page 9
At the margin, next to lines 16–19, at 2:211

Because dubious things are small, one calls a [breaks off][49]

Sheet inserted after page 10
[21] Obverse

[20:26] The simple human being has very early a sentiment of what is right, but very late or never a concept thereof. That sentiment must be developed long before the concept. If one teaches him early to develop according to rules, he will never feel the sentiment

Once the inclinations are developed, it is difficult to represent the good or ill in other circumstances. Because I will now, without an everlasting enjoyment, waste away from boredom, I imagine this also to be the case with the Swiss who grazes his cows in the mountains. I <And the latter> cannot ~~me~~ imagine how a human being who has had enough could still desire something more. One ~~ste~~ can hardly conceive how, in such a low state, this lowness does not fill him with pains. On the other hand, if the rest of [R26] the human beings are infected with the ills of delusion, some cannot imagine how this delusion could be acquired by them. The noble man imagines that the ills of the disrespect caused by having one's glamor stolen can oppress a citizen, and the latter does not understand how the

[20:27] former could have become accustomed to count certain delightful things among his needs.

The sovereign who granted nobility wanted to give something that could serve certain persons in lieu of all other opulence. After all, they have the tidbit of nobility. Let the rest of the mob have the money

Can anything be more perverse than already to speak of the other world to children who have barely stepped into this one.

*[Related by signs to page 10, line 18]

others also tire of it. One does not listen long to precocious speeches. A human being who does not neglect himself at all becomes burdensome. Too much attentiveness to oneself looks embarrassing

---

[49] The Academy Edition does not include this fragment.

[22] Obverse, opposite page 11, at 2:211

Just as fruit, when it is ripe enough, breaks away from the tree and falls
to the earth to let its own seeds take root, so the mature human being
breaks away from his parents, transplants himself, and becomes the root
of a new generation.[50]

The man must depend on no one else, so that the woman depends [20:28]
entirely on him.

It must be asked how far inner moral grounds can bring a human being.
It̶ They will perhaps bring him so far, that, in a state of freedom without
great temptations, he is good, but if the injustice of others or the force
of delusion does violence to him, then this inner morality does not have
enough power. He must have *religion*, and encourage himself [R27] by
means of the rewards of a future life; and human nature is not capable
of an immediate moral purity. But if, in a supernatural manner, purity
were produced in him, then the future rewards would no longer have the
quality of motivations

The difference between a false and a healthy morality is that the former
seeks only antidotes for ills, while the latter takes care that the causes of
this ill are not there at all

Reputation, if it indicates sublimity, is that which shimmers, if it
indicates beauty, it is the pretty, or, also, the decorated of finery if it is
contrived

Among all kinds of finery there is also the moral. The sublime with
respect to rank consists in this, that it includes much dignity; the beautiful
means [̶u̶n̶r̶e̶a̶d̶a̶b̶l̶e̶ ̶w̶o̶r̶d̶] here the becoming

The reason why those of nobility commonly pay poorly

[23] Page 11
Upper margin, at 2:211

It is a great harm[51] for the genius if the critique is prior to the art. If, in
a nation, exemplars come in that blind it before it has developed its own
talents.

---

[50] *Geschlecht*
[51] The word in German here is "Schade." We suspect that Kant omitted an "n" at the end of this
word. Thus, we translate the word as "harm." However, Kant might also have forgotten an "n"
after the first three letters of the word, in which case the word would have to be translated as
"shame."

Lower margin

[20:29]   Sublime disposition that overlooks trivialities and notices the good among deficiencies.   tobacco[52]

Sheet inserted after page 12
[24] Obverse, at 2:212

It is unnatural that a human being should spend the great part of his life in order to teach one child how it should live some day. Such tutors as *Jean Jacques* are therefore artificial. In the simple state only a few services are provided for a child; as soon as he has a bit of strength [R28] he carries out small, useful actions of the adult, as with the countryman or the craftsman, and gradually learns the rest.

It is therefore seemly that a human being spend his life teaching so many at once [how] to live that the sacrifice of his own life is by contrast not to be considered. Schools are therefore necessary. But in order for them to be possible, one must raise[53] *Émile*. One would wish that Rousseau would show how schools can arise from this.

Preachers in the country could begin this with their own children and those of their neighbors. Taste ~~is~~ does not depend on our needs. The man must already be civilized if he is to choose a wife according to taste.

[20:30]   One shall not be very refined, for thereby only small traits are noticed; the big ones will only become apparent to the simple and coarse eye.

It is a burden for the understanding to have taste. I must read Rousseau for so long that the beauty of [his] expressions no longer disturbs [me], and only then can I finally examine him with reason.

That great people only glitter in the distance, that a sovereign is greatly diminished among his valets, stems from the fact that no human being is great

What constitutes a great hindrance to the doctrine of the happy eternity, and which lets one assume that the latter would be hardly adequate

---

[52] The German word here is "Tobak," and not "Tabak." In German, one calls something "starker Tobak" when one judges it to be a bit too strong.

[53] The German word here is "ziehen," which one usually would translate as "to pull." In this context, however, "ziehen" should probably be understood as "erziehen" (*"to raise," "to educate"*) or "aufziehen" (*"to raise," "to grow"*). One could also import a preposition and translate this as "draw on *Émile*" (cf. Guyer, ed., 2005).

to our state, is that those who believe [in] it do not become less arduous about the happiness of this life, which yet would have to happen if our vocation would involve taking it as the great basis for our actions

[25] Obverse, opposite page 13, at 2:212

If I now wanted to put myself into a great although not total independence [20:31] from human beings, I would have to be able to be poor without [R29] feeling it, and be able to be thought of as lowly without minding it. But if I were a rich man I would primarily add freedom from things and from human beings to my pleasures. I would not overload myself with things such as guests, horses, [and] underlings, about whose loss I would have to worry. I would have no jewels, because I can lose them, etc. I would neither my clothes adapt myself[54] to the delusion of others, so that it would not really harm me, for example, reduce my acquaintance, but not so that it gives me comfort.

How freedom in the proper sense (the moral, not the metaphysical) would be the supreme *principium* of all virtue and also of all happiness

It is necessary to see how late art, daintiness and the civilized constitution are to be found, and how they never are found in some regions of the world (for example, where there are no domestic animals) so that one distinguishes that which is foreign and contingent to nature from that which is natural to it. If one considers the happiness of the savage it is not in order to return to the woods, but only in order to see what one has lost while gaining elsewhere; so that, among in the enjoyment and exercise of social opulence, one would not, with unhappy and unnatural inclinations, cling to the former, and would remain a civilized human being of nature. That consideration serves as the standard. For nature never makes a human being into a citizen, and his inclinations [and] endeavors are merely aimed at the simple state of life.

With most other creatures, it appears to be their main purpose that they live and that their species should live. If I presuppose this in the case of the human being, then I must not condemn the basest savage.

---

54 The German phrase here is "mich einrichten," which one could also translate as "to make myself at home."

[26] Page 14
Next to lines 4–8

Greek *profile*
a fat body
of great size
huge wigs[55]

Sheet inserted after page 14
[27] Obverse

[20:32]   [R30] How, out of *luxury*, civil religion and also religious coercion (at least, with every new transformation) finally becomes necessary

The mere natural religion does not at all suit a state, rather *skepticism* would sooner do so

Anger is a very benign sentiment of weak human beings. An inclination to suppress it brings about irreconcilable hate. Women, clerics. One does not always hate the one at whom one is angry. Benignity of the human beings who are angry. Pretended mannerliness conceals anger and makes false friends.

For such a weak creature as the human being, the partly necessary, partly voluntary, ignorance of the future is very suitable

I can never convince another except by means of his own thoughts. I must, therefore, presuppose that the other has a good and correct
[20:33]   understanding, otherwise it is futile to hope that he can be won over by my reasons. Likewise I can morally move no one except by means of his own sentiments; I must, therefore, presuppose that the other one has a certain *Bonitaet*[56] of heart, for otherwise he will never feel abhorrence <at> my portrayal of vice and never feel ~~praise~~ incentives in himself at my praise of virtue. But since it would be impossible that some *morally* correct sentiments would be in him, and that he could assume his sentiments to be in unison with those of the whole human race, if his evil were evil through and through, I must grant him partial goodness therein, and must depict the slippery resemblance of innocence and crime as deceptive.[57]

---

[55] In the Academy Edition, these lines appear as one line, below at 20:33, right before the paragraph reading "The supreme reason . . ." See footnote 57.

[56] Latin for "goodness."

[57] In the Academy Edition, the remark beginning with "Greek profile" on R29 above appears after this sentence. See footnote 55.

[28] Obverse, opposite page 15, at 2:213

[R31] ~~It cou~~ The supreme reason to create is because it is good. From this it must follow that since God, with his power and his great cognition, finds himself good, he also finds it good to *actualize* everything that is possible thereby. Second, that he has satisfaction in everything that is good for something, the most [satisfaction], however, in that which aims at the greatest good. The first is good as a consequence, the second as a ground. [20:34]

~~B[ecause]~~ Because revenge presupposes that human beings who hate each other remain close, if one could instead remove oneself as one wanted the reason for taking revenge would fall away; hence, revenge cannot be in nature, because the latter does not presuppose that human beings are confined next to each other. But it is very natural that anger is a very necessary ~~passion~~ quality and one very suited to a man; that is, if it is not a passion (which is to be distinguished from an *affect*)

One cannot imagine the agreeableness of something that one has not tasted, like the Carib detested salt, to which he had not gotten accustomed[58]

Agesilaus and the Persian satrap despised each other; the former said, "I know the Persian voluptuousness, but mine is unknown to you"; he was wrong[59]

The goods of soft opulence and of delusion; the latter come from the comparative estimation in sciences, in honor, etc.

Christianity says that one shall not devote one's heart to temporal things; by this it is now also understood that one shall early on prevent no one[60] from acquiring such devotion. But to first nurture inclinations

---

[58] The source of Kant's observation here could be *Allgemeine Historie der Reisen zu Wasser oder Lande; oder Sammlung aller Reisebeschreibungen* (see footnote 42): "The Caribs never eat salt, not because they lack it, since they have natural salt mines on every island, but rather it is not their taste" (vol. XVII [1759], p. 482).

[59] Agesilaus, King of Sparta (444–360 BC). Kant's source for this anecdote is probably Rousseau, who writes in his *Second Discourse*, "I know the delights of your country, said Brasidas to a Satrap who was comparing the life of Sparta with that of Persepolis, but you cannot know the pleasure of mine" (*Second Discourse*, Part II, § 38, in *The Discourses and Other Early Political Writings*, ed. Victor Gourevitch, Cambridge University Press, 1997, pp. 177–78; cf. Herodotus' *Historiae* VII, 135 and Plutarch's *Apophthegmata Laconica*, 255 F). Brasidas was a Spartan general who fought during the Archidamian War.

[60] The German word here is "keiner." However, Kant may have meant to write "einer" ("*anyone*").

and then to expect supernatural assistance to rule them, that is to tempt God.

[R32]

[29] Page 16
At the margin, next to lines 8–12, at 2:214

The adventurous taste parodies.
Hudibras parodies grimaces[61]
cutely sublime. [unreadable word][62]

Sheet inserted after page 16
[30] Obverse

Graduated scale: freedom, equality, honor. (Delusion) Attention, hence-forth he loses his entire life.

[20:35]   Two touchstones of the difference between the natural and the unnat-ural: 1. Whether it is proper to that which one cannot change, 2. Whether it can be common to all human beings or only to a few with the oppression of the rest

A certain great monarch in the North has, as one says, civilized his nation – would that God had wanted him to bring morals into it – this way, however, everything he did was political welfare and moral corruption[63]

I can make no one better except by means of the remnant of good that is in him; I do not want to make any one more prudent except by means of the remnant of prudence that is in him

Vicious ones can be looked upon with affability, because vices come to them quite externally through our corrupted constitution

---

[61] *Hudibras*, by Samuel Butler (1612–80), was published in three parts in 1663, 1664, and 1678. The work was mentioned as an example of ridicule in *The Spectator* (number 249). For details of its reception in Germany, see Harvey M. Thayer, "*Hudibras* in Germany," *PMLA* 24 (1904): 547–84.

[62] In the Academy Edition, this and the preceding two lines appear on page 20:37, before the paragraph that starts "All incorrect estimations..." below. See footnote 65.

[63] Kant refers to Charles XII of Sweden (1682–1718), whose life Voltaire described in his *Histoire de Charles XII* (available in English as *History of Charles XII with a Life of Voltaire*, ed. Lord Macaulay and Thomas Carlyle, Honolulu: University Press of the Pacific, 2002).

From the feeling of equality arises the idea of justice, both the idea of the ~~suffer~~ obliged as well as the idea of the obliging. The former is the obligation towards others, the latter is the felt obligation of others towards me.

In order for the latter to have a standard in the understanding, we are [20:36] able to put ourselves in the place of others in thoughts, and, in order for there to be no lack of motivations for this, [R33] we will be moved through *sympathy* for the misfortune and distress of others just as through our own.

This obligation will be recognized as something whose lack in another would let me consider him my enemy, and would make me hate him. Never is anything more outrageous than injustice; all other ills that we endure are nothing in comparison. Obligation only concerns the necessary self-preservation ~~and the~~ in so far as it exists in accordance with the preservation of the species; all the rest are favors and goodwill. Still, I will hate everyone who sees me struggling in the ditch and coldheartedly passes by.

Kindnesses occur only due to inequality. For, by kindness, I understand a readiness to cause something good even in those cases where universal natural sympathy would be an insufficient ground for it. Now, it is simple-minded and natural to sacrifice as much leisureliness as I provide for another, because one human being counts as much as another. If I therefore should be willing, I must judge myself more harshly with respect to discomforts than another, [and] I must regard that, which I spare another, as a great ill and that, which I suffer myself, as a small one. A man would despise another if he showed such kindnesses towards him.

The first inequality is of a man and a child, and of a man and a woman. In a certain way, he considers it an obligation not to sacrifice anything to them, since he is strong, and they are weak.

*Linked by signs to page 16, line 2, at 2:213

The seemingly noble is ~~reputation~~ decency.[64] The seemingly magnificent, shimmer. The seemingly beautiful [is] made up. The beautiful is either [20:37] engaging or pretty.

---

[64] Here we follow Rischmüller's "Das scheinbar Edle ist der ~~Ansehen~~ Anstand" instead of the Academy Edition's "Das scheinbar Edle ist der Anstand. Ansehen."

[31] Reverse, opposite to page 17, at 2:214

[65]All incorrect estimations of that which does not belong to the purposes of nature also destroys [*sic*] the beautiful harmony of nature. Because one [R34] holds the arts and sciences to be so very important, one decries those that do not have them, and brings us to injustices that we would not commit if we were to regard them as more equal to us.

If something is not ~~ultimately~~ suitable to the length of a lifetime, nor to its epochs, nor to the great part of all human beings, if it further is subject very much to chance, and is only possible with difficulty, it does not belong to the happiness and perfection of the human race.[66] How many centuries have passed by before there were genuine sciences, and how many nations are there in the world that will never have them.

[20:38]

One must not say that nature calls us to the sciences, because it has given us capacities for them; for what concerns pleasure can be merely artificial. Since the availability of the sciences has been proven, one rather is to judge that we have a capacity of the understanding ~~go~~ that goes further than our vocation in this life; thus, there will be another life. If we seek to develop these here we will fill our post badly. A caterpillar that would feel that it ought to become a butterfly.

Scholars believe that everything is for their sake. Nobles as well. If one has traveled through barren France one can find comfort again at the *Academy* of sciences[67] or at respectable societies, just as in Rome one can find delight to the point of drunkenness in the splendor of the churches and antiquities, if one has happily gotten away from all the beggars in the state of the Church

[20:39]

Precisely for the preceding reason, one should judge that those who want to know too much prematurely here will be, over there, castigated with imbecility as punishment. Just as a prematurely clever child either dies or withers and becomes dumb at an immature age.

A human being may become as artful as he wants, he still cannot force nature to follow other laws. He must either work for himself or [R35]

---

[65] In the Academy Edition, the three lines beginning "The adventurous taste . . . " (on R32) appear here. See footnote 62.

[66] *menschliches Geschlecht*

[67] The French Academy of Sciences was established by Louis XIV, formalizing what had previously been an informal group of scholars meeting together under the patronage of Jean-Baptiste Colbert. In the eighteenth century it contributed to scientific advances through its publications and served as counselor to those in power.

others for him. And this work will rob others of as much of their happiness as he wants to increase his own beyond the average

If some want to enjoy without working then others will have to want to work without enjoying

Inserted sheet after page 20
[32] Obverse, 2:215

One can promote welfare either by allowing desires to expand and striving to satisfy them; one can promote rectitude if one allows the inclinations of delusion and opulence to grow and strives towards moral incentives to resist them. With both of these challenges, however, there is another solution, namely not allowing these inclinations to arise. Finally, one can also promote good conduct by setting aside all immediate moral *goodness* and merely taking the commands of a rewarding and punishing lord as a basis.

The ill for human beings inherent in science is above all that the greatest part of those who want to adorn themselves with it do not acquire any improvement of their understanding, but only a perversion of it, not to mention that for most of them it only serves as an instrument of vanity. The utility that the sciences have either consists in opulence, e.g., mathematics, or in the hindrance of those ills that they themselves have brought on, or also in a certain kind of modesty as a by-product.

The concepts of civil and of natural justice and the sentiment of obli- [20:40] gation that arises from them are almost exactly opposite. If I beg from a rich man who has won his fortune through extortion from his peasants and give this to the very same poor, then in a civil sense I perform a very generous action, but in the natural sense only a common obligation.

In universal opulence, one complains about the divine government and [20:41] about the government of the king. One does not consider that, concerning the [R36] latter, the very same ambition and immoderacy that controls the citizen can have no other form on the throne than what it has 2. that such citizens cannot be governed otherwise. The subject wants the master to overcome his inclination of vanity in order to promote the good of his lands and does not consider that, in the view of his inferiors, this demand could be made on him with the very same right. First of all, be wise, righteous, and moderate yourself, these virtues will soon rise to the throne and make the prince good as well. Look at the weak princes who, in such times, can show kindness and generosity; they hardly can exercise these without greater injustice towards others, because they put generosity into nothing other than the distribution of a bounty that one has stolen from others. The freedom that a prince accords to think and write in such a way as I am doing now is probably worth as much as many benefits [leading] to a greater opulence, because through that freedom all of this ill can yet be ameliorated.

[33] Reverse, opposite pages 21, at 2:216

The greatest concern of the human being is to know how properly to fulfill his station in creation, and to rightly understand what one must be in order to be a human being. But if he gets to know gratifications that are above or beneath him, or gets to know moral qualities that [are] yet his, which indeed flatter him but which but for which he is not organized, then and which oppose the (layout), the constitution that nature has suited to him, if he gets to know moral qualities that shimmer there, then he will disturb the beautiful order of nature, only to bring harm to himself and others, because he will have left his post, he knows [that he] cannot be content with that which is noble for, since he does not let himself be satisfied – to be that for which he is destined – since he steps out of the sphere of a human being, he is nothing, and the gap that he opens spreads his own ruin to the neighboring members.

[20:42]   Among the harms perpetrated by the flood of books in which our part of the world is annually drowned, not the least is that the actually useful ones that from time to time swim on the wide abyss of learnedness [R37] ocean of book-learning are overlooked, and under must share the fate of fugacity with the other chaff and. The inclination to read a lot in order to say that one has read. The habit not to dwell long on a book and [breaks off]

    Opulence brings human beings together into the city; *Rousseau* wants to bring them to the country

    The ills related to the developing immoderateness of human beings quite replace themselves. The loss of freedom and the exclusive power of a ruler is a great misfortune, but it will just as much be an orderly

[20:43]   system; indeed, there really is more order, though less happiness, than in free states. Softness in morals, idleness and vanity bring forth sciences. These give a new ornament to the whole, prevent much evil, and if they are raised to a certain level they ameliorate those ills that they themselves have perpetrated.

One of the greatest harms of science is that it takes away so much time that the youth are neglected in morals

Second, that it so accustoms the mind to the sweetness of *speculation* that good actions are omitted[68]

Page 21
[34] Upper margin

Moral beauty, simplicity, sublimity. Justice; righteousness is simplicity. The passion of the sublime is enthusiasm. In love, virtuous. Friendship. Beautiful ideal.

Sheet inserted after page 22
[35] Obverse

The first impression that an <understanding> reader <who does not only read out of vanity or in order to pass the time> acquires from the writings of Mr. *J. J. Rousseau* [R38] is that he has encountered an ~~great~~ uncommon acuity of the mind, a noble impetus of genius and a sensitive soul in such a high degree as ~~probably hardly at any times~~ has perhaps never before been possessed by a writer of any age or any people. ~~The next judgment that initially arises concerns the~~ The impression that follows next is bewilderment at strange and absurd opinions, which oppose what is generally held so much that one could easily form the suspicion that, ~~through his~~ by means of his extraordinary talents, the author ~~wanted to show, <only prove> excite admiration~~ only wanted to prove ~~the~~ the ~~power of a charming wit and through a~~ magical power of eloquence and ~~play the strange man~~ play the ~~the~~ eccentric ~~in order for him~~ who stands out among all rivals in wit because of ~~the~~ a disarming <invisible making> novelty. The third thought, to which one comes only with difficulty because it happens only rarely   [20:44]

One must teach youth to honor the common understanding for moral as well as logical reasons.

---

[68] The Academy Edition has the two preceding clauses as one sentence.

I myself am a researcher by inclination. I feel the entire thirst for cognition and the eager restlessness to proceed further in it, as well as the satisfaction at every acquisition. There was a time when I believed this alone could constitute the honor of humankind, and I despised the rabble who knows nothing. *Rousseau* has set me right. ~~I~~ This blinding prejudice vanishes, I learn to honor human beings, and I would feel by far less useful than the common laborer if I did not believe that this consideration could impart a value to all others in order to establish the rights of humanity.

[20:45]   It is very ridiculous to say that you shall love other people, one rather must say that you have good reason to love your neighbor. This holds even for your enemy.

Virtue is strong; thus, what debilitates and makes one soft by pleasures, or makes one dependent upon delusion, is opposed to virtue.[69] What makes life contemptible or even hateful to us does not lie in nature. What makes vice easy and virtue difficult does not lie in nature.

[R39] Universal vanity makes it so that one says only of those who never understand how to live (for themselves) that they know how to live

It is not at all conducive to happiness to extend the inclinations to the level of opulence, for since there are ~~many~~ uncommonly many cases where circumstances are unfavorable for these inclinations [and] against a desired situation, they constitute a source of displeasure, grief and worry, of which the simple human being knows nothing

It also does not help here to preach noble endurance.

[36] Reverse, opposite page 23, at 2:217

If <there> is any science ~~necessary to the human being~~ that the human being ~~truly~~ needs, it is that which teaches him properly to fulfill [and] <hold> the position that has been assigned to him in creation, and from which he can learn what ~~he~~ one must be in order to be a human being. Suppose he had become familiar with ~~betraying~~ deceptive temptations ~~above or~~ above or beneath him that, without being noticed, had brought him away ~~from~~ from his <typical> position, then this instruction would [20:46] lead him back again to the state of a human being; ~~and~~, however small or imperfect he may then find himself, he still will be quite good for his

---

[69] The Academy Edition has a paragraph break here.

assigned post, because he is ~~neither more nor less than~~ <exactly> what he ought to be.

The mistake of saying ~~one knows none~~ "this is universal among us, [and] therefore universal in general" is easily avoided by intelligent people. But the following judgments seem more plausible: "Nature has given us the opportunity for pleasure, why do we not want to use it"; "we have the capacity for sciences, nature calls us to seek them"; we feel in us a ~~moral~~ voice that speaks to us that this is noble and righteous, or that this is a duty to do so"[70]

Everything passes by us in a river, and the changeable taste and the different forms of human beings make the entire game [R40] uncertain and deceptive. Where do I find fixed points of nature that the human being can never disarrange, and that can give him signs as to which bank he must head for

That all magnitude is only relative and that there is no *absolute* magnitude is seen from the following. I measure in the sky by means of the diameter of the earth, the earth's diameter by means of miles, miles by means of feet, the latter by means of their relation to my body   [20:47]

[37] Page 23
At the margin, next to lines 11–12, at 2:217

Friendship, young people

At the margin, next to lines 16–18

Self-respect, equality

Inserted sheet after page 24
[38] Obverse, at 2:217

The question is ~~which qualities~~ which condition suits the human being, an inhabitant of the planet that orbits the sun at a distance of 200 diameters of the sun.

---

[70] The last sentence could also be translated as "We feel in us a ~~moral~~ voice that speaks to us; this is noble and righteous; this is a duty to act in such a way."

Just as little as I can ascend from here to the planet Jupiter, so little do I demand to have qualities that are proper only to that planet. He who is so wise with respect to another place in creation is a fool with respect to the one he inhabits

I do not at all have the ambition of wanting to be a seraph; my pride is only this, that I am a human being

[20:48]   The one sentence is difficult to sort out: that does not lie <or it lies> in nature, i.e., nature has given no drives for it, rather they are artificial; no such afflictions are innate, but they have grown accidentally[. T]he other sentence is easier: that does not conform with nature, i.e., that opposes whatever really lies in nature. [R41] Rousseau more often proceeds according to the former, and since human nature has now acquired such a desolate form, the natural foundations become dubious and unrecognizable

The moderate citizen can form no concept of what, then, the courtier, who, exiled to his estates can live as he pleases, can lack; meanwhile the latter grieves to death.

Many people have *theology* and no religion except perhaps in order to apologize for great acts of viciousness someday when they are threatened by the horrors of hell

On the value of this life in itself or and immediately and on the value of this life only as a means to another life

The life of those that only enjoy without consideration and morals appears to have no value <A sign of crude taste nowadays is that one requires so much pretty make-up; now, the finest taste is in simplicity.>[71]

With people and animals, a certain average size has the most strength

<In a civilized state, one becomes clever very late; indeed, one could say with Theophrastus that it is a shame that one then ceases to live when one hopes for success.>[72,73]

---

[71] This sentence appears in the Academy Edition below on page 20:49. See footnote 74.

[72] This sentence appears in the Academy Edition below on page 20:49. See footnote 74.

[73] Theophrastus (372–287 BC). Cicero, in *Tusculan Disputations* (Book III, § 69), explains:
They say that Theophrastus, on his deathbed, reproached Nature for giving a long life to stags and ravens but a short one to humans, since for us it would have made a great difference, while to them it makes no difference at all. For if humans had had a longer lifespan, we might have perfected every discipline and schooled ourselves in every branch of knowledge. And so he complained about being snuffed out just when he had begun to understand those things. (*Cicero on the Emotions*, trans. Margaret Graver, University of Chicago Press, 2002, pp. 30–31)

Moral taste with respect to sexual inclination, since in that everyone wants to appear to be quite refined or even pure

[74]Truth is not the main perfection of social life; beautiful illusion here, [20:49] as in painting, drives it much further. On taste in marrying

[39] Reverse, opposite page 25, at 2:218

[R42] The certainty in ~~[unreadable word]~~ moral judgments by means of a comparison with the moral feeling is just as great as the [certainty] with logical sentiment; and through analysis I will make it as certain to a human being that lying is repulsive as that a thinking body is incoherent. Deception with respect to a moral judgment occurs in the same fashion as it does with respect to a logical one, but the latter is still more frequent

Concerning the metaphysical foundations of aesthetics, the different [20:50] immoral feeling – concerning the foundations of moral world-wisdom[75] the different moral feeling – of human beings according to [their] difference in sex, age, education and government, race and climate is to be noted

On the religion of a woman – on bold facial expression. A certain timidity, suspicion, etc. suits them well. Their loquacity, use

Why difference in rank is mostly shown among women.

The woman is closer to nature. A man who knows how to live — what sort of woman will he marry

On Rousseau's attempt to move the best talents through love[76]

Women educate their men themselves; they can attribute it to themselves if they turn out badly.

---

74 The Academy Edition places the sentences beginning "A sign of crude taste" and "In a civilized state" here. See footnotes 71 and 72.

75 In eighteenth-century Germany, the term "Weltweisheit" was briefly adapted for the discipline of philosophy itself. See Werner Schneiders, "Akademische Weltweisheit: Die Deutsche Philosophie in Zeitalter der Aufklärung," in *Frankreich und Deutschland in 18.Jahrhundert*, ed. Gerhard Sauder and Jochem Schlobach, Heidelberg: Winter, 1986, pp. 25–44; Holly Wilson, *Kant's Pragmatic Anthropology: Its Origin, Meaning, and Critical Significance*, Albany, NY: SUNY Press, 2006; John Zammito, *Kant, Herder, and the Birth of Anthropology*, University of Chicago Press, 2002. Kant later used the term specifically to highlight the sort of wisdom that he sought to give students through his practical disciplines of physical geography and anthropology.

76 In Book v of *Émile*, Rousseau attempts to show how love could successfully develop Émile's best talents. See too *Julie*, where St. Preux's love for *Julie* arguably develops his talents as well.

The one who is foolishly accommodating becomes a grumpy husband
On the empty longing through a disproportionate, and for human
beings poorly suited, feeling for the sublime. Novels.

Rousseau pulled his sweetheart to the village[77,78]

[20:51]   [R43] A marriage of an overly refined <exquisite> man to a *coquette.*

One imagines two marriages, one of which is, so to say, of a respectable
kind, and the other domestic.

Moral taste is inclined to imitation; moral principles rise above this.
Where there are courts and great distinctions among human beings,
everything is given over to taste; in republics it is otherwise. Therefore, taste in social gatherings is more refined in the former and cruder
in the latter. One can be very virtuous and have little taste. If social
life is to grow, taste must be extended, because the agreeableness of
social gatherings must be easy; principles, though, are difficult. Among
women, this taste is easiest. The moral taste easily agrees with illusion,
[20:52]   the principle does not. Swiss, Dutch, French, imperial cities. Suicide in
Switzerland

Taste for mere virtue is a bit crude; if it is refined, then it must be able
to try it [virtue] mixed with folly

Sheet inserted after page 26
[40] Obverse, at 2:218

What the finer part of mankind calls life is a quaint weaving of trifling
~~pleasures~~ <diversions, boring distractions>, even more plagues — of
vanity and a whole swarm of ludicrous diversions. The loss of the same,
the loss of the same [*sic*] is regarded [as] death, commonly, though, even
much worse than death, (a human being who knows how to live), who
has lost the taste for it has become dead to [all] pleasure

Fine coarse feeling. Fine self-acting *ideal*, at times *chimerical.* One has
reason not to refine his feeling very much, first in order not to open the
gates to pain. Second, in order to be close to the useful

---

[77] The Academy Edition does not set this line on its own, and instead has it immediately after the
previous sentence.

[78] Rousseau's model couples, Sophie and Émile in *Émile* and Julie and Wolmar in *Julie*, live in
villages.

Sufficiency and simplicity demand a coarser feeling and make [one] happy

[R44] The beautiful is loved, the noble respected

The ugly ~~hated~~ with disgust, the ignoble despised[79]

The courage of a woman to follow the man in misfortune and his affectionateness. The man feels himself in his wife, and communicates no pain to her; an affectionate, a braver man

Short people are supercilious and hot tempered, tall [ones] are calm [20:53]

The natural human being is moderate, not on account of future health (for he foresees nothing), but on account of present well-being

One reason that ladies are haughty towards each other is that they are more similar to each other, because the basis of the noble class is in men. The reason that they are embarrassed and rivalrous around one another is that ~~they~~ the happiness of men does not arise as much from pleasure as from merits, ~~but this from pleasure and from~~, whereby they make their happiness themselves, whereas the former [the ladies] are made happy by others. Their essential inclination to please is based on this

The reason why the excesses of lust are sensed so sharply is because they concern the grounds of *propagation*, that is, the preservation of the species; and because this is the only thing women are good for, therefore, it constitutes their highest perfection, whereas their own preservation depends on men

The capacity to create utility with fertility is limited for a woman and broadened for a man.

[41] Reverse, opposite page 27, at 2:218

Opulence causes one to draw a great distinction between one woman and another

One does not satisfy desires through loving, but through marrying; they are at the same time the purest

[R45] The mark of sociableness is not to prefer oneself to another every [20:54] time. To prefer another to oneself every time is weak. The idea of equality *regulates* everything

---

[79] The Academy Edition has the two preceding fragments as one sentence.

In society and in *meetings*,[80] simplicity and equality ease them and make them pleasant

Control delusion and be a man so that your wife esteems you highest among all human beings; thus, be yourself no servant of the opinions of others.

In order for your wife to honor you, she should not see in you a slave of the opinions of others. Be domestic; in your society, there shall not prevail opulence, but taste – comfort, and not exuberance – rather a choice of guests than of dishes

— It would be better for women if they really worked.

[20:55]   A good of delusion consists in the fact that only opinion is sought after, but the thing itself is either regarded with indifference or even hated. The first delusion is that of honor. The second of avarice. The latter only loves the opinion that he could have many goods of life with his money, though without ever wanting it in earnest as well

One who is not convinced by what is obviously certain is a blockhead. One who is not moved by what is obviously a duty is a villain.

— A dull head and corrupt heart.

That the drive for honor comes from the desire for equality is to be seen from this. Would a savage search for another in order to show him his advantages? If he can be without him, he will enjoy his freedom. Only if he must be together with him, will he attempt to outdo him, therefore the desire for honor is mediate

The desire for honor is just as immediate as the miser's desire for money. Both originate in the same way

[42] Page 27
Lower margin, at 2:219

[R46] The Arcadian shepherd's life and our chivalrous life of the court are both of bad taste and unnatural, though alluring.[81] For true pleasure

---

[80] The German word here is "Tractamenten," which one could also translate as "remunerations."

[81] Arcadia is a region of Greece in the Peloponnesus that takes its name from the mythological character Arcas and is the mythological home of the god Pan. A remote, mountainous region, in both antiquity and the Renaissance it has been portrayed as a place of refuge from civilization and as the epitome of pastoral simplicity in which people, usually represented by the shepherd,

can never take place where one makes it into one's occupation. The recreations of someone with an occupation, which are rare, short and without preparation, are alone lasting and of genuine taste. A woman, because she now has nothing to do but to seek distractions, irritates herself and gets a bad taste for men, who do not always know to satisfy this thwarted inclination

Sheet inserted after page 28
[43] Obverse, at 2:219

Others' love of honor is so highly valued because it indicates so much [20:56] renunciation of other advantages

The question is whether, in order to move my *affects* or those of others, I shall take a position outside the world or in it. I answer that I find it [the position] in the state of nature, i.e., of freedom

Women have female virtues

Of compassion it is only to be noted that it must never rule, but must be *subordinated* to the capacity and reasonable desire to *do* good. He who cannot do without much or is lazy has an idle compassion.

The natural human being without religion is much to be preferred to [20:57] the civilized ones with merely natural religion. For the latter's morality would have to have high degrees if it were to provide a counterweight to his corruption.

Meanwhile, a civilized human being without any religion is much more dangerous

For, in the natural state, no correct concept of [R47] God can arise at all and the false one that one makes himself is harmful. Consequently, the theory of natural religion can be true only where there is science; therefore, it cannot bind all human beings[82]

Natural theology, natural religion. A supernatural theology can nevertheless be combined with a natural religion. Those who believe Christian ~~religion~~ theology nevertheless have only a natural religion in so far as the morality is natural. The Christian religion is supernatural with respect

---

live unsophisticated but happy lives. Virgil described Arcadia as a kind of idyllic paradise in his *Eclogues* (see especially the fourth, seventh, and tenth eclogues).

[82] This phrase could also be translated as "therefore, it cannot unite all human beings."

to the doctrine and also the powers to exercise it. How little do the usual Christians have cause to pause over the natural [one][83]

The cognition of God is either *speculative*, and this is uncertain and liable to dangerous errors, or moral through faith, and this conceives of no other qualities in God except those that aim at morality. This faith is either natural or supernatural; the former is [breaks off]

[44] Reverse
Opposite page 29, at 2:219

Providence is primarily to be praised in that it accords quite well with the present state of human beings, namely, that their foolish wishes do not conform to [its] direction, that they suffer for their follies, and nothing wants to harmonize with the human being who has stepped out [20:58] of the order of nature. If we consider the needs of animals [and] plants, with these providence agrees. It would be quite inverted if the divine governance were to alter the order of things according to the delusion of human beings, just as it alters itself. It is just as natural that, as far as he has deviated from there, everything must seem to be inverted to him according to his degenerate inclinations.

Out of this delusion arises a kind of theology as a phantasm of opulence (for this is always ~~fraught with~~ soft and superstitious) and a certain shrewdness and cleverness to intertwine through subjugation the highest being into one's businesses and plans.

[R48] *Diagoras.*[84]

Newton saw for the very first time order and regularity combined with great simplicity, where before him disorder and [a] poorly matched manifold was found; and since then comets run in geometrical courses.[85]

---

[83] In German, this sentence is ambiguous. It could also be translated as "How little have the usual Christians to pause over the natural cause."

[84] Diagoras was a Greek poet and sophist of the fifth century BC. Pierre Bayle refers to Diagoras as an example of a "theoretical atheist"; see his 1697 *Dictionaire historique et critique*, which was translated into German as the *Historisches und Critisches Wörterbuch* (Leipzig, 1740–41). See *Dictionary Historical and Critical of Mr. Peter Bayle*, New York: Garland, 1984, or *Historical and Critical Dictionary, Selections*, trans. Richard Popkin, Indianapolis: Hackett, 1991, p. 405. See also Cicero, *On the Nature of the Gods*, Book. I, ch. 1, 23, 42; and Book III, ch. 37.

[85] The *Principia mathematica* (1687) of Sir Isaac Newton (1642–1727) unified diverse phenomena (such as terrestrial and heavenly motions of bodies) within a single universal theory of gravitation. This work also provided the theoretical framework that allowed Edmund Halley to predict the appearance of a comet in 1758.

Rousseau discovered for the very first time beneath the manifold of forms adopted by the human being the deeply hidden nature of the same and the hidden law, according to which providence is justified by his observations. Before that the objection of Alfonso and Manes still held. After Newton and Rousseau, God is justified, and henceforth Pope's theorem is true[86]

[20:59]

[45] Page 30
At the margin, next to lines 12–15, at 2:220

Agreeable melancholy
  true virtue cries

Sheet inserted after page 32
[46] Obverse, at 2:221

The savage stays beneath the nature of a human being. The opulent one roams further outside of its limits and the morally contrived one goes above it.

[20:60]

On friendship in general

On the beautiful and noble of company and of hospitality; simplicity, magnificence

If something keeps a youth who has turned into a man from becoming a father, if something hinders one from enjoying life, even though it is short, and urges one to prepare for the future life in order to lose the

---

[86] King Alfonso X of Castile (1221–84) questioned the notion of a natural order. Leibniz explains, [There are] writers who hold that God could have done better. That is more or less the error of the famous Alfonso, King of Castile, who was elected King of Romans by certain Electors, and originated the astronomical tables that bear his name. This prince is reported to have said that if God in making the world had consulted him he would have given God good advice. Apparently the Ptolemaic system, which prevailed at that time, was displeasing to him. He believed therefore that something better planned could have been made, and he was right. But if he had known the system of Copernicus, with the discoveries of Kepler, now extended by knowledge of the gravity of the planets, he would indeed have confessed that the contrivance of the true system is marvelous. (*Theodicy*, II, § 193)

Manes, also known as Manichaeus, of third-century Persia, taught that there were two gods: one evil and one good. Kant also alludes here to Alexander Pope's dictum, "Whatever is, is right," from his *Essay on Man* (1733–34), line 294. For an extensive discussion of relevant passages in Newton and Rousseau, see Rischmüller, pp. 198–211.

present one,[87] if something demands that we hate life, or find it unworthy or short, then it does not lie in nature

[R49] Male strength does not express itself in forcing oneself to accept the injustice of others when one can drive it back, but in bearing the heavy yoke of necessity, as well as abiding the deprivations as a sacrifice for freedom or for whatever else it is that I love. The acceptance of insolence is a monkish virtue

[20:61]   The *sanguine*[88] accepts insults, because he fears the vast extent of avenging them

The foolishness of vaingloriousness consists in one who esteems others to be so important that he believes their opinion to give him such great value nevertheless despising them so much that he also views them to be nothing compared to himself

parallel to penuriousness

[47] Reverse, opposite page 33, at 2:221

The *art* of *appearing* agrees very well with the character of the beautiful. For since the beautiful does not aim at the useful, but at mere opinion – since, by the way, the thing itself that is beautiful becomes disgusting if it does not appear to be new – the art of giving an agreeable appearance with respect to things is very beautiful, since the simplicity of nature is always the same. The female sex possesses this art to a high degree, which also constitutes our entire happiness. Through this the deceived husband

[20:62]   is happy, the lover or companion sees English[89] virtues and much to conquer and believes himself to have triumphed over a strong enemy. Dissimulation is a perfection of ladies but a vice in men.

Frankness complies with the noble; it pleases even if it is clumsy but goodhearted to a woman

The choleric person is honored in his presence and criticized in his absence; he has ~~few~~ no friends at all. The melancholic, few and good, the sanguine, many and careless

[R50] The choleric person makes faces full of secrets

---

[87] Here we follow the Academy Edition and provide a comma. Rischmüller has a sentence break here.
[88] *Sangvineus*   [89] *englische*. This term could also be translated as "angelic."

If one bears in mind that man and woman constitute a moral whole, then one must not ascribe the same qualities to them, but instead ascribe to one those qualities that the other is missing

<They do not have as much sentiment for the beautiful as the man does, but more vanity>[90]

A woman endeavors to acquire still much more love than men. The latter content themselves with pleasing roughly one, but the former everyone. If this inclination is poorly understood, then there arises a person of universal devotion

[48] Page 33
Lower margin, at 2:222

All arousing delights are feverish, and deadly exhaustion and dull feeling follow upon ecstasies of joy. The heart is used up and sensation becomes coarse

Inserted sheet after page 34
[49] Obverse, at 2:222

<The melancholic is just and rancorous about injustice.>

Anger is a good-natured passion in the simplicity of nature, but it makes   [20:63]
a fool in the silly vanities of society.

The melancholic who is choleric is terrible. Extinguished blue eyes filled the pale face of Brutus.[91] (On humor, mood, hypochondria. The woman and a ~~soft~~ dreamer have moods.) The melancholic who is sanguine is cowardly, depressed, afraid of people, jealous. (The sanguineous person is *gallant*.) The melancholic loves more strongly and is less loved by women, because women are changeable. The choleric person is a schemer of state, mysterious, and important in trifles; the sanguineous one turns

---

[90] In the Academy Edition, this sentence occurs after the following one.
[91] Brutus could refer to Marcus Brutus (85–42 BC), son-in-law of Cato the Younger (see footnote 8) and famous as one of the principle assassins of Julius Caesar. More likely, it refers to (Lucius) Junius Brutus (b. 509 BC), a founder of the Roman Republic who is described in Voltaire's tragedy *Brutus*, which appeared in French in 1730 and which vividly portrays the scene in which Junius Brutus famously chooses to put to death his own son for treason against the Republic. In the eighteenth century, Junius Brutus was often seen as a sort of philosopher willing to sacrifice himself for the Republic, a kind of analogy to Cato. See Remark at 20:123.

[R51] important things into jokes. The melancholic-sanguineous person is a hermit or penitent in religion; the melancholic-choleric [breaks off]

[20:64]   The sanguine-choleric is valiant as a choleric, vain as a sanguine person, driven to fame, ~~without~~ and yet polite, loves change and is brave therein; for this reason he gives prestige to his pranks, ~~him~~ only greatly loves the coquette and ~~it mingles~~ his wife very much from the viewpoint of how she pleases others. The melancholic is domestic, the choleric person a courtier. The sanguine one ~~one a~~ thrusts himself into every jolly company. In misfortune, the melancholic-choleric person is bold and desperate; the sanguine one is in tears and disheartened; the choleric one is ashamed of being kept; the choleric-sanguine one distracts himself through amusement and is content, because he seems to be happy. In clothing, the melancholic-sanguineous person is tidy, but ~~dir~~ something is always missing. The choleric-sanguine one [is] of good choice with carelessness, the phlegmatic one is dirty, the melancholic-choleric one is pure and simple

[50] Reverse, opposite page 35, at 2:222

Before one asks about the virtue of women, one must first ask whether they need such a thing. In the state of simplicity, there is no virtue. With men, to protect strong ~~G~~ inclinations and honesty;[92] with women, loyal devotion and flattery.

In the opulent state, the man must have virtue, the woman honor.

One can hardly put the movement of fine moral sentiments or decoration (moral yeomanry. Alongside the pomade tin, the [writings of]

[20:65]   Gellert)[93] in the place of domestic occupation, and one who weaves a gown for her husband always shames the gallant lady, who in place of this reads a tragedy.

Longings.

In conversation the melancholic is still and serious. The sanguine person [R52] talks a lot when one jokes and changes the subjects. The choleric one tries to set the tone and plays hard to get. The choleric one

---

[92] In the original German text, it is a bit unclear whether Kant relates honesty to men or to women.

[93] Christian Fürchtegott Gellert (1715–69), professor of philosophy and writer of hymns, fables, comedies, and the novel *Die Schwedische Gräfin*.

laughs forced by propriety; the sanguine one by habit and friendliness; the melancholic one still laughs when everything has stopped.

When both sexes degenerate, the degeneration of man is still far worse

One who likes none but excessively raging expressions has a dull feeling; one who likes no one except very beautiful persons, only screaming colors [and] only great heroic virtues has a dull feeling. One who notices the gentle style of writing, the noble simplicity in morals [and] the hidden charm has a tender feeling. The feeling becomes more tender during one's middle age, but also gradually weaker. The tender feeling is not as strong as the coarse one

[51] Page 36
At the margin, next to line 18f., at 2:223

Valiant

Inserted sheet after page 36
[52] Obverse, at 2:222

Good consequences are to be sure marks of morality, but not ~~always those~~ the only ones, because they cannot always be recognized with certainty. How many good consequences some lies could have.

The ground of the *potestatis legislatoriae divinae*[94] is not in kindness, for then the motivation would be gratitude (*subjective* moral ground, kind of feeling) and hence not strict duty. The ground of the *potestatis legislatoriae*[95] presupposes inequality, and has the result that ~~the~~ a human being loses a degree of freedom with respect to another. This can only [20:66] happen if he himself sacrifices his will to that of another; if he does this with respect to all his actions, he makes himself into a *slave*. A will that is subjected to that of another ~~is~~ [is] imperfect ~~because the h~~ and contradictory, for the human being has *spontaneitatem*;[96] if he is subjected to the will of a human being [R53] (although he himself can choose) then he is ugly and contemptible; but if he is subjected to the will of God, then he is in accordance with nature. One must not perform actions out of obedience to a human being that one could perform out of inner

[94] Latin for "divine legislative power." [95] Latin for "legislative power."
[96] Latin for "spontaneity."

motivations, and demanding obedience, where inner motivations would have done everything, produces *slaves*.

The body is mine for it is a part of my I[97] and is moved by my faculty of choice. The entire animated or unanimated world that does not have its own faculty of choice is mine, in so far as I can compel it and move it according to my faculty of choice. The sun is not mine. The same holds for another human being, therefore nobody's property is a *Proprietat* or an exclusive property. But in so far as I want to appropriate something exclusively to myself, I will, at least, not presuppose the other's will or his action as being opposed to mine. I will therefore perform those actions that designate what is mine, cut down the tree, mill it, etc. The other human being tells me that this is his, for through the actions of his faculty of choice, it belongs to his own self, as it were.

[20:67]

[53] Reverse, opposite page 37, at 2:223

A will that is to be good must not cancel itself out[98] if it is taken universally and reciprocally; for the sake of this, the other will not call his own what I have worked upon, since otherwise he would presuppose that his will moved my body

Thus, when a human being calls some things his own, he thereby *tacitly* promises in similar circumstances, through his will, not about something [breaks off]

The obedience of the child to the parents is not based 1. on gratitude 2. on the fact that they cannot sustain themselves, for that would be based on utility, but rather because they have no completed will of their own, and it is good to be directed by the will of others. But since so far they are an affair[99] of the parents, because they only live through their [parents'] faculty of choice, thus it is morally good to be ruled by them. As soon as they can ~~educate~~ nourish themselves, obedience ends.

[20:68] [R54] We belong to the divine affairs, as it were; we exist through Him and His will. There are some things that can be in accordance with God's will that would not be at all good from inner motivations, e.g., to slay one's son. The *goodness* of obedience now depends on this. My will is always subordinated to the will of God in its determinations; thus, it agrees with

---

[97] *meines Ichs*　　[98] *sich selbst aufheben*　　[99] *Sache*

itself best when it agrees with the divine will; and it is impossible ~~that~~ for that, which is evil, to be in accordance with the divine will.

The woman seeks pleasure and expects necessities from others. The man seeks necessities and expects pleasure from the woman. If both seek necessities they probably are in agreement, but penurious; if both seek pleasure they are foolish

A man finds more pleasure in giving a woman amenities than a woman does, but the latter wants to appear to be giving rather than enjoying; because the former is surely her main purpose, in contrast, she admits to having received the necessities

[54] Page 38
Lower margin, at 2:224
*[Through signs related to inserted sheet after page 38]

One sees that this is true from the fact that a woman prefers herself, for she always wants to rule; a man, however, prefers his wife, for he wants to be ruled; he even makes for himself an honor thereof

Inserted sheet after page 38
[55] Obverse, at 2:223

I do not know what solace those who consider their imagined needs to be just and natural can find in a providence that denies them their fulfillment. I, of whom I certainly know that I suffer no ills but those which I bring upon myself, and that it only depends on me to become happy through the kindness of divine order, will never grumble about them

[R55] <Why must one speak French in order to be polite. *Dames Messieurs. Chapeaux Cornetten.**>[100]

Now, if a woman marries a twenty-year-old man, she takes herself a fop. The reason for this, among others, is that he has not yet become acquainted with the deceptive art of women to appear better and more agreeable than they are. Therefore, he makes a poor husband, because he always believes that he probably could have chosen better, or also

---

[100] French for "Ladies Gentlemen. Hats Cornets."

[20:69] because he has really fallen for her and chosen poorly. But if with more age he knows the sex and sees the futile appearance, he returns to simplicity, where according to nature he already could have been at the beginning. Hence the path to a good marriage goes through wantonness – an observation that is very unpleasant, especially because it is true

The time of maturity of a lord and of a farmer is never different. A woman is never mature without a man.

Men are much more in love than women,*[101] which also is natural. But [20:70] if the latter grow in the art of appearing – an appearance which however ends in marriage – then from this must emerge a kind of deceived reluctance in marriage, which finds less agreeableness than it had expected. It is not good to make a future husband fall too much in love; one must save something for the future.

*The expression (the woman) is certainly polite and seems to prove that they were previously in a special room together with one another, as is still the case in England now.

[56] Reverse, opposite page 39

The art of doing without, i.e., of not letting inclinations germinate in oneself, is the means to happiness; hence one can either seek to acquire honor, i.e., the high opinion of others, or strive to do without it entirely and be indifferent towards it.

That the choleric person is angry stems from his love of honor because he [R56] always believes [himself] to be insulted; the reasonable one desires[102] nothing but equality and has little occasion to be angry.

In those lands where women are not beautiful they are treated tyrannically, as among savages, because the weak one must inspire inclination or else get oppressed

[20:71] The main ground of lasting beauty is illusion. Make-up. A kind of untruth that is lovelier than truth. *Corregio* departed from nature[103]

---

[101] The German word here is "Frauenzimmer," which literally translates as "women-room."
[102] The German word here is "begeht," which translates as "commits." We assume that Kant forgot here an "r" and actually meant to write "begehrt," which translates as "desires."
[103] Antonio Allegri Correggio (1494–1534), artist. Kant most likely was familiar with Correggio's works from Raphael Mengs' *Gedanken über die Schönheit and über den Geschmack in der Malerei* (Zurich, 1762) and Johann Joachim Winckelmann's *Abhandlung von der Empfindung des Schönen*

Women gladly love bold men – and these modest, decent men. Judgment of a woman by *Bayle*.[104] *Hercules* endeared himself more to *Omphale* through his 72 girls than through his spinning.[105]

As far as sex is concerned, women are more of a bawdy taste, men more of a fine one. They love civilities and ~~court~~ manners more in order to display their own vanity.

Whether the savage has had taste, the one whom the eating-houses[106] pleased best [breaks off]

When the inclinations of women and men grow equally, they nevertheless must come into *disproportion*, namely, that the latter have less capacity in *proportion* to their inclination

Inserted sheet after page 40
[57] Obverse, at 2:224

In everything that pertains to beautiful or sublime sentiment, we do best if we let ourselves be led by the examples of the ancients. In sculpture, architecture, poetry, and oratory the ancient mores and the ancient political constitution. The ancients were closer to nature: we have much frivolous or opulent or servile corruption between ourselves and nature. Our age is the *seculum*[107] of beautiful trivialities, *bagatelles* or sublime *chimeras*.

---

in der Kunst (Dresden, 1763). Mengs contrasts Correggio with both Raphael and Titian. Whereas the latter two painters stick closely to nature,

> [Correggio] began to study almost only the imitation of Nature, and since he pursued more a grateful and pleasing genius, than a perfect one, he found out the way at the beginning, by means of uniformity, and depriving his drawing of every angular and acute part. When he advanced in the art he was convinced by the clareobscure, that grandeur adds much to the pleasing parts; then he began to relinquish the minutiae and to aggrandize the form, by imitating entirely the angles, and thus he produced a kind of sublime taste even in design, which was not always conformable to truth . . . In general his design was not too just, but great, and pleasing. One ought not to depreciate the studious painter, but it is necessary also to try to cull the honey from those flowers, that is to say to avail of those beauties which are to be found in nature, wherever the circumstance and quality of things permit it. When Correggio has sometimes designed any part of a beautiful object, he has joined the beautiful by way of imitation. (*The Works of Anthony Raphael Mengs, first painter to His Catholic Majesty Charles III*, ed. José Nicolás de Azara, London: R. Faulder, 1796, pp. 50–51)

[104] Pierre Bayle (1647–1706), the French philosopher, theologian, and critic who especially influenced Voltaire and writers of encyclopedias. See footnote 84 above. It is unclear what Kant has in mind by Bayle's judgment of women.
[105] See above, footnote 23.   [106] *Garküchen*   [107] Latin for "age."

[R57] *Character* in society

[20:72] The sanguineous person goes where he is not invited; the choleric one does not go where he is not invited in accordance with propriety; the melancholic one ~~doesn't come at all~~ prevents [himself from] not being invited at all. In society, the melancholic is still and pays attention; the sanguine one speaks what occurs to him; the choleric one makes comments and interpretations. Concerning domestic nature, the melancholic is ~~frugal~~ <stingy> [and] penurious; the sanguineous one is a bad host.[108] The choleric one is acquisitive, but magnificent. The generosity of the melancholic is magnanimity, of the choleric one is boasting, of the sanguine is thoughtlessness.

The melancholic person is jealous; the choleric one, power-hungry; the sanguine one, occupied with courting

The *coquette* is an excellent *maîtresse*, but no wife at all, except for a Frenchman.

On providence. The fools that forsake the order of nature are astonished about providence, that it does not improve its terrible consequences; *Augustine* with his *crapula*.[109] *pag. 37*

[20:73] Union is possible where one can be whole without the other, e.g., between two friends, and where neither is subordinated to the other. There can also be union in exchange or in *contracts* of a way of life. But unity depends on only two constituting a whole together in a natural way with respect to needs as well as what is agreeable. This exists with a man and a woman. Yet, here unity is tied to equality. The man cannot enjoy a single pleasure of life without the woman, and the latter can enjoy no necessities without the man. This also constitutes the difference between

---

[108] The Academy Edition has a comma here.

[109] Aurelius Augustine (354–430), Bishop of Hippo. In his *Confessions*, Augustine writes, "I hear the voice of my God commanding: 'Let not your heart be overcharged with surfeiting and drunkenness.' Drunkenness is far from me. Thou wilt have mercy that it does not come near me. But 'surfeiting' sometimes creeps upon thy servant. Thou wilt have mercy that it may be put far from me" (Book x, ch. 31). The quoted phrase here is from Luke 21:34. The term "surfeiting" is, in Augustine and in the Latin Vulgate, "crapula." Kant may also be alluding to a reference from Bayle's discussion of the possibility that Augustine was a heavy drinker and the difficulty of translating the term "crapula" (see *Dictionary Historical and Critical of Mr. Peter Bayle*, pp. 567–68). While referencing one French scholar (Couffin) who translates *crapula* as "eating . . . to excess," Bayle focuses on an extensive analysis of the speculations of a physician, Mr. Petit, who claims that *crapula* should be translated as "hangover," raising questions about how Augustine could have avoided drunkenness but still suffered hangovers.

their characters. According to his inclination, the man will seek necessities solely in accordance with his judgment and pleasure in accordance with the pleasure of the woman, and further make the latter into necessities. The woman will seek pleasure according to her taste and leave the necessities to the man.

[58] Back side, opposite page 41, at 2:225

[R58] In countries where societies mostly consist of men, one values personal merit according to understanding, fidelity and the useful zeal of friendship or also of common utility. Where they are always intermingled with women, according to wit, suavity, jest, amusements, *Medisance*.[110] In the case of the old Germans ~~it must~~, before French mores corrupted us, women must have been in special rooms as in England. [20:74]

A man who has a wife is *complete*, detaches himself from his parents, and is alone in the state of nature. He is so disinclined to associate himself with others, that he even fears the approach of others. Therefore, the state of war. *Hobbes*[111]

The embarrassment and blushing that the ladies of fine manners do not need to have in themselves is very charming and particular to the sex, but where it still is encountered, there she is a good bulwark of chastity

Female grace. Femininities are laudable in a woman; if she has masculinities, then it is a reproach

In marrying, the infatuated blindness disappears so that the woman misses the unlimited reign over the heart of the man and the rank of

---

[110] French for "malicious gossip."
[111] In his *Leviathan*, Hobbes famously wrote of the state of nature:

> In the nature of man, we find three principal causes of quarrel. First, competition; secondly, diffidence; thirdly, glory.
>
> The first maketh men invade for gain; the second, for safety; and the third, for reputation. The first use violence, to make themselves masters of other men's persons, wives, children, and cattle; the second, to defend them; the third, for trifles, as a word, a smile, a different opinion, and any other sign of undervalue, either direct in their persons or by reflection in their kindred, their friends, their nation, their profession, or their name.
>
> Hereby it is manifest that during the time men live without a common power to keep them all in awe, they are in that condition which is called war; and such a war as is of every man against every man.
>
> . . . In such a condition . . . the life of man [is] solitary, poor, nasty, brutish, and short. (*Leviathan*, ch. 13, ¶¶ 6–9)

goddess that she has had before the marriage. But the man does not feel himself ruled anymore as much as he was and wishes. The woman loses more in vanity, the man more in tenderness. The fantasy of infatuation had instilled even more exaggerated concepts in the man than in the woman

<The woman then wished to still rule as before, while the man wished to be ruled. The woman sees herself as being coerced to flatter, the man finds no other inclination in himself than kindness>

The man is stronger not only according to build, but also in principles and in the steadfastness to endure something; therefore, his clothes must be so, the woman's must be *delicate* and fettled

[20:75]   [R59] Taste in the choice of company. Taste for virtue, friendship.[112] One turns more on taste than on bare necessities

Inserted sheet after page 42
[59] Obverse, at 2:225

Nature has equipped women to make affectionate and not to be affectionate

They ~~have~~ are never equal to men in true tenderness, which can be seen in the fact that all women want to rule and the most reasonable men let themselves be dominated; now he who, in spite of being stronger himself, reluctantly surrenders his power must yet have more tenderness than she who is aware that it happens reluctantly, and yet prefers herself to the other

Women are more for lustful love, men are more for affectionate love. All widows marry, but not all widowers. No woman must marry a man who is vain

[20:76]   At best union can occur in the case of equality, but never unity; since there must be unity in marriage, everything must be ruled by one, the man or the woman. Now, it is inclination and not the understanding that rules here. Thus, the inclination of either the man or the woman can rule; the latter is the best

---

[112] Kant here omits any punctuation, making it ambiguous whether the sentence translates as "Taste for virtue, friendship" or as "Taste for virtue [in] friendship."

War can only bring about virtues if it is patriotic, i.e., if it does not serve to gain money and support, but to preserve oneself, and if the soldier again becomes a citizen

[60] Reverse, opposite page 43, at 2:225

Lustful love is the ground of sexual inclination. Hence, everything beautiful and sublime in this love is only a phantasm if this is not presupposed. The husband must be a man by night and day. This remark also serves to warn of affectionate and highly respectful love between the sexes, for the latter more often degenerates into the outbreak of lust.

[R60] The woman must be kept from being unfaithful through [20:77] goodheartedness love and honor; if she the if man does not win her affection, then he can hardly count on her [sense of] duty. That is a reason why women must be met with kindness. For they have, by the way, a widely extended capacity.[113]

The difference between he who requires little because he lacks little and he who requires little because he can do without a lot. *Socrates.*[114] The enjoyment of a pleasure that is not a necessity; i.e., whatever one can spare is agreeableness. One who If, however, it is taken for a need, then it is concupiscence. The state of a human being who can do without is moderation, that of the one who counts what is very dispensable among his needs is opulence.

The contentment of a human being arises either from the fact that he satisfies many inclinations through many things that are agreeable, or from the fact that few he has not let many inclinations sprout, and therefore is content with a few satisfied needs. The state of the one who is content because he does not know things that are agreeable is moderate simple moderation, that of the one who knows them, but voluntarily[115] dispenses with them because he fears the unrest that arises from them, is wise moderation. The former demands no self-constraint and privation,

---

[113] There is an unreadable line here in Kant's remarks.
[114] In his *Dreams of a Spirit-Seer* (1766), Kant writes "reason, matured by experience into wisdom, serenely speaks through the mouth of *Socrates*, who, surrounded by the wares of a market-fair, remarked: *How many are the things of which I have no need*" (2:369, in *Theoretical Philosophy 1755–1770*, ed. David Walford, Cambridge University Press, 1992, p. 355). Walford cites Diogenes Laertius, *Vitae philosophorum* II, xxv for the original source of this anecdote.
[115] *willkürlich*

but the latter does; the former is easy to seduce, the latter has been seduced and is safer with respect to future [seduction]. The state of a human being without displeasures, therefore, because he does not know of greater pleasures being possible for \<him\>, and thus does not desire [them].

Virtue does not at all consist in prevailing over acquired inclinations under special circumstances, but in seeking to get rid of such inclinations and thus ~~doing without~~ learning to do without them gladly. It [20:78] does not consist in quarreling with natural inclinations, but in making it so that one has none but natural ones, for then one can always satisfy them

Inserted sheet after page 44
[61] Obverse, at 2:226

[R61] The characters of human nature are the degenerations of their vocation, in the same way the necessity of war, dominance and subservience of religions and of science

It is the question whether the noble and why it does not agree more[116] with the useful than the beautiful [does]

Women will always prefer a man with masculine appeal who is wild, for they always believe that they will rule him. Most of the time they are right about this, and this excuses them if they fail. This is also the beautiful side of the female sex, that they can rule men

One will perhaps find more among men who deserve the gallows than women who get drunk

[20:79]   If one wants to maintain the fantastical [aspect] of love in the married state, then jealousies and adventures must take place; if one wants to maintain the courting, then the wife must be a *coquette*; if both should fall away, only the simplicity of nature remains

In countries that are rich and monarchical, where many have nothing to do with their private businesses of self-interest and with public businesses of the state, everything comes down to the skillfulness of society. From there arises politeness. In England there are rich people, but

---

[116] Here we follow Rischmüller's "warum es nicht mehr... verträgt" rather than the Academy Edition's "warum es sich mehr... verträgt".

they have to do with the state; in Holland they are intertwined with self-interest
On fashionable casts of mind

A woman is always ready to betray a lover who is highly respectful and to give herself in secret to him who, without much ado, is bold and enterprising. In the state of simplicity the man rules over the woman; in the state of opulence, the woman rules over the man. The finer taste of free association makes it necessary

[62] Reverse, opposite page 45, at 2:226

[R62] *Sensus subjecti bene vel male <affectio> afficiendi* ~~The~~ *potestas leg-*   [20:80]
islatoria non nititur amore sed reverentia et facultate morali exterorquendi facultas logica leges ferendi (propter sapientiam) non est moralis[117]
The still and peaceful serenity in the beautiful is turned inward with a man, outward with a woman
Pelisson and *Madame Sévigné*[118]

Bold attitude and courting or disarming smile. <On the habit of women of adopting an earnest decency.>
Who himself is devoid of sentiments (that is, has feelings for judging but not for needs) can much more easily maintain them permanently in others. Therefore, the woman must be less affectionate
Because we have so much vain *Jalousie*,[119] friends are also rivals. Therefore, friendship can only take place with needs
Light and warmth appear to differ from each other as sound and wind; light and color as sound and tone. Taut strings ~~can~~ must make *undulationes.*[120] A coal fire in the hearth is a space empty of ether, which goes out through the chimney; since thereby ether is now being freed in

---

[117] Latin for "The legislative power of affecting the subject's sense in a good way or in a bad way does not depend on love but on respect and on the moral power of necessitation; the logical faculty of making laws (in accordance with wisdom) is not moral."
[118] Paul Pelisson-Fontanier (1624–93), French philosopher and member of the Academy in Paris. Madame de Sévigné, or Marie Rabutin de Sévigné (1626–96) famously said of Pelisson: "Pelisson abuses the privilege men have of being ugly" (See Kant's *Anthropology*, 7:298).
[119] French for "jealousy."   [120] Latin for "undulations."

all the surrounding bodies, they give warmth. Those who receive it in such a way ~~are~~ become warm ~~those who give it are e~~ [breaks off]

[20:81] The question is whether, when bodies become warm, they let go of fire or take it in. It depends on whether bodies, in absolute coldness, are saturated with fire, for then ~~are~~ a warm body becomes cold if it absorbs fire, and it heats a body that it forces to let go of fire. Is a heated oven devoid of fire? Yes, it gradually absorbs the fire into itself, thereby releases the fire in others and makes them warm and becomes cold itself. In this way, the suns ~~and also those~~ are the spaces most empty of the fire element. The dispersion of light can thereby also be comprehended, for it is easier that the intrusion into [R63] an empty space should be followed endlessly by a thread of agitated matter than that an impact should.

$$
\begin{array}{ccc}
29 & 29 & 29 \\
\underline{12} & \underline{33} & \underline{14} \\
58 & 87 & 116 \\
\underline{29} & \underline{87} & \underline{294} \\
 & 957 & 406 \\
 & 12 & 122 \qquad 34 \\
 & & 36 \\
 & & 4 \qquad\; 8
\end{array}
$$

Inserted sheet after page 46
[63] Obverse

In this way, light might perhaps be a movement towards the sun rather than one away from it

Sound, although air is squeezed out of the lungs, can perhaps be generated through the recession of air rather than through the driving away [of it]

[20:82] Fire above a body (earth) makes it cold underneath; but only to a certain extent, for it releases the fire element from the closest one, the more remote one partly attracts ~~so~~ this already released fire element to itself; thus, many poles arise.

a x y b c d

Let there be fire at *a*; the fire element is released before *b*, but it continuously becomes weaker than at *y* and *x*; the movement from *b* to *a*, which breaks into the empty space, is weaker than [the one that] is pulled from *b* in order to move towards *c*; thus *bc* becomes *attractive* and consequently cold; only by breaking in, does it accumulate in *c*, ~~and this *e*~~ although with delayed movement, so that *c*, indeed, is positively warm – i.e., lets fire go – but beyond *c* towards *d* [it gets] negative again.

[R64] The sun warms the earth, i.e., makes it so that the fire in it releases itself ~~hence it must from the upper~~ or rather that there is a space empty of fire on the earth; assume now a body being placed high in the air, the body is then in a space full of fire; thus, no fire comes out of itself [or] into itself and ~~it is~~ because it does not let go of any such element

[64] Reverse, opposite page 47, at 2:227

The true concept of fire seems to consist in this, that in heating the fire does not pass from the warm into the cold, but from the cold into the warm; ~~hence~~ in cooling, the body that is becoming cold is put in a state of absorbing, and fire passes into it. ~~From this it follows that when a body warms it pulls fire from the other into itself, and just thereby gradually diminishes its state of absorbing, i.e., the body itself gradually becomes colder. In contrast~~ From this it follows that only the body that warms others becomes cold, and conversely the one that becomes cold warms others, for it cannot warm without releasing the fire in others, ~~i.e.,~~ but the more it fills itself, the less it is in a state to release it in others. Yet, if a body becomes cold, it falls into a state of absorbing and thereby warms others. A body is cold with respect to others if it cools them, i.e., fills others with the fire element, and thus diminishes their state of absorbing by ~~its~~ becoming warm itself, i.e., by releasing fire. Comets are, among all heavenly bodies, those which are most full of the fire element. They come into the empty space of the ether, or rather their elemental fire, which rises behind them, is strongly released

<If there is a fire in the hearth, then the air in all [of its] expanse, and also the nearby bodies, will become warm. Because the fire is freed out of the air, remote [objects], however, attract it and become cold. Or so: the ether that is rushing by makes waves and is denser in some place than before, hence the body found there will suck rather than aspirate>

[20:83]

All the contrived rules for a wife exist in order to prevent others from not pleasing us more or making us lustful.[121] Constrain your own concupiscence and your wife will be enough for you.

[20:84] [R65] A valiant woman is something wholly different from a romanic[122] beauty, the latter is best for a lover, the former for a husband. German women are valiant, French women *coquettes* who

A good housewife is honorable for the husband, how a *gallant* lady wants to earn this name

A man must show some contemptuousness with respect to his finery; it must be seen that he has worn the hat. His cuffs must not worry him

If I should choose a wife, I want to take one who does not have much wit, but feels it.

The corruption of our time can be boiled down to this, that no one demands to be content with himself, or also good, but instead to appear so

One complains that marriages are not as good as the unmarried state. The reason for this is above. One never enjoys oneself.

Inserted sheet after page 48
[65] Obverse

[20:85] *Poena est vel politica vel moralis. Prior ut causa impulsiva est ratio omissionis posterior causatum commissionis. Moralis est proprie afflictiva vel vindica-tiva sed habet etiam rationem medii ad correctionem vel peccatoris respectu antecedentium vel futurorum demeritorum.*[123]

The cause of all moral punishment is this. All evil action would never happen if it were sensed through moral feeling with as much aversion as it deserves. But if it is carried out, then it is a proof that physical stimulation

---

[121] We assume that Kant actually meant to say here that the rules exist in order to prevent others from pleasing us more, instead of saying that they exist in order to prevent others from not pleasing us more.

[122] *romanische*; see footnote 25.

[20:85] [123] Latin for "Punishment is either political or moral. As a motivating cause, the first is the reason for omission, the latter is the cause of commission. Moral punishment is strictly speaking afflictive or vindicative, but it also has the function of being a means for improvement of the sinner in view of either previous or future misdeeds."

[unreadable word] has sweetened it and the action has seemed good; but now it is nonsensical and ugly that what is morally evil should yet be good on the whole; consequently, in the outcome, a physical evil must make good for the absence of aversion that was missing in the action.

<To a certain extent, it is fortunate that marriages become difficult, because if [R66] they became frequent, the masters would multiply and injustice would become still more common>

Women are far cleverer in judging male merits and their weaknesses of which one can make use, than men are among each other. Men, by contrast, more easily see the value of a woman than a woman sees that of another, but they do not as easily see the shortcomings as a woman sees those of another. Thus, women rule over men and deceive them more easily than the other way around. It is easy to deceive a man, but not the other way around. Traitor. You don't love me anymore, you believe more in what you see, etc.; no man can say such a thing to a wife.

she even sees what he does not see himself and sees correctly[124]

They rightly carry out such intrigues in retaliation for the injustice we show them, in that we want them chaste and have been unchaste ourselves

<The reason why there are so many cuckolds is because the time of the debaucheries of men has ended and that of women has begun.> [20:86]

[66] Reverse, opposite page 49, at 2:228

It is very good that the woman is chosen; she herself cannot choose

Why aging seems so terrible to a woman, [but] not to men, for the sublime applies to the latter

Youth is a great perfection for a woman in marriage; one still loves her afterwards in old age for the sake of the memory of her youth. That elderly women marry comes about because of our injustice.

Women are all avaricious except where vanity is stronger; they are all *devout* and acquiescent to the clerics. The honor of a man resides in his judgment of himself, that of a woman in the judgment of others

[R67] If a man were found by whom I was hated, it would worry me. [20:87] Not as if I were afraid of him, but because I would find it hideous to have something in oneself that could become a reason for hate in others, for

---

[124] The Academy Edition has this line at the end of the preceding paragraph.

I would suspect that another could not have developed a dislike without any apparent reason at all. Therefore, I would seek him out, I would make myself better known to him, and after I ~~the disadvantages~~ would have seen some benevolence toward me having developed in him, I would let ~~it~~ <myself> be satisfied with this without ever wanting to take advantage of it. But if I saw it as inevitable that common and raffish prejudices, a wretched envy or an even more contemptuous [and] jealous vanity make it impossible to entirely avoid all hatred, well then I would say to myself, it is better that I be hated than that I be despised. ~~Hatred~~ This motto is based on an entirely different ground than that which self-interest concocts for us, [namely that] I want to be envied rather than pitied. ~~Who~~ The hatred of my fellow citizens does not nullify their concept of equality, ~~but of the~~ but contempt makes me small in the eyes of others and always causes a very annoying delusion of inequality. Yet, it is much more harmful to be despised than to be hated.

[67] Page 50
At the margin, next to lines 11–13, 2:229

They laugh easily and gladly, and it increases their charms

Inserted sheet after page 50
[68] Obverse, at 2:229

Female pride. Male pride

The corrupted woman was *Arria Margaretha* Maultasch[125]

It is not appropriate that a woman makes the man happier by something other than her person. With her money a woman buys herself a jester or a tyrant

The greatest perfection is domesticity

---

[125] Arria was a Roman who became famous for committing suicide with her husband while in prison. See Pliny the Younger, *Complete Letters*, trans. P. G. Walsh, Oxford University Press, 2006, pp. 74–76; here Letters of Pliny the Younger, 3.16. Margarete von Tirol (1318–69), whose castle at Terlan was named "Maultasch." That Margarete is "degenerate" comes from both her autocratic style of government and her infamous marriage: Kaiser Ludwig IV supported her efforts to obtain a divorce from her first husband so that Margarete could marry Ludwig's son and thereby expand the power base of the Wittelsbach throne. The marriage in 1342, done without regard to the canonical law of the time, caused such a sensation that the entire affair led to the deposing of King Ludwig IV four years later (see Rischmüller, p. 223).

[R68] <Women[126] are incomparably able to control their countenance, [20:88] [they] have more accent, [they are] eloquent>

The human being has his own inclinations, and ~~they~~ in virtue of his power of choice he has a hint from nature to arrange his actions in accordance with these. Now, there can be nothing more horrendous than that the action of a human being shall stand under the will of another. Hence no antipathy can be more natural than that which a human being has towards slavery. For this reason a child cries and becomes bitter if it has to do what others want without one having bothered to make it attractive to him. And it[127] only wishes to be a man soon and to operate according to its will. What new servitude toward things must it[128] impose in order to introduce the latter[?][129]

Already in her build, a woman is equipped so that she will be sought after, i.e., that she will know how to provoke advances and be clever at yielding or also at refusing. Hence she would have to know how to win over but also how to conceal desires in order to prevent disdain. [20:89] Therefore, she can adopt a decent and cool[130] nature more easily than a man, can pretend excellently, and is equipped with all qualities for always appearing as what she should be. She is therefore soberly eloquent, never imprudent, etc.

Shamefulness is never a ground of chastity, but something that in place of the latter, by means of the incentive of propriety, generates the very same effects

A woman wants men to be enterprising in matters of love

[69] Reverse, opposite page 51, at 2:229

The sweetness that we find in respecting beneficence towards human beings is an effect of the feeling of the universal well-being that would occur in the state of freedom

The refinement of times is an adeptness at deceiving and our *academies* [20:90] furnish a great multitude of swindlers.

---

[126] Rischmüller does not offer a noun for this sentence; the noun "women" (*Frauenzimmer*) is taken from the Academy Edition.
[127] *es*   [128] *sie*
[129] Here we follow Rischmüller's "muss sie erheben" (68) rather than the Academy Edition's "muss sich erheben" (20:88).
[130] *kaltsinnig*

[R69] Drunkenness is the failing of a man
Roughness
~~Defiance~~ Anger

The law-giving power of God with respect to the first human being ~~is~~ is based on property. The human being was freshly placed in the world, all trees belonged to God and he forbade him one of them.

This *idea* ended. The law-giving power of God over the Jewish people is grounded in the social contract. God wanted to lead them out of Egypt and give them another country if they obeyed him;*when they subsequently had kings, God still reserved supremacy for himself, and the kings were only satraps or vassals. In the New Testament, this ground comes to an end. The universal ground of the law-giving power of God is presupposed, but the bindingness is grounded only in a kindness, which does not want to make use of any severity. Thus, in genuine Christianity, this is wholly annihilated with respect to the law-giver, and the Father is introduced

* <At that time, he was not a God of human beings, but of the Jews>

Paul judges that the law only produces reluctance, because it ~~the incli~~ makes it so that one unwillingly does what has been commanded, and indeed this is how things are. For this reason he sees the law as abolished by Christ and only [sees] grace, namely a ground to love God quite from one's heart, which is not possible according to nature, and by means of which actions will be brought to morality and not to *theocratic politics*.

[70] Page 51
At the margin, next to lines 22–25, at 2:230

Is generally unclean as *Magliabechi*;[131] she is disguised by a loose mouth. As my brother says [breaks off]

---

[131] Antonio Magliabecchi, (1633–1714), librarian to Grand Duke Cosimo III of Tuscany, was famously slovenly in his personal life. Kant's source for the reference to Magliabecchi's unseemliness is an article in Christian Gottlieb Jöcher's 1751 *Allgemeines Gelehrten-Lexicon*:
    He was of a quite poor external appearance, and always carried in the winter-time a coal lamp for warmth, on which he often managed to burn his hands and clothes. To sleep, he attended to coarse books. His library was horrible, and he was so eager in reading his books that he never took care to change his clothes so as not to lose time that could be spent reading; hence his clothing also was not all too respectable. At night he sent his servant home, and as was his habit read until he fell asleep in his

Lower margin

One can hate him who is right, but one is forced to respect him highly. [20:91]
 [R70] Selfishness fights against common utility. The latter acquires
love from inclination

[71] Page 52
At the margin, next to lines 6–11, at 2:230

Yet men may always devote troublesome and sleepless nights to their
research if the woman only knows how she is supposed to rule them.

Inserted sheet after page 52
[72] Obverse

<On the mutterings against providence>
 On freedom
 In whatever state he finds himself, the human being is dependent
on many <external> things ~~partially in order to satis~~. ~~On means of
nourishment, the impressions of the air, of the sun~~. He always depends on
some things because of his needs, on others because of his concupiscence,
and since he <surely> is the administrator of nature but not its master,
he must <rather> ~~often acquiesce to the yoke of necessity and yield to
the order of nature and accommodate himself to its laws, according to
its laws, if it~~ accommodate himself to its coercion, because he does not [20:92]
find that it will always accommodate itself to his wishes. But what is

chair or threw himself, still clothed, on his bed; hence it also sometimes happened
that his coal-pot set fire to his bed and the many books on it, and he would have to
call to his neighbors for help. (Quoted from Rischmüller, p. 223)
In an anthropology lecture from 1772–3, Kant is reported to have said of Magliabecchi:
What the ground/degree of learnedness relates to, from this one finds wonderful
things . . . A librarian of the Duke of Florenz – *Maleabesche Magliabecchi* – had an
extraordinary learnedness, who initially was a peasant youth who everywhere sought
books whereever he could catch them. He was first with a gardener, then with a
bookseller, where he learned to read and his happy learnedness manifested itself;
everything that he read, he retained; at last because of his expansive reading, he
would be chosen as librarian to the learned world. He was the oracle of Europe, when
one could not find out a spot, one asked *Maleabechen* and he could say that the spot
would be found in this or that book, in a library in Constantinople, in such and such
section, on such and such page. Nevertheless, this *Magliabecchi* was uncommonly
dirty. He wore pants that were so filthy that he sometimes wrote his thoughts on
them with a pin. (*Anthropologie Euchel 1772–3*, pp. 128–29; Academy Edition vol. 25)

much harder <and more unnatural> than this yoke of necessity is the ~~dependence~~ subjection of one human being under the will of another human being. There is no misfortune more terrible to him who ~~is~~ would be accustomed to freedom – [who] <would have enjoyed the good of freedom> – than to see himself delivered ~~under~~ to a creature of his own kind, who could force him ~~to surrender his own will~~ to do what he wants. ~~There is also no doubt that~~ [breaks off]

~~It must~~ It also ~~necessarily~~ <requires> a very long habituation to ~~have made when~~ make <the> ~~the horrible~~ terrible thoughts of subservience tolerable, because everyone must feel it in himself that even though there are many adversities that one may not always want to cast off at the risk of one's life, still in the choice between slavery and the risk of death there ~~would be no doubt that the first attempt his free~~ would [R71] be no reservation about preferring the latter.

[73] Obverse, opposite page 53, at 2:230

The cause of this is also very clear and rightful. All other ~~ills of nature follow law~~ ills of nature are still subject to certain laws that one gets to know in order subsequently to choose how far one wants to give into them or be subjected to them. The heat of the burning sun, the harsh winds, the motions of the water still allow the human being to devise something that will protect him against them or at least [breaks off]

But the will of every human being is ~~upon~~ the effect of his own drives [and] inclinations, ~~and true or imagined welfare~~ and agrees only with his own true or imagined welfare. But if I was free before, nothing can present a more dreadful prospect of sorrow and despair to me than that in the future my state shall not reside in my own will, but in the will of another. ~~I only conceive of the extreme coldness~~ Today it is extremely cold, I can go out or stay at home, whichever I prefer; but the will of another does not determine what is most agreeable to me on this occasion, but what is most agreeable <to him>. I want to sleep so he wakes me. I want to rest or play, and he forces me to work. The wind that rages outside may well force me to flee to a cave, but here or elsewhere it finally leaves me in peace, but my master seeks me out, and since the cause of my misfortune has reason, he is far more skillful at tormenting me than all elements. Even if I presume that he is good, who guarantees me that he will not

[20:93]

change his mind. The motions of matter hold to a certain determinate rule, but the obstinacy of the human being is without any rule

[74] Page 53
At the margin, next to lines 15–23, at 2:230

Those who regard the marital excesses as trifles that would deserve no contumely or ~~punishment~~ revenge make the strongest satires of marriage, because then ~~it~~ the state of marriage itself is not different [R72] from gallantry, from that of the most indifferent sort. [20:95]

Lower margin

The woman takes a satire of her sex as a joke, because she knows well that the mockery of the little shortcomings of her sex actually applies to the men themselves, who only love her all the more for the sake of them; but a satire of marriage insults them all, because this seems to be more serious, and because they also feel there is some truth in this reproach. But if such a principle got the upper hand, her sex would be degraded to men's power of choice.

Inserted sheet after page 54
[75] Obverse, at 2:230

<On the rightful expression "gentlemen" [*meine Herren*]>[132]

In subjection there is ~~also someth~~ not only something externally dangerous but ~~something~~ also a certain ugliness and a contradiction that at the same time indicates its unlawfulness. An animal is not yet a complete being because it is not conscious of itself; and its drives and inclinations may be opposed by another or not, it surely feels its ill, but it [the ill] disappears for it in a moment, and it does not know of its own existence.[133] But that the human being himself should, as it were, need no soul and should have ~~through a~~ no will of his own, and that another soul should move my limbs is absurd and perverse: Also in our constitutions [20:93]

---

[132] In German, "Herr" can mean "mister" (as a title of address), "gentleman" or "lord." In the Academy Edition, the preceding three paragraphs appear after the sentence beginning "There may quite well be . . . " below . See footnote 136.

[133] *Dasein*

[20:95]

every human being who is subordinated to a great degree is contemptible to us—[breaks off]

Livery

<Instead of freedom appearing to elevate me above the cattle, it places [R73] me even beneath them, since I can more easily be coerced>

Someone like that is, as it were, by himself,[134] nothing but the house-ware of another. ~~it~~ I could just as well indicate my respect to the boots of the master as to his lackey. In short, the human being who is dependent in this way is no longer a human being; he has lost this rank, he is nothing except another human being's belonging.

[20:94]

Subjection and freedom ~~often are~~ are commonly admixed to a certain degree, ~~the master~~ and ~~it does not always mean the m~~ one depends on the other. But even the small degree of dependence is much too great an ill not naturally to terrify. This feeling is very natural but one can also greatly weaken it. The power to withstand other ills can become so small that slavery seems a lesser ill than adversity. Nevertheless, it is certain that in human nature it stands above [breaks off]

Indeed, the cattle are coerced by the human beings, but the human being by the delusion[135] of the human being

The momentary violence of an attack is much less than servitude

[76] Reverse, opposite page 55, at 2:231

There may quite well be stimulations that the human being prefers to freedom for a moment, but he certainly must feel sorry right after that.[136]

[20:95]   Society makes it so that one evaluates oneself only comparatively. If others are not better than me, I am good; if all are worse, I am perfect.

[20:96]   Comparative evaluation is still distinguished from honor.

~~If~~ Chastity cannot be a lack of amorous passion, [R74] since then it really is a flaw, namely if this passion is too small for the whole purpose; but it is good in so far as it is appropriate to age <and> estate, but this *Bonitaet*[137] is not moral.

---

[134] *vor sichs*
[135] Here we follow the Academy Edition's "Wahn" as opposed to Rischmüller's "Wan."
[136] In the Academy Edition, the three paragraphs beginning "Those who regard the marital excesses..." appear here. See footnote 132.
[137] *goodness*

To preserve chastity ~~in a man~~ is either an immediate shamefulness (a concern to make one's sexual character contemptible) or a mediate one – a consequence of the general concept of honor. The latter is either merely a concern to bring no dishonor upon oneself – and this is a means of preserving virtue against which much ado could be made – or a tender irritability of an inner self-reproach in so far as it is connected with sincerity and not able to conceal itself, that is, shows itself in blushing; this quality is the best means of preservation.

We have all sorts of drives that should serve us as means to serve [20:97] and more often immediately rule others. First, comparing ourselves with others in order for us to be able to evaluate ourselves; from this arises the falsity of evaluating one's worth comparatively, [i.e.,] arrogance, and of evaluating one's happiness in just the same way, [i.e.,] jealousy. Second, putting ourselves in the place of another in order for us to know what he feels ~~and judges~~. From this arises blind pity, which also brings justice into disorder. Third, ~~others us in the~~ investigating the judgments of others because this can correct the truth of ours morally as well as logically. From this arises the desire for glory. Fourth, acquiring and saving oneself all sorts of things for enjoyment; from this arises greed, which is miserly.[138]

One says that ambition is the final weakness of the wise. I believe that in so far as the wisdom is not of the kind that presupposes old age the love of women is the final weakness.

[77] Page 56
Marginal notes next to lines 9–14, at 2:231

[139]That a woman possesses femininities is no ill, but that they be encoun- [20:99] tered in a man surely is one. Likewise, it is a biting mockery rather than a word of praise that a woman possesses masculinity

Next to lines 18–22

[R75] A woman restricts the heart of a man; and one usually loses a friend when he marries

---

[138] *karg*
[139] From here until the start of 20:102, the page order of Rischmüller and the Academy Edition are substantially different. We have followed Rischmüller's order and pagination.

Lower margin

Thus the man is a dandy[140] in the marital state

Inserted sheet after page 56
[78] Obverse, at 2:231

[20:97] The naming of *dames*[141] and *chapeaux*,[142] although it is a fashionable trifle in the social interaction among Germans, indicates quite well the foolishness in taste that creeps in among us, and that makes us into a mimic

[20:98] of the most ridiculous customs of a *nation*[143] that is lively and clownish in its own character. The everlasting social interaction of the French with women is in accordance with their character, yet this is not so with the Germans. Our women also do not have by far the lively *coquetterie* of the French. Therefore, this manner of association must always be somewhat vulgar. They are still proud here

Since women are weak, they are much less capable of virtue; but they have that which can make it dispensable

Virtue becomes ever more necessary, but also ever more impossible in our present constitution

Since virtue shows strength, it must be suitable for warlike states, more for *Rome* than *Carthage*.

Unity in society is not possible among many

If we count the labors of another among [our] needs, why not also his wife

Men only evaluate their worth in relation to one another if they are in society: women [evaluate theirs] only in relation to men, because now every charming quality discovered or pretention to win over questions every other's [R76] courting claim; thus, they strongly disparage each other

Every well-mannered woman seeks to charm the entire sex, even though she does not mean to profit thereby. This is because, since they should be sought after, they must possess a general inclination to please;

---

[140] *Laffe*   [141] French for "ladies."   [142] French for "hats."
[143] Kant uses here the French term "nation."

for if this were restricted, she might fall for him who does not want her. In marriages, this inclination steps beyond its restrictions

[79] Reverse, opposite page 57, at 2:232

<On the amenities that one makes into a need and vice versa. Ideal [20:100] pleasures. Chimerical ones that deceive in [their] fulfillment>

1. On need and amenities. Rest, change, boredom
On opulence and sufficiency. Preparation, foresight
On ambition.
<On courage and cowardice, health and sickness>
On the ~~fine and~~ goods of delusion. Stinginess[144]
On sexual inclination. On science

On fine and crude sentiments
On foresight
On the human being of simplicity
On the natural human being in comparison with the civilized one; <on the extent of the welfare of both>
On the value of human nature
[R77] One who is free values himself more than one who is slavish
Dependence on violence is not as disreputable as the [dependence] on delusion
<On industriousness and laziness>
On the opulence of civilized human beings.
On the sciences, on healthy and fine understanding   [20:101]
On enjoyment and delusion, *prevoiance*[145] <On the capacity of enjoyment and of delusion>
On welfare and misery
<moral>
On generosity and guiltiness
On the drive for acquisition or for defense. War
On truth and lies. On propriety and righteousness
On friendship. On the perfection of human nature

[144] *Kargheit*   [145] French for "foresight."

On sexual inclination
  Virtue, religion. On the natural and artificial state, education

The officer who became embarrassed – or who pretended to become so –
by the gaze of *Louis* XIV. expressed the sentiment of a slave.[146] The
embarrassment of a man with respect to a woman does no harm to his
noble qualities; his boldness is here crude indifference. A woman must not
be embarrassed in consideration of male virtue, *conscia decoris Venus*.[147]
Her noble propriety is calm and gentle, not bold. I revere the beautiful
girl in a noble or princely person.

  [R78] If he already talks of virtue all the time, he is corrupt; if he
constantly talks of religion, he is [corrupt] to the most extreme degree

  The clergymen in the country could hold large schools for the education
of children

[80] Page 57
Upper margin, at 2:232

[20:99]   Beauty is commanding. Merit [unreadable word] peaceful and yielding.
The wife sustains the affectionateness of the man through jealousy

At the margin, next to lines 2–19

The man from whom escapes a tear that has been held back with difficulty.
Therefore, his pain, which he compresses in his chest, chokes him if
tender wistfulness moves him and the effort to bear it unwaveringly shines
forth in his behavior. A woman can let her grief out in lamentations with
propriety and relieves herself [of] her sentiment. She also passes easily
[20:100]   from pain to joy, even if the former has been serious, which is good for
a beautiful sex as well. The man loves more affectionately, the woman
more steadily.

---

[146] In *The Age of Louis XIV*, Voltaire offers an anecdote of an officer who was embarrassed by the
gaze of Louis XIV: "The awe which he [Louis XIV] inspired in those who spoke with him
secretly flattered the consciousness of his own superiority. The old officer who became confused
and faltered in his speech when asking a favour, finally breaking off with 'Sire, I have never
trembled thus before your enemies,' had no difficulty in obtaining what he asked" (Voltaire, *Age
of Louis XIV*, pp. 267–68).
[147] Latin for "Venus is conscious of her propriety."

Inserted sheet after page 58
[81] Obverse, at 2:232

On inequality [20:102]

Once this has begun, the ill of oppression is not nearly so great as that the minds of the oppressed become abject and value themselves lowly. A peasant is a much viler human being and has cruder vices than a savage who lacks everything, and just the same [holds for] a common worker.

If I went into the workshop of a craftsman, I would not wish that he could read my thoughts. I dread this comparison; he would realize the great inequality in which I stand to him. I recognize that I cannot live a single day without his industriousness, that his children are brought up to be useful people.

On the defensive passions.

[R79] Although the human being hates no other human being by nature, he does indeed fear him. Hence he is on his guard, and the equality that he thinks he is losing every moment brings him to arms. The state of war[148] soon begins. But since it is based on a noble ground, it [20:103] surely brings forth great ills but no ignominy. It is less likely to dishonor human nature than a slavish peace*

Virtue that depends on strength also can last long only in warlike states. The English still have the most virtue among all European nations. ~~They are~~ Their *luxury* is acquired through hard work and is wasted with savagery

*Our present war aims only at the acquisition of money and *luxury*. That of the Ancients [aimed] at equality and the predominance, not of wealth, but of power; with the latter virtue can still subsist

[82] Reverse, opposite page 59, at 2:233

Everything that unnerves kills virtue at its sources.

The female sex is closer to nature than the male. For the present age is the age of propriety, of beauty, of good behavior. But those are her specific inclinations

---

[148] Here we follow Rischmüller's "Der Stand des Krieges" as opposed to the Academy Edition's "Der Stand des Kriegers."

[20:104] The male sex has come to an end, and the noble qualities no longer endure after everything has degenerated into ornamentation

The state of virtue is a violent one; thus, it can only be encountered in a violent state of the commonwealth.

To a certain degree, the opulent life increases [the number of] human beings. Women cease to work, they have more children. ~~they~~ There are enough prostitutes who want to suckle children or poor women who neglect their own and raise the children of the noble, etc. Opulence of an even greater degree makes for a stagnation in growth[149] and finally a dimunition. From this arises poverty. But before this begins, or when it emerges, the greatest vices occur

[R80] On *religion* in the natural state.

One must not regard savages without religion as people who are to be subordinated to our [people] with religion. For one who does what God wills him to do – by means of the incentives God put in his heart – is obedient to Him without knowing of His existence.[150] One who recognizes God, but who is brought to such actions only through the naturally good *morality*, has theology, or if he honors God for the sake of his *morality*, then this is only a *morality* whose object has been broadened. If their faith is not alive Christians can become blessed just as little as those who have no revelation at all; but with the former something more has happened than what naturally takes place.

Inserted sheet after page 60
[83] Obverse, at 2:233

If Diogenes had cultivated the field instead of rolling his barrel, he would have been great.[151]

---

[149] The German word here is "Vermehrung." This word could also be translated as "reproduction."
[150] Here Kant echoes St. Paul's letter to the Romans (2:14–15): "When the Gentiles, which have not the law, do by nature the things contained in the law, these, having not the law, are a law unto themselves, which shows the work of the law written in their hearts."
[151] Diogenes (b. 323 BC), student of Antisthenes. Kant's source for this anecdote was probably the preface to Mendelssohn's *Philosophical Writings*: "Diogenes once saw the citizens of Corinth busy with enormous war preparation and, in order not to be the only indolent soul in the city, he rolled his peaceful barrel up and down the streets" (Moses Mendelssohn, *Philosophical Writings*, ed. Daniel Dahlstrom, Cambridge University Press, 1997, p. 3). See too Bayle's entry on Diogenes in his *Dictionary*. The ancient source is probably Diogenes Laertius, *The Lives of the Philosophers*.

One must not ban any books now; that is the only way ~~the harm~~ that [20:105] they destroy themselves. We have now come to the point of return. If one lets them flood, rivers form their own banks. The dam that we set against them serves only to make their destructions unending. For the authors of useless things have as their excuse the injustice of others.

In states where industriousness concerning things of necessity ~~no honor~~ is not honored and highly esteemed, where the people who engage in such trades do not value themselves, there a man without honor is the worst good-for-nothing, dissolute, deceptive, insidious, and thieving. But where the simplicity of nature rules, honor can very well be done without.

See there, honor wreaks much ill, and then[152] it also serves as a means to prevent the greatest excesses of the very same [ill]. The sciences wreak much ill, and then they also serve as a means to better their own evil. War creates more evils than it takes away [R81], but to a certain extent it brings about the state of equality and noble courage. In [20:106] such a way corruption as well as virtue cannot endlessly rise in human nature

[84] Reverse, opposite page 61, at 2:234

He who is not proud himself watches the game of vanity among noble ladies with no small pleasure

Shamefulness, frailty. Embarrassment.

Satire never improves; thus, even if I had the talents for it, I would not make use of them. The vanity of a woman is either that of her sex or that of her status.

The pride of sex or of status

Because nobility and the honor based upon it merely depend on the arbitrary choice[153] of princes, pride in them is very foolish. <He who is angry and strong does not hate>

That the drive for honor only arises from the idea of equality can be [20:107] seen from this: 1. because as far as another is stronger, yet only appears not to make any comparison, we surely fear him ~~but we~~ (from which esteem arises), but we do not hate him 2. that the inclination to show one's worth to superiors is noble, but to equals or inferiors is ~~contemptible~~

---

[152] Reading "dann" here for "denn."   [153] *Willkühr*

<worthy of hate>; and that a human being who does not value himself is despised.

The highest peak of fashionable taste is <when young men [become] refined early,> acquire vulgar boldness, ~~the~~ but the young woman soon casts aside reserved modesty and has learned early how to play the game of *coquetterie* with liveliness. For ~~thereupon we~~ this is necessarily the most charming manner, which catches the eye the most; in such a society, a reasonable man looks like a dolt or a pedant, a ~~decent~~ modest and decent woman like a common landlady, and the finer part of society plays the role of courtiers. Thus, those of common taste soon withdraw [R82], and reason and domestic virtue are old, rusted ~~quality~~ memorials of taste, ~~that~~ kept for remembrance. But as with all ills that one can never bring to the highest point without the scale turning to the other side, here again stagnation and return is found. For gradually the women who have practiced the female art long before marriage will exercise this freedom with great ease in a state where they can do it with security. Men, warned by such examples, instructed by the very seduction that they themselves have instigated, and in anticipation of a wild vanity that will never let them rest, love the marriages of others but complicate their own. Contempt for the beautiful sex follows the adoration [of it] and ~~one~~, what is most terrible for it, the male sex is prudent so as to no longer be deceived by [20:108] them. The greatest obstacle to the male sex's ability to return to happy simplicity is the female sex.

[85] Page 61
Upper margin, at 2:234

I plant human beings. Propriety. A helpful instinct of chastity.

Marginal notes at lines 1–4

Men are exceedingly easy to deceive, women are not.

Lower margin

Old-fashioned seclusion also has its troubles. Social interaction becomes speechless, full of stiff *ceremony*, [and of] rustic and sodden prudery.

The vanity and the juggler's game of gallant social interaction serve, to an extent, to put passion ~~under~~ to sleep through the shifting games of distraction and to divert [it] with the finery of fashion and empty vanity, instead of solitude introducing there that which society had forbidden.

Inserted sheet after page 62
[86] Obverse, at 2:234

[R83] Blushing is a beautiful quality of women, and it is not impudence that ~~makes~~ destroys blushing; rather, she who does not easily blush easily becomes impudent and wanton

 There are by far more men who have reason to praise the generosity of [20:109] (those) women who do not use the legal privilege that nature gives them to fulfill the fair demand on their husband, if need be, through other men than there are men who can complain [about it]. With so many enervated ~~persons~~ men, a foolish or chimerical honor-project[154] ~~is~~ arises, in which they want to turn marriage into friendship and demand great virtues of the wife for a self-overcoming of those impulses that are quite fair and that the former cannot satisfy

 A woman is able to make men virtuous, but is not also virtuous [herself]. Strange as it is, they are even the greatest means of chastity in men, for nothing makes an otherwise flighty man more chaste than love toward a girl.

 A woman has a quick concept of everything concerning *sentiments*[155] but she does not feel them. For instance, take a heroic virtue: the man will consider when he is supposed to practice it himself, the woman, however, when it is done toward her or done by her husband. ~~Imagine a~~ Speak of great discretion and she will think of such a lover. Thus, some virtues that have no noticeable tendency toward her sex will not be respected by them (for instance, the simplicity of nature)

 This is excellent, for the woman is the whetstone of virtue, *frangere vix cotis,*[156] etc., and male virtue would also have ~~toward~~ no object of use if the woman were so herself, for then she would be able to do without

---

[154] *Ehrprojekt* [155] Kant uses here the French term "sentiments."
[156] Latin for "the whetstone breaks with difficulty."

Perhaps this is a secret cause, on account of which we always attach ourselves to women in such a way, whether we want to or not

[87] Reverse, opposite page 63, at 2:235

[20:110] [R84] Absolute cold is where a body is saturated with fire, absolute warmth where it has let go of all fire, which is possible, i.e., since the *attraction* is exactly equal to the *expansive force* of the same

Whether I can impute[157] *anteactum*[158] to a morally changed human being

If a body draws fire from others it warms them, if it lets it go it cools them.

If the warmth is in *a*, then *a* is put into the absorbing state through the loss of its fire element. Thus, there must be coldness in *b* as more fire element is there to be encountered and is attracted by the parts themselves; because the fire element ~~will be drawn into *b* there will emerge an empty space in *c*, in *c* therefore~~ will be accumulated in *b*, it must spread itself out and yield an empty space in *c*, which will be warm, and so forth. On the *ethereal* waves in warmth, on those in light. Yet this distinction can only last for a short time.

[20:111] If water is above fire, then there is an empty space underneath; hence, if the water has let go all the fire – i.e., boils – then, if one removes it, [the fire] must ~~absorb [at the bottom] – i.e., heat – and at the top~~ leave at the bottom and absorb at the top because the movement was once given to the element;[159] thus, it is hot at the top and cool at the bottom. In boiling, bubbles, which ascend, must develop at the bottom; the fire element, which releases itself, is not able to pass through copper as quickly as through water and gathers in bubbles; in these, vapors emerge and soar while constituting an elastic medium.

---

[157] The German word here is "imputieren," which is a Germanization of the French verb "imputer."
[158] Latin for "prior deed."
[159] Given his theory of fire, Kant must have meant to write here that "the fire must leave at the bottom and be absorbed at the top."

All bodies vitrify and are *comparatively* empty of fire element; therefore, while light produces warmth in others, at its innermost it here yields only light, that is, not so much a discharge of ether as an adjustment of it.

Inserted sheet after page 64
[88] Obverse

[R85] The magnitude of punishment is either to be evaluated *practically*, namely, that it be great enough to prevent the action, and then no greater punishment is allowed; but a punishment as great as is physically necessary is not always morally possible.

Or its magnitude is evaluated in moral *proportion*: e.g., of the man who [20:112] kills another in order to take his money, it will be judged that, because he has valued another's life as less than ~~his own~~ money, one must also value his life less than the amount of money settled for anyone else's life

Few care about deceiving their prince, which is a sign that they feel the injustice of the government

    <*timor indolis ingenui est filialis altera servilis*>[160]

Indoles est <respectu motivorum> vel ingenua vel ~~servilis~~ abiecta haec vel tanquam mercenarii vel tanquam mancipii[161]

On the method of morality: since one regards ~~all~~ the qualities that are now common to all human beings from birth on as natural (not originating from sin) and extracts from that the rules as to how they can be good in [this] state, [one] does not err even if the *supposition* could be false. In this way, I can say that the human being of nature, who does not know of God, is not evil

Because God was a political law-giver in the Old Testament, he also gave political reasons for rewards and punishments, but not moral ones, except in later times. <A prince cannot put a reward on all of his laws because he himself has nothing>

---

[160] Latin for "The fear of a noble character is either that of a child or that of a servant."

[161] Latin for "Character <with regard to motives> is either noble or ~~servile~~ abject, the latter is that of a mercenary or that of a slave." (In the Academy Edition, the order of these two sentences is reversed.)

Indoles ingenua est vel amoris vel reverentiae dominatur prior in evangelio posterior in lege. Amor non poterat in veteri testamento locum habere ideo tum reverentia. In novo testamento amor non potest nisi divinitus oriri[162]

[89] Reverse, opposite page 65, at 2:235

[20:113]   [R86] On the *Republic* of *Geneva*; on *Rousseau's* peculiar way of life.[163]
Love is either lustful <corporeal> or moral <spiritual>

Toward women something of the first is always intermingled, it can also be toward the elderly, or else they will only be valued as men. ~~Toward chi~~ Fathers spoil daughters, and mothers spoil sons

All follies have this in common with each other, that the images that ~~there~~ they allure float in the air and have no support or stability. You marry a woman without wit, without manners, without birth and family, what a decline of your taste. Oh, that is not the rule of my taste, you may answer. But what will the people say, consider how the world will judge you. Before I get involved with this important difficulty, I ask you first ~~what then are such peo~~ what one understands by such people and the world whose opinion is decisive for my happiness. Those are, one answers me, a multitude of persons in which each is just as distressed [by] what people
[20:114]   want to say, and I belong among the number of these so-called people whose judgment is so important. Oh, I answer, we people altogether do not at all want to bother each other about the opinion of another any longer because it robs us of enjoyment; for now we understand each other, or I, at least, understand all of you; I ~~want~~ am no *comedian* who is paid by applause.

Conceit and stingy greed are never to be healed.

Women are never generous; this is also entirely proper, for since they are not actually the ones who acquire, but the ones who save, it would be wrong ~~because~~ if they gave away for nothing because that is an affair of gentlemen. But they are only subordinated gentlemen; and although they never want to be, nature still retains its rights. Yet they invest in finery

---

[162] Latin for "The noble character is either that of love or that of reverence; the first dominates in the Gospels, the second in the Law. Love could not have had a place in the Old Testament, thus there was reverence. In the New Testament love cannot exist unless it comes from God."

[163] See Rousseau's *Confessions*. Rousseau was, at various times in his life, a citizen of Geneva, and his *Discourse on the Origin of Inequality* is dedicated "To the Republic of Geneva." For the rumors circulated in the 1760s regarding Rousseau's lifestyle, see Rischmüller, pp. 233–34.

because this does not appear to them to be given away and they rightfully *use*[164] that which belongs to men collectively

Inserted sheet after page 66
[90] Obverse, at 2:236

[R87] Error is never more useful than truth, all things considered, but ignorance often is

The understanding of children is the one that only judges that which is [20:115] currently useful to it. The masculine understanding judges about future use; the aged understanding ~~judges about~~ despises current use and has an imagined use as purpose, which will never exist in the future. With respect to the understanding, women are indeed children and, with respect to the future, they are given to stinginess in spite of all foresight.[165] With respect to the future, the valiant man acquires <his> own powers and sacrifices his concerns to others rather than being distressed by external circumstances. In the household, an admirable unity arises out of this.

If one merely depends on things then one does not require much reason but only understanding

Arrogance for the sake of religion is the most ridiculous, for the thought[166] that others do not become blessed should make me sympathetic and helpful rather than arrogant. Arrogance for the sake of money is common and coarse because it is based on that which easily passes from one to another; thus, it is crude. That for the sake of freedom is noble and proud. That for the sake of birth ~~and for the sake of rank~~ is finer because it is permanent, and that for the sake of office is the most admissible.

[91] Reverse, opposite page 67, at 2:236

The Jews, Turks, and Spaniards have arrogance of religion; they are also either treacherous if they are cowardly or tyrannical if they are powerful. The Dutch [are arrogant] for the sake of money, the English for the sake of freedom and power. The conceit of nations because of their great monarch causes vanity, and vanity also brings about [a] monarchical constitution. A proud nation is free; a coarse and industrious one also free

---

[164] *tractiert*   [165] The Academy Edition has a paragraph break here.   [166] *Vorstellung*

and money-grubbing. Spanish arrogance will show a spirit of persecution in all religions, and so also with the Turks.

[R88] Where there are many nobles and many obedient [to them], there is partly flattery and otherwise arrogance, as with the Poles.

[20:116]   A woman only cares for delight but not for the necessity of life. Therefore, they let the man take care of the needs, while they take care of taste. And in religion they let others determine what is true, while they are intent on imitating it fashionably with good form.

I want to note one more thing (but this is said just among us men): through their behavior, they can make [others] more chaste than they themselves are and ~~without~~ console themselves over the loss of an inclination through the satisfaction of vanity by having instilled great respect. Women ~~wants a~~ like to see a strong man ~~serves~~ so that they seem to be coerced in a good way

The woman makes of men what she wants; she has formerly made heroes and now makes monkeys. Whether she makes reasonable men is to be doubted; the latter cannot be formed by others at all, but must become so by themselves

[20:117]   On taste **for** society in distinction from that **in** society

Sheet inserted after page 68
[92] Obverse, at 2:237

The capacity for pleasure and displeasure is feeling in general. Lack of feeling [breaks off]

The capacity for pleasure and displeasure in things that do not belong to needs [is] taste. The latter is coarse taste in so far as it ~~in~~ is close to needs; the refined one is the true taste in that which is remote from needs. ~~In so far this refined~~

~~The feeling for things that a gre which presuppose greater perfection of the understanding is ideal.~~

[R89] In so far as the powers of the soul must not be merely passive but active and creative,[167] taste is called spiritual and ideal (when the noblest feeling is not moved by external sensation but by that which one creates for it)

---

[167] *dichtend*

With regard to morality, feeling either merely ~~belongs~~ remains with the needs, i.e., obligation, or it goes further; in the latter case it is sentiment[168]

The beautiful and the sublime in the highest degree are closely related. If they are to be felt, both presuppose the soul at peace. ~~Thus~~ Yet they are [20:118] so different that if busyness, ~~is increasing~~ cheerfulness, and liveliness are increasing the beautiful shines forth; if they end and peaceful contentment shows through, the sublime stands out. In the early morning, the former; in the evening, the latter.

In its lesser forms, the beautiful is related to the change out of varying novelty. The sublime, with constancy, oneness, and inalterability. With beauty, manifoldness; with the noble, unity

[93] Reverse, opposite page 69, at 2:237

Only the dispensable is beautiful, but the noble can be combined with the useful. Yet in moral matters, ~~that~~ the noble must not be considered from the viewpoint of usefulness. Blossoms are beautiful, fruit is useful.*
In these refined sentiments it is presupposed that the human being does not depend on things through bare necessity, otherwise the refined taste ~~are~~ is foolish. <Enchanted by beauty, astonished by sublimity>

The beautiful in a lesser degree is agreeable and pretty, if ~~great not~~ [20:119] sublimity disappears, [it is] cute.[169] If the beautiful is imitated, it is decorated ~~adornment~~, like golden hens.

~~The sublime is in a lesser~~ [breaks off]

[R90] With the feeling of the sublime, the powers of a human being seem to become stretched, as it were; with the beautiful, they contract.

The taste that extends itself with respect to the immediate sexual inclination is the lustful one and is a sign of corruption with respect to [breaks off]

There are moral and nonmoral necessities (obligations), which one presupposes before there is talk of beauties. ~~Before one~~ Sciences inside the head are for some human beings as useless as hair powder on top of the same. And as it would be quite foolish to have flour on [one's] curls and none in one's soup, so it is incongruous to know dispensable arts ~~without~~ and to misconceive those that constitute the welfare of life.

---

[168] *Sentiment*   [169] *niedlich*

Before we think of civilities, we must first be truthful and honest. It is peculiar that the lover bothers himself over a free woman before he knows whether she is also faithful. Before we ask for generosity[170]

* <Spring ~~is beautiful~~ and girls are beautiful; autumn and wives are useful. <The usefulness of girls [consists in] that they are *sterile*>>

Inserted sheet after page 70
[94] Obverse

we must remind ourselves [of] obligation. Stop, brazen ones – shouted the merchant.[171]

Good manners with inner improbity, the suavity of women without domesticity is like ~~beautiful~~ many ribbons and a dirty shirt.

The common opinion that previous times were better comes from the ill that one feels and the presupposition that otherwise everything would be good.

[20:120] [R91] Clothes are only signs of comfort and excess with respect to life. They must not be made so that they draw attention exclusively to themselves. (Garish colors are repugnant to the eye, which gets attacked too much.) Likewise with rank and title. Those who have little worth themselves are doomed to golden frames.

In marriage, mere love without respect is already enough to attach the man to the woman, and mere respect without love is enough to attach the woman to the man. Thus, although understanding and merits have little effect on the woman outside of marriage, the most harmonious marriage is still the one where the man instills respect through understanding, even if the ages are different. *Wolmar*[172]

I would like to be the happy Saint-Preux rather than the one who courts a wife[173]

---

[170] In Rischmüller, the sentence breaks off here. In the Academy Edition, it continues with "we must remind ourselves," below. See footnote 171.

[171] The Academy Edition reads this fragment as continuous with the one beginning nine lines above, "Before we consider civilities . . ."

[172] In Rousseau's *Julie*, Julie eventually marries Wolmar, a much older man whom she greatly respects for his virtue and understanding.

[173] In Rousseau's *Julie*, St. Preux begins the book courting Julie as his wife, but ends content with her marriage to Wolmar.

[95] Reverse, opposite page 71, at 2:238

The correct cognition of the construction of the world according to Newton[174] is perhaps the most beautiful product of inquisitive human reason; meanwhile, Hume notes that the philosopher can easily get distracted in this delightful rumination by a little brunette maiden, and that rulers are not moved to despise their conquests because of the smallness of the earth in comparison to the universe. The cause is that it is indeed beautiful but unnatural to lose oneself outside of the circle that heaven has fixed for us. It is the same with the sublime contemplations of the heaven of the blessed. [20:121]

If light had a streaming movement, then its strength when striking a slanted surface ~~not~~ and the warming would not behave like the square of the sine of the inclination, but like its *cube*.

That the poles do exert attraction at all is clear from the experiment of *Bougeurs* who put a magnetic needle on a piece of copper[175]

Inserted sheet after page 72
[96] Obverse

[R92] The Spectator says that the fool and the clever one are different in that the former thinks aloud, etc.[176] This is a very correct remark typical of our present kind of prudence. Now, because both sexes progress *proportionately*[177] in this and the female one generally surpasses the male

---

[174] See footnote 85 above.

[175] Pierre Bouguer (1698–1758) was a French scientist who wrote *Optical Treatise on the Gradation of Light* (1729) and *The Figure of the Earth* (1749), which drew on experiments performed in Peru to give determination of the Earth's shape and gravitational attraction.

[176] See *The Spectator* (number 225). *The Spectator* was a periodical, written by Joseph Addison and Richard Steele during 1711–14, devoted to commentary on the literature and life of eighteenth-century England. It was enormously influential and was published in book form. It first appeared in German as *Der Zuschauer* in 1749–51. Letter 225, written by Addison, begins as follows:
> I have often thought if the Minds of Men were laid open, we should see but little Difference between that of the Wise Man and that of the Fool. There are infinite *Reveries*, numberless Extravagancies, and a perpetual Train of Vanities which pass through both. The great Difference is that the first knows how to pick and cull his Thoughts for Conversation, by suppressing some, and communicating others; whereas the other lets them all indifferently fly out in Words. This sort of Discretion, however, has no Place in private Conversation between intimate Friends. On such Occasions the wisest Men very often talk like the weakest; for indeed the Talking with a Friend is nothing else but *thinking aloud*.

[177] *proportionirlich*

one in the art of appearance, woman must now be much more perfect in this and dominate.

[20:122] That the anticipation of death is not natural is to be seen from the fact that the consideration of death accomplishes nothing at all against the inclination to make preparations as if one were to live long, ~~and from this~~ and the human being makes arrangements at the end of his life as seriously as if he would not live at all.[178] From this, vanity and the thirst for glory after death may originate because the natural human being flees shame and knows nothing of death. Hence the natural drive extends beyond death, which surprises it

In morals as in the art of medicine, that doctor is best who teaches me how I can be above diseases and remedies. This art is easy and simple. But the one that allows all corruption and removes it afterwards is artificial and complicated.

The *odium theologorum*[179] has its ground in that it is held to be contrary to the propriety of the clergy to express the fast and vigorous movements of anger, and since this is suppressed it degenerates into secret bitterness. Parallel with women and *Indians*.

[97] Reverse, opposite page 73, at 2:239

Gigantism is a disease; one could ask whether it is not also so with respect to intellectual qualities; at any rate it seldom makes [one] happy. *Cato,*
[20:123] *Brutus.*[180] Gigantic plans without power and insistence are like children whose heads are too big. Premature prudence. *Margarethe Maultasch.*[181]

[R93] I praise mediocrity. Good, content citizen.

Difficult relationship between rank and *talents. Alexander* had large weapons left behind, not in order to form the opinion of the Indians[182]

---

[178] We assume that Kant actually meant to write here that the human being makes arrangements at the end of his life as seriously as if he would not die at all.

[179] *Odium theologorum*, which literally means "theological hatred," was a term for the antipathy that arises from theological disputes.

[180] Regarding Cato and Brutus, see above, footnotes 8 and 91.

[181] See footnote 125 above regarding Margarete Maultasch.

[182] Here we follow Rischmüller's "nicht um den Indianern die Meinung zu machen" (R93) rather than the Academy Edition's "nicht um den Indianern die Wenigen zu nehmen" (20:123).

about of the gigantic size of his army, but rather in order to confirm it.[183]

Tender taste is wounded (screaming) by the very strong prominence of gaiety, of affectation, [and] of loquacity and loves peaceful and gentle beauty.

Coarse taste (is very different from lack of feeling) requires stronger stimulation, vivaciously brought out, and shows its wear and tear. Old, exhausted lover. <Whether the youth that loves tragedies would not have a coarse taste.>

ugly and nasty.

The ideal of beauty may very well be preserved in hope but not in possession. <Wantons become very skeptical with respect to the chastity of women and make others so as well> [20:124]

I do not know whether it is true what they say about the very extended loyalty ~~wom~~ of married women in the most civilized nations and let those judge who know it from experience. This much I do know, that if all sentiments grow beyond their boundaries, the female capacity, which is not so restricted, will go much further than the male.

Nothing can replace the loss of female grace, not even the noblest propriety.

Outside of marriage, debauchery is most dangerous for the female sex to conceal by all arts; for the male one it is so within marriage. Hence one can already suspect prior to any experience that the female sex will be reserved before marriage and excessive in marriage, vice versa, though, with the male sex.

[R94]

---

[183] In his life of Alexander, Plutarch writes that Alexander the Great "could not refrain from leaving behind him [in India] various deceptive memorials of his expedition, to impose upon aftertimes, and to exaggerate his glory with posterity, such as arms larger than were really worn, and mangers for horses, with bits and bridles above the usual size, which he set up, and distributed in several places" (*Plutarch's Lives, vol.* II, ed. Arthur Hugh Clough, New York: Modern Library, 2001, p. 189). In *The Spectator* (number 127), Addison writes, "You know, Sir, it is recorded of Alexander the Great, that in his *Indian* Expedition he buried several Suits of Armour, which by his Direction were made much too big for any of his Soldiers, in order to give Posterity an extraordinary Idea of him, and make them believe he had commanded an Army of Giants."

[98] Page 74
At the margin, next to lines 14–21, at 2:239

The woman seems to lose more than the man because with the former the beautiful qualities end, yet with the man the noble ones remain. The old woman seems to be no longer good for anything.[184]

Inserted sheet after page 74
[99] Obverse, at 2:239

All pleasures that are connected to the fulfillment of needs are called coarse. Drinking, sleeping, eating, and cohabitation. The last is considered so crude that *Tiresias* had to endure an unpleasant encounter with *Juno* because he attributed it primarily to the female sex.[185]

Thus, taste always attaches to that which actually is no bare necessity. From this it follows that if resemblance to nature is the requirement in painting – e.g., *landscapes*,[186] *portraits*[187] – then this nature must be captured; for the rest, ideal pleasures constitute the noblest. Nature is not good enough for our pleasure. In addition to this, softness and tenderness [20:125] of our organs, indeed our imagination. Hence painting can very well depart from nature, like *poetry* and *theatrical* action.

---

[184] In the Academy Edition, this paragraph appears below at 20:125, after the sentence beginning "Unity is in accordance with . . . " See footnote 188.

[185] For the story of Juno and Tiresias, see Ovid, *Metamorphoses*, III, 316–38. As Ovid explains there: Jupiter, expansive with wine, set aside his onerous duties, and relaxing, exchanging pleasantries, with Juno, said "You gain more than we do from the pleasures of love." She denied it. They agreed to ask learned Tiresias for his opinion. He had known Venus in both ways. Once, with a blow of his stick, he had disturbed two large snakes mating in the green forest, and, marvelous to tell, he was changed from a man to a woman, and lived as such for seven years. In the eighth year he saw the same snakes again and said "Since there is such power in plaguing you that it changes the giver of a blow to the opposite sex, I will strike you again, now." He struck the snakes and regained his former shape, and returned to the sex he was born with. As the arbiter of the light-hearted dispute he confirmed Jupiter's words. Saturnia, it is said, was more deeply upset than was justified and than the dispute warranted, and damned the one who had made the judgment to eternal night. But, since no god has the right to void what another god has done, the all-powerful father of the gods gave Tiresias knowledge of the future, in exchange for his lost sight, and lightened the punishment with honor. (trans. Anthony Kline, available online at http://etext.virginia.edu/latin/ovid/trans/Ovhome.htm)
Kant discusses the same story with different emphasis in *Dreams of a Spirit-Seer* 2:341.
[186] *Naturalien*   [187] *Portraits*

Truth is more of an obligation than beauty. Thus, one must conceal obligation in order to be beautiful.

The tenderness of the nerves is one of the governing determinations of taste, for the degree of *contrast* or of *affect* – the hardness of sensations – will thereby be restricted, etc.

Harmony arises from the agreement of the manifold, in *music* just as in *poetry* and painting. These are points of rest for some nerves

Unity is in accordance with comfort in so far as it is connected with *activity*, which desires manifoldness.[188]

[R95]

[100] Reverse, opposite page 75, at 2:240

On refinement and the extent of these sentiments [20:126]

The sense of the eye provides long and tender albeit very ideal pleasures; displeasure is small except in sex. Horror [is] great.

The sense of hearing effects enduring pleasures. But only through change is [breaks off] less ideal but very lively, the displeasures are small and short-lived. The sense of smell gives a bit of ideal pleasure; they are short in pleasure and strong and short. Strong in displeasure, for disgust requires change.

The sense of taste is not at all ideal; it is great in pleasure but short and broken off – [it] requires change (without bare necessity). Displeasure is far more sensitive and [so is] disgust.

The sense of feeling is short and exhaustive in lust, short and sensitive in warmth [and] in titillation; in pain it can last long and be great. [It] can easily be outweighed by the understanding (except for the sexual inclination).

The sense of vision reveals most moral things, but then also the sense of hearing

That in marriages the chastity of women is harder to preserve than [20:127] that of men stems from the fact that their capacity to give is greater than that of men; hence the fantastical desires can go further in their case.

---

[188] In the Academy Edition, the remark beginning "The woman seems to lose more . . ." (at R94) comes here. See footnote 184.

Inserted sheet after page 76
[101] Obverse

On the old physiognomic characters in comparison with the moral ones

Beautiful and gallant actions primarily consist in those [R96] to which one has no obligation. Obligation is a kind of moral need; whatever relates itself more closely to it is simple.

All *affects* that elicit tenderness and moral sentiment must be taken from the determinations[189] of a human being; therefore [breaks off]

Because if one already presupposes beauty as necessary it becomes a kind of need, thus simplicity is also possible with the beautiful and the sublime

[20:128] Because after all such sentiments for the beautiful, which sometimes are stronger than needs, it requires a great art to achieve the simplicity of nature, even though it is superfluous – since one only does not want to depart from it – yet still great, therefore [this simplicity] is a special kind of the sublime

A pampered feeling, which is not strong enough for simplicity, is female. Nature at peace is the greatest beauty (yet trickling brooks) because they lull the human to sleep), grazing herds of cattle. Hence the evening [is] even more moving than the morning

Gaiety is not beautiful [and] also does not last. On the agreement of beautiful faces and beautiful bodies with the soul

[102] Reverse, opposite page 77, at 2:241

The free enjoyment of lustful inclination and the unconcealed discovery of its *object* nullifies everything ideal that can be spread through inclination; therefore, it is so difficult to preserve the ideal pleasures in marriages. Unless one concedes dominance to the wife.

[20:129] Some persons please more if one is away from them, others if one is more present; the former are better suited for the ideal pleasures of marriage

When fantastical love pairs well with knightly virtue.

---

[189] *Bestimmungen*

[R97] Novels end with marriages <and the history[190] begins>; how-ever, they still can be prolonged beyond them through jealousy, for instance, a wife who is a *coquette* of her husband and of others

All female beauty is spread by the sexual drive, for suppose you ~~exp~~ realize that a woman has a certain ambiguity of her sex, all your infat-uations will cease, although this does nothing to the pleasant qualities, which you believe to enchant you alone.

A pregnant woman is obviously useful but not so beautiful. Maiden-hood is useless but agreeable

Sheet inserted after page 78
[103] Obverse, at 2:241

It is quite bad that we do not at all want to allow women to be ugly, even when they are old.　　　　　　　　　　　　　　　　　　　　　　　　　[20:130]

Because needs are common, the domesticity of a woman is considered a thing to be dismissed among *gallant* men.

If the main work arises from the pleasures then the latter become flat.

I love the French as such but not the Germans when they imitate them.

Some women misuse the permission that women have to be ignorant

In proportion to their power to do evil, princes are by far less corrupt than the common man.

Inner honor. Self-esteem. External honor as a means to insure oneself of the former. Therefore, a man of honor. *honestas*[191] External honor as a means is true, as the end a delusion. The former concerns advantage either for self-preservation, equality, or preservation of the species. The [R98] desire for honor (immediate) either concerns the opinion of important perfections (*patriotism*[192]) and is called ambition, or concerns trifles and is called vanity. The consciousness of one's honor, which one believes oneself to be in possession of, and that without measuring oneself against others, is called pride. Dignity.[193] *Gallantry* is either of pride or of vanity; the former of a *petitmaitre*,[194] the latter of a fop. The proud one who

---

[190] *Geschichte*　　　[191] Latin for "honor."
[192] Kant uses here the French word "patriotism" and not the German word "Patriotismus."
[193] The Academy Edition offers a paragraph break here.
[194] Regarding the term "petitmaitres," see footnote 2 above.

[20:131]   despises others is arrogant. ~~The vain one~~ if he wants to show that through pomp [it is] presumptuous. The arrogant one who shows his disdain is pompous

[104] Reverse, opposite page 79, at 2:242

The honor of a man with respect to a woman is courage, and that of a woman chastity. These points are peculiar. When the age[195] becomes soft then the honor of the former is sweetness, and that of the latter understanding and boldness; the former makes the romanic,[196] the latter the affected and courtly or fashionable

Because philosophy is not a thing of bare necessity but of agreeableness, hence it is strange that one wants to restrict ~~from~~ it through painstaking laws

Because the man in courtship[197] chooses the woman as his ruler, he poeticizes her [as being] very admirable, since one will hardly submit to a wretched idol; conversely, the woman wants to dominate. Spectator, black monkey.[198] *Applies*[199] to the hidden secret of all tender inclination toward the sex

The strongest ~~preferences~~ pleasures become flat first

What it means to be domestic; to make a need out of society. Boredom.

[20:132]   The housewife is honorable. The beautiful propriety of her domestic care, intermixed with cleanliness and ornament; [she] must not appear to prefer being out of the house rather than at home

The man is the one who solicits, the woman the one who chooses; that is the point of making [R99] oneself scarce. Shall she choose the romanic[200] dreamer, the fool in his finery, or the selfish and phlegmatic – unfeeling – one.

---

[195] *seculum*   [196] *romanische*. See footnote 25 above.   [197] *brünstig*

[198] For the relationship between *The Spectator*, monkeys, and the lustful man, see *The Spectator* number 127. That letter as a whole deals with the (enormous) size of the hoops in petticoats at the time. The reference to the black monkey comes at the end of the letter: "When I survey this new-fashioned *Rotonda* in all its Parts, I cannot but think of the old Philosopher, who after having entered into an *Egyptian* Temple, and looked about for the Idol of the Place, at length discovered a little Black Monkey Enshrined in the midst of it, upon which he could not forbear crying out, (to the great Scandal of the Worshippers) What a magnificent Palace is here for such a Ridiculous Inhabitant!"

[199] *appliziert*   [200] *romanischen*. See footnote 25 above.

Saint-Evremond wanted to choose a wife and chose a *coquette*.[201] That happened because he was from a country where every woman is a *coquette*, though not toward her husband.[202]

The man who does not make his amusements into his business but into recreation, who knows how to live – i.e. who does not make acquisition but its enjoyment his aim – who likes the peaceful pleasure of company and friendship, he is a man

All pleasures become insipid if they are not recreations but occupations. The wife and the husband who have something to do will not become tired of another

The wife[203] possesses the skill of always being a woman[204] much more than the husband [that of being a man], but will she not prefer to employ this skill elsewhere than with her husband, who is insipid to her

[105] Page 79
Marginal note at lines 3–4, at 2:242

The standard of happiness is the household

Marginal notes at line 10 – lower margin, at 2:242

I walk ~~out~~ from a blooming field and the Arcadian valleys to barren fields[205]

The novel ends and the history begins. Henceforth the magical haze, [20:133] <through> which the enamored madness had seen its idol, gradually disperses. The marriage-bed receives a human [R100] girl, and she, otherwise worshiped as a goddess, as ~~a~~ a wife stifles the protest of her slave the next morning. ~~Thereupon the understanding husband drinks the salubrious water.~~ The lover, previously intoxicated by his imaginations, wakes from a beautiful reverie and [breaks off]

---

[201] Charles de Saint-Evremond (1613–1703). The French writer lived with Ninon de Lenclos, was condemned in the light of his satirical writings, and fled to England, where he died. His collected works first appeared in London in 1705. In Kant's time, Saint-Evremond was still an oft-quoted figure.

[202] Here we follow Rischmüller's "wo jede Ehefrau eine *Coquette* ist aber nicht gegen ihren Mann" [R99] as opposed to the Academy Edition's "wo jede Ehefrau eine *Coquette* ist launisch gegen ihren Mann". [20:132]

[203] *Frau*   [204] *Weib*   [205] See footnote 81 above.

The sight of blossoms.   A *gallant* person always blossoms

[106] Page 80
Upper margin, at 2:242

Love is a unity   Solomon never loved.[206] The

Inserted sheet after page 80
[107] Obverse, at 2:242

Beauty is without utility because the latter is a pressing of a thing to other purposes, thus it indicates no perfection complete in itself. Hence the more useful things are, the more corners they show, so to speak, as means to adapt themselves to other connections; the curve of a sphere is perfect in itself

Gallantry: a new kind of beauty of manners.   *Politesse.*[207]

[20:134] The former is a certain sweetness in pleasing behavior, the latter a certain good-natured cautiousness

The former is affected, the latter peaceful and composed. Not every woman is beautiful in the physical or intellectual sense, but *gallantry* meets them all with that subjection that is shown by him who, through his inclination, is ruled by a weaker one

The sentiment for the beauty of young boys constituted the origin of Greek love – the ~~disgraceful~~ most disgraceful passion ~~that ever has been and in the nature~~ that has ever ~~perverse~~ stained <human> nature, and that [passion] no doubt deserved that ~~the~~ its criminals be turned over to the revenge and scolding of women, ~~who~~ etc.

[R101] The permitted illusion is a kind of untruth that is not then a lie; it is an inducement for ideal pleasures whose object is not in things

---

[206] King Solomon, son of David, who lived around 1000 BC and became King of Israel in 967 BC. Traditionally, Solomon is viewed as the author of the biblical book Song of Songs (or Song of Solomon), an erotic song describing courtship and consummation between two lovers. Renowned for his wisdom and power, the later half of Solomon's reign was plagued by accusations that his many wives and concubines of other faiths led him to idolatry. His history is recorded in 2 Kings 1–11 and 2 Chronicles 1–9.

[207] French for "politeness."

Illusion in a large gathering, as if all these were cleverer than one

He who thought himself the president in the marriage-bed wanted to contrive something that could make him strong against the befuddling magical power of illusion

Illusion is so compatible with the beautiful – but not with the noble – that even if one becomes aware of it, it still pleases. To appear as clever, pious, hearty, honest

[108] Reverse, opposite page 81, at 2:243

Benevolence is a calm inclination to regard the happiness of others as an object of one's joy and also as a motive of one's actions. Compassion is an *affect* of benevolence toward the needy, according to which we imagine [20:135] that we would do what is in our power to help them; it is thus for the most part a chimera, because it is neither always in our power nor in our will. The citizen is compassionate toward others who are oppressed by the prince. The nobleman is compassionate toward another nobleman, but himself hard on the peasants.

With opulence the fantasy of the love of humanity *cultivates*[208] itself and the capacity and appetite reduces itself. The simple human being attends to no other except to him he can help

The understanding brings about no increase of the moral feeling; in this sense, he who ratiocinates only has rather cooled-off *affects* and is more cool-minded, consequently less evil and less good. The morally good rather makes [one] reasonable

One has long tried to explain the feeling of pleasure in the ridiculous. In nature nothing is ridiculous

[R102] One demands illusion with respect to clerics and women; the [20:136] former shall appear to take no part in frivolous pleasures, the latter [shall appear to have] no inclination for lustful intimacy at all. Thereby one makes them deceitful

[The] illusion of religion as it is finally taken for the thing itself. Then [it] is a delusion.

---

[208] *excolirt*

One must pay respect to clerics for the sacrifice of so many freedoms and pleasures. (They are within boundaries almost as narrow as those a woman is in)

One must deal attentively with both because both do not have on their side either the capacity or the propriety in order to boldly resist an insult

Inserted sheet after page 82
[109] Obverse, at 2:243

The formal aspect of all perfection consists in manifoldness (in addition[209] duration and strength) and unity; it can also give pleasure by itself.

Sensitive.   Insensitive.

[20:137] The will is perfect in so far as in accordance with the laws of freedom it is the greatest ground of the good in general. The moral feeling is the feeling of the perfection of the will.

Whether God is the originator of all *morality*, i.e., whether we can distinguish good from evil only through the recognized will of God

Sulzer[210] says that what facilitates and promotes the natural efficacy of the soul touches me with pleasure. This says only that it promotes the natural striving after pleasure

Unius corruptio est alterius generatio.[211] Through smell, nature has wanted to warn us of rottenness as the greatest ground of the dissolution and the ferment of the destruction of animals.

[R103] The man is stronger than the woman in all capacities; yet he is weaker with respect to inclination, which he cannot tame as well, and also with respect to the excitability of his tenderness and confidence. The

---

[209] The German term here is "wozu," which one could also translate as "for the purpose of."

[210] Johann Georg Sulzer (1720–79) was a Swiss philosopher and critic, whose *Recherches sur l'origine des idées agréables et désagréables* (1751) appeared in German as *Theorie der angenehmen und unangenehmen Empfindungen* (*Theory of Agreeable and Disagreeable Feelings*). Sulzer was an important philosopher of feeling and aesthetics, and he translated many of Hume's works into German. Sulzer was also the professor who proposed the theme for which Kant wrote his *Inquiry Concerning the Distinctness of the Principles of Natural Theology and Morality*.

[211] Latin for "The corruption of one is the generation of another."

woman is weaker with respect to power but also more cool-headed and therefore more capable

Among all [inclinations], sexual inclination adopts the most *ideal* embellishment

One reason why women soon show off their great understanding is that one accommodates them in the choice of subjects; thus they finally believe that there are no others.

Women have a very swift but no systematic conception; they quickly grasp something as much as is necessary to talk about it and believe that there is nothing better

[110] Reverse, opposite page 83, at 2:244

On the means to measure the dryness and humidity of the air

With women, my generosity makes me into a slave; with men, my cowardice [20:138]

The very great respect for human beings is based on chimerical merits that we ascribe to others

That *author*[212] who said that when he observes a grave man in his serious or sublime appearance, he moderates his blind reverence through the representation of his familiarity with women or with the common necessity. He would not have needed this representation. However, this appears to be why the Roman church has forbidden clerics from having wives

The free will (of someone with needs) is good for itself if it wants everything that contributes to its perfection (pleasure), and good for the whole if at the [R104] same time it desires the perfection of all. However destitute[213] the human being who has this will may be, the will is still good. Other things may be useful; other human beings may do a lot of good in a certain action through a lot of power and a small degree of will; yet the ground of willing the good is still uniquely and solely moral.

---

[212] Kant may be thinking here of Montaigne (*Essays*, Book III, ch. 2, "Of Repentance"), who says, "We much more aptly imagine an artisan upon his close-stool, or upon his wife, than a great president venerable by his port and sufficiency" (trans. Charles Cotton).

[213] *unvermögend*

[20:139]   The mathematician[214] and the philosopher: they differ in that the former requires *data* from others while the latter examines them himself. Hence the former can prove <from> any revealed religion.

The fable of the swallow that wanted to catch birds there[215]

Inserted sheet after page 84
[111] Obverse, at 2:244

The French only love laughing beauty, the *Italians* only stirring beauty.

A selfish (lustful) human being needs a person whom he can love; a generous (affectionate) one needs a person who loves him, i.e., whom he can make happy through his compliant behavior

With respect to her unhappiness in marriage, no woman will readily admit that the long fasting in her marital gratification offends her, for the woman always wants to appear to only give and not to need; if they appear to be in need of this an inequality will arise out of it because otherwise they are already in need of the man with respect to all other things.

Her refusal is a kind of beautiful untruth

[20:140]   All things, if they are only recognized as they are, have little that is agreeable in them; they elevate the sentiment only by appearing [to be] what they are not; all ideal pleasures are promoted through the art of appearing. If a woman could always appear as she liked, [R105] this skill would be very loveable; now the ill lies in that the thing comes and the illusion disappears

[112] Reverse, opposite page 85, at 2:245

He who does more than he owes is called kind; in so far as he has no obligation at all to the other, who ~~him nevertheless~~ nevertheless has nothing but obligations to him, he is merciful

A natural human being can be merciful toward no one, for he has obligations toward everyone. However, he can be merciful toward a captured enemy

---

[214] *Mathematikus*

[215] Rischmüller suggests that this is a reference to La Fontaine's fable "The Swallow and the Little Birds" (Book I, no. 8), in which a swallow warns birds of the hunger of the coming winter, but the birds pay no attention to the warning.

In our condition, when general injustice is established, the natural rights of the lowly cease; thus, the latter are only debtors; the nobles owe them nothing. Therefore, these nobles are called merciful lords. He who requires nothing from them but justice and can hold them to their [20:141] obligations does not need this subjection

A woman's modest (*civil*) behavior, if she is equal, is an obligation; female grace is kindness and must be asked for, not demanded. Therefore, noble ladies can certainly be called merciful women, but their husbands not merciful lords. If she is defiant and pompous, then she commits an offense against her obligation; if she is indifferent then she is treated[216] as equal.

On common and rustic faces

What maintains the delusion[217] of the inequality of classes is, among other things, that the lowly themselves imagine this [inequality to exist], on account of which a bourgeois woman feels the lowliness in herself, hates it and shows her disquiet, which the pride of the noble [breaks off]

<A merciful lord who has no money is an absurdity,[218] but a merciful lady without money can certainly exist>[219]

[R106] On the "He," "Her," and "She"[220]
On even and uneven numbers
On the feeling of youth[221]

On the reasons why he who pays is thanked although he does not ~~do~~ give more than he gets. Only money makes it this way. (*Pope*'s joke:[222] if there were no money.[223]) For he who has money is richer than the one who has goods because he has the choice. He who sells dispensable things

---

[216] *tractiert*   [217] *Wahne*   [218] *Unding*
[219] In the Academy Edition, this fragment comes after the paragraph below beginning "On the reasons why he who pays . . . ". See footnote 225. [20:141]
[220] The German phrase here goes "Vom Er Ihr und Sie," which one could also translate as "On the 'He,' 'Your,' and 'You.'"
[221] *Jugend Gefühl*
[222] Here we follow the Academy Edition's "*popes* Schertze" rather than Rischmüller's "Pope Schertze."
[223] The reference may be to Alexander Pope's "Of the Use of Riches" in his *Moral Essays*, letter 3 (in *The Works of Alexander Pope*, ed. Joseph Warton, London: J. F. Dove, 1822, p. 235). The essay as a whole is a satire on the value of wealth. In one part of the satire Pope specifically critiques the effects of paper money in making bribery easier, and remarks, "Oh, that such bulky bribes as all can see / Still encumbered Villainy" (lines 49–50), following this suggestion with a series of allusions to the difficulties that other nations would have bribing British officials without paper money.

(*gallantry*-grocer, *caffetier*[224]) and lives on this must be more polite than his customer, but not he who sells necessary things, especially if he always finds a customer[225]

Sheet inserted after page 86
[113] Obverse, at 2:245

[20:142] A married man acquires and deserves more esteem than a single man or an old bachelor.

A wife [is] more than a girl. A widow [is] also more than a girl. The reason is because the vocation is then completed and also the other persons appear to be in need, i.e., a girl wants to have a husband (without difficulties), but a wife never wants to be a girl. Moreover, an encounter <with> a wife[226] is looked upon equivocally, and it is the same, only the other way around, with the husband[227]

He who is supposed to teach others how to be wise with little knowledge must know a lot. It is very much to wish for that this art become further *cultivated.* Dumb and wise ignorance [breaks off]

The habit of representing the deity on the model of princes has brought forth many false concepts of *religion,*[228] for example, insults. The honor of God [breaks off]

[20:143] If I presuppose that everything in the relations between the sexes goes amiss then there are two possibilities: 1. that the girl is abstinent and debauched as a wife, 2. that the girl is debauched and abstinent as a wife. The second is more in accordance with nature, the first with the age [R107] of propriety, for ~~the wife~~ if the wife gives birth it will seem every time as if her husband is the father.

Among friends, each can talk about himself, because the other attends to it as if it concerns himself; among people and friends *of fashion,*[229] one must never talk about oneself (also not in books); unless one wants to say something of oneself that can be laughed about.

---

[224] French for "coffee purveyor."

[225] In the Academy Edition, the fragment beginning "A merciful lord" appears after this paragraph. See footnote 219.

[226] Here and throughout this paragraph, the German *Frau* (wife) could also be translated simply as "woman."

[227] Here and throughout this paragraph, the German *Mann* (husband) could also be translated simply as "man."

[228] *Religionsbegriffe*   [229] *nach der Mode*

In fashionable society I must regard each as exclusively self-loving; therefore I must praise no one who is present nor anyone absent, and thus must either joke or *slander*[230] in order for it to be *interesting*. <*Slander*[231] is based in part on the drive for equality. *Ostracism. Aristides.*[232]>

[114] Reverse, opposite page 87, at 2:245

The capacity to recognize something as a perfection in others does not   [20:144] yet bring about the consequence that we ourselves feel pleasure in it. But if we have a feeling for finding pleasure in this, then we will also be moved to desire it and to apply our powers to it. Thus, it is to be asked whether we feel pleasure immediately in the well-being of others or whether the immediate appetite actually lies in the possible exercise of our power to promote it. Both are possible, but which is real[?] Experience teaches that a human being in the simple state regards the happiness of others with indifference, but if he has promoted it, it pleases him infinitely more. The ill of others is commonly just as indifferent, but if I have caused it, it displeases just as if it has been done by another. And concerning the affectionate instincts of compassion and sympathy, we have reason to believe that they are merely great strivings to mitigate the ills of others, taken from the self-approval of the soul, which bring about these sentiments.

We take pleasure in certain perfections of ours, but much more if we ourselves are the cause. Most of all if we are the freely acting cause.

---

[230] *medisieren*   [231] *Medisance*

[232] Ostracism was the Greek law whereby citizens voted to ban a fellow citizen from Athens for ten years. It was first enforced in 487 BC. Introduced by Cleisthenes, the law proved absolute for Aristides (540–c. 467), who in 483 was banned for opposing Themistocles' plan to turn Athens into a great naval power. As Plutarch explains,

> Themistocles spread a rumor amongst the people that, by determining all matters privately, [Aristides] had destroyed the courts of judicature and was secretly making way for a monarchy in his own person . . . Moreover the spirit of the people, now grown high, and confident with their late victory, naturally entertained feelings of dislike to all of more than common fame and reputation. Coming together, therefore, from all parts into the city, they banished Aristides by ostracism, giving their jealousy of his reputation the name of fear of tyranny. For ostracism was not the punishment of any criminal act, but was speciously said to be the mere depression and humiliation of excessive greatness and power; and was in fact a gentle relief and mitigation of envious feeling, which was thus allowed to vent itself in inflicting no intolerable injury, only a ten years' banishment. (*Plutarch's Lives*, vol. I, pp. 441–42)

See too Bayle's entry on Aristides in *Dictionary Historical and Critical of Mr. Peter Bayle*, pp. 459–60.

[20:145] To subordinate everything to the free faculty of choice is the greatest perfection. And the perfection of the free [R108] faculty of choice as a cause of possibility is far greater than all other causes of the good even if they would bring about the actuality [of the good]

[115] Page 88
Upper margin, at 2:246

With the French, the thought ~~is sooner ready than the~~ <does not mature by means of> reasons, indeed it does not await their development and examination. The German seeks reasons for all thoughts and improves; [he] is patient

Under line 17, at 2:246

[20:146] The French demand almost as much leniency as women. *Maupertuis*[233]

Inserted sheet after page 88
[116] Obverse, at 2:246

<Habitu>
actionis ex voluntate singulari est solipsismus Moralis
—   —   communi — justicia   —[234]

The feeling of pleasure and displeasure concerns either that with respect to which we are passive or else ourselves as an active *principium*[235] of good and evil through freedom. The latter is moral feeling. Past physical evil ~~offends~~ delights us, but [past] moral evil grieves us, and the kind of joy we take in the good that befalls us is entirely different from that we take in what we do.

We have little feeling for whether the condition of another is evil or good except in so far as we feel capable of alleviating the former [or] promoting the latter. Sympathy is an instinct that works only on rare and very important occasions; its other effects are artificial.

---

[233] Pierre Moreau de Maupertuis (1698–1759), French physician and mathematician who in 1741 was invited by Frederick the Great to become a member of the Academy of the Sciences in Berlin, and who served as president of that academy from 1745 to 1753.
[234] Latin for "<Habit> The attitude of an action from a single will is moral solipsism; [the attitude of an action from the] common [will is moral] justice."
[235] Latin for "principle."

[R109] Since the greatest inner perfection and the perfection that arises from it consist in the subordination of all of the capacities and receptivities to the free faculty of choice, the feeling for the *Bonität*[236] of the free faculty of choice must be immediately much different from and also greater than all of the good consequences that thereby can be *brought about*.[237]

This faculty of choice contains ~~either~~ the merely individual will as well as the general will, or the human being considers himself at the same time in *consensu*[238] with the general will.

That which is necessary through the general will is an obligation, what [breaks off]

[117] Reverse, opposite page 89, at 2:246

Since the human being of nature needs little – and the more he needs (*egenus*[239]) the more miserable he is – the human being is perfect in so far as he can do without; but in so far as he still has a lot of power left to promote the needs and happiness of others ~~he is~~ he has a feeling for a will that is beneficent beyond itself. Since the faculty of choice, in so far as it is also useful to the acting subject, is physically necessary with regard to bare necessity, it has no immediate *goodness*. Hence the moral *goodness* of action is unselfish.

In the state of nature, one cannot be selfish, but also not for the common good; friendships however are possible in the same [state]

Male adolescence[240] is more open to friendship because it is more unselfish, more affectionate, more <benevolent>, and more honest than the later [age]

On happiness in all human ages. Youthful flightiness ~~prevents~~ and restlessness prevent much pleasure. The old one has fewer lively inclinations, but he satisfies the calm ones. Yet we must not interchange the positions of life [20:147]

[R110] One already has biased attitudes towards a nation that has the same language. Prussian, Livonians.[241] Likewise the total diversity of languages causes *national* hatred. But, if the speech of the mob in one

---

[236] A Germanized version of the Latin for "goodness." [237] *actuiert*
[238] Latin for "agreement." [239] Latin for "needy." [240] *Jünglingsalter*
[241] Livonia, a region now split between Estonia and Latvia, was part of the Russian empire in the eighteenth century. See Voltaire's *History of Charles XII*.

language comes close to the speech of the rulers in the other then it causes contempt. But all of this at a distance.

Inserted sheet after page 90
[118] Obverse, at 2:247

Sensus internus voluptatis et taedii est prior appetitione et aversatione quia receptivitas gaudendi aut aversandi subjecto inest quanquam adhuc objecti hujus sensus ignarus sit ut ignoti nulla est cupido. Appetitio vel est primitiva vel derivativa prior est varia etiam qua qualitatem. Sensus internus si allegatur ut principium probandi logicum legis moralis est qualitas occulta si ut facultas animae cuius ratio ignoratur est phaenomenon[242]

[20:148]   A *pactum*[243] is not possible between a *domino*[244] and a *mancipio*.[245] God entered into an alliance with humans because they do not have a sufficient *practical* concept of his *dominio*,[246] and so that they are led by the *analogy* with the *pacto* of men, and not to abhor the authoritative strictness.

A virtuous action is at all times a morally good action that occurs or at least has occurred reluctantly

Omnis bonitas conditionalis actionis est vel sub conditione possibili (uti problemata) vel actuali (uti regulae prudentiae quilibet vult sanus esse) sed in bonitate mediata vel conditionali τ velle absolute non est bonum nisi adsint vires et circumstantiae temporis loci. Et in tantum quatenus voluntas est efficiens est bonum sed poterit haec bonitas etiam qua voluntatem solam spectari. si desint vires tamen est laudanda voluntas in magnis voluisse sat est et perfectio haec absoluta quatenus utrum aliquid inde actuatur nec ne est indeterminatum dicitur moralis[247]

---

[242] Latin for "The inner sense of pleasure and displeasure precedes desire and aversion, since the receptivity to the enjoyment and aversion lies in the subject, even if it, the subject, does not have any knowledge of the object of this sense, as there cannot be a desire for something unknown. Desire is either original or derived; the former also varies with respect to quality. The inner sense, if it is held to be a logical principle for the judgment of the moral law, is an occult quality; if it is a faculty of the soul whose ground is unknown, then it is a phenomenon."

[243] Latin for "contract."   [244] Latin for "lord."

[245] Latin for "slave."   [246] Latin for "lordship."

[247] Latin for "All conditional goodness of an action depends on either a possible condition (as in problems) or on an actual one (as in the rules of prudence, [e.g.] everyone wants to be reasonable), but in mediate or conditional goodness the absolute will is not good if the powers and circumstances of time and place are lacking. And insofar as the will is effective it is good, but one can also consider this goodness with respect to the will alone; even if the powers should be

[119] Reverse, opposite page 91, at 2:247

<The woman can abstain much more with regard to pleasures [and] needs, but not with regard to vanity>

[R111] The equilibrium of sentiments is the soul at peace. This smooth   [20:149]
surface is only disturbed through passions. It is a main ground of happiness not only to feel agreeable, but also to be conscious of this in one's entire condition, which is hindered <by> strong sentiment

The natural human being is spared this disquiet through lack of feeling
*Contentment with respect to needs is called simplicity. In so far as agreeable things themselves are counted among necessities it is partly beautiful and partly noble simplicity.

Where dispensability appears with respect to necessities, combined with the effort to produce things that are agreeable, that is contrived; with respect to the beautiful [it is] ornamented [and] decorated; with respect to the sublime [it is] magnificent [and] grandiose.

Taste, indeed, does not concern needs, but it must not prevent them, as in the case of luxuriousness.

Regularity accords with simplicity, for if ~~the one~~ the rule did not determine the kind of connections, it would be so contingent and indeterminate that it would also contradict the needs. For example, *symmetry.* Following in pairs. Thus, among that which is interconnected, it serves to assign to each thing its purpose.

<What is agreeable can greatly oppose necessities, but when they agree with them, then there is beautiful simplicity. The needs of human beings are closely related to the ease of thinking and representing something. From this comes the agreeableness of order. *Symmetry.*>

Inserted sheet after page 92
[120] Obverse, at 2:248

<*in Deo simul est subjectiva*>[248]

    Bonitas actionis liberae objectiva vel quod idem est necessitas objectiva est [R112] *vel conditionalis vel categorica prior est bonitas actionis tanquam*

---

lacking, the will is still praiseworthy. With regard to great deeds, it suffices to have willed them. And this absolute perfection, whether something is effected by it or not, is called moral."

[248] Latin for "In God it is at the same time subjective."

[20:150]   *medii posterior tanquam finis illa igitur mediata haec immediata illa continet*
necessitatem practicam problematicam haec pp[249]

Actio libera conditionalis bona non est ideo categorie necessaria. e.g. liber-
alitas mea aliis egenis est utilis ergo oportet esse liberalem Minime. Sed si quis
vult esse aliis utilis esto liberalis. Si autem actio ~~utili~~ liberalitatis ingenuae non
solum aliis sed et in se bona sit tum est obligatio.[250]

De sensu morali et possibilitate oppositi[251]

Adstrinxit quidem providentia sensum moralem publicae ut universali util-
itati ut et privato commodo ita tantum ~~quemad modum~~ ut arbitrii bonitas non
judicetur tantum valere quantum valet[252]

When I say that this action will bring me more honor than the other, I
mean to say that I appeal to the universal judgment that the judgment I
pass on my own action is grounded.

[20:151]   Controversies in world-wisdom[253] have the benefit that they promote
the freedom of understanding and arouse mistrust towards the doctrine[254]
itself, which was supposed to be constructed upon the ruins of another.
In refuting, one is still so happy [breaks off]

In most languages simplicity and stupidity mean almost the same. That
is because a human being of simplicity is easily betrayed by a human being
of artifice whom he considers to be as honest as himself

[121] Reverse, opposite page 93, at 2:248

There is always so much talk about virtue. But one must eliminate injustice before one can be virtuous. One must suppress leisureliness,[255] opulence, and everything that oppresses others while elevating me, so that I

[20:150]
[249] Latin for "The goodness of a free action is objective, or what is the same, the objective necessity
is either conditional or categorical. The former is goodness of an action as means, the latter as
an end; hence the former is mediated, the latter is unmediated; the former contains a practical,
problematic necessity, the latter, etc."
[250] Latin for "A free action that is conditionally good is not for that reason a categorical necessity,
e.g., my liberality to another person who is destitute is useful, and therefore one ought to be
liberal. By no means [does this follow]. But if someone wants to be useful to another, he will have
to be liberal. If, however, an action of genuine liberality is not only good for another but good in
itself, then it is an obligation."
[251] Latin for "On the moral sense and the possibility of its opposite."
[252] Latin for "Indeed providence has so connected moral sense to public and universal utility as well
as to private advantage that the goodness of the free will is not esteemed as highly as it is actually
worth."
[253] *Weltweisheit*   [254] *Lehrbegriff*   [255] *Gemächlichkeiten*

am not one of all those who oppress their own kind. All virtue is impossible without this decision.

All virtue is grounded on ideal feeling. Hence, in the state of opulence, no virtue is found in a human being who has merely corporeal feeling; in the state of nature, however, simplicity in straightforward sentiments and simplicity in mores[256] subsist together quite well

[R113] Where the lengths of days <throughout the year> are more   [20:152] equal, one ~~serves~~ is more orderly; thus in France and England more than in Petersburg. For, since here, on a bright day in summer, one at best can wake up late, one does so also in winter.

It is funny that opulence now makes the [upper] ranks poor, especially the princes

The misery of human beings is not to be bewailed, but to be laughed at: *Democritus*[257]

Swift's linen weaver, etc.[258]

Among all vanities the most common is that one wants to appear to be happy; hence one ~~admit~~ pretends that one does not want to do something good (for example, marrying, serving the commonwealth) rather than that one cannot do it; because he who does without that something or refrains from it is merely happy according to his own will in so far as he has sufficient capacity to satisfy his desires

Inserted sheet after page 94
[122] Obverse, at 2:249

We can see other worlds in the distance, but gravity forces us to remain   [20:153] on the earth; we still can see other perfections of the spirits above us, but our nature forces us to remain human beings.

---

[256] *Sitten*
[257] See too Kant's lectures on anthropology, where Kant explains, "We would rather be an object of hatred than of ridicule. It is better to be a Heraclitus than a Democritus" (*Anthropologie Phillipi 1772–3*, p. 14; Academy Edition vol. 25). In Lucian's *Philosophies for Sale*, the philosophers Democritus and Heraclitus are both put up for sale. As one "buyer" puts it, "My god! What a contrast! This one [Democritus] won't stop laughing, and the other one looks as if he's in mourning" (in *Selected Satires of Lucian*, ed. Lionel Casson, New York: Norton Library, 1968, p. 321; see too Seneca, *De Ira* 10.2.5). For an analysis of the early modern reception of the image of Democritus as "laughing philosopher," see Christoph Luthy, "The Fourfold Democritus on the Stage of Early Modern Science," *Isis* 91(2000): 443–79, especially pp. 455–61.
[258] Jonathan Swift (1667–1745), the British satirist most famous for *Gulliver's Travels*. Here Kant refers to Swift's work *Epilogue to a Play for the Benefit of the Weavers in Ireland*.

Because in society all mine and thine depends on *pacta*,[259] yet these [depend] on keeping one's word, love of truth is the *foundation*[260] of all social virtue, and lying is the main vice against others next to robbery, murder and *stuproviolatio*[261]

If human beings subordinate *morality* to religion (which is also only possible and necessary in the case of the oppressed rabble) they thereby become hostile, hypocritical, [and] slanderous; but if they subordinate religion to *morality*, then they are kind, benevolent, and just

[R114] <All choice must concern future taste>

True marriage in its perfection, poeticized marriage in its perfection. Perfect happiness, peace

The human being in his perfection is not in the state of ~~simplicity, and likewise not in~~ sufficiency, nor in the state of opulence, but in the return from the latter state to the former. Remarkable character of human nature. This most perfect state rests on the tip of a hair; the state of ~~nature can~~ simple and original nature does not last long; the state of renewed nature is more lasting, but never as innocent.

very social women do not blush anymore, and if they are untrue [they blush] even less than men; the *étourdi*[262] who does not blush

A great proof of opulence is that now entire states are becoming constantly poorer. National debt. Standing armies

[20:154]   All amusements intoxicate, i.e., prevent one from not feeling the entire sum of happiness[263]

[123] Reverse, opposite 95, at 2:249

It is to be asked whether all of morality could not be deduced through the soul at peace – [which is] indeed to be understood with respect to the natural human being. Delightful things and excesses are opposed to peace. The sexual inclination finds its peace only in marriage. To offend

---

[259] Latin for "contracts."   [260] *Fundament*
[261] Latin for "rape."   [262] French for "scatterbrain."
[263] We assume that Kant actually meant to say here that all amusements prevent one from feeling the entire sum of happiness instead of saying that they prevent one from not feeling this sum.

others unsettles oneself. *Affects* in general unsettle. It is horrible that through this *morality* no other human being benefits*[264]

Religion determines the way of life of the Jews. For since they are always concerned about being forced to [adapt to] another, they detest every way of life in which they would not have enough freedom to avoid it. Therefore, they do not cultivate the field

* <Except that this is already a great virtue[:] to do no evil.>

In the case of this soul at peace, friendship is no *enthusiasm*, sympathy [is] no soft-heartedness, gentleness not *ceremony*. Desire, no longing. The feeling soul at peace is therefore not inactive according to the body or the understanding, but only according to desires and pleasures

[R115] In flourishing countries, the innkeepers and workers are polite and try to serve, but the customers and guests are commanding, and there is, so to speak, more industry than money, i.e., the money itself has an inner *principium*[265] of its increase. In poor countries, there is still more money than industry.   [20:155]

In rich countries, the merchants (*en detail*[266]) are cold-minded and ~~it is~~ the customer is fair without haggling, because there are just as many wares as money; in poor [countries], there are more wares than money, and the merchants are groveling.

[124] Page 95
Lower margin

In all nations, the habit of drinking among men has ceased as soon as social gatherings were adorned with women. The Greeks drank; the old Germans [and] Prussians. The English still drink because the women are more separated. It would still be good in the case of special women. Our way of life is nowadays *Arcadian*, as it were;[267] one always socializes, and love and play entertain them. But black sorrow, discord, and tedium rule at home

---

[264] In the original German text this sentence is ambiguous. That is, the phrase "kein andrer Mensch einen Nutzen hat" could also be translated as "no other human being has a use."

[265] Latin for "principle."   [266] French for "in detail."   [267] See footnote 81 above.

Inserted sheet after page 96
[125] Obverse, at 2:250

Why an old woman is an object of disgust for both sexes except when she is very cleanly and not a *coquette.*

Necessitas actionum <objectiva (bonitatis)> vel est conditionalis (sub conditione alicujus boni appetiti) vel categorica prior est problematica ~~[unreadable word]~~ *et si appetiones quae spectantur tanquam conditiones necessariae actionis non solum ut possibiles sed ut actuales spectantur est necessitas prudentiae. Ad [R116] eam cognoscendam necesse erit omnes dignoscere animi humani appetiones et instinctus ut fieri possit. computatio quid sit pro inclinatione subjecti melius. et hoc quidem non solum pro praesenti sed et futuro statu. Necessitas categorica actionis tanti non constat sed poscit solum applicationem facti ad sensum moralem*[268]

[20:156]   *Poterit equidem in quibusdam vitae conditionibus mendacium esse admodum utile ideoque per regulam prudentiae mentiendum sed ad hoc requiritur vasta astutia et sagacitas consectaria si moraliter consideratur per simplicitatem moralem illico cognoscitur quod factu opus sit*[269]

Quantumvis ~~modo~~ *falsiloquium aliis aliquando admodum sit utile tamen erit mendacium nisi ad illud incumbat obligation stricta hinc videre est* ~~falsi~~ *veracitatem non a Philantropia sed a sensu juris quo fas ac nefas distinguimus pendere. Hic sensus autem originem ducit a mentis humanae natura per quam* ~~quo se bonum~~ *quid sit bonum categorice (no utile) judicat non ex privato commodo <nec ex alieno> sed eandem actionem ponendo in aliis si oritur* ~~contradictio~~ *oppositio et contrarietas displicet si harmonia et consensus placet. Hinc facultas stationum moralium ut medium heuristicum. Sumus enim a natura sociabiles et quod improbamus in aliis in nobis probare sincera mente*

---

[268] Latin for "The necessity of actions <their objective (goodness)> is either conditional (under the condition of some desired good) or categorical. The former is problematic and, if the desires that are seen as necessary conditions of actions are seen as not only possible but actual, this is a necessity of prudence. In order to know this, it will be necessary to know all of the drives and instincts of the human soul so that a calculation may be made about what is better for the inclination of the subject. And this indeed not only for the present, but also for the future state. The categorical necessity of an action does not depend on so much; rather, it requires only the application of the facts to moral feeling."

[20:156]   [269] Latin for "In certain situations in life a lie can be exceedingly useful, and thus lying will be in accordance with the rule of prudence, but for this, extensive astuteness and the shrewdness that follows from it is required. If one considers it morally, on the basis of moral simplicity, it will be immediately known what one should do."

non possumus. Est enim sensus communis veri et falsi non nisi ratio humana generatim tanquam criterium veri et falsi et sensus boni vel mali communis criterium illius. Capita sibi opposita certitudinem logicam corda moralem tollerent.[270]

Bonitas voluntatis ~~[unreadable word]~~ *ab effectibus et earum immediata*   [20:157]
voluptate repetita est vel privatae vel publicae utilitatis et prior rationem habet in indigentia posterior in potentia boni prior propriae utilitatis posterior communis utilitatis instinctus ambo simplicitati naturali conformes. Sed voluntatis tanquam principii liberi bonitas non quatenus proficiscuntur illae utilitates inde sed quatenus in se sunt possibiles cognoscitur. Et ~~non~~ *aliorum felicitas pro ratione* [breaks off][271]

[126] Reverse, opposite page 97, at 2:250

Obligation <the natural one towards human beings> has a certain measure; the duty of love has none. The former consists in this that nothing happens anymore other than what I myself have let another want, and that I give him only what is his; [R117] consequently, everything, after such an action, is equal. (Sympathy is excepted from this.)

If I promise him something, then I rob him of something, for I have created a hope that I do not fulfill. If he is in hunger and I do not help him, then I have violated no obligation. But if I gladly desired to receive

---

[270] Latin for "As much as false testimony might sometimes be useful to others, it is still a lie if no strict obligation necessitates it. From this, one can see truthfulness does not depend on philanthropy, but on the sense of justice, through which we learn to distinguish what is permitted from what is forbidden. This sense, however, has its origin in the nature of the human mind, through which one judges what is ~~in itself good~~ categorically good (not useful), not according to private benefit or benefit to others, but through supposing the same action in others; if a contradiction and contrast then arises, it displeases; if harmony and unison arise, they please. Hence the ability to put oneself in the place of others [functions] as a heuristic means. Indeed we are by nature social and could not sincerely approve in ourselves of what we criticize in others. The common sense of true and false is indeed nothing other than human reason taken generally as the criterion of true and false, and the common sense of good and evil is the criterion of the latter. Opposing minds would eliminate logical certainty, opposing hearts, moral certainty."

[271] Latin for "The goodness of the will ~~[unreadable word]~~ is derived from the effects of private or   [20:157]
public use and from the immediate pleasure in them, and the former has its basis in need, the latter in the power for the good; the former is related to one's own utility, the latter to general utility; both feelings conform to natural simplicity. But the goodness of the will as a free principle is recognized not insofar as such forms of utility arise from it, but insofar as they are possible in themselves. And ~~not~~ the happiness of others for the reason" [breaks off].

[20:158] from others in case that I should be hungry myself – even on the *condition* of paying it back – then it would be an obligation to satisfy [them]. ~~I~~ A robber certainly wishes that he may be *pardoned*, but knows well that he would not pardon if he were the judge. The judge punishes, although he knows that if he were the *delinquent*[272] he would not want to be punished, but ~~hinder~~ with punishment it is different. The deprivation of life does not happen through the judge, but through the criminal, because of his misdeed. No one, if he is in need, can imagine that if he were a rich man, he would help every needy person

In primo hominis statu ~~obligatio~~ <obedientia> ipsius erat tanquam mancipii deinde tanquam subditi post tanquam filii et facultas ~~legislatori~~ legislatoria tanquam domini, principis, patris[273]

Obligans tanquam dominus <despota> mancipium causas impulsivas non nisi poenas statuit obligans princeps subditum (legitimum) praemia et poenas obligans pater tanquam filium non nisi amorem et praemia. Ratio obligandi prior est ~~s~~ servitium naturale et debitum secunda rationes morales pacti continet tertium omnia priora ac internam simul moralitatem complectitur[274]

Christ sought to bring human beings to simple sufficiency through *religion*, [that is], in that he presented to them the glory of heaven; his speeches could only produce perverse concepts among the Jews, because the latter ~~for no other price~~ all along founded[275] their religion only on empty concepts, and constructed the latter [their religion] on no other *condition* than the reestablishment of their kingdom[276]

All truthfulness presupposes an idea of equality; hence the Jews, who in their opinion have no duty at all towards others, lie and deceive without having any pangs of conscience. *haereticis non est fides*[277]

[R118]

---

[272] In the Academy Edition this term is not italicized.

[273] Latin for "In the first state of the human being, his ~~obligation~~ obedience was that of a slave, then that of a subject, hereafter that of a son; the ~~law-giving~~ law-giving power was that of a master, of a prince, of a father."

[274] Latin for "Whoever put slaves under obligation to himself as a master (despot), set only punishments as incentives; the prince who put his (legitimate) subject under obligation set rewards and punishments [as incentives]; the father who put his son under obligation set only love and rewards [as incentives]. The ground of obligation is natural servitude and debt in the first case; the second contains the moral grounds of a contract; the third contains all of the previous and, at the same time, an inner morality."

[275] *setzen*   [276] *Reich*   [277] Latin for "In heretics there is no faith."

[127] Page 98
Upper margin, at 2:250

Honor cannot be a basic drive; otherwise, one who engages in drinking and fighting (*dueling*), while they are in fashion, would be justified, because he concerns himself with the opinion of others[278]

Inserted sheet after page 98
[128] Obverse, at 2:250

Women are by nature much more domestic than men because they have [20:159] children to nurse. Our *gallant* women who do not have any [children] and our maidens who know that they will never nurse are not domestic because it is not necessary. Their beautiful disposition for tidy housekeeping and for the care of a sick person, and likewise for the thrifty use of acquisitions [breaks off]

Male dignity and female grace get lost in society. *Madame Montagu*[279]

Authors[280] seem to be thorough if they dispense with all wit, just as coarse people seem to be honest

Just as one deceives oneself through the appearance of wealth, so a woman at last believes herself actually to have those virtues to the appearance of which she has devoted herself at the beginning.

~~*Duels* orig~~[281]

It takes more to be good as a common human being than to be a good prince. If he is just not exceptionally evil, then he is already good for that purpose.

No matter how much understanding he has, the young man full of [20:160] sentiment will easily be persuaded by the female illusion and wants to be deceived; he is, in all seriousness, submissive and meek. The ~~wan~~ experienced and smart wanton has long ago understood the mirage of

---

[278] In the Academy Edition, this sentence comes on 20:160, after the paragraph beginning "*Epicurus* seems to me . . . " See footnote 284.

[279] Mary Wortley Montagu (1689–1762). At the age of 20 she published translations from Greek and wooed Alexander Pope, who wrote numerous poems and epigrams in her honor. In 1711 she married Pope and accompanied him, first to Turkey and then throughout Asia and Africa. Between 1716 and 1718 Montagu wrote elegant accounts of her travels, which circulated among her friends and were published in 1763 as *Letters of the Right Honourable Lady M—y W—y M—e: Written, during her Travels in Europe, Asia, and Africa, to Persons of Distinction, Men of Letters, Etc. in different parts of Europe*. Her writings appeared in German in 1764.

[280] *Verfasser*   [281] ~~*Duelle Urspr*~~

illusion; he therefore is bold, unabashed, and because he relieves the other sex from the coercion of being careful about decency he is agreeable to it.

[R119] *Duels* have their true origin in the time of *gallantry* from the inclinations of women, for when it comes to general courtship, the beauty chooses the most hearty one[282] and triumphs over her rivals through this, that her lover is horrible to theirs. When it comes to insults that befall her, he cannot sustain himself in her reckoning other than through strong-heartedness.[283]

Who would want to take away propriety from women

Epicurus seems to me to be different from *Zeno* in that the former conceived of the virtuous soul at peace to be victorious after having overcome moral hindrances, while the latter [conceived of the soul to be victorious] in fighting and in practice. *Antisthenes* did not have such a high idea; he wanted that one should only reflect on vain ostentation and false happiness and choose to be a simple man rather than a great one[284,285]

[129] Reverse, opposite page 95, at 2:251

Quatenus meae voluntati res modificabilis paret mea est sed possum meam voluntatem alteri veluti devincire[286]

Obligation is communal selfishness *in aequilibrio*[287]

[20:161] *officium est vel beneplaciti* ~~discretionary~~ *vel debiti actiones priores sunt moraliter spontaneae posteriores moraliter coactae. (haec differt a coactione politica) voluntas est vel propria hominis vel communis hominum.*[288]

---

[282] *den Herzhaftesten*   [283] *Herzhaftigkeit*

[284] In the Academy Edition, the sentence beginning "Honor cannot be a basic drive..." comes here. See footnote 278.

[285] Epicurus (341–271 BC), Greek philosopher. Epicurus famously identified pleasure and the absence of pain as the highest good in life. For a comparison of Epicurus to Zeno, see Cicero, *Tusculan Disputations* III, 28. For Antisthenes, see footnote 35 above.

[286] Latin for "An object is mine insofar as it is subject to be modified according to my will, but I can, so to speak, transfer my will to another."

[287] Latin for "in equilibrium."

[288] Latin for "Duty is either chosen ~~discretionary~~ or imposed. The former actions are morally spontaneous, the latter are morally coerced. (This differs from political coercion.) The will is either the particular will of a human being or the general will of humankind."

~~*Obigatio ex communi hominum*~~[289]
(necessarium aliquod est ex voluntate bona hominis propria vel communi)[290]
<fas nefas>[291]

~~*Voluntas*~~ *Actio spectata secundum voluntatem hominum communem* ~~est~~
*si sibimet ipsi contradicat est externe moraliter impossibilis (illibitum) fac
me alterius* ~~domin~~ *frumentum occupatum ire tam si spetco hominem neminem*
[R120] *sub ea conditione ut sibi ipsi eripiatur quod acquisit acquirere velle quod
alterius est idem secundum privatum volo et secundum publicum aversor.*[292]

*Quatenus enim aliquid a voluntate alicujus plenarie pendet eatenus impos-
sibile est ut sibi ipsi contradicat (objective). Contradiceret autem voluntas
divina sibimet ipsi si vellet homines esse quorum voluntas opposita esset voluntati ipsius. Contradiceret hominum voluntas sibimet ipsi si vellent quod ex
voluntate communi abhorrerent.*[293]

Es autem voluntas communis is statu collisionis praegnantior propria[294]

Actionis <~~hypothetica~~> necessitas <conditionalis> ut medii ad finem pos-   [20:162]
sibilem est **problematica** *ad finem actualem est necessitas <categorica>*
prudentiae *necessitas categorica es* **moralis.**[295]

It belongs to *morality* to make *stationes;*[296] first, in the judgment of
others about the deed (from this, if it becomes an instinct, ambition arises
and goes further than the means for determining legitimacy); secondly,
in ~~judgment~~ the sentiment of others, so that one feels their distress or
their happiness (hence moral *sympathy* arises as an instinct)

---

[289] Latin for ~~"the obligation from that which is common to [all] human beings".~~
[290] Latin for "(Anything necessary arises from the specific good will of a human being or from the general [will].)"
[291] Latin for "<Right [and] wrong.>"
[292] Latin for "An action that contradicts itself, when considered from the perspective of the general will of human beings, is externally morally impossible (forbidden). Suppose I were about to take the fruits of another. If I then see that, under the condition that what one acquires will soon be snatched away, nobody wants to acquire anything, then I will desire another's goods from the private point of view while rejecting them from the public one."
[293] Latin for "In so far as something depends entirely on the will of a subject, it is impossible that it [the will of a subject] contradicts itself (objectively). The divine will, however, would contradict itself if it willed there to be human beings whose will was opposed to its own will. The will of human beings would contradict itself if they willed something that they would abhor according to their general will."
[294] Latin for "In the case of a collision, however, the universal will is weightier than the individual one."
[295] Latin for "The <~~hypothetical~~> <conditional> necessity of an action as a means to a possible end is **problematic**, [as a means] to an actual end it is the <categorical> necessity of **prudence**, the categorical necessity is **moral**."
[296] Latin for "stations."

The origin of the love of honor regarding the beauty of actions thus lies in a badly understood *medio*[297] of *directing* one's own *morality*, which falsely becomes an end

The origin of the love of honor regarding the judgment of physical qualities lies in the means to freedom, preservation of oneself and [one's own] kind.

[130] Page 99, lower margin, at 2:251

To compare oneself to others is a means, yet to make comparative greatness or worth into one's intention is perverse and the origin of envy

[R121] Bravery is only a means; the savage values it as an end.

Eventually, one happily can place honor in drinking and in vices

[131] Page 100, upper margin, at 2:251

Man and woman do not have the same *sentiment* and also should not have it, but just from this arises the unity, not of the *identity*, but of the *subordination* of inclinations, since each feels that the other is necessary to him for the greatest perfection. Friendship presupposes *sentiments* that agree[298]

Inserted sheet, after page 100
[132] Obverse, at 2:251

In the case of a great corruption of mores, maidens keep themselves chaste and women live in excess, because the latter then only act against obligation, while the former act against propriety

<It is already an honor not to be despised.>

[20:163] ~~The drive to~~ I need things or also human beings. Honor is either mediate or immediate. In the first case, it is a drive of enjoyment; in the second, of delusion. In the first case, the ~~imaginary~~ needs are either true or imaginary, to which honor is a means, and the first [is] either in the natural or ~~unnat~~ the degenerate state. Needs for things in the natural state <to procure them for oneself> do not require honor (because everyone can

---

[297] Latin for "means" or "way."

[298] In the Academy Edition, this paragraph appears after the paragraph beginning "I need things . . ." at 20:163. See footnote 300.

procure them for himself); but in order to preserve them and oneself, they demand that others have an opinion of our equality, so that our freedom does not suffer, since we can seek our needs as we please. Man's natural need of **acquisition** is a woman. For this, he needs the opinion not of superiority over but of equality with other men, and he also easily acquires this. In both cases, however, the human being will raise the drive of real honor[299] above equality, partly [so] that freedom [should] be more secure, partly because he begins to prefer one woman over another, so that she will also prefer him. Finally, in the state of ~~opulence~~ <inequality>, the [R122] drive of honor will either be that of true needs or of artificial ones. In Sparta, it was ~~such a~~ a true one because by means of it one remained free, but in an opulent country, where freedom is lost, it becomes all the more necessary. At the same time, the honor of delusion arises primarily with respect to sex, to which, in the end, the honor that is a means of enjoyment gets sacrificed[300]

[20:164]

[133] Reverse, opposite page 101, at 2:252

~~Voluntary~~ Slavery is either that of force or that of blindness. The latter is based either on the dependence on things (opulence) or on the delusion of other human beings (vanity). The latter is more incongruous and also harder than the former because things are much more in my own power than the opinions of others, and it is also more despicable

The loss of freedom is grounded either on dependence or on subservience. In the first case, one is ruled by means of one's inclination (either to things or to human beings, as in love and friendship, [and] parental love) or contrary to one's inclinations. The former is a consequence of weak opulence, the latter, however, of fearful cowardice and is a consequence of the first

[20:165]

The drive of honor with respect to [one's] sex also becomes pure delusion in the end. And honor, which is supposed to promote self-preservation, promotes this pure delusion, and vanity is a cause of the lack of marriage.[301]

---

[299] *Trieb der realen Ehre*

[300] In the Academy Edition, the paragraph beginning "Man and woman do not have the same *sentiment* . . ." (R121) appears here. See footnote 298.

[301] The German "Ehelosigkeit" translates into "lack of marriage," but Kant may have meant to write "Ehrlosigkeit," which translates into "lack of honor."

With a woman, the drive of honor is directed ~~merely~~ solely at sexual union, and by means of the same at needs, because she must be sought; since this is not necessary with men, she will only be attracted by business, and thus can sooner resolve[302] to lack honor

That which very much proves the *fantastical nature* of love is that one loves the beloved object more in its absence than in its presence; with friendship, it is different.

[R123]

[134] Page 102
Upper margin

The drive of honor is grounded on the drive for equality and the drive for unity. Two powers that move the animal world, as it were. The instinct for unity is either unity in judgments and thoughts or also in inclinations. The former brings about logical perfection, the latter moral one.

Left margin, at 2:252

The only naturally necessary good of a human being in relation to the will of others is equality (freedom) and, with respect to the whole, unity. Analogy: Repulsion, through which the body fills its own space just as everyone [fills] his own. Attraction, through which all parts combine into one.

[20:166]   The truth of a perfection consists in the magnitude of the pleasure that is not exclusive with regard to itself and with regard to other greater ones. If falsity could be durable and more pleasurable than truth, then the pleasure from this deception would be a true pleasure, though a false cognition

Lower margin, at 2:252

The natural instincts of active benevolence towards others consist in love towards the [other] sex and towards children. That towards other human beings merely concerns equality and unity

---

[302] *resolvieren*

There is unity in the *sovereign* state but not equality; if the latter is combined with unity ~~of uni~~, then it constitutes the perfect *republic*

Inserted sheet at page 102
[135] Obverse, at 2:252

[R124] The drive to evaluate oneself merely comparatively, with respect to one's worth as well as with respect to one's welfare, is far more widespread than the drive for honor, and contains the latter within itself. It does not lie in nature and is an indirect result of the use of the means to know one's own state better through the comparison with others. Ambition, which is a spur of science, arises from the comparison of our judgment with the judgment of others; thus as a means [ambition] presupposes esteem for the judgment of others

The Indians are remarkably calm and not violent
The South Americans --------- indifferent and phlegmatic
The Negroes ---------- very careless and vain
The Europeans --------- lively and hot-tempered

The *affects* of the Indians are nevertheless still stronger than [those] of the Europeans
    A reason why Montesquieu was able to say so many excellent things is that he presupposed that those who introduced customs or gave laws   [20:167] would have had a reasonable ground in each case[303]
    The main intention of Rousseau is that education be free and also make a free human being
    We must honor common understanding and common taste

---

[303] Charles de Montesquieu (1689–1755), whose work *The Spirit of Laws* was written in 1748. In the preface to that work, Montesquieu explains,
> I began by examining men, and I believed that, amidst the infinite diversity of laws and mores, they were not led by their fancies alone.
>
> I have set down the principles, and I have seen particular cases conform to them as if by themselves, the histories of all nations being but their consequences, and each particular law connecting with another law or dependent on a more general one . . .
>
> I did not draw my principles from my prejudices but from the nature of things . . . Each nation will here find the reasons for its maxims . . . (Montesquieu, *The Spirit of the Laws*, ed. Anne Cohler et al., Cambridge University Press, 1989, p. xliii)

A woman does not like to give away, in contrast, she takes. No one knows contentment; everyone asserts delightfulness in its place. <Golden rain in the lap of Danae. Jupiter a bull. In *Amphitryon*, Alcmene was honest>[304]

How education helps public regulation[305] is to be seen from the fact that the former makes many goods, e.g., silk [and] gold, etc., entirely dispensable, whereas the latter prohibits in vain because it only offends thereby

[R125] A woman loves less affectionately than a man or otherwise she would not claim dominance over him and ~~demand~~ obviously prefer herself to him. She is also aware that she tolerates more affection; if the man does not have this refined sentiment, he is called clumsy and hard by her

Marriage gives no other ideal pleasure than mere sympathy[306]

[20:168] Illusion is sometimes better than truth, for the pleasure from the former is a true pleasure. Make-up; if one knows it [the illusion], then it is no longer a deception.

[136] Reverse, page 103, at 2:253

Living long and little or living short and much; living much in enjoyment or in action. Both in the greatest ratio is the best.

That the capacity for life decreases from the 16th year on

It is to be noted that we do not value the *Bonität*[307] of an action because it is useful to another, or otherwise we would not value it more highly than the utility it creates.

---

[304] For the story of Danae, see Ovid, *Metamorphoses* IV, 613. Danae was the daughter of Acrisius, King of Argos. When it was prophesied to Acrisius that Danae would have a son who would kill him, he locked her up in a bronze cave when she became fertile. Jupiter came to her in the form of a shower of gold and impregnated her. She then gave birth to Perseus. For the "bull," see Ovid, *Metamorphoses* II, 833–75. Jupiter assumes the form of a bull in order to abduct Europa, whom he then rapes in a scene famously depicted by Paulo Veronese in his "Rape of Europa" (*c.* 1570). For the case of Alcmene, see Molière's 1668 comedy *Amphitryon* (a version of the similarly titled play by the Roman poet Plautus), which depicts the classic story wherein Jupiter takes on the form of the Theban general Amphitryon and seduces his newly wedded wife, Alcmene. For Alcmene, see too Apollodorus *Biblioteca* II.iv.8–9. All three seduction stories are mentioned in Ovid's account of Arachne's web (*Metamorphoses* VI, 103–28).

[305] *Policey*   [306] *Teilnehmung*

[307] A Germanized version of the Latin for "goodness."

The moral feeling *applied*[308] to one's own actions is conscience

Providence probably gave us this feeling for the sake of universal perfection, yet in such a way that the latter is not thought of in its greatness, just as we have the sexual drive for reproduction without *intending* it.

De stationibus:[309]	*Physicis*	the moon is inhabited	[20:169]
	Logicis	in absence, *egoism*	
	Moralibus	in absence, *solipsisimus moralis*[310]	

statio moralis vel per instinctum. Sympathia vel misericordia
vel per intellectum[311]

[R126] Magnetic force is probably based on the heterogeneity (*diversa gravitas specifica*[312]) of ethereal matter, of which iron is full (the earth is full of iron), [and] whereby the heavier [thing] sinks downward

Hence the magnetic quality reveals itself more in length – e.g., more if a clump of iron is long and *vertical* instead of thick and short – precisely because the *quantity* of ether must here provide greater difference in density. One can assume that the little clumps that have their *negative* and *positive* pole are small.

Inserted sheet after page 104
[137] Obverse, at 2:253

Electricity consists of particles that have been rubbed off; the magnetic [force] does not. Hence the latter is penetrating and works in proportion to mass; the former does not.

The two poles of the same sign[313] repel each other because two elastic   [20:170]
ether-spheres of similar density push themselves, but [in the case of those poles that are] not of the same sign one [pole] will be engulfed by the others – because it is of a lighter kind (already according to its elements, not merely *ob rarefactionem*[314]) – and the magnet will be pulled

The needle's heavy end sinks into the universal magnetic atmosphere and the other end rises

---

[308] *applizirt*   [309] Latin for "on stations."   [310] Latin for "moral solipsism."
[311] Latin for "Moral position, either through instinct. Sympathy or pity. Or through intellect."
[312] Latin for "diverse specific gravity."   [313] *gleichnamigen*
[314] Latin for "by virtue of rarefaction."

The sensitive soul at peace, in faces, in societies, in eloquence
Poetry in marriages and the sexual drive[315]
The difference of the sexes
Blessedness and cheerfulness

Perhaps that the moon, by affecting the electrical (refringing[316]) matter that extends much higher, brings about the great causes of the winds and of the ebb and flow
Perhaps that it is itself the compressed heavenly air;[317] from the *centro gravitates coeli*[318] to the *centro*[319] of the earth.

[20:171]   [R127] <*Paris*, the seat of science and of the ridiculous, also contains *petit Maitressen*[320]>

Etourderie[321] (tasteless brazenness) rises above the effort at appearance[322] and expresses only a certain boisterous reliability with respect to that which can please. The petitmaitre is an *étourdi*[323] who is *gallant*, but he must appear to be well known in the great world. He has good luck with women. The Germans travel to France to become *étourdi*, but they achieve only the appearance of a brazen jester. The *coquette* expresses the awareness of her rule over the hearts of men and makes their caresses into her toys.[324] The *petitmaitre* and the *coquettes* are never in love, but both pretend to be so. A dandy is actually a fool for fancy clothing[325] and is very different from the *petitmaitre* who even *affects* free carelessness.

[138] Reverse, opposite page 105, at 2:254

~~Were the~~ I suppose magnetic matter to be a sphere of heterogeneous ether, which however in each expanse contains all species one beneath
[20:172]   the other, although the denser parts [are] closer to the center of the earth,

---

[315] The Academy Edition has the two preceding lines as one sentence, not on separate lines as above.
[316] The German here is *"refringirende."* According to Adickes (see note at 14:97), "This probably can only mean: denser than the aether . . . so that therefore light particles are refracted upon entry into the electrical matter."
[317] *Himmelsluft*   [318] Latin for "sky's center of gravity."
[319] Latin for "center."   [320] French for "little mistresses." See footnote 2 above.
[321] French for "thoughtlessness."   [322] *Bemühung zu scheinen*
[323] French for "scatter-brain."
[324] The last part of this sentence could also be translated as "makes her caresses into their toys".
[325] *Putznarr*

the lighter ones above. If this *ether-sphere* shared a *centrum* with the earth, then no *direction* toward the poles would take place; were its centrum on the axis, then no *declination* would take place. For, ~~since~~ because the intersection of the horizons of two spheres is a circle – upon which the needle must stand perpendicularly if it shall sink as deep as possible into the magnetic circle[326] – yet all these circles run *parallel* with the *equator*, then the needles will hold the *meridian*.

If this *centrum* is not in the axis, then there is only *linea expers variationis*[327] where the meridian of the earth coincides with the *meridiano magnetico*.[328] ~~It~~ Now, because the ~~axis~~ magnetic axis lies in such a way on a plane with the earth's axis that the meridian that goes through the earth's poles also goes through the magnetic ones, the *linea expers variationis* would be a meridian at all times. Now, should it not be a meridian, then the magnetic horizon must be spheroid or else irregular; in that case, however, the magnetic attractions must not [R128] point to the *centro* of the magnetic spheroid, but instead also diverge from it. Suppose that this oblateness comes from the centrifugal force of the earth; then ~~in such~~ the size of the divergence from the magnetic *centro* will be to the divergence from the *centro* of the earth as the [force of] gravity[329] is to the conducting magnetic force. Therefore, the magnetic horizon can be bent in very different ways, and not only the *inclination*, but also the *declination* can be very diverse.

Inserted sheet after page 106
[139] Obverse, at 2:254

Moral delusion consists in one's really taking opinion about a possible moral perfection to be real.

We have selfish and altruistic sentiments. The former are older than the latter, and the latter are first generated in the sexual inclination. A human being is needy, but also has power over needs. He [who is] in [20:173] the state of nature is more capable of altruistic and active sentiments; he [who is] in a state of opulence has imaginary needs and is selfish. One sympathizes more with the ill – particularly the injustice – that others suffer than with their welfare. The sympathetic sentiment is true if it is

---

[326] *Kreis*   [327] Latin for "line without variation."
[328] Latin for "magnetic meridian."   [329] *Schweere*

equal to the altruistic powers, otherwise it is chimerical.[330] It is universal in an indeterminate way in so far as it is directed to one among all those whom I can help, or in a determinate way, towards helping everyone who suffers; the latter is chimerical. Good-heartedness arises through the *culture* of moral but inactive sentiments and is a moral delusion. On the ~~negat~~ private good-heartedness to do no evil and to fulfill one's obligation towards justice

The morality that wants nothing but unselfishness is chimerical, as is the one that is sympathetic to imagined needs. The morality that affirms selfishness alone is crude

The *officia beneplaciti*[331] can never entail that one robs oneself of one's own needs, but the *officia debiti*[332] surely can, for these are moral needs

[20:174] [R129] Virtue carries along with it a natural wage, although not in goods of opulence, but [in goods] of sufficiency

It is possible to conceive of a most perfect human being of nature, but not of artifice

The former takes care not to impose some obligations on himself. And also the latter

[140] Reverse, opposite page 107, at 2:255

The sweetness of current need is chimerical

Friendship of agreeableness or of needs. They must be equal, otherwise it is not called friendship, but enjoyment

Friendship is always reciprocal, hence not between father and child, and since the wife never desires the man's well-being as much as the latter desires hers, marriage is only closely related to the most perfect friendship.

In the state of opulence, marriages must cease to become friendships.

The friendship of delusion that consists in reciprocal good wishes
[20:175] without effect is foolish but beautiful, that of sociable friendliness and concordant sentiments is the most common, but such [a person] is a socializer,[333] perhaps **open-hearted** and discreet, but no friend.

---

[330] The Academy Edition offers a comma here.   [331] Latin for "duties of benevolence."
[332] Latin for "duties of obligation."
[333] Here we follow Rischmüller's "ein Gesellschafter" [R129] as opposed to the Academy Edition's "in Gesellschaften".

The education of Rousseau is the only means to help civil society flourish again. For since opulence constantly increases – from which arise need, oppression and contempt of the classes – laws can accomplish nothing against this, as in Sweden. Thereby all governments also become more orderly and wars more infrequent. *Censors* should be instituted; but where will the first ones come from[?] Switzerland [is] the only country. Russia.[334]

[R130] The doubt that I assume is not dogmatic, but a doubt of post-ponement. Zetetics[335] (ζητεῖν) searchers. I will raise the reasons from both sides. It is amazing that one worries about danger from that. Speculation is not a matter of bare necessity. Knowledge with respect to the latter is secure. The method of doubt is useful because it *preserves* the mind, not to act according to speculation, but according to common sense[336] and *sentiment*. I seek the honor of *Fabius Cunctator*.[337]

Truth has no value in itself, it is all the same whether an opinion about the inhabitation of many worlds is true or false. One must not confuse truth with truthfulness. Only the manner in which one arrives at truth has a determinate value, because that which leads to error can also do so in practical matters

If the pleasure from the sciences is supposed to be the motive, then it is all the same whether it is true or false. In this, the ignorant and precocious have an advantage over the reasonable and cautious. The final end is to find the human being's vocation

[141] Page 107
Lower margin, at 2:255

The opinion of inequality also makes human beings unequal. Only the doctrine of Mr. *Rousseau* can bring it about that even the most learned   [20:176]

---

334 In his *Letter to d'Alembert*, Rousseau argues against the establishment of a theater in Geneva (a city-state presently in Switzerland), and there points out that even censors will not protect against the corrupting influence of the theater: "the Drama will turn the Censors to ridicule or the Censors will drive out the actors" (Jean-Jacques Rousseau, *Letter to d'Alembert and Writings for the Theatre*, ed. Allan Bloom et al., Lebanon: University Press of New England, 2004, p. 306). For more on Rousseau and censorship, see too *The Social Contract*, Book IV, ch. 7.

335 *Zetetici*. The Greek that follows transliterates to *zetein*.   336 *gesunder Verstand*

337 Quintus Fabius Maximus Verruscosus (280–203 BC), Roman commander and consul five times from 233 to 209 BC. He was called Fabius "Cunctator" ("Delayer") because he avoided open battle against the more powerful Hannibal in Italy. These delaying tactics prevented Hannibal from sacking Rome.

philosopher, with his knowledge, earnestly regards himself, without help from religion, as no better than the common man.

Inserted sheet after page 108
[142] Obverse, at 2:255

What a miserable condition it is when oppression is so universal and common that an industrious and honest human being cannot merely demand justice, but instead must beg for mercy. The more we misconceive of our obligations, when we are not yet entirely corrupted, the more favors remain for us; we especially neglect obligations toward some and give favors to others.

[R131] In order for the weakness of women in the active qualities to be counterbalanced by something, nature has made men weak in so far as they very much surrender themselves to illusion and let themselves be easily deceived. The man is inclined to form great conceptions of a beloved object and to feel himself unworthy, as it were, with respect to her. Yet the woman commonly imagines herself worthy of courtship and forms no fantastical ideas of the man's superiority. They soon believe that they are able to take command over the man's heart. The man is inclined [20:177] to value his wife or his lover higher than himself, the woman never. If one merely considers the sex's intention, then the woman obviously rules and is more clever. The generous one believes more easily than the selfish and weak one.

The *Gallantry* (of men) is the art of appearing to be in love.[338] Women's *coquetterie* is the art of giving the appearance of the inclination to conquer. Both are ridiculous in marriages. ~~If the women and men~~ The art of appearing virtuous is propriety, and especially that of appearing chaste; modesty, refined and selective in taste, prudery, appearing affable, *politesse*,[339] refinement.[340] ~~If this~~ The persons who understand the arts best make the worst marriages

If appearance ~~of marriage~~ is employed for the purpose of marriage, then it is still good; if it lasts after marriage, then it is very ridiculous. Yet men demand such women, who, as they say, do them credit, who are sought after, who one would gladly like to take from them.

---

[338] *die Kunst verliebt zu scheinen*   [339] French for "politeness."   [340] *Geschliffenheit*

[143] Reverse, opposite page 109, at 2:255

*est obligatio stricta erga dominum ex obsequio <reverentia> erga benefactorem
ex amore in novo foedere licet deum amare in veteri revereri*[341]

Bodies are either positive, transparent, or *negative (reflecting)*, or zero   [20:178]
(black). All bodies on the surfaces are both at the same time, especially
small lamellae.

The small lamellae of iron magnets have this quality and pull themselves in whole clumps with their opposite poles. Electrical bodies only
have it on the surface

[R132] <In the case of women, book-reading occurs in order to appear
learned>

    <The marriage that has no illusion, likewise honorableness >

*jus cum sit complexus ~~regularum~~ obligationum debiti habitus Actionum ~~cum
jure~~ ex rationibus juris determinandarum est justicia quae vel vel est obligantis
(activa) vel obligati (passiva). Prior ~~necessitate actiones aliorum non nisi juri
adaequatas haec tales et in tantum quales et in quantum ratio juris postulat.
Posterior est habitus actiones actiones suas~~ exigit actiones aliorum ~~conformiter
robore quantenus~~ <ad quas quales> per rationes juris necessitantur Posterior
~~se ipsum determinat a legi~~ est habitus se ad actiones determinandi quae per
rationes juris ~~sunt~~ ab aliis necessitantur: [unreadable phrase] ~~Utrumque potest
esse a~~ Si actionum habitus sit justitiae adaequatus prior erit justicia severa
posterior [breaks off]*[342]

    *Habitum ~~actionum~~ officiorum limites justiciae activae excedentium
Aequitas, justiciae passivae itidem*[343]

---

[341] Latin for "There is a strict duty toward the Lord out of obedience <reverence>, toward the
benefactor out of love; in the new covenant, one can love God, in the old covenant, one can
revere Him."

[342] Latin for "While the law is the sum of the ~~common~~ obligations related to that which is owed, the
disposition of actions ~~with the law~~ that should be determined by reasons of law constitutes justice,
which is either that of the one who obligates (active) or that of the one who is obligated (passive).
The former ~~necessitates the actions of others only if they correspond to the law, [and] this in
such a way and to the extent that the ground of the law demands it. The latter is the disposition
to actions to one's own actions~~ requires actions of others ~~in conformity with the strength insofar
as~~ <insofar as they are> necessitated by reasons of law. The latter ~~of determining oneself from
the law~~ is the disposition to determine oneself to actions that ~~are~~ are necessitated by others for
reasons of law: . . . ~~both can be from~~ If the disposition of actions corresponds to justice, then the
former will be strict justice, the latter." [breaks off].

[343] Latin for "The state ~~of actions~~ of duties that exceeds the limits of active justice [is] equity; it is
the same [regarding those duties] of passive justice."

Indoles[344]

[20:179] <The illusion of friendship. *Aristotle* –;[345] if we wake, we have *mundum communem*[346]>

De sententia respectu juris civilis summum jus summa injuria. respectu civis vera non respectu judicis[347]

<A young husband is not good because he has not yet considered the falsity of appearance>

Hume believes that the clergy very much practice the art of appearing.[348] Truth is only suitable in a nightdress; in the suit *of the parade*[349] appearance [is suitable]. To appear to be all sorts of things in clothes. Make-up.

Alexander v. *Antipater*; purple interior[350]

Envy ceases when I can wipe away the deceiving appearance of others' happiness and perfection

---

[344] Latin for "predisposition" or "character."

[345] For Aristotle's account of friendship, see his *Nicomachean Ethics*, Book VIII.

[346] Latin for "a common world."

[347] Latin for "Regarding the sentence in civil law, 'the greatest right, the greatest wrong': It is true with respect to the citizen, but not with respect to the judge."

[348] In his "Of National Characters" (1748), Hume wrote:

> Though all mankind have a strong propensity to religion at certain times and in certain dispositions; yet are there few or none, who have it to that degree, and with that constancy, which is requisite to support the character of this profession. It must, therefore, happen, that clergymen, being drawn from the common mass of mankind, as people are to other employments, by the views of profit, the greater part, though no atheists or free-thinkers, will find it necessary, on particular occasions, to feign more devotion than they are, at that time, possessed of, and to maintain the appearance of fervor and seriousness, even when jaded with the exercises of their religion, or when they have their minds engaged in the common occupations of life. They must not, like the rest of the world, give scope to their natural movements and sentiments: They must set a guard over their looks and words and actions: And in order to support the veneration paid them by the multitude, they must not only keep a remarkable reserve, but must promote the spirit of superstition, by a continued grimace and hypocrisy. This dissimulation often destroys the candor and ingenuity of their temper, and makes an irreparable breach in their character. (David Hume, *Essays Moral, Political, Literary*, ed. Eugene Miller, Indianapolis: Liberty Fund, 1987, p. 96)

[349] *Habit de Parade*

[350] In *The Advancement of Learning*, Francis Bacon, in a series of praises of Alexander the Great, records the following:

> Consider further, for tropes of rhetoric, that excellent use of a metaphor or translation, wherewith [Alexander] taxed Antipater, who was an imperious and tyrannous governor; for when one of Antipater's friends commended him to Alexander for his moderation, that he did not degenerate as his other lieutenants did into the Persian pride, in uses of purple, but kept the ancient habit of Macedon, of black: "True (saith Alexander), but Antipater is all purple within." (Book I, ch. 7, § 17, in Francis Bacon, *The Advancement of Learning and New Atlantis*, ed. Arthur Johnston, Oxford: Clarendon Press, 1974, p. 50; cf. Erasmus' *Apophthegms* iv.17)

[R133] On the means of imagining a president or a dignified man with his wife

[144] Page 110
Upper margin, at 2:256

The most perfect woman. Understanding and brave, reasonable, if she is voluntarily[351] excused from ratiocination. <Clever, wise – witty, refined> The exemption from domestic affairs makes foolish women <*gallant.*> Foolish women.

He who knows how to satisfy his desire is clever; he who knows how to master it is wise. World-wisdom[352]

Left margin, next to lines 21–28

Costs and expenses.[353] These are expenses if one loses the pleasures that one can get for money or work and thus also [loses] the latter. The [20:180] miser has the greatest expenses; he who knows how to live so, with the expenditure of all money, [has] the greatest profit. Also avaricious. To use it every time for one's contentment (not delightfulness).[354]

Lower margin, between the text and the closing vignette

Just as the size of a human being cannot grow above the mean without his becoming weaker, and also cannot remain below the mean without his being too weak, so it is with ethical and delicate[355] qualities

Lower margin, under the vignette

Greek Roman face. Characters of *nations* in social interaction: the Spanish, French, Germans, [and] English

That our youths and men are[356] still so childish is because they did not have enough permission to be children earlier. Thus, the trees whose

---

[351] *willkürlich*   [352] *Weltweisheit*. See footnote 75 above.   [353] *Kosten und Unkosten*
[354] Here we follow Rischmüller's "Geitzig auch. jede Zeit sie zu seiner Zufriedenheit (nicht Erget-zlichkeit) zu verwenden" [R133] instead of the Academy Edition's "Geitzig auf jede Zeit sie zu seiner Zufriedenheit (nicht Ergetzlichkeit) zu verwenden".   [20:180]
[355] *zierlich*   [356] Here we follow Rischmüller's "seyn" instead of the Academy Edition's "sehen."

blossoms were not allowed to burst forth properly in the spring bloom in [R134] the fall

[145] Inside of the back cover

Simplicity is either ignorant or reasonable and wise simplicity

In all moral *definitions*, the expression *mediocritas*[357] is very wretched and indefinite – e.g., *in parsimonia*[358] – for it only indicates that there is a degree that is not good on account of its size, without saying how large the good would have to be.

This *mediocritas aurea*[359] is a *qualitas occulta*[360]

Difference between: he knows how to appear or he knows how to live.

[20:181] One could say that metaphysics is a science of the limits of human reason

The doubts of the same do not remove useful certainty, but useless certainty

Metaphysics is useful in that it removes the appearance that can be harmful

In metaphysics, it is partiality not to also think from the opposite side, and it [is] also a lie not to say it; in actions it is different

One only falls in love with illusion, but one loves truth. If one should reveal the illusion of most human beings, then they would seem like that bride of whom one says that [when] she had taken off her beautiful silken eyebrows, a pair of ivory teeth, excellent ringlets and a few handkerchiefs that had supported her bosom, and had wiped off her make-up, her astonished lover [breaks off]

Illusion demands refinement and art, truth demands simplicity and peace. According to Swift, everything in the world is clothes[361]

---

[357] Latin for "the mean."   [358] Latin for "in parsimony."
[359] Latin for "the golden mean."   [360] Latin for "occult quality."
[361] In his *Tale of a Tub* (§ 2), a satire on religious excesses, Swift writes,
> The worshippers of this deity had also a system of their belief which seemed to turn upon the following fundamental. They held the universe to be a large *suit of clothes* which *invests* everything; that the earth is invested by the air; the air is invested by the stars; and the stars are invested by the *primum mobile*. Look on this globe of earth, you will find it to be a very complete and fashionable *dress*. What is that which some call *land* but a fine coat faced with green, or the sea but a waistcoat of water-tabby? Proceed to the particular works of the creation, you will find how curious *Journeyman* Nature hath been to trim up the *vegetable* beaux; observe how sparkish a periwig adorns the head of a *beech*, and what a fine doublet of white satin is worn by the *birch*.

The most ridiculous is this: that one creates illusion toward others for so long that one oneself imagines it to be true; this is what children do with *religion*. Illusion, when the one who intends it takes it for the thing itself, is delusion.[362]

The illusion that the woman *intends* as a means to the attainment of marital love is no delusion, but [it] surely is aside from this condition. On the art of making the easy difficult

Loose Sheets to the *Observations on the Feeling of the Beautiful and Sublime*[363] [20:183]

The inclination of women toward novels perhaps comes about because they wish that love were the sole inclination by which men are ruled.

Just as the greatest excess that arises from free government ultimately amounts to throwing everything into slavery and finally poverty, so the **unnatural** freedom of the female sex and the agreeableness that they thereby enjoy and impart must at last amount to making them completely despicable and finally to making them into slaves.

Mr. Hume believes that a woman who has no knowledge of the history of her fatherland or of Greece and Rome cannot ever keep company with people of understanding.[364] Yet he does not consider that they are not there to serve men as support for cogitation but as support for the

---

To conclude from all, what is man himself but a *micro-coat*, or rather a complete suit of clothes with all its trimmings? As to his body there can be no dispute, but examine even the acquirements of his mind, you will find them all contribute in their order towards furnishing out an exact dress. To instance no more, is not religion a *cloak*, honesty a *pair of shoes* worn out in the dirt, self-love a *surtout*, vanity a *shirt*, and conscience a *pair of breeches*, which, though a cover for lewdness as well as nastiness, is easily slipped down for the service of both. (Jonathan Swift, *A Tale of a Tub and Other Works*, ed. Angus Ross, Oxford University Press, 1986, p. 36)

[362] *Wahn*

[363] Rischmüller's edition does not include the loose sheets. We take them from the Academy Edition.

[364] In his "Of the Study of History," Hume writes,

An extensive knowledge of this kind belongs to men of letters; but I must think it an unpardonable ignorance in persons of whatever sex or condition, not to be acquainted with the history of their own country, together with the histories of ancient Greece and Rome. A woman may behave herself with good manners, and have even some vivacity in her turn of wit; but where her mind is so unfurnished, 'tis impossible her conversation can afford any entertainment to men of sense and reflection. (David Hume, *Essays Moral and Political*, ed. Eugene Miller, Indianapolis: Liberty Fund, 1987, p. 236)

recuperation from it. History is of no use without a degree of philosophy, even if it were just moral philosophy. In this, however, the woman only needs the part of history that concerns that morality which relates to her sex.

The woman, because she always wants to rule, takes herself a fool without reservation.

The valiant wife wants to be honored through her husband; the vain wife does not ask for this honor but wants to catch the [public] eye herself. The *coquette* has the intention of inspiring inclinations, even though she has none herself; it is a mere game of vanity.

All inclinations are either exclusive or sympathetic.[365] The former are selfish, the latter are altruistic. However, self-love[366] and self-esteem are not exclusive according to their nature; but egoism[367] and self-conceit are. The love of women is exclusive with respect to other men in accordance with the law of nature. The purely lustful drive or the amorous rage can even be exclusive with respect to the object of love, hence rape, Herod, etc.[368] The immediate drive for honor is exclusive with respect to honor. The quality of the mind to desire in objects everything exclusively, where this drive is not justified by nature, is called envy. Envy is a kind of balefulness. But emulation – a sadness about inequality – can probably only concern an imagined inequality; in any case, it is then only a perverse application of a good law of nature. The drives that are sympathetic are

[20:184]

---

[365] *teilnehmend*   [366] *Selbstliebe*   [367] *Eigenliebe*

[368] Kant could be referring to Herod the Great (73–4 BC) or to Herod Antipas (20 BC–29 AD). In neither case is there a clear instance of rape, however. Herod the Great suspected his wife Miriamne of having an affair with his uncle Joseph, and he eventually killed both Joseph and Miriamne. In *The Antiquities of the Jews* (trans. William Whiston), Josephus writes of Herod the Great:

> This much troubled him, to see that this surprising hatred of his wife to him was not concealed, but open; and he took this so ill, and yet was so unable to bear it, on account of the fondness he had for her, that he could not continue long in any one mind, but sometimes was angry at her, and sometimes reconciled himself to her; but by always changing one passion for another, he was still in great uncertainty, and thus was he entangled between hatred and love, and was frequently disposed to inflict punishment on her for her insolence towards him; but being deeply in love with her in his soul, he was not able to get quit of this woman. In short, as he would gladly have her punished, so was he afraid lest, ere he were aware, he should, by putting her to death, bring a heavier punishment upon himself at the same time. (Book xv, ch. 7, § 7)

Herod Antipas, son of Herod the Great, famously had John the Baptist beheaded for the sake of his daughter-in-law Salome, with whom he became infatuated (see Mark 6:14–29).

the best: only in the case of sexual drives must sympathy concern only the object of the amorous inclination.

Women's refusals are to them an irresistible drive to create illusion; those men who have not yet become extremely wanton have the quality that they are very easily deceived by this illusion; this relation holds the strength of the reciprocal inclination within bounds.

The moral state, when the taste for a great amount of artificial pleasures and charms is missing, is simplicity; the [moral state] in which this taste is acquired is virtue; heroic virtue however even aims at the overcoming of needs. Thus, one can be good without virtue. Correct judgment, which is acquired through experience that depends on needs, is understanding; if taste extends to many things and the manifoldness of the issue is magnified, then reason – indeed, even fine reason – is necessary. But healthy reason is that fine reason, which returns to that which is necessary to judge and know. One can be very understanding without great fineness of reason.

Simple taste easily gets out of hand and moral simplicity is easily deceived due to a lack of knowledge of seductive temptation; hence the greatest perfection is [breaks off]

The woman who has acquired no particular taste for all those distractions, *gallantries* and vanities can be good without virtue and understanding without brooding.[369] If she is pulled from the midst and from the seat [20:185] of these fine pleasures, then thousands of enticements affect her and she needs virtue in order to be a good woman.

In domestic life, in company that is spirited, good-hearted and calm, no witticism,[370] no books and courtly manners[371] and ratiocination is needed, but if so much refined taste, concupiscence, and fashion is acquired, then reason is required in order to prevent one from becoming a foolish woman.

The most perfect woman would be the one who knows the various fine delights of life, manners [and] gallantry in their beautiful charms, and has taste, but, through reasonable insight into their uselessness, voluntarily readies herself for domesticity and simplicity, and knows how to constrain herself through virtue.

A woman needs even more virtue in marriage than a man, especially if the necessity of modest appearance has gone completely out of fashion

---

[369] *klügeln*   [370] *Witzeley*   [371] *Hofkentnis*

and gallant freedom, as innocent as it may sound, emerges. For she has a safer game, as one can easily guess, and will be more solicited.[372]

One can presuppose in accordance with the rule of prudence that one never encounters that which is extremely rare and, where it is encountered, hard to recognize; for this reason it is not at all in accordance with prudence to let oneself be guided by this deceitful pleasantness of women

Elderly persons very much love jokes and that which arouses laughter; youth falls in love with the moving tragic that arouses strong sentiments. What is the cause[?]

I find this mistake [to be] almost universal: that one does not ponder the shortness of human life enough. It is surely perverse to have it in mind in order to despise human life and in order to look only toward the future one. But [one should have it in mind] so that one may live right at his [20:186] position and not postpone it [life] too far through a foolish fantasy about the plan of our actions. The epitaphs of various ancients lend themselves to the encouragement of lustful and opulent enjoyment and of avaricious greediness for pleasure. But if well understood, it [the epitaph] only serves to liberate the mind through sufficiency from the rule of such drives that entangle us in preparations whose enjoyment is not in proportion with the efforts due to the brevity of life. The consideration of the nearness of death is agreeable in itself and a *corrective* for bringing human beings toward simplicity and for helping them towards the sensitive peace of the soul, which begins as soon as the blind ardor, with which one previously chased after the imagined objects of one's wishes, ceases.

The woman who is constantly busy with taking care of choice finery must be kept in this practice in marriage. For, since she has maintained no inclination for cleanliness and agreeableness except to please others, she will become foul and swinish if she lives alone with her husband.

In society, the man is more preoccupied with the contemplation of that which pleases him in a woman, while the woman [focuses] more on that which pleases men in herself.

All pleasures of life have their great charm while one hunts after them; [their] possession is cold and the enchanting spirit has evaporated. So, the acquisitive merchant has thousands of pleasures while he earns money. If he considers enjoying it after earning it thousands of worries will torment

---

[372] *aufgefordert*

him. The young lover is extremely happy [when] in hope, and the day on which his happiness rises to its highest also brings it to a decline again.

A certain calm self-confidence combined with the marks of respect and modesty secures trust and goodwill; in contrast, a boldness that appears to give little respect to others brings about hate and reluctance

In *disputes*, a calm attitude of the mind combined with kindness and leniency toward the opponent is a sign that one is in possession of the power through which the understanding is certain of its victory. Just as Rome sold the fields on which Hannibal stood. [20:187]

When facing the eyes of a large crowd, few human beings will endure their mockery and contempt with a calm mind, even if they know that those [in the crowd] are all ignorant fools. The great crowd always creates awe, indeed, even the audience shivers with fright at the false step of him who compromises himself in their presence, although each individual, if he were alone with the speaker, would find little disparaging in his disapproval. But if the great crowd is absent, a composed man can very well regard their judgment with complete indifference.

With regard to a beautiful object, an intense passion, an embarrassment and a languishing longing adorns the man very well; in the case of a woman, though, calm affectionateness. It is not good that the woman offers herself to the man or anticipates his declarations of love. For he who alone has the power must necessarily be dependent upon her who has nothing but charms, and the latter must be conscious of the value of her charms, otherwise there would be no equality but slavery

The mechanical in laughter is the vibration of the diaphragm and the lungs, as well as the contorted face, since the mouth is pulled from elsewhere, etc. Women and fat people like to laugh. One laughs most violently when one is supposed to behave seriously. One laughs most strongly about him who looks serious. Strong laughter is tiring [and] breaks into tears, as sadness does. Laughter that is aroused by tickling is at the same time very exhausting, but that [which is aroused] through imagination amuses, though it can lead to *convulsions*. [One] about whom I laugh myself, then[373] if I suffer damages from him, I can no longer be mad. The recollection of the ridiculous gives much pleasure and also does not wear off as easily as other agreeable stories. The Abbé *Terrasson* with the cap on his head.[374] [20:188]

---

[373] Reading *dann* for *denn*.   [374] See footnote 13 above.

The ground of laughter seems to consist in the trembling of quickly pinched nerves, which propagates through the entire *system*; other pleasures come from uniform movements of the fluid of the nerves. Thus, if I hear something that has an appearance of a prudent purposeful relation, but which entirely cancels itself out in trifles, then the nerve that is bent towards one side becomes repelled and trembling, as it were. Indeed, I would not want to wager, yet I will attest it any time.

Pelisson who should have been painted instead of the devil.[375]

Sexual inclination is either amorous need or amorous concupiscence. In the state of simplicity, the former rules and thus [there is] no taste yet. In the state of artifice the amorous concupiscence becomes either one of the enjoyment of all or one of ideal taste. The latter constitutes lustful immoderateness. In all of this two things are to be noted. The female sex is either mingled with the male sex in free company or excluded. If the latter is the case then no moral taste occurs, but at the most, simplicity (lending the Spartans' wives[376]), or it is a lustful delusion, as it were, an amorous greed to possess much for enjoyment without being able to really enjoy any of it; Salomon.[377] In the state of simplicity, mutual need ruled. Here is need on one side and lack on the other. There was fidelity without temptation; here guards of chastity, which is not possible in itself. In the free interaction of both sexes, which is a new invention, concupiscence grows, but so does moral taste. One of the qualities of this drive is that it probably underlies the ideal charms but must always be carried on as [20:189] a kind of secret; from this arises a kind of modest propriety even with respect to strong desires, without which the latter would be common and, in the end, liable to tedium. Second, that the female sex takes on the illusion as if it were not a need in her case; this is necessary if the amorous inclination is supposed to remain combined with ideal pleasures

---

[375] Paul Pelisson-Fontanier (1624–93), French philosopher and member of the Academy in Paris. See footnote 118 above.

[376] Sparta was a Greek city-state famous for its legendary founder Lycurgus and for its military valor. Spartans were strictly segregated by the sexes, with men under 30 typically not allowed to see even their wives in daylight. Polybius reports that "among the Lacedaemonians [Spartans] it was a hereditary custom and quite usual for three or four men to have one wife or even more if they were brothers, the offspring being the common property of all, and when a man had begotten enough children, it was honorable and quite usual for him to give his wife to one of his friends" (*The Histories of Polybius* XII.6b.8, trans. W. R. Paton for the Loeb Classical Library, 1922–).

[377] King Solomon (see footnote 206 above). According to 1 Kings 11:3, King Solomon had seven hundred wives and three hundred concubines.

and moral taste in the state of artifice. In lustful passion this illusion is not necessary at all. Hence female acquiescence merely appears to be either forced or a sign of favor

A young man who expresses no amorous inclination at all will be indifferent in the eyes of the woman.

Whether [or not] there really can be a use for religion that immediately pertains to future blessedness, still the most natural first [use of religion] is that it arranges mores[378] in such a way that they are good for fulfilling one's station in the present world, so that one thereby becomes worthy of the future one. For things that concern fasting, ceremony, and chastening,[379] those have no use for the present world. But if this internal use is to be achieved, *morality* must be refined[380] before religion.

Montesquieu says that it would be entirely unnatural for a woman to rule a house but that it could very well happen that she should rule a country.[381]

If mores are entirely simple and all luxury[382] is banned, then the man rules; if public affairs are in the hands of a few and the majority of men become idle, then women leave their solitude and have great influence over men. If women *inspire* virtue and *romanic*[383] esteem in men, then they rule the man hereafter in the household through kindness; if they do not win him through *coquetterie* before they have seduced him and turned him into a fool, then they will rule him imperiously and willfully. In a good marriage both have only one will and that is the will of the wife; likewise in a bad marriage, but with the distinction that the husband

---

[378] *Sitten*   [379] *Casteyen*   [380] *excolirt*
[381] In *The Spirit of the Laws*, Book VII, § 17, Montesquieu writes,
> On Administration by Women. It is against reason and against nature for women to be mistresses in the house, as was established among the Egyptians, but not for them to govern an empire. In the first case, their weak state does not permit them to be preeminent; in the second, their very weakness gives them more gentleness and moderation, which, rather than the harsh and ferocious virtues, can make for good government.
>
> In the Indies government by women turns out very well; it is established that, if the males do not come from a mother of the same blood, a daughter whose mother is of royal blood succeeds to the throne. She is given a certain number of people to help her carry the weight of the government. According to Mr. Smith, government by women also turns out very well in Africa. If one adds to this the examples of Muscovy and of England, one will see that they succeed equally well in moderate government and in despotic government. (Montesquieu, *The Spirit of the Laws*, ed. Anne Cohler et al., Cambridge University Press, 1989, p. 111)

[382] *Luxus*   [383] *romanische* (see footnote 25 above).

agrees with the will of the wife in the first case, [while] in the second case he opposes her, yet is outweighed.

[20:190]   This is the age of the rule of women, but with little honor because they degrade the man in his worth. They first make him vain, yielding, and foolish, and after they have deprived him of the dignity of male honor, they have no obstacle. In all marriages, women rule, but also over men of worth.

There are two paths in the Christian religion, in so far as it is supposed to improve *morality*: 1. beginning with the revelation of mysteries, in that one expects a sanctification of the heart from a divine supernatural influence; 2. beginning from the improvement of morality according to the order of nature and, after the greatest possible effort spent on this, expecting supernatural assistance according to the divine order of his decrees expressed in revelation.

For it is not possible by beginning with revelation, to expect moral improvement from this instruction as a result according to the order of nature.

The *refined*[384] view into the future, if it is carried out to the end, namely [to] the goal of imminent death, brings its own *remedium*[385] with it. For why should one torment oneself with many concerned preparations given that death will soon interrupt them

A man easily develops high esteem toward a woman who captures him, while the woman for her part has more inclination than respect. Hence it comes about that the man expresses a kind of generosity in overcoming his own lustful inclination, without which many women would be seduced. A tempted wanton is a dangerous man among women.

It is good that, although the sensitive heart at peace is always beautiful, the affect of love nevertheless suits the man very well before marriage, while quiet submissiveness suits the woman: so that the man can appear to be in love without the least bit of bad manners,[386] yet the woman only appears to love.

[20:191]   It is strange that women have so much attentiveness and memory in things pertaining to ornament, propriety, and *politesse*,[387] while men have so little.

---

[384] *excolirt*   [385] Latin for "remedy."   [386] *Anstand*   [387] French for "politeness."

One is not compassionate with respect to the grief and distress of another but with respect to those in so far as their causes are natural and not imagined. Therefore a craftsman has no compassion for a *bankrupt* merchant who is degraded to the position of a broker or a servant because he does not see that the merchant lacks anything other than imagined necessities. A merchant has no compassion for a courtier who has fallen from grace and must live on his own estates after the loss of his posts.[388] Yet if both are regarded as benefactors of humanity, then one does not consider the ills according to one's own sentiment, but according to the sentiment of the other. But the merchant has compassion for the downfall of another who is otherwise honest if he obtains no advantage from it because he has just the same imagined need as the other. At the most, one also has compassion in the case of an otherwise gentle woman for her grief about imagined misfortune, because one despises a man for his weakness in such a case, but not a woman. But everyone has compassion for the ill that is opposed to true needs. From this it follows that the good-heartedness of a human being of much opulence will contain a very extensive compassion, while that of the human being of simplicity will contain a very restricted one. One has unlimited compassion for one's children

The more extensive the compassion is, when the powers remain the same, the more idle it is; the more the imagined needs also grow here, the greater is the obstacle of the remaining capacity to do good. Hence the goodwill of the opulent state becomes a mere delusion

There is no sweeter idea than idleness[389] and no activity [sweeter] than that which is aimed at pleasure. This is also the *object* that one has before one's eyes if one wants to sit down in peace, but all of this is a phantasm. He who does not work dies of boredom and is, at the most, numbed by delightful things and exhausted, but never refreshed and satisfied

[20:192]

The drive for honor with respect to those qualities whose higher value can make the judgment of others resolute[390] and universal is ambition; the drive for honor with respect to the less significant qualities, about which the judgment of others [is] frivolous and changeable, is vanity.

Self-esteem, humility. The scornful laughter that is worthy of being laughed at [should] be hated rather than despised.

---

[388] *Chargen*   [389] *Nichtstuerei*   [390] *angelegentlich*

Self-esteem pertains to equality, and the latter leads to respect if it is badly understood.

Why incapacity is regarded as even more ignominious than an evil will, namely in such cases where incapacity also cancels out the good consequences at the same time

That the desire for honor is partly based on the condition of equality can be seen from the fact that nobles greatly despise the judgment of the lower ones. One sees that it is based on the sexual drive because the contempt of a woman is very offensive

Essay
on the Maladies of the Head

[2:257]

Essay
on the Maladies of the Head

The simplicity and frugality of nature demands and forms only common concepts and a clumsy sincerity in human beings; artificial constraint and the luxury of a civil constitution hatches punsters and subtle reasoners, occasionally, however, also fools and swindlers, and gives birth to the wise or decent semblance by means of which one can dispense with understanding as well as integrity, if only the beautiful veil which decency spreads over the secret frailties of the head or the heart is woven close enough. Proportionately as art advances, reason and virtue will finally become the universal watchword, yet in such a way that the eagerness to speak of both can well dispense instructed and polite persons from bothering with their possession. The universal esteem which both praised properties are accorded nevertheless shows this noticeable difference that everyone is far more jealous of the advantages of the understanding than of the good properties of the will, and that in the comparison between stupidity and roguery no one would hesitate a moment to declare his preference for the latter; which is certainly well thought out because, if everything in general depends on art, fine cleverness cannot be dispensed with, but sincerity, which in such relations is only obstructive, can well be done without. I live among wise and well-mannered citizens, that is to say, among those who are skilled at appearing so, and I flatter myself that one would be so fair as to credit me with as much finesse that even if I were presently in possession of the most proven remedies for dislodging [2:260] the maladies of the head and the heart, I would still hesitate to lay this old-fashioned rubbish in the path of public business, well aware that the beloved fashionable cure for the understanding and the heart has already made desirable progress and that particularly the doctors of the understanding, who call themselves logicians, satisfy the general demand very well since they made the important discovery: that the human head is actually a drum which only sounds because it is empty. Accordingly, I see nothing better for me than to imitate the method of the physicians, who believe they have been very helpful to their patient when they give his malady a name, and will sketch a small onomastic[1] of the frailties of the head, from its paralysis in *imbecility* to its raptures in *madness*; but in order to recognize these loathsome maladies in their gradual origination, I find it first necessary to elucidate their milder degrees from *idiocy* to *foolishness*, because these properties are more widespread in civil relations and lead nonetheless to the former ones.

The *dull head* lacks wit; the *idiot* lacks understanding. The agility in grasping something and remembering it, likewise the facility in expressing it properly, very much depend on wit; for that reason he who is not stupid can nevertheless be very dull, in so far as hardly anything gets into his head, even though afterward he may be able to understand it with a greater maturity of judgment; and the difficulty of being able to express oneself proves nothing less than the capacity of the understanding, it only proves that wit is not performing enough assistance in dressing up the thought with all kinds of signs of which several fit it most aptly. The celebrated Jesuit *Clavius*[2] was run out of school as incapable (because according to the testing procedure of the understanding employed by tyrannical schoolmasters,[3] a boy is useful for nothing at all if he can write neither verses nor essays[4]). Later he came upon mathematics, the tables turned, and his previous teachers were idiots compared to him. The practical judgment concerning matters, such as the farmer, the artist, or the seafarer, etc., need it, is very different from judgment one possesses about the techniques with which human beings deal with one another. The latter is not so much understanding as craftiness, and the lovable

---

[1] From the Greek for "study of proper names."

[2] Latinized name of Christoph Schlüssel (1537–1612), a famous mathematician who was involved in the institution of the Gregorian calendar.

[3] *Orbile*; word coined after the name of Horace's teacher, Orbilius Pupillus, to designate a school tyrant.

[4] *Schulchrien*; a *chreia* (Greek) is a collection of useful sayings; the term was also used for expository writing according to a rhetorical model taught in school.

lack of this highly praised capacity is called *simplicity*. If the cause of this is to be sought in the weakness of the power of judgment, then such a human being is called a *ninny*,[5] *simpleton*, etc. Since intrigue and false devices have gradually become customary maxims in civil society and have very much complicated the play of human actions, it is no wonder when an otherwise sensible and sincere man for whom all this cunning is either too contemptible to occupy himself with it or who cannot move his honest and benevolent heart to make himself such a hated concept of human nature were to get caught everywhere by swindlers and give them much to laugh about – so that in the end the expression "a good man" designates a simpleton no longer in a figurative manner but directly, and occasionally even designates a cuckold.[6] For in the language of rogues no one is a sensible man but the one who holds everyone else for no better than what he himself is, namely a swindler.

The drives of human nature, which are called passions when they are of a high degree, are the moving forces of the will; the understanding only comes in to assess both the entire result of the satisfaction of all inclinations taken together from the end represented and to find the means to this end. If, e.g., a passion is especially powerful, the capacity of the understanding is of little help against it; for the enchanted human being sees very well indeed the reasons against his favorite inclination, but he feels powerless to give them active emphasis. If this inclination is good in itself and the person is otherwise reasonable, except for the overweighing penchant obstructing the view of the bad consequences, then this state of fettered reason is *folly*. A *foolish person* can have a good deal of understanding even in the judgment concerning those actions in which he is foolish; he must even possess a good deal of understanding and a good heart before being entitled to this milder appellation for his excesses. The *foolish person* can even be an excellent adviser for others, although his advice has no effect on himself. He will become shrewd only through damage or through age, which however only displaces one folly to make room for another one. The amorous passion or a great degree of ambition have always made foolish persons of many reasonable people. A young girl compels the formidable *Alcides*[7] to pull the thread on the

[2:261]

---

[5] *Tropf*
[6] *H –*; the translation assumes that Kant's elliptic designation is a discrete abbreviation for *Hahnrei*.
[7] Nickname of *Heracles*; the reference is to Heracles' stay with the Lydian princess Omphale, who made him wear women's clothes.

distaff, and Athen's idle citizens send *Alexander* with their silly praise to the end of the world. There are also inclinations of lesser vehemence and generality which nevertheless do not lack in generating folly: the building demon, the inclination to collect pictures, book mania. The degenerate human being has left his natural place and is attracted by everything and supported by everything. To the foolish person there is opposed the *shrewd man*; but he who is without folly is a *wise man*. This *wise man* can perhaps be sought for on the moon; possibly there one is without passion and has infinitely much reason. The insensitive person is safe from folly through his stupidity; to ordinary eyes, however, he has the mien of a wise person. *Pyrrho* saw a pig eating calmly from his trough on a ship in a storm while everyone was anxiously concerned and said pointing to it: "Such ought to be the calm of a wise person."[8] The insensitive one is *Pyrrho*'s wise person.

If the predominant passion is odious in itself and at the same time insipid enough to take for the satisfaction of the passion precisely that which is contrary to the natural intention of the passion, then this state of reversed reason is *foolishness*. The foolish person understands the true intention of his passion very well, even if he grants it a strength that is able of fettering reason. The *fool*, however, is at the same time rendered so stupid by his passion that he believes only then to be in possession of the thing desired when he actually deprives himself of it. *Pyrrhus*[9] knew very well that bravery and power earn universal admiration; he followed the drive for ambition and was nothing more than for what *Kineas* held him, namely a foolish person. However, when *Nero*[10] exposes himself to public mockery by reciting wretched verses to obtain the poet's prize and still says at the end of his life: *quantus artifex morior!*,[11] then I see in this feared and scorned ruler of Rome nothing better than a fool. I hold that every offensive folly is properly grafted on to two passions, arrogance and greediness. Both inclinations are unjust and are therefore hated, both are insipid in their nature, and their end destroys itself. The arrogant person expresses an unconcealed presumption of his advantage over others by a clear disdain for them. He believes that he is honored when he is

---

[8] Pyrrho of Elis (*c.* 365–360 to *c.* 275–270 BC), founder of Greek skepticism. The anecdote can be found in Diogenes Laertius, *Lives and Doctrines of the Eminent Philosophers*, IX, 68.

[9] Pyrrhus (319–272 BC), king of Epirus, who campaigned extensively but never won a lasting victory.

[10] Nero Claudius Caesar (37–68), Roman Emperor.   [11] Latin for "What an artist dies with me!"

hissed at, because there is nothing clearer than that his disrespect for others stirs up their vanity against the presumptuous person. The greedy person believes that he needs a great deal and cannot possibly do without the least of his goods; however, he actually does without all of them by [2:263] sequestering them through parsimony. The delusion of arrogance makes in part *silly*, in part *inflated fools*, according to whether silly inconstancy or rigid stupidity has taken possession of the empty head. Stingy avarice has from time immemorial given occasion for many ridiculous stories which could hardly be more strangely concocted than they actually occured. The foolish person is not wise; the fool is not clever. The mockery that the foolish person draws on himself is amusing and sparing, the fool earns the sharpest scourge of the satirist, yet he still does not feel it. One may not fully despair that a foolish person could still be made shrewd. But he who thinks of making a fool clever is washing a Moor. The reason is that in the former a true and natural inclination reigns which at most fetters reason, but in the latter a silly phantom reigns that reverses reason's principles. I will leave it to others to decide whether one has actual cause to be troubled about *Holberg*'s strange prediction, namely that the daily increase in fools is a matter of concern and gives rise to fears that they could eventually get it into their heads to found the fifth monarchy.[12] Supposing, however, that they were up to this, they might nevertheless not get too excited at that because one could easily whisper in the other's ear what the well-known jester of a neighboring court yelled to the students who ran after him as he rode through a Polish town in fool's attire: "You gentlemen, be industrious, learn something, because if we are too many, then we all can no longer have bread."

I come now from the frailties of the head which are despised and scoffed at to those which one generally looks upon with pity, or from those which do not suspend civil community to those in which official care provision takes an interest and for whom it makes arrangements. I divide these maladies in two, into those of impotency and into those of reversal. The first come under the general appellation of *imbecility*, the second under the name of the *disturbed mind*. The imbecile finds himself in a great impotency of memory, reason, and generally even of sensations. This ill is for the most part incurable, for if it is difficult to remove the

---

[12] A reference to the eschatological vision of the four realms or monarchies preceding the divine governance of the world in the prophet Daniel (Daniel 7:15–27).

[2:264] wild disorders of the disturbed brain, then it must be almost impossible to pour new life into its expired organs. The appearances of this weakness, which never allow the unfortunate person to leave the state of childhood, are too well known for it to be necessary to dwell long on this.

The frailties of the disturbed head can be brought under as many different main genera as there are mental capacities that are afflicted by it. I believe to be able to organize them all together under the following three divisions: first, the reversal of the concepts of experience in *derangement*, second, the power of judgment brought into disorder by this experience in *dementia*, third, reason that has become reversed with respect to more universal judgments in *insanity*. All remaining appearances of the sick brain can be viewed, it seems to me, either as different degrees of the cases mentioned or as an unfortunate coalition of these ills among one another, or, finally, as the engrafting of these ills on powerful passions, and can be subordinated under the classes cited.

With respect to the first ill, namely derangement, I explain its appearances in the following way. The soul of every human being is occupied even in the healthiest state with painting all kinds of images of things that are not present, or with completing some imperfect resemblance in the representation of present things through one or another chimerical trait which the creative poetic capacity draws into the sensation. One has no cause at all to believe that in the state of being awake our mind follows other laws than in sleep. Rather it is to be conjectured that in the former case the lively sensible impressions only obscure and render unrecognizable the more fragile chimerical images, while they possess their whole strength in sleep, in which the access to the soul is closed to all outer impressions. It is therefore no wonder that dreams are held for truthful experiences of actual things, as long as they last. Since they are then the strongest representations in the soul, they are in this state exactly what the sensations are in being awake. Now let us suppose that certain chimeras, no matter from which cause, had damaged, as it were, one or other organ of the brain such that the impression on that organ had become just as deep and at the same time just as correct as a sensation could make it,

[2:265] then, given good sound reason, this phantom would nevertheless have to be taken for an actual experience even in being awake. For it would be in vain to set rational arguments against a sensation or that representation which resembles the latter in strength, since the senses provide a far greater conviction regarding actual things than an inference of reason.

At least someone bewitched by these chimeras can never be brought by reasoning to doubting the actuality of his presumed sensation. One also finds that persons who show enough mature reason in other cases nevertheless firmly insist upon having seen with full attention who knows what ghostly shapes and distorted faces, and that they are even refined enough to place their imagined experience in connection with many a subtle judgment of reason. This property of the disturbed person, due to which, while being awake and without a particularly noticeable degree of a vehement malady, he is used to representing certain things as clearly sensed of which nevertheless nothing is present, is *derangement*. The deranged person is thus a dreamer in waking. If the usual illusion of his senses is only in part a chimera, but for the most part an actual sensation, then he who is in a higher degree predisposed to such reversal is a *fantast*. When after waking up we lie in an idle and gentle distraction, our imagination draws the irregular figures such as those of the bedroom curtains or of certain spots on a near wall, into human shapes, and this with a seeming correctness that entertains us in a not unpleasant manner but the illusion of which we dispel the moment we want to. We dream then only *in part* and have the chimera in our power. If something similar happens in a higher degree without the attention of the waking person being able to detach the illusion in the misleading imagination, then this reversal lets us conjecture a fantast. Incidentally, this self-deception in sensations is very common, and as long as it is only moderate it will be spared with such an appellation, although, if a passion is added to it, this same mental weakness can degenerate into actual fantastic mania. Otherwise human beings do not see through an ordinary delusion to what is there but rather what their inclination depicts for them: the natural history collector sees cities in florentine stone, the devout person the passion story in the speckled marble, some lady sees the shadow of two lovers on the moon in a telescope, but her pastor two church steeples. Fear turns the rays of the [2:266] northern light into spears and swords and in the twilight a sign post into a giant ghost.

The fantastic mental condition is nowhere more common than in hypochondria. The chimeras which this malady hatches do not properly deceive the outer senses but only provide the hypochondriac with an illusory sensation of his own state, either of the body or of the soul, which is, for the most part, an empty whim. The hypochondriac has an ill which, regardless which place it may have as its main seat, nevertheless in all likelihood migrates incessantly through the nerve tissue to all parts of the body. It draws above all a melancholic haze around the seat of the soul such that the patient feels in himself the illusion of almost all maladies of which he as much as hears. Therefore he talks of nothing more gladly than of his indisposition, he likes to read medical books, he recognizes everywhere his own misfortunes; in society he may even suddenly find himself in a good mood, and then he laughs a lot, dines well and generally has the look of a healthy human being. As regards his inner fantastic mania, the images in his brain often receive a strength and duration that is burdensome for him. If there is a ridiculous figure in his head (even if he himself recognizes it as only an image of fantasy) and if this whim coaxes an unbecoming laugh out of him in the presence of others without him indicating the cause of it, or if all kinds of obscure representations excite a forceful drive in him to start something evil, the eruption of which he himself is anxiously apprehensive about, and which nevertheless never comes to pass: then his state bears a strong resemblance to that of the deranged person, except that it is not that serious. The ill is not deeply rooted and lifts itself, in so far as the mind is concerned, usually either by itself or through some medication. One and the same representation affects the sensation in quite different degrees according to the different mental state of human beings. Therefore there is a kind of fantastic mania that is attributed to someone only because the degree of the feeling through which he is affected by certain objects is judged to be excessive for the moderate, healthy head. In this regard, the *melancholic* is a fantast with respect to life's ills. *Love* has quite a number of fantastic raptures,

[2:267] and the fine artifice of the ancient governments consisted in making the citizens into fantasts regarding the sense of public well-being. If someone is more excited by a moral sensation than by a principle, and this to a larger extent than others could imagine according to their own insipid and often ignoble feeling, then he is a fantast in their opinion. Let us place *Aristides*[13] among usurers, *Epictetus*[14] among courtiers and *Jean-Jacques Rousseau*[15] among the doctors of the Sorbonne. I think I hear loud derision and a hundred voices shout: *What fantasts!* This two-sided appearance of

---

[13] Athenian statesman and soldier (fifth century BC) with a reputation for honesty already among his contemporaries.
[14] Stoic philosopher (*c.* 55–*c.* 135), who had grown up as a slave.
[15] French-Swiss philosopher (1712–78), who was very much at odds with academic philosophy and education, as represented preeminently by the University of Paris, known as the Sorbonne.

fantasy in moral sensations that are in themselves good is *enthusiasm*, and nothing great has ever been accomplished in the world without it. Things stand quite differently with the *fanatic* (*visionary*, *enthusiast*). The latter is properly a deranged person with presumed immediate inspiration and a great familiarity with the powers of the heavens. Human nature knows no more dangerous illusion. If its outbreak is new, if the deceived human being has talents and the masses are prepared to diligently accept this leaven, then even the state occasionally suffers raptures. Enthusiasm leads the exalted person to extremes, *Muhammad* to the prince's throne and *John of Leyden*[16] to the scaffold. To a certain extent, I can also count the disturbed *faculty of recollection* among the reversedness of the head, in so far as it concerns the concepts of experience. For it deceives the miserable person who is afflicted by it through chimerical representations of who knows what a previous state, which actually never existed. Someone who speaks of the goods that he alleges to have possessed formerly or of the kingdom that he had, and who otherwise does not noticeably deceive himself with regard to his present state, is a deranged person with regard to recollection. The aged grumbler, who strongly believes that the world was more orderly and the human beings were better in his youth, is a fantast with regard to recollection.

Up to this point the power of the understanding is not actually attacked in the disturbed head, at least it is not necessary that it be; for the mistake actually resides only in the concepts. Provided one accepts the reversed sensation as true, the judgments themselves can be quite correct, even extraordinarily reasonable. A disturbance of the understanding on the contrary consists in judging in a completely reversed manner from otherwise correct experience; and from this malady the first degree is *demen-* [2:268] *tia*, which acts contrary to the common rules of the understanding in the immediate judgments from experience. The *demented person* sees or remembers objects as correctly as every healthy person, only he ordinarily explains the behavior of other human beings through an absurd delusion as referring to himself and believes that he is able to read out of it who knows what suspicious intentions, which they never have in mind. Hearing him, one would believe that the whole town is occupied with him. The market people who deal with one another and by chance

---

[16] A Dutch tailor and merchant (1509–36), who became the leader of the short-lived anabaptist kingdom in Munster, Westphalia.

glance at him are plotting against him, the night watchman calls out to play pranks at him, in short, he sees nothing but a universal conspiracy against himself. The *melancholic* is a gloomy person who is demented with respect to his sad or offensive conjectures. But there are also all kinds of amusing dementia, and the amorous passion flatters itself or is tormented with many strange interpretations that resemble dementia. An arrogant person is to a certain measure a demented person who concludes from the conduct of others staring at him in scorn that they admire him. The second degree of the head that is disturbed with respect to the higher power of cognition is properly reason brought into disorder, in so far as it errs in a nonsensical manner in imagined more subtle judgments concerning universal concepts, and can be called *insanity*. In the higher degree of this disturbance all kinds of presumed excessively subtle insights swarm through the burned-out brain: the contrived length of the ocean, the interpretation of prophecies, or who knows what hotchpotch of imprudent brain teasing. If the unfortunate person at the same time overlooks the judgments of experience, then he is called *crazy*. But there is the case where there are many underlying correct judgments of experience, except that, due the novelty and number of consequences presented to him by his wit, his sensation is so intoxicated that he no longer pays attention to the correctness of the connection of these judgments. In that case often a very glittering semblance of dementia arises that can exist along with great *genius* to the extent that slow reason is no longer able to accompany the excited wit. The state of the disturbed head that makes it unreceptive to outer sensations is *amentia*; in so far as rage rules in the latter it is called *raving*. Despair is a temporary dementedness in someone who is [2:269] hopeless. The raging vehemence of a disturbed person is generally called *frenzy*. The frantic, in so far as he is demented, is *mad*.

The human being in the state of nature can only be subject to a few follies and hardly any foolishness. His needs always keep him close to experience and provide his sound understanding with such easy occupation that he hardly notices that he needs understanding for his actions. Indolence moderates his coarse and common desires, leaving enough power to the small amount of the power of judgment which he needs to rule over those desires to his greatest advantage. From where should he draw the material for foolishness, since, unconcerned about another's judgment as he is, he can be neither vain nor inflated? Since he has no idea at all of the worth of goods he has not enjoyed, he is safe from the absurdity of stingy avarice, and because not much wit finds entrance to his head, he is just as well secured against every craziness. In like manner the disturbance of the mind can occur only seldom in this state of simplicity. Had the brain of the savage sustained some shock, I do not know where the fantastic mania should come from to displace the ordinary sensations that alone occupy him incessantly. Which dementia can well befall him since he never has cause to venture far in his judgment? Insanity, however, is surely wholly and entirely beyond his capacity. If he is ill in the head, he will be either idiotic or mad, and this, too, should happen most rarely, since he is for the most part healthy because he is free and in motion. The means of leavening for all of these corruptions can properly be found in the civil constitution, which, even if it does not produce them, nevertheless serves to entertain and aggravate them. The understanding, in so far as it is sufficient for the necessities and the simple pleasures of life, is a *sound understanding*, however, in so far as it is required for artificial exuberance,[17] be it in enjoyment or in the sciences, is the *refined understanding*. Thus the sound understanding of the citizen would already be a very refined understanding for the natural human being, and the concepts which are presupposed by a refined understanding in certain estates are no longer suited for those who are closer to the simplicity of nature, at least in terms of their insights, and those concepts usually make fools out of them when they take them over. Abbot *Terrasson* differentiates somewhere the ones of a disturbed mind into those who infer correctly from false representations and those who infer wrongly from correct representations.[18] This division seems to be in agreement with the propositions advanced earlier. In those of the first type, the fantasts or deranged persons, it is not the understanding that properly suffers but only the faculty that awakens the concepts in the soul of which the power of judgment afterward makes use by comparing them. These sick people can be well opposed by judgments of reason, if not to put an end to their ill, at least still to ease it. However, since in those of the second kind, the demented and insane persons, the understanding itself is attacked, it is not only foolish to reason with them (because they would not be demented if they could grasp these rational arguments),

[2:270]

---

[17] *gekünstelte Üppigkeit.* Elsewhere in this volume, *Üppigkeit* is generally translated as "opulence."
[18] Jean Terrasson (1670–1750), French classicist and philosopher, and member of the Académie Française.

but it is also extremely detrimental. For one thus gives their reversed head only new material for concocting absurdities; contradiction does not better them, rather it excites them, and it is entirely necessary in dealing with them to assume an indifferent and kind demeanor, as though one did not notice at all that their understanding was lacking something.

I have designated the frailties of the power of cognition *maladies of the head*, just as one calls the corruption of the will a *malady of the heart*. I have also only paid attention to their appearances in the mind without wanting to scout out their roots, which may well lie in the body and indeed may have their main seat more in the intestines than in the brain, as the popular weekly journal that is generally well known under the name of The Physician, plausibly sets forth in its 150th, 151st, and 152nd issues.[19] I can not even in any way convince myself that the disturbance of the mind originates from pride, love, too much reflection, and who knows what misuse of the powers of the soul, as is generally believed. This judgment, which makes of his misfortune a reason for scornful reproaches to the diseased person, is very unkind and is occasioned by a common mistake according to which one tends to confuse cause and effect. When one pays attention only a little to the examples, one sees that first the body suffers, that in the beginning, when the germ of the malady develops unnoticed, an ambiguous reversedness is felt which does not yet give suspicion of a disturbance of the mind, and which expresses itself in strange amorous whims or an inflated demeanor or in vain melancholic brooding. With time the malady breaks out and gives occasion to locate its ground in the immediately preceding state of the mind. But one should rather say that the human being became arrogant because he was already disturbed to some degree, than that he was disturbed because he was so arrogant. These sad ills still permit hope of a fortunate recovery, if only they are not hereditary, and it is the physician whose assistance one chiefly has to seek in this. Yet, for honor's sake, I would rather not exclude the philosopher, who could prescribe the diet of the mind – but on the condition that, as

[2:271]

[19] See *Der Arzt. Eine medicinische Wochenschrift*, Part VI, Hamburg, 1761. The journal was authored and edited by Johann August Unzer of Altona near Hamburg. The contributions to which Kant refers are: "Vom Zusammenhang des Verstandes mit der Verdauung" (Of the connection of the understanding with digestion) (in issue 150); "Beweis, dass alle Arten des Unsinns durch die Verbesserung der Verdauung curirt werden müssen" (Proof that all kinds of mental deficiency must be cured by the improvement of the digestion) (in issue 151); "Derselbe Beweis insbesondere von einigen hitzigen Deliris" (The same proof in particular of some feverish deliria) (in issue 152).

also for most of his other occupations, he requires no payment for this one. In recognition, the physician would also not refuse his assistance to the philosopher, if the latter attempted now and then the great, but always futile cure of foolishness. He would, e.g., in the case of the frenzy of a *learned crier* consider whether cathartic means taken in strengthened dosage should not be successful against it. If, according to the observations of *Swift*,[20] a bad poem is merely a purification of the brain through which many detrimental moistures are withdrawn for the relief of the sick poet, why should not a miserable brooding piece of writing be the same as well? In this case, however, it would be advisable to assign nature another path to purification so that he would be thoroughly and quietly purged of the ill without disturbing the common wealth through this.

---

[20] Jonathan Swift (1667–1745), whose satirical poetics *Peri bathou or Anti-Sublime*, containing the idea referred to by Kant, had been published in a German translation in 1733.

Inquiry Concerning the Distinctness of the Principles
of Natural Theology and Morality

Inquiry Concerning the Distinctness of the Principles   [2:273]
of Natural Theology and Morality

Being an answer to the question proposed for consideration by the Berlin
Royal Academy of Sciences for the year 1763

Verum animo satis haec vestigia parva sagaci
Sunt, per quae possis cognoscere caetera tute[1]

Introduction   [2:275]

The question proposed for consideration is such that, if it is appropriately answered, higher philosophy must as a result acquire a determine form. If the method for attaining the highest possible degree of certainty in this type of cognition has been established, and if the nature of this kind of conviction has been properly understood, then the following effect will be produced: the endless instability of opinions and scholarly sects will be replaced by an immutable rule which will govern didactic method and unite reflective minds in a single effort. It was in this way that, in natural science, *Newton's* method transformed the chaos of physical hypotheses into a secure procedure based on experience and geometry.[2] But what

---

[1] Latin for "But to a wise spirit these small clues will be sufficient: by their means you can safely come to know the rest." From Lucretius, *De rerum natura*, 1, 402–03. The regulations governing the prize essay competition required that all entries be submitted anonymously and identified only by a motto. Kant's motto was the above quotation from Lucretius.

[2] See Newton's *Principia mathematica* (1687). See too the present volume footnote 85 to Kant's *Remarks* (at 20:58).

method is this treatise itself to adopt, granted that it is a treatise in which metaphysics is to be shown the true degree of certainty to which it may aspire, as well as the path by which the certainty may be attained? If what is presented in this treatise is itself metaphysics, then the judgment of the treatise will be no more certain than has been that science which hopes to benefit from our inquiry by acquiring some permanence and stability; and then all our efforts will have been in vain. I shall, therefore, ensure that my treatise contains nothing but empirical propositions which are certain, and the inferences which are drawn immediately from them. I shall rely neither on the doctrines of the philosophers, the uncertainty of which is the very occasion of this present inquiry, nor on definitions, which so often lead to error. The method I shall employ will be simple and cautious. Some of the things I shall have to say may be found to be lacking in certainty; but such things will only have an elucidatory function and will not be employed for purposes of proof.

[2:276]
First Reflection: General comparison of the manner in which certainty is attained in mathematical cognition with the manner in which certainty is attained in philosophical cognition

§ I   *Mathematics arrives at all its definitions synthetically, whereas philosophy arrives at its definitions analytically*

There are two ways in which one can arrive at a general concept: either by the *arbitrary combination* of concepts, or by *separating out* that cognition which has been rendered distinct by means of analysis. Mathematics only ever draws up its definitions in the first way. For example, think arbitrarily of four straight lines bounding a plane surface so that the opposite sides are not parallel to each other. Let this figure be called a *trapezium*. The concept which I am defining is not given prior to the definition itself; on the contrary, it only comes into existence as a result of that definition. Whatever the concept of a cone may ordinarily signify, in mathematics the concept is the product of the arbitrary representation of a right-angled triangle which is rotated on one of its sides. In this and in all other cases the definition obviously comes into being as a result of *synthesis*.

The situation is entirely different in the case of philosophical definitions. In philosophy, the concept of a thing is always given, albeit confusedly or in an insufficiently determinate fashion. The concept has to be analyzed; the characteristic marks which have been separated out and the concept which has been given have to be compared with each other in all kinds of contexts; and this abstract thought must be rendered complete and determinate. For example, everyone has a concept of time. But suppose that that concept has to be defined. The idea of time has [2:277] to be examined in all kinds of relation if its characteristic marks are to be discovered by means of analysis: different characteristic marks which have been abstracted have to be combined together to see whether they yield an adequate concept; they have to be collated with each other to see whether one characteristic mark does not partly include another within itself. If, in this case, I had tried to arrive at a definition of time synthetically, it would have had to have been a happy coincidence indeed if the concept, thus reached synthetically, had been exactly the same as that which completely expresses the idea of time which is given to us.

Nonetheless, it will be said, philosophers sometimes offer synthetic definitions as well, and mathematicians on occasion offer definitions which are analytic. A case in point would be that of a philosopher arbitrarily thinking of a substance endowed with the faculty of reason and calling it a spirit. My reply, however, is this: such determinations of the meaning of a word are never philosophical definitions. If they are to be called definitions at all, then they are merely grammatical definitions. For no philosophy is needed to say what name is to be attached to an arbitrary concept. *Leibniz* imagined a simple substance which had nothing but obscure representations, and he called it a *slumbering monad.*[3] But, in doing so, he did not define the monad. He merely invented it, for the concept of a monad was not given to him but created by him. Mathematicians, on the other hand, it must be admitted, sometimes have offered analytic definitions. But it must also be said that for them to do so is always a mistake. It was in this way that *Wolff* considered similarity in geometry: he looked at it with a philosophical eye, with a view to subsuming the geometrical concept of similarity under the general

---

[3] Cf. Leibniz, *Principes de la nature et de la grace*; also *Monadologie* §§ 20 and 24; also Baumgarten, *Metaphysica* (1739), § 401. The Leibniz selections are both available in *Leibniz: Philosophical Essays*, ed. Roger Ariew and Daniel Garber, Indianapolis: Hackett, 1989, pp. 206–24.

concept. But he could have spared himself the trouble. If I think of figures, in which the angles enclosed by the lines of the perimeter are equal to each other, and in which the sides enclosing those angles stand in identical relations to each other – such a figure could always be regarded as the definition of similarity between figures, and likewise with the other similarities between spaces. The general definition of similarity is of no concern whatever to the geometer. It is fortunate for mathematics that, even though the geometer from time to time gets involved in the business of furnishing analytic definitions as a result of a false conception of his task, in the end nothing is actually inferred from such definitions, or, at any rate, the immediate inferences which he draws ultimately constitute the mathematical definition itself. Otherwise this science would be liable to exactly the same wretched discord as philosophy itself.

[2:278] The mathematician deals with concepts which can often be given a philosophical definition as well. An example is the concept of space in general. But he accepts such a concept *given* in accordance with his clear and ordinary representation. It sometimes happens that philosophical definitions are given to him from other sciences; this happens especially in applied mathematics. The definition of fluidity is a case in point. But, in a case like that, the definition does not arise within mathematics itself, it is merely employed there. It is the business of philosophy to analyze concepts which are given in a confused fashion, and to render them complete and determinate. The business of mathematics, however, is that of combining and comparing given concepts of magnitudes, which are clear and certain, with a view to establishing what can be inferred from them.

§ 2   Mathematics, in its analyses, proofs, and inferences examines the universal under signs in concreto; *philosophy examines the universal by means of signs* in abstracto

Since we are here treating our propositions only as conclusions derived immediately from our experiences, I *first of all* appeal, with regard to the present matter, to arithmetic, both the general arithmetic of indeterminate magnitudes and the arithmetic of numbers, where the relation of magnitude to unity is determinate. In both kinds of arithmetic, there are posited first of all not things themselves but their signs, together with the special designations of their increase or decrease, their relations *etc.* Thereafter, one operates with these signs according to easy and certain rules, by means of substitution, combination, subtraction, and many kinds of transformation, so that the things signified are themselves completely forgotten in the process, until eventually, when the conclusion is drawn, the meaning of the symbolic conclusion is deciphered. *Secondly*, I would draw attention to the fact that in geometry, in order, for example, to discover the properties of all circles, one circle is drawn; and in this one circle, instead of drawing all the possible lines which could intersect each other within it, two lines only are drawn. The relations which hold between these two lines are proved; and the universal rule, which governs the relations holding between intersecting lines in all circles whatever, is considered in these two lines *in concreto*.

If the procedure of philosophy is compared with that of geometry it becomes apparent that they are completely different. The signs employed in philosophical reflection are never anything other than words. And words can neither show in their composition the constituent concepts of which the whole idea, indicated by the word, consists; nor are they capable of indicating in their combinations the relations of the philosophical [2:279] thoughts to each other. Hence, in reflection in this kind of cognition, one has to focus one's attention on the thing itself: one is constrained to represent the universal *in abstracto* without being able to avail oneself of that important device which facilitates thought and which consists in handling individual signs rather than the universal concepts of the things themselves. Suppose, for example, that the geometer wishes to demonstrate that space is infinitely divisible. He will take, for example, a straight line standing vertically between two parallel lines; from a point on one of these parallel lines he will draw lines to intersect the other two lines. By means of this symbol he recognizes with the greatest certainty that the division can be carried on *ad infinitum*. By contrast, if the philosopher wishes to demonstrate, say, that all bodies consist of simple substances, he will first of all assure himself that bodies in general are wholes composed of substances, and that, as far as these substances are concerned, composition is an accidental state, without which they could exist just as well; he will then infer, therefore, that all composition in a body could be suspended in imagination, but in such a way that the substances, of which the body consists, would continue to exist; and since that which remains of a compound when all composition whatever has been canceled is simple, he will conclude that bodies must consist of simple substances. In this case, neither figures nor visible signs are capable of expressing either the thoughts or the relations which hold between them. Nor can abstract reflection be replaced by the transposition of signs in accordance with rules, the representation of the things themselves being replaced in this procedure by the clearer and the easier representation of the signs. The universal must rather be considered *in abstracto*.

§ 3   In mathematics, unanalyzable concepts and indemonstrable propositions are few in number, whereas in philosophy they are innumerable

The concepts of magnitude in general, of unity, of plurality, of space, and so on, are, at least in mathematics, unanalyzable. That is to say, their analysis and definition do not belong to this science at all. I am well aware of the fact that geometers often confuse the boundaries between the different sciences, and on occasion wish to engage in philosophical speculation in mathematics. Thus, they seek to define concepts such as those just mentioned, although the definition in such a case has no

[2:280] mathematical consequences at all. But this much is certain: any concept is unanalyzable with respect to a given discipline if, irrespective of whether or not it be definable elsewhere, it need not be defined, not, at any rate, in this discipline. And I have said that concepts are rare in mathematics. I shall go still further and deny that, strictly speaking, any such concepts at all can occur in mathematics; by which I mean that their definition by means of conceptual analysis does not belong to mathematical cognition – assuming, that is, that it is actually possible elsewhere. For mathematics never defines a given concept by means of analysis; it rather defines an object by means of arbitrary combination; and the thought of that object first becomes possible in virtue of that arbitrary combination.

If one compares philosophy with this, what a difference becomes apparent. In all its disciplines, and particularly in metaphysics, every analysis which can occur is actually necessary, for both the distinctness of the cognition and the possibility of valid inferences depend upon such analysis. But it is obvious from the start that the analysis will inevitably lead to concepts which are unanalyzable. These unanalyzable concepts will be unanalyzable either in and for themselves or relatively to us. It is further evident that there will be uncommonly many such unanalyzable concepts, for it is impossible that universal cognition of such great complexity should be constructed from only a few fundamental concepts.

For this reason, there are many concepts which are scarcely capable of analysis at all, for example, the concept of a *representation*, the *concepts of being next to each other* and *being after each other*. Other concepts can only be partially analyzed, for example, the concepts of *space*, *time*, and the many *different feelings* of the human soul, such as the feeling of the *sublime*, the *beautiful*, the *disgusting*, and so forth. Without exact knowledge and analysis of these concepts, the springs of our nature will not be sufficiently understood; and yet, in the case of these concepts, a careful observer will notice that the analyses are far from satisfactory. I admit that the definitions of *pleasure* and *displeasure*, of *desire* and *aversion*, and of numberless other such concepts, have never been furnished by means of adequate analyses. Nor am I surprised by this unanalyzability. For concepts which are as diverse in character as this must presumably be based upon different elementary concepts. The error, committed by some, of treating all such cognitions as if they could be completely analyzed into a few simple concepts is like the error into which the early physicists fell. They were guilty, namely, of the mistake of supposing that all the matter of which nature is constituted consists of the so-called four elements – a view which has been discredited by more careful observation.

Furthermore, there are only a few fundamental *indemonstrable propositions* in mathematics. And even if they admit of proof elsewhere, they are [2:281] nonetheless regarded as immediately certain in this science. Examples of such propositions are: *the whole is equal to all its parts taken together*; *there can only be one straight line between two points*, and so forth. Mathematicians are accustomed to setting up such principles at the beginning of their inquiries so that it is clear that these are the only obvious propositions which are immediately presupposed as true, and that all other propositions are subject to strict proof.

If a comparison were to be made between this and philosophy, and, in particular between this and metaphysics, I should like to see drawn up a table of the indemonstrable propositions which lie at the foundation of these sciences throughout their whole extent. Such a table would constitute a scheme of immeasurable scope. But the most important business of higher philosophy consists in seeking out these indemonstrable fundamental truths; and the discovery of such truths will never cease as long as cognition of such a kind as this continues to grow. For, no matter what the object may be, those characteristic marks, which the understanding initially and immediately perceives in the object, constitute the *data* for exactly the same number of indemonstrable propositions, which then form the foundation on the basis of which definitions can then be drawn up. Before I set about the task of defining what space is, I clearly see that, since this concept is given to me, I must first of all, by analyzing it, seek out those characteristic marks which are initially and immediately thought in that concept. Adopting this approach, I notice that there is a manifold in space of which the parts are external to each other; I notice that this manifold is not constituted by substances, for the cognition I wish to acquire relates not to things in space but to space itself; and I notice that space can only have three dimensions *etc.* Propositions such as these can well be explained if they are examined *in concreto* so that they come to be cognized intuitively; but they can never be proved. For on what basis could such a proof be constructed, granted that these propositions constitute the first and the simplest thoughts I can have of my object, when I first call it to mind? In mathematics, the definitions are the first thought which I can entertain of the thing defined, for my concept of the object only comes into existence as a result of the definition. It is, therefore, absolutely absurd to regard the definitions as capable of proof. In philosophy, where the concept of the thing to be defined is given to [2:282] me, that which is initially and immediately perceived in it must serve as an indemonstrable fundamental judgment, for since I do not yet possess a complete and distinct concept of the thing, but am only now beginning to look for such a concept, it follows that the fundamental judgment cannot be proved by reference to this concept. On the contrary, such a judgment serves to generate this distinct cognition and to produce the definition sought. Thus, I shall have to be in possession of these primary fundamental judgments prior to any philosophical definition of the things under examination. And here the only error which can occur beforehand is that of mistaking a derivative characteristic mark for one which is primary and fundamental. The following reflection will contain some considerations which will put this claim beyond doubt.

§ 4 *The object of mathematics is easy and simple, whereas that of philosophy is difficult and involved*

The object of mathematics is magnitude. And, in considering magnitude, mathematics is only concerned with how many times something is posited. This being the case, it is obvious that this science must be based upon a few, very clear fundamental principles of the general theory of magnitudes (which, strictly speaking, is general arithmetic). There, too, one sees the increase and decrease of magnitudes, their reduction to equal factors in the theory of roots – all of them originating from a few simple fundamental concepts. And a few fundamental concepts of space effect the application of this general cognition of magnitudes to geometry. In order to convince oneself of the truth of what I am saying here all one needs to do is contrast, for example, the ease one has in understanding an arithmetical object which contains an immense multiplicity, with the much greater difficulty one experiences in attempting to grasp a philosophical idea, in which one is trying to understand only a little. The relation of a *trillion* to unity is understood with complete distinctness, whereas even today the philosophers have not yet succeeded in explaining the concept of freedom in terms of its elements, that is to say, in terms of the simple and familiar concepts of which it is composed. In other words, there are infinitely many qualities which constitute the real object of philosophy, and distinguishing them from each other is an extremely strenuous business. Likewise, it is far more difficult to disentangle complex and involved cognition by means of analysis than it is to combine simple given cognitions by means of synthesis and thus to establish conclusions. I know that there are many people who find philosophy a great deal easier than higher mathematics. But what such people understand by philosophy is simply what they find in books which bear the title. The outcome of the [2:283] two inquiries shows the difference between them. Claims to philosophical cognition generally enjoy the fate of opinions and are like the meteors, the brilliance of which is no guarantee of their endurance. Claims to philosophical cognition vanish, but mathematics endures. Metaphysics is without doubt the most difficult of all the things into which man has insight. But so far no metaphysics has ever been written. The question posed for consideration by the Royal Academy of Sciences in Berlin shows that there is good reason to ask about the path in which one proposes to search for metaphysical understanding in the first place.

Second Reflection: The only method for attaining the highest possible degree of certainty in metaphysics

Metaphysics is nothing other than the philosophy of the fundamental principles of our cognition. Accordingly, what was established in the preceding reflection about mathematical cognition in comparison with philosophy will also apply to metaphysics. We have seen that the differences which are to be found between cognition in mathematics and cognition in philosophy are substantial and essential. And in this connection, one can say with Bishop *Warburton* that nothing has been more damaging to philosophy than mathematics, and in particular the *imitation* of its method in contexts where it cannot possibly be employed. The *application* of the mathematical method in those parts of philosophy involving cognition of magnitudes is something quite different, and its utility is immeasurable.

In mathematics I begin with the definition of my object, for example, of a triangle, or a circle, or whatever. In metaphysics I may never begin with a definition. Far from being the first thing I know about the object, the definition is nearly always the last thing I come to know. In mathematics, namely, I have no concept of my object at all until it is furnished by the definition. In metaphysics I have a concept which is already given to me, although it is a confused one. My task is to search for the distinct, complete, and determinate concept. How then am I to begin? *Augustine* said: "I know perfectly well what time is, but if someone asks me what it is I do not know."[4] In such a case as this, many operations have to be performed in unfolding obscure ideas, in comparing them with each other, in subordinating them to each other and in limiting them by each other. And I would go as far as to say that, although much that is true and much that is penetrating has been said about time, nonetheless no real definition has ever been given of time. For, as far as the nominal definition is concerned, it is of little or no use to us, for even without the nominal definition the word is understood well enough not to be misused. If we had as many correct definitions of time as there are definitions to be found in the books devoted to the subject, with what certainty could inferences be made and conclusions drawn. But experience teaches us the opposite.

[2:284]

In philosophy and in particular in metaphysics, one can often come to know a great deal about an object with distinctness and certainty, and even establish reliable conclusions on that basis prior to having a definition of

---

[4] See Saint Augustine, *Confessions*, XI, 14: "What, therefore, is time? If no one asks me what it is, I know; if I wish to explain what it is to someone who has asked me about it, I do not know what it is."

that object, and even, indeed, when one had no intention of furnishing one. In the case of any particular thing, I can be immediately certain about a number of different predicates, even though I am not acquainted with a sufficiently large number of them to be able to furnish a completely determinate *concept of the thing*, in other words, a definition. Even if I had never defined what an *appetite* was, I should still be able to say with certainty that every appetite presupposed the representation of the object of the appetite; that this representation was an anticipation of what was to come in the future; that the feeling of pleasure was connected with it; and so forth. Everyone is constantly aware of all this in the immediate consciousness of appetite. One might perhaps eventually be able to arrive at a definition of appetite on the basis of such remarks as these, once they had been compared with each other. But as long as it is possible to establish what one is seeking by inference from a few immediately certain characteristic marks of the thing in question, and to do so without a definition, there is no need to venture on an undertaking which is so precarious. In mathematics, as is known, the situation is completely different.

In mathematics, the significance of the signs employed is certain, for it is not difficult to know what the significance was which one wished to attribute to those signs. In philosophy generally and in metaphysics in particular, words acquire their meaning as a result of linguistic usage, unless, that is, the meaning has been more precisely determined by means of logical limitation. But it frequently happens that the same words are employed for concepts which, while very similar, nonetheless conceal within themselves considerable differences. For this reason, whenever such a concept is applied, even though one's terminology may seem to be fully sanctioned by linguistic usage, one must still pay careful attention to whether it is really the same concept which is connected here with [2:285] the same sign. We say that a person *distinguishes* gold from brass if, for example, he recognizes that the density to be found in the one metal is not to be found in the other. We also say that an animal distinguishes one kind of provender from another if it eats the one and leaves the other untouched. Here, the word "distinguishes" is being used in both cases even though, in the first case, it means "recognize the difference," which is something which can never occur without *judging*, whereas in the second case it merely signifies that *different actions are performed* when different representations are present, and in this case it is not necessary that a judgment should occur. All that we perceive in the case of the animal is that it is impelled to perform different actions by different sensations; and that is something which is perfectly possible without its in the least needing to make a judgment about similarity or difference.

From all this there flow quite naturally the rules which govern the method by which alone the highest possible degree of metaphysical certainty can be attained. These rules are quite different from those which have hitherto been followed. They promise, if they are adopted, to produce a happier outcome than could ever have been expected on a different path. The *first* and the most important *rule* is this: one ought not to start with definitions, unless that is, one is merely seeking a nominal definition, such as, for example, the definition: that of which the opposite is impossible is necessary. But even then there are only a few cases where one can confidently establish a distinctly determinate concept right at the very beginning. One ought, rather, to begin by carefully searching out what is immediately certain in one's object, even before one has its definition. Having established what is immediately certain in the object of one's inquiry, one then proceeds to draw conclusions from it. One's chief concern will be to arrive only at judgments about the object which are true and completely certain. And in doing this, one will not make an elaborate parade of one's hope of arriving at a definition. Indeed, one will never venture to offer such a definition, until one has to concede the definition, once it has presented itself on the basis of the most certain of judgments. The *second rule* is this: one ought particularly to distinguish those judgments which have been immediately made about the object and relate to what one initially encountered in that object with certainty. Having established for certain that none of these judgments is contained in another, these judgments are to be placed at the beginning of one's inquiry, as the foundation of all one's inferences, like the axioms of geometry. It follows from this that, when one is engaged in metaphysical

[2:286] reflection, one ought always particularly to distinguish what is known for certain, even if that knowledge does not amount to a great deal. Nonetheless, one may experiment with cognitions which are not certain to see whether they may not put us on the track of certain cognition; but care must be taken to ensure that the two sorts of cognition are not confused. I shall not mention the other rules of procedure which this method has in common with every other rational method. I shall merely proceed to render these rules distinct by means of examples.

The true method of metaphysics is basically the same as that introduced by *Newton* into natural science and which has been of such benefit to it. *Newton's* method maintains that one ought, on the basis of certain experience and, if need be, with the help of geometry, to seek out the rules in accordance with which certain phenomena of nature occur. Even if one does not discover the fundamental principle of these occurrences in the bodies themselves, it is nonetheless certain that they operate in accordance with this law. Complex natural events are explained once it has been clearly shown how they are governed by these well-established rules. Likewise in metaphysics: by means of certain inner experience, that is to say, by means of an immediate and self-evident inner consciousness, seek out those characteristic marks which are certainly to be found in the concept of any general property. And even if you are not acquainted with the complete essence of the thing, you can still safely employ those characteristic marks to infer a great deal from them about the thing in question.

Example of the only certain method for metaphysics illustrated by reference to our cognition of the nature of bodies

For the sake of brevity, I refer the reader to the proof which is briefly given at the end of Section 2 of the First Reflection. I do so with a view to first establishing here as my foundation the proposition: all bodies must consist of simple substances. Without determining what a body is, I nonetheless know for certain that it consists of parts which would exist even if they were not combined together. And if the concept of a substance is an abstracted concept, it is without doubt one which has been arrived at by a process of abstraction from the corporeal things which exist in the world. But it is not even necessary to call them substances. It is enough that one can, with the greatest certainty, infer from them that bodies consist of simple parts. The self-evident analysis of this proposition could easily be offered, but it would be too lengthy to present here. Now, employing [2:287] infallible proofs of geometry, I can demonstrate that space does not consist of simple parts; the arguments involved are sufficiently well known. It follows that there is a determinate number of parts in each body, and that they are all simple, and that there is an equal number of parts of space occupied by the body, and they are all compound. It follows from this that each simple part of the body (each element) occupies a space.

Suppose that I now ask: What does "occupying a space" mean? Without troubling myself about the essence of space, I realize that, if space can be penetrated by anything without there being anything there to offer resistance, then one may, if need be, say that there was something in this space but never that the space was being occupied by it. By this means I cognize that a space is occupied by something if there is something there which offers resistance to a moving body attempting to penetrate that same space. But this resistance is impenetrability. Accordingly, bodies occupy space by means of impenetrability, But impenetrability is a *force*, for it expresses a resistance, that is to say, it expresses an action which is opposed to an external force. And the force which belongs to a body must also belong to the simple parts of which it is constituted. Accordingly, the elements of every body fill their space by means of the force of impenetrability. However, I proceed to ask whether the primary elements are not themselves extended since each element in the body fills a space? At this juncture, I can for once introduce a definition which is immediately certain. It is the definition, namely, that a thing is *extended* if, when it is posited in itself (*absolute*), it fills a space, just as each individual body, even if I imagine that nothing existed apart from it, would fill a space. However, if I consider an absolutely simple element, then, if it is posited on its own (with no connection with anything else), it is impossible that there should exist within it a multiplicity of parts existing externally to each other, and impossible that it should occupy a space *absolute*. It cannot, therefore, be extended. However, the cause of the element occupying a space is the force of impenetrability which it directs against numerous external things. I therefore realize that whereas the multiplicity of its external action flows from that fact, multiplicity in respect of inner parts does not. Hence, the fact that it occupies a space in the body (*in nexu aliis*[5]) is not the reason for its being extended.

I shall just add a few words in order to reveal the shallowness of the proofs offered by the metaphysicians when, in accordance with their custom, they confidently establish their conclusions on the basis of definitions which have been laid down once and for all as the foundation of their argument. The conclusions instantly collapse if the definitions are defective. It is well known that most *Newtonians* go further than *Newton* himself and maintain that bodies, even at a distance, attract each other

[2:288]

---

[5] Latin for "in connection with other bodies."

immediately (or, as they put it, through empty space). I do not propose to challenge the correctness of this proposition, which certainly has much to be said for it. What, however, I do wish to say is that metaphysics has not in the least refuted it. First of all, bodies are *at a distance* from each other if they *are not touching* each other. That is the exact meaning of the expression. Now, suppose that I ask what I mean by "touching". Without troubling about the definition, I realize that whenever I judge that I am touching a body I do so by reference to the resistance which the impenetrability of that body offers. For I find that this concept originates ultimately from the sense of touch. The judgment of the eye only produces the surmise that one body will touch another; it is only when one notices the resistance offered by impenetrability that the surmise is converted into certain knowledge. Thus, if I say that one body acts upon another immediately *at a distance* then this means that it acts on it immediately, but not by means of impenetrability. But it is by no means clear here why this should be impossible, unless, that is, someone shows either that impenetrability is the only force possessed by a body, or at least that a body cannot act on any other body immediately, without at the same time doing so by means of impenetrability. But this has never yet been proved, nor does it seem very likely that it ever will be. Accordingly, metaphysics, at least, has no sound reason to object to the idea of immediate attraction at a distance. However, let the arguments of the metaphysicians make their appearance. To start with, there appears the definition: The immediate and reciprocal presence of two bodies is touch. From this it follows that if two bodies act upon each other immediately, then they are touching each other. Things which are touching each other are not at a distance from each other. Therefore, two bodies never act immediately upon each other at a distance *etc.* The definition is surreptitious. Not every immediate presence is a touching, but only the immediate presence which is mediated by impenetrability. The rest is without foundation.

I shall now proceed with my treatise. It is clear from the example I have adduced that both in metaphysics and in other sciences there is a great deal which can be said about an object with certainty, before it has been [2:289] defined. In the present case, neither body nor space has been defined, and yet there are things which can be reliably said of both. What I am chiefly concerned to establish is this: in metaphysics one must proceed analytically throughout, for the business of metaphysics is actually the analysis of confused cognitions. If this procedure is compared with the procedure which is adopted by philosophers and which is currently in vogue in all schools of philosophy, one will be struck by how mistaken the practice of philosophers is. With them, the most abstracted concepts, at which the understanding naturally arrives last of all, constitute their starting point, and the reason is that the method of the mathematicians, which they wish to imitate throughout, is firmly fixed in their minds. This is why there is a strange difference to be found between metaphysics and all other sciences. In geometry and in the other branches of mathematics, one starts with what is easier and then one slowly advances to the more difficult operations. In metaphysics, one starts with what is the most difficult: one starts with possibility, with existence in general, with necessity and contingency, and so on – all of them concepts which demand great abstraction and close attention. And the reason for this is to be sought chiefly in the fact that the signs for these concepts undergo numerous and imperceptible modifications in use; and the differences between them must not be overlooked. One is told that one ought to proceed synthetically throughout. Definitions are thus set up right at the beginning, and conclusions are confidently drawn from them. Those who practice philosophy in this vein congratulate each other for having learnt the secret of thorough thought from the geometer. What they do not notice at all is the fact that geometers acquire their concepts by means of *synthesis*, whereas philosophers can only acquire their concepts by means of *analysis* – and that completely changes the method of thought.

If philosophers, having entered the natural path of sound reason, first seek out what they know for certain about the abstracted concept of an object (for example, space or time); and if they refrain from claiming to offer definitions; and if they base their conclusions on these certain *data* alone, making sure that, even though the sign for the concept in question has remained unchanged, the concept itself has not undergone modification whenever its application has changed – if philosophers adopt this approach then, although they may not, perhaps, have quite so many opinions to *hawk* around, the views they do have to offer will be of sound value. I should like to adduce one more example of this latter procedure. Most philosophers adduce as examples of obscure concepts those which we have in deep sleep. *Obscure* representations are representations of which we are not conscious. Now, some experiences show that we also have representations in deep sleep, and since we are not conscious of them it follows that they were obscure. In the case before us here, the term

[2:290]

"*consciousness*" is ambiguous. Either one is not conscious that one has a representation, or one is not conscious that one has had a representation. The former signifies the obscurity of the representation as it occurs in the soul, while the latter signifies nothing more than that one does not remember the representation. Now, all that the example adduced shows is that there can be representations which one does not remember when one is awake; but from this it by no means follows that they may not have been clearly present in consciousness while one was sleeping. A case in point would be the example, adduced by *Sauvage*,[6] of the person suffering from catalepsy, or the ordinary actions of sleepwalkers. People have a tendency to jump too readily to conclusions, without paying attention to differing cases and investing the relevant concept with a significance appropriate to each respective instance. This may explain why, in the present case, no attention has been paid to what is probably a great mystery of nature: the fact, namely, that it is perhaps during sleep that the soul exercises its greatest facility in rational thought. The only objection which could be raised against this supposition is the fact that we have no recollection of such rational activity when we have woken up; but that proves nothing.

Metaphysics has a long way to go yet before it can proceed synthetically. It will only be when analysis has helped us towards concepts which are understood distinctly and in detail that it will be possible for synthesis to subsume compound cognitions under the simplest cognition, as happens in mathematics.

Third Reflection: On the nature of metaphysical certainty

§ I   Philosophical certainty is altogether different in nature from mathematical certainty

One is certain if one knows that it is impossible that a cognition should be false. The degree of this certainty, taken objectively, depends upon

---

[6] Kant is alluding to an observation published by Francois Boissier de Sauvages (a disciple of the vitalist, Georg Ernst Stahl) in the *Mémoires de l'Académie des sciences de Paris* for the year 1742: a German translation appeared in the *Hamburger Magazin* (vol. 7, pp. 489–512) in 1745 under the title "*Betrachtungen über die Seele in der Erstarrung und Schlafwanderung*" (Observations on the soul in catalepsy and sleepwalking).

[2:291]   the sufficiency in the characteristic marks of the necessity of a truth. But taken subjectively, the degree of certainty increases with the degree of intuition to be found in the cognition of this necessity. In both respects, mathematical certainty is of a different kind to philosophical certainty. I shall demonstrate this with the greatest possible clarity.

The human understanding, like any other force of nature, is governed by certain rules. Mistakes are made, not because the understanding combines concepts without rule, but because the characteristic mark which is not perceived in a thing is actually denied of it. One judges that that of which one *is not conscious* in a thing *does not exist*. Now, *firstly*, mathematics arrives at its concepts synthetically; it can say with certainty that what it did not intend to represent in the object by means of the definition is not contained in that object. For the concept of what has been defined only comes into existence by means of the definition; the concept has no other significance at all apart from that which is given to it by the definition. Compared with this, philosophy and particularly metaphysics are a great deal more uncertain in their definitions, should they venture to offer any. For the concept of that which is to be defined is given. Now, if one should fail to notice some characteristic mark or other, which nonetheless belongs to the adequate distinguishing of the concept in question, and if one judges that no such characteristic mark belongs to the complete concept, then the definition will be wrong and misleading. Numberless examples of such errors could be adduced, and for that very reason I refer only to the above example of touching. *Secondly*, mathematics, in its inferences and proofs, regards its universal knowledge under signs *in concreto*, whereas philosophy always regards its universal knowledge *in abstracto*, as existing alongside signs. And this constitutes a substantial difference in the way in which the two inquiries attain to certainty. For since signs in mathematics are sensible means to cognition, it follows that one can know that no concept has been overlooked, and that each particular comparison has been drawn in accordance with easily observed rules *etc*. And these things can be known with the degree of assurance characteristic of seeing something with one's own eyes. And in this, the attention is considerably facilitated by the fact that it does not have to think things in their universal representation; it has rather to think the signs as they occur in their particular cognition which, in this case, is sensible in character. By contrast, the only help which words, construed as the signs of philosophical cognition, afford is that of reminding us of the universal concepts which they signify. It is at all times necessary to be immediately aware of their significance. The pure understanding [2:292] must be maintained in a state of constant attention; how easy it is for the characteristic mark of an abstracted concept to escape our attention without our noticing, for there is nothing sensible which can reveal to us the fact that the characteristic mark has been overlooked. And when that happens, different things are taken to be the same thing, and the result is error.

What we have established here is this: the grounds for supposing that one could not have erred in a philosophical cognition which was certain can never be as strong as those which present themselves in mathematics. But apart from this, the intuition involved in this cognition is, as far as its exactitude is concerned, greater in mathematics than it is in philosophy. And the reason for this is the fact that, in mathematics, the object is considered under sensible signs *in concreto*, whereas in philosophy the object is only ever considered in universal abstracted concepts; and the clarity of the impression made by such abstracted concepts can never be as great as that made by signs which are sensible in character. Furthermore, in geometry the signs are similar to the things signified, so that the certainty of geometry is even greater, though the certainty of algebra is no less reliable.

§ 2   *Metaphysics is capable of a certainty which is sufficient to produce conviction*

Certainty in metaphysics is of exactly the same kind as that in any other philosophical cognition, for the latter can only be certain if it is in accordance with the universal principles furnished by the former. We know from experience that, even outside mathematics, there are many cases where, in virtue of rational principles, we can be completely certain, and certain to the degree of conviction. Metaphysics is nothing but philosophy applied to insights of reason which are more general, and it cannot possibly differ from philosophy in this respect.

Errors do not arise simply because we do not know certain things. We make mistakes because we venture to make judgments, even though we do not know everything which is necessary for doing so. A large number of errors, indeed almost all of them, are due to this latter kind of overhastiness. You have certain knowledge of some of the predicates of

[2:293] a thing. Very well! Base your conclusions on this certain knowledge and you will not go wrong. But you insist on having a definition at all costs. And yet you are not sure that you know everything which is necessary to drawing up such a definition; nonetheless, you venture on such an undertaking and thus you fall into error. It is therefore possible to avoid errors, provided that one seeks out cognitions which are certain and distinct, and provided that one does not so lightly lay claim to be able to furnish definitions. Furthermore, you could also establish a substantial part of an indubitable conclusion, and do so with certainty; but do not, on any account, permit yourself to draw the whole conclusion, no matter how slight the difference may appear to be. I admit that the proof we have in our possession for establishing that the soul is not matter is a good one. But take care that you do not infer from this that the soul is not of a material nature. For this latter claim is universally taken to mean not merely that the soul is not matter, but also that it is not a simple substance of the kind which could be an element of matter. But this requires a separate proof – the proof, namely, that this thinking being does not exist in space in the way in which a corporeal element exists in space, that is to say, in virtue of impenetrability; it also requires proof that this thinking being could not, when combined with other thinking beings, constitute something extended, a conglomerate. But no proof has actually been given yet of these things. Such a proof, were it to be discovered, would indicate the incomprehensibility of the way in which a spirit is present in space.

§ 3   The certainty of the first fundamental truths of metaphysics is not of a kind different from that of any other rational cognition, apart from mathematics

The philosophy of *Crusius* has recently claimed to give metaphysical cognition quite a different form.[7] It has done so by refusing to concede to the law of contradiction the preeminent right to be regarded as the supreme and universal principle of all cognition. *Crusius* introduced a large number of other principles which were immediately certain and indemonstrable, and he maintained that the correctness of these principles could be established by appeal to the nature of our understanding,

---

[7] Kant is alluding to Christian August Crusius (1715–75), *Weg zur Gewissheit* (1747).

employing the rule that what I cannot think as other than true is true. [2:294]
Such principles include: what I cannot think as existing has never existed;
all things must be somewhere and somewhen, *etc*. I shall briefly indicate
the true character of the first fundamental truths of metaphysics; at the
same time, I shall offer a brief account of the true content of *Crusius's*
method, which is not as different from that of the philosophy contained
in this treatise as may, perhaps, be thought. On this basis, it will also be
possible to establish in general the degree of possible certainty to which
metaphysics can aspire.

All true propositions must be either affirmative or negative. The *form*
of every *affirmation* consists in something being represented as a characteristic mark of a thing, that is to say, as identical with the characteristic
mark of a thing. Thus, every affirmative judgment is true if the predicate
is *identical* with the subject. And since the *form* of every *negation* consists
in something being represented as in conflict with a thing, it follows that
a negative judgment is true if the predicate *contradicts* the subject. The
proposition, therefore, which expresses the essence of every affirmation
and which accordingly contains the supreme formula of all affirmative
judgments, runs as follows: to every subject there belongs a predicate
which is identical with it. This is the *law of identity*. The proposition
which expresses the essence of all negation is this: to no subject does
there belong a predicate which contradicts it. This proposition is the *law
of contradiction*, which is thus the fundamental formula of all negative
judgments. These two principles together constitute the supreme universal principles, in the formal sense of the term, of human reason in
its entirety. Most people have made the mistake of supposing that the
law of contradiction is the principle of all truths whatever, whereas in
fact it is only the principle of negative truths. Any proposition, however,
is indemonstrable if it is immediately thought under one of these two
supreme principles and if it cannot be thought in any other way. In other
words, any proposition is indemonstrable if either the identity or the contradiction is to be found immediately in the concepts, and if the identity
and the contradiction cannot or may not be understood through analysis
by means of intermediate characteristic marks. All other propositions are
capable of proof. The proposition, a body is divisible, is demonstrable,
for the predicate and the subject can be shown by analysis and therefore indirectly: a body is *compound*, but what is compound is *divisible*,
so a *body* is divisible. The intermediate characteristic mark here is *being* [2:295]

compound. Now, in philosophy there are, as we have said above, many indemonstrable propositions. All these indemonstrable propositions are subsumed under the formal first principles, albeit immediately. However, in so far as they also contain the grounds of other cognitions, they are also the first material principles of human reason. For example: *a body is compound* is an indemonstrable proposition, for the predicate can only be thought as an immediate and primary characteristic mark in the concept of a body. Such material principles constitute, as *Crusius* rightly says, the foundation of human reason and the guarantor of its stability. For, as we have mentioned above, they provide the stuff of definitions and, even when one is not in possession of a definition, the *data* from which conclusions can be reliably drawn.

And *Crusius* is also right to criticize other schools of philosophy for ignoring these material principles and adhering merely to formal principles. For on their basis alone it really is not possible to prove anything at all. Propositions are needed which contain the intermediate concept by means of which the logical relation of the other concepts to each other can be known in a syllogism. And among these propositions there must be some which are the first. But it is not possible to invest some propositions with the status of supreme material principles unless they are obvious to every human understanding. It is my conviction, however, that a number of the principles adduced by *Crusius* are open to doubt, and, indeed, to serious doubt.

This celebrated man proposes setting up a supreme rule to govern all cognition and therefore metaphysical cognition as well. The supreme rule is this: *What cannot be thought as other than true is true, etc.* However, it can easily be seen that this proposition can never be a ground of the truth of any cognition. For, if one concedes that there is no other ground of truth which can be given, apart from the impossibility of thinking it other than true, then one is in effect saying that it is impossible to give any further ground of truth, and that this cognition is indemonstrable. Now, of course, there are many indemonstrable cognitions. But the feeling of conviction which we have with respect to these cognitions is merely an avowal, not an argument establishing that they are true.

Accordingly, metaphysics has no formal or material grounds of certainty which are different in kind from those of geometry. In both [2:296] metaphysics and geometry, the formal element of the judgments exists in virtue of the laws of agreement and contradiction. In both sciences, indemonstrable propositions constitute the foundation on the basis of which conclusions are drawn. But whereas in mathematics the definitions are the first indemonstrable concepts of the things defined, in metaphysics, the place of these definitions is taken by a number of indemonstrable propositions which provide the primary data. Their certainty may be just as great as that of the definitions of geometry. They are responsible for furnishing either the stuff, from which the definitions are formed, or the foundation, on the basis of which reliable conclusions are drawn. Metaphysics is as much capable of the certainty which is necessary to produce conviction as mathematics. The only difference is that mathematics is easier and more intuitive in character.

Fourth Reflection: Concerning the distinctness and certainty of which the fundamental principles of natural theology and morality are capable

§ I   The fundamental principles of natural theology are capable of the greatest philosophical certainty

Firstly, distinguishing one thing from another is easiest and most distinct if the thing in question is the only possible thing of its kind. The object of natural religion is the unique first cause; its determinations are such that they cannot easily be confused with those of other things. But the greatest conviction is possible when it is absolutely necessary that these and no other predicates belong to a thing. For in the case of contingent determinations it is generally difficult to discover the variable conditions of its predicates. Hence, the absolutely necessary being is an object such that, as soon as one is on the right track of its concept, it seems to promise even more certainty than most other philosophical cognition. In this part of my undertaking, all that I can do is consider the possible philosophical cognition of God in general; for if we were to examine the philosophical theories relating to this object which are actually current, we should be taken too far afield. The chief concept which here offers itself to the metaphysician is that of the absolutely necessary existence of [2:297] a being. In order to arrive at this concept, the metaphysician could first of all ask the question: *Is it possible that absolutely nothing at all should exist?* Now, if he realizes that, were absolutely nothing at all to exist, then no *existence* would be given and there would be *nothing to think* and there would be no *possibility* – once that is realized, all that needs to be investigated is the concept of the existence of that which must constitute the ground of all possibility. He will develop this idea and establish the determinate concept of the absolutely necessary being. I do not wish to become involved in a detailed investigation of this project, but I shall say this much: as soon as the existence of the unique, most perfect and necessary Being is established, then the concepts of that Being's other determinations will be established with much greater precision, for these determinations will always be the greatest and most perfect of their kind; they will also be established with much greater certainty, for the only determinations which will be admitted will be those which are necessary. Suppose, for example, that I am to determine the concept of the divine *omnipresence*. I have no difficulty in recognizing the following fact. The Being, upon which everything else depends – for it is itself independent – determines through its presence the *place* of everything else in the world; it does not, however, determine *for itself* a place among those things, for if it did it would belong to the world as well. Therefore, strictly speaking, God does not exist in any *place*, although He is present to all things in all the *places in which things exist*. Likewise, I realize that, whereas the things in the world which follow upon one another are in His power, nonetheless He does not in virtue of that fact determine for Himself a moment of time in this series; as a consequence, nothing is past or future in relation to God. If, therefore, I say that God foresees the future, this does not mean that God sees that which *relative to Him is future*. It rather means that God sees that which, relative to certain things in the world, is future, that is to say, that which follows upon a state of those certain things in the world. From this it can be seen that cognitions of the future, the past and the present are not, relative to the action of the divine understanding, different from each other; God rather cognizes them all as actual things in the universe. This foreknowledge can be imagined much more determinately and with much greater distinctness in God than in a thing which belongs to the totality of the world.

Metaphysical cognition of God is thus capable of a high degree of certainty in all those areas where no analogon of contingency is to be encountered. But when it comes to forming a judgment about His free actions, about providence, or about the way in which He exercises justice and goodness, there can only be, in this science, an approximation to certainty, or a certainty which is moral. For there is still a great deal of obscurity surrounding the concepts which we have of these determinations, even when they occur in ourselves.

§ 2   *The fundamental principles of morality in their present state are not*   [2:298]
capable of all the certainty necessary to produce conviction

In order to make this claim clear I shall merely show how little even the fundamental concept of *obligation* is yet known, and how far practical philosophy must still be from furnishing the distinctness and the certainty of the fundamental concepts and the fundamental principles which are necessary for certainty in these matters. The formula by means of which every obligation is expressed is this: one *ought* to do this or that and abstain from doing the other. Now, every *ought* expresses a necessity of the action and is capable of two meanings. To be specific: either I ought to do something (as a *means*) if I want something else (as an *end*), or I *ought immediately* to do something else (as an *end*) and make it actual. The former may be called the necessity of the means (*necessitas problematica*), and the latter the necessity of the ends (*necessitas legalis*). The first kind of necessity does not indicate any obligation at all. It merely specifies a prescription as the solution to the problem concerning the means I must employ if I am to attain a certain end. If one person tells another what actions he must perform or what actions he must abstain from performing if he wishes to advance his happiness, he might perhaps be able, I suppose, to subsume all the teachings of morality under his prescription. They are not, however, obligations any longer except in the sense, say, in which it would be my obligation to draw two intersecting arcs if I wanted to bisect a straight line into two equal parts. In other words, they would not be obligations at all; they would simply be recommendations to adopt a suitable procedure, if one wished to attain a given end. Now since no other necessity attaches to the employment of means than that which belongs to the end, all the actions which are prescribed by morality under the condition of certain ends are contingent. They cannot be called obligations as long as they are not subordinated to an end which is necessary in itself. Take the following examples: I ought to advance the total greatest perfection; or: I ought to act in accordance with the will of God. To whichever of these two principles the whole practical philosophy is to be subordinated, the principle chosen must, if it is to be a rule and ground of obligation,

command the action as being immediately necessary and not conditional upon some end. And here we find that such an immediate supreme rule of all obligation must be absolutely indemonstrable. For it is impossible, by contemplating a thing or a concept of any kind whatever, to recognize or infer what one ought to do, if that which is presupposed is not an end, and if the action is a means. But this cannot be the case; if it were, our principle would not be a formula of obligation; it would be a formula of problematic skill.

Having convinced myself after long reflection on this matter, I can now briefly show the following. The rule: perform the most perfect action in your power, is the first *formal ground* of all obligation to act. Likewise, the proposition: abstain from doing that which will hinder the realization of the greatest possible perfection, is the first *formal ground* of the duty to *abstain from acting*. And just as, in the absence of any material first principles, nothing flowed from the first formal principles of our judgments of the truth, so here no specifically determinate obligation flows from these two rules of the good, unless they are combined with indemonstrable material principles of practical cognition.

It is only recently, namely, that people have come to realize that the faculty of representing the *true* is *cognition*, while the faculty of experiencing the *good* is *feeling*, and that the two faculties are, on no account, to be confused with each other. Now, just as there are unanalyzable concepts of the true, that is to say, unanalyzable concepts of that which is encountered in the objects of cognition, regarded in itself, so too there is an unanalyzable feeling of the good (which is never encountered in a thing absolutely but only relatively to a being endowed with sensibility). One of the tasks of the understanding is to analyze and render distinct the compound and confused concept of the good by showing how it arises from simpler feelings of the good. But if the good is simple, then the judgment: "This is good," will be completely indemonstrable. This judgment will be an immediate effect of the consciousness of the feeling of pleasure combined with the representation of the object. And since there are quite certainly many simple feelings of the good to be found in us, it follows that there are many such unanalyzable representations. Accordingly, if an action is immediately represented as good, and if it does not contain concealed within itself a certain other good, which could be discovered by analysis and on account of which it is called perfect, then the necessity [2:300] of this action is an indemonstrable material principle of obligation. Take for example the principle: love him who loves you. This is a practical principle which is, it is true, subsumed, albeit immediately, under the supreme formal and affirmative rule of obligation. For since it cannot be further shown by analysis why a special perfection is to be found in mutual love, it follows that this rule has not been proved practically. In other words, the rule has not been proved by tracing it back to the necessity of another perfect action. It is rather subsumed immediately under the universal rule of good actions. It is perhaps possible that the example I have adduced does not present the matter with sufficient distinctness and persuasiveness. However, the limits of a treatise such as the present one – limits which, perhaps, I have already overstepped – do not permit me the completeness I would wish. An immediate ugliness is to be found in the actions, which conflicts with the will of Him, from Whom all goodness comes and to Whom we owe our existence. This ugliness is clearly apparent, provided that we do not straightaway focus our attention on the disadvantages, which may, as consequences, accompany such behavior. Hence, the proposition: do what is in accordance with the will of God, is a material principle of morality. Nonetheless, it is formally though immediately subsumed under the supreme universal formula, of which mention has already been made. In both practical and in theoretical philosophy one must avoid lightly taking for indemonstrable that which in fact is capable of proof. Notwithstanding, those principles, which as postulates contain the foundations of all the other practical principles, are indispensable. *Hutcheson* and others have, under the name of moral feeling, provided us with a starting point from which to develop some excellent observations.

It is clear from what has been said that, although it must be possible to attain the highest degree of philosophical certainty in the fundamental principles of morality, nonetheless the ultimate fundamental concepts of obligation need first of all to be determined more reliably. And in this respect, practical philosophy is even more defective than speculative philosophy, for it has yet to be determined whether it is merely the faculty of cognition, or whether it is feeling (the first inner ground of the faculty of desire) which decides its first principles.

[2:301]

Postscript

Such are the thoughts I surrender to the judgment of the Royal Academy of Sciences. I venture to hope that the reasons presented here will be of some value in clarifying the subject, which was what was requested. In what concerns the care, precision and elegance of the execution: I have preferred to leave something to be desired in that respect, rather than to allow such matters to prevent my presenting this inquiry for examination at the proper time, particularly since this defect is one which could easily be remedied should my inquiry meet with a favorable reception.

M. Immanuel Kant's Announcement of the Program of
his Lectures for the Winter Semester 1765–1766

[2:303]

M. Immanuel Kant's Announcement of the program of his Lectures for the Winter Semester 1765–1766

[2:305]

There is always a certain difficulty involved in the instruction of young people, and it is this: the knowledge one imparts to them is such that one finds oneself constrained to outstrip their years. Without waiting for their understanding to mature, one is obliged to impart knowledge to them, which, in the natural order of things, can only be understood by minds which are more practiced and experienced. It is this which is the source of the endless prejudices of the schools – prejudices which are more intractable and frequently more absurd than ordinary prejudices. And it is this, too, which is the source of that precocious prating of young thinkers, which is blinder than any other self-conceit and more incurable than ignorance. This difficulty, however, is one which cannot be entirely avoided, and the reason is this. In an epoch which is characterized by an elaborately complex social organization, a knowledge of higher things is regarded as a means to advancement and comes to be thought of as a necessity of life. Such knowledge ought by nature, however, really to be regarded merely as one of life's adornments – one of life's inessential beauties, so to speak. Nonetheless, even in this branch of instruction, it is possible to make public education more adapted to nature, even though it will not be possible to bring it into perfect harmony with it. The natural progress of human knowledge is as follows: first of all, the understanding develops by using experience to arrive at intuitive judgments, and by their means to attain to concepts. After that, and employing reason, these concepts come to be known in relation to their grounds and consequences. Finally, by means of science, these concepts come to be known as parts of a well-ordered whole. This being the case, teaching must follow exactly the same path. The teacher is, therefore, expected to develop in his pupil firstly the man of *understanding*, then the man of *reason*, and finally the man of *learning*. Such a procedure has this advantage: even if, as usually happens, the pupil should never reach the final phase, he will still have benefited from his instruction. He will have grown more experienced and become more clever, if not for school then at least for life.

[2:306]

If this method is reversed, then the pupil picks up a kind of reason, even before his understanding has developed. His science is a borrowed science which he wears, not as something which has, so to speak, grown within him, but as something which has been hung upon him. Intellectual aptitude is as unfruitful as it ever was. But at the same time it has been corrupted to a much greater degree by the delusion of wisdom. It is for this reason that one not infrequently comes across men of learning (strictly speaking, people who have pursued courses of study) who display little understanding. It is for this reason, too, that the academies send more people out into the world with their heads full of inanities than any other public institution.

The rule for proceeding is, therefore, as follows. Firstly, the understanding must be brought to maturity and its growth expedited by exercising it in empirical judgments and focusing its attention on what it can learn by comparing the impressions which are furnished by the senses. It ought not to venture any bold ascent from these judgments and concepts to higher and more remote judgments and concepts. It ought rather to make its way towards them by means of the natural and well-trodden pathway of the lower concepts, for this path will gradually take it further than any bold ascents ever could. But all this should be done, not in accordance with that capacity for understanding which the teacher perceives, or thinks he perceives in himself, and which he mistakenly presupposes in his pupils, but rather in accordance with that capacity for understanding which must of necessity be generated in that faculty by the practice which has just been described. In short, it is not *thoughts* but *thinking* which the understanding ought to learn. It ought to be *led*, if you wish, but not carried, so that in the future it will be capable of *walking* on its own, and doing so without stumbling.

The peculiar nature of philosophy itself demands such a method of teaching. But since philosophy is strictly speaking an occupation only for those who have attained the age of maturity, it is no wonder that difficulties arise when the attempt is made to adapt it to the less practiced capacity of youth. The youth who has completed his school instruction has been accustomed *to learn*. He now thinks that he is going to *learn philosophy*. But that is impossible, for he ought now to learn to philosophize. Let me explain myself more distinctly. All the sciences which can be learned in the strict sense of the term can be reduced to two kinds: the *historical* and the *mathematical*. To the first there belong, in addition to history proper, natural history, philology, positive law, etc. In everything historical, it is one's own experience or the testimony of other people which constitute what is actually given and which is therefore available for use, and which may, so to speak, simply be assimilated. In everything mathematical, on [2:307] the other hand, these things are constituted by the self-evidence of the concepts and the infallibility of the demonstration. It is thus possible in both types of knowledge to learn. That is to say, it is possible to impress either on the memory or on the understanding that which can be presented to us as an already complete discipline. In order, therefore, to be able to learn philosophy as well there must already be a philosophy which actually exists in the first place. It must be possible to produce a book and say: "Look, here is wisdom, here is knowledge on which you can rely. If you learn to understand and grasp it, if you take it as your foundation and build on it from now on, you will be philosophers." Until I am shown such a book of philosophy, a book to which I can appeal, say, as I can appeal to *Polybius* in order to elucidate some circumstance of history, or to *Euclid* in order to explain a proposition of mathematics – until I am shown such a book, I shall allow myself to make the following remark. One would be betraying the trust placed in one by the public if, instead of extending the capacity for understanding of the young people entrusted to one's care and educating them to the point where they will be able in the future to acquire a more mature insight *of their own* – one would be betraying the trust placed in one by the public, if, instead of that, one were to deceive them with a philosophy which was alleged to be already complete and to have been excogitated by others for their benefit. Such a claim would create the illusion of science. That illusion is only accepted as legal tender in certain places and among certain people. Everywhere else, however, it is rejected as counterfeit currency. The method of instruction, peculiar to philosophy, is *zetetic*, as some of the philosophers of antiquity expressed it (from ζητειν). In other words, the method of philosophy is the method of *enquiry*. It is only when reason has already grown more practised and only in certain areas, that this method becomes *dogmatic*, that is to say, *decisive*. The philosophical writer, for example, upon whom one bases one's instruction, is not to be regarded as the paradigm of judgment. He ought rather to be taken as the occasion for forming one's own judgment about him, and even, indeed, for passing judgment against him. What the pupil is really looking for is proficiency in the method of reflecting and drawing inferences *for himself*. And it is that proficiency alone which can be of use to him. As for the positive knowledge which he may also perhaps come to acquire at the same time – that must be regarded as an incidental consequence. To reap a superabundant harvest of such knowledge, he needs only to plant within himself the fruitful roots of this method.

If one compares the above method with the procedure which is commonly adopted and which differs so much from it, one will understand a number of things which would otherwise strike one as surprising. For example: why is there no other kind of specialized knowledge which exemplifies so many *masters* as does philosophy? Many of those who have [2:308] learned history, jurisprudence, mathematics, and so forth, nonetheless modestly disclaim that they have learned enough to be able to teach the subject themselves. But why, on the other hand, is it rare to find someone who does not in all seriousness imagine that, in addition to his usual occupation, he is perfectly able to lecture on, say, logic, and moral philosophy, and other subjects of the kind, should he wish to dabble in such trivial matters? The reason for this divergence is the fact that, whereas in the former science there is a common standard, in the latter science each person has his own standard. It will likewise be clearly seen that it is contrary to the nature of philosophy to be practiced as a means to earning one's daily bread – the essential nature of philosophy is such that it cannot consistently accommodate itself to the craze of demand or adapt itself to the law of fashion – and that it is only pressing need, which still exercises its power over philosophy, which can constrain it to assume a form which wins it public applause.

In the course of the present semester which has just begun, I propose to hold private lectures on the following science, which I intend to handle in an exhaustive fashion.

1. Metaphysics. I have sought to show in a short and hastily composed work[a] that this science has, in spite of the great efforts of scholars, remained imperfect and uncertain because the method peculiar to it has been misunderstood. Its method is not *synthetic*, as is that of mathematics, but *analytic*. As a result, that which is simple and the most universal in mathematics is also what is easiest, whereas in the queen of the sciences it is what is most difficult. In mathematics, what is simple and universal must in the nature of things come first, while in metaphysics it must come at the end. In mathematics one begins the doctrine with the definitions; in metaphysics one ends the doctrine with them; and so on in other respects. For some considerable time now I have worked in accordance with this scheme. Every step which I have taken along this path has revealed to me both the source of the errors which have been committed, and the criterion of judgment by reference to which alone those errors can be avoided, if they can be avoided at all. For this reason, I hope that I shall be able in the near future to present a complete account of what may serve as the foundation of my lectures in the aforementioned science. Until that time, however, I can easily, by applying gentle pressure, induce A. G. Baumgarten, the author of the textbook on which this course will be based – and that book has been chosen chiefly for the richness of its contents and the precision of its method – to follow the same path. Accordingly, after a brief introduction, I shall begin with   [2:309] *empirical psychology*, which is really the metaphysical science of *the human being* based on experience. For in what concerns the term "soul," it is not yet permitted in this section to assert that he has a soul. The second part of the course will discuss *corporeal nature* in general. This part is drawn from the chapters of the *Cosmology* which treat of *matter* and which I shall supplement with a number of written additions in order to complete the treatment. In the first of these sciences (to which, on account of the analogy, there is added empirical zoology, that is to say, the consideration of animals) we shall examine all the organic phenomena which present themselves to our senses. In the second of these sciences we shall consider everything which is *inorganic* in general. Since everything in the world can be subsumed under these two classes, I shall then proceed to

---

[a] The second of the treatises published by the *Berlin Academy of Sciences* on the occasion of the award of the prize for the year 1763. [Kant is here referring to his *Inquiry*, included in the present volume.]

ontology, the science, namely, which is concerned with the more general properties of all things. The conclusion of this enquiry will contain the distinction between *mental* and *material* beings, as also the connection or separation of the two, and therefore *rational psychology*. The advantage of this procedure is this: it is the already experienced student who is introduced to the most difficult of all philosophical investigations. But there is another advantage as well: in every reflection, the abstract is considered in the form of a concrete instance, furnished by the preceding disciplines, so that everything is presented with the greatest distinctness. I shall not have to anticipate my own argument; in other words, I shall not have to introduce anything by way of elucidation which ought only to be adduced at a later stage – an error which is both common and unavoidable in the synthetic method of presenting things. At the end there will be a reflection on the cause of all things, in other words the science which is concerned with God and the world. There is one other advantage which I cannot but mention. Although it is a product of accidental causes, it is not, however, to be lightly esteemed. It is an advantage which I hope will accrue from the employment of this method. Everyone knows with what eagerness the spirited and volatile youth attend the start of a course, and how subsequently the lecture theatres grow gradually increasingly empty. Now, I am assuming that what ought not to happen will, in spite of all reminders, continue to happen in the future. Nonetheless, the aforementioned method of teaching has a utility of its own. The student, whose enthusiasm has already evaporated even before he has got to the end of empirical psychology (though this is scarcely to be expected if such a procedure as the one I have described is adopted) will, nonetheless, have benefited this much: he will have heard something which he can under-

[2:310] stand, on account of its easiness; and he will have heard something which he can enjoy, in virtue of its interest; and he will have heard something which he can use, because of the frequency with which it can be given an application in life. On the other hand, if he should be deterred from proceeding further by ontology, which is difficult to understand, that which he might perhaps have grasped if he had continued could not have been of any further use to him at all.

2. *Logic.* Of this science there are really two kinds. The first kind is a critique and canon of *sound understanding*. In one direction, it borders on crude concepts and ignorance, and, in the other, it borders on science and learning. It is with this type of logic that all philosophy, at the start of

academic instruction, ought to be prefaced. It is, so to speak, a quarantine (if the expression be permitted) which must be observed by the apprentice who wishes to migrate from the land of prejudice and error, and enter the realm of a more enlightened reason and the science. The second kind of logic is the critique and canon of *real learning*. The only way in which it can be treated is from the point of view of the sciences of which it is supposed to be the organon. The purpose of such a treatment is to make the procedure employed by the science concerned more consonant with the rules, and to render the nature of the discipline itself, as well as the means for improving it, accessible to the understanding. In this way, I shall add at the end of the metaphysics a reflection on the method which is peculiar to it, and which can serve as an organon of this science. This reflection would have been out of place at the beginning, for it is impossible to make the rules clear, unless there are some examples to hand by means of which the rules can be elucidated *in concreto*. The teacher must, of course, be in possession of the organon, before he presents his account of the science in question, so that he can be guided by it; but he must never present the organon to his audience except at the end of his presentation. The critique and the canon of the whole of philosophy in its entirety, this complete logic, can therefore only have its place in instruction at the end of the whole of philosophy. The reason is this. It is the knowledge of philosophy, which we have come to acquire, and the history of human opinions which alone make it possible for us to reflect on the origin both of its insights and of its errors. And it is this alone which enables us to draw up a precise ground plan, on the basis of which an edifice of reason, which is permanent in duration and regular in structure, can be erected.

I shall be lecturing on logic of the first type. To be more specific, I shall base my lectures on *Meier's* handbook, for he has, I think, kept his eye focused on the limits of the intentions which we have just now mentioned. And he also stimulates us to an understanding, not only of [2:311] the cultivation of reason in its more refined and learned form, but also of the development of the ordinary understanding, which is nonetheless active and sound. The former serves the life of contemplation, while the latter serves the life of action and society. And in this, the very close relationship of the materials under examination leads us at the same time, in the *critique of reason*, to pay some attention to the *critique of taste*, that is to say, *aesthetics*. The rules of the one at all times serve to elucidate the rules of the other. Defining the limits of the two is a means to a better understanding of them both.

3. Ethics. Moral philosophy[1] has this special fate: that it takes on the semblance of being a science and enjoys some reputation for being thoroughly grounded, and it does so with even greater ease than metaphysics, and that in spite of the fact that it is neither a science nor thoroughly grounded. The reason why it presents this appearance and enjoys this reputation is as follows. The distinction between good and evil in actions, and the judgment of moral rightness, can be known, easily and accurately, by the human heart through what is called sentiment, and that without the elaborate necessity of proofs. In ethics, a question is often settled in advance of any reasons which have been adduced – and that is something which does not happen in metaphysics. It will not, therefore, come as a surprise that no one raises any special difficulties about admitting grounds, which only have some semblance of validity. For this reason, there is nothing more common than the title of a moral philosopher, and nothing more rare than the entitlement to such a name.

For the time being, I shall lecture on *universal practical philosophy* and the *doctrine of virtue*, basing both of them on *Baumgarten*. The attempts of *Shaftesbury*, *Hutcheson* and *Hume*, although incomplete and defective, have nonetheless penetrated furthest in the search for the fundamental principles of all morality. Their efforts will be given the precision and the completeness which they lack. In the doctrine of virtue I shall always begin by considering historically and philosophically what *happens* before specifying what *ought to happen*. In so doing, I shall make clear what method ought to be adopted in the study of the human being. And by *human being* here I do not only mean *the human being* as he is distorted by the mutable form which is conferred upon him by the contingencies of his condition, and who, as such, has nearly always been misunderstood even by philosophers. I rather mean the unchanging *nature* of human beings, and his distinctive position within the creation. My purpose will be to establish which perfection is appropriate to him in the state of *primitive* innocence and which perfection is appropriate to him in the state of *wise* innocence. It is also my purpose to establish what, by contrast, the rule of human behavior is when, transcending the two types of limit, he strives to attain the highest level of physical or moral excellence, though falling

[2:312]

---

[1] *Die moralische Weltweisheit*

short of that attainment to a greater or lesser degree. This method of moral enquiry is an admirable discovery of our times, which, when viewed in the full extent of its program, was entirely unknown to the ancients.

4. *Physical geography*. Right at the beginning of my academic career, I realized that students were being seriously neglected, particularly in this respect: early on they learned the art of subtle argumentation but they lacked any adequate knowledge of historical matters which could make good their lack of *experience*. Accordingly, I conceived the project of making the history of the present state of the earth, in other words, geography in the widest sense of the term, into an entertaining and easy compendium of the things which might prepare them and serve them for the exercise of practical reason, and which might arouse within them the desire to extend even further the knowledge which they had begun to acquire in their study of the subject. The name which I gave to the discipline, constituted by that part of the subject on which my chief attention was at the time focused, was that of *physical geography*. Since then I have gradually extended the scheme, and I now propose, by condensing that part of the subject which is concerned with the physical features of the earth, to gain the time necessary for extending my course of lectures to include the other parts of the subject, which are of even greater general utility. This discipline will therefore be a *physical, moral,* and *political* geography. It will contain, *first of all,* a specification of the remarkable features of *nature* in its three realms. The specification will, however, be limited to those features, among the numberlessly many which could be chosen, which particularly satisfy the general desire for knowledge, either because of the fascination which they exercise in virtue of their rarity, or because of the effect which they can exercise on states by means of trade and industry. This part of the subject, which also contains a treatment of the natural relationship which holds between all the countries and seas in the world, and the reason for their connection, is the real foundation of all history. Without this foundation, history is scarcely distinguishable from fairy stories. The *second* part of the subject considers *the human being*, throughout the world, from the point of view of the variety of his natural properties and the differences in that feature of the human being which is moral in character. The consideration of these things is at once very important and also highly stimulating as well. Unless these matters are considered, general judgments about the human being would scarcely be possible. The comparison of human beings with each

[2:313]   other, and the comparison of the human being today with the moral state of the human being in earlier times, furnishes us with a comprehensive map of the human species. *Finally,* there will be a consideration of what can be regarded as a product of the reciprocal interaction of the two previously mentioned forces, namely, the condition of the *states* and nations throughout the world. The subject will not be considered so much from the point of view of the way in which the condition of states depends on accidental causes, such as the deeds and fates of individuals, for example, the sequence of governments, conquests, and intrigues between states. The condition of states will rather be considered in relation to what is more constant and which contains the more remote ground of those accidental causes, namely, the situation of their countries, the nature of their products, customs, industry, trade, and population. Even the reduction, if I may use the term, of a science of such extensive prospects to a smaller scale has its great utility. For it is only by this means that it is possible to attain that unity without which all our knowledge is nothing but a fragmentary patchwork. In a sociable century, such as our own, am I not to be permitted to regard the stock which a multiplicity of entertaining, instructive, and easily understood knowledge offers for the maintenance of social intercourse as one of the benefits which it is not demeaning for science to have before its eyes? At least it cannot be pleasant for a man of learning frequently to find himself in the embarrassing situation in which *Isocrates,* the orator, found himself: urged on one occasion when he was in company to say something, he was obliged to reply: *What I know is not suitable to the occasion; and that which is suitable to the occasion I do not know.*

   This is a brief indication of the subjects on which I shall be lecturing in the university in the course of the coming semester which has just started. I thought it necessary to say something in this connection in order to explain my method, where I have now found it opportune to make some alterations. *Mihi sic est usus: Tibi ut opus facto est, face. (Terence).*[2]

---

[2] Latin for "For my part, such is my practice; you, for your part, do what you deem fitting." [From Terence *Heautontimoroumenos* ("The Self-Tormentor"), line 80.]

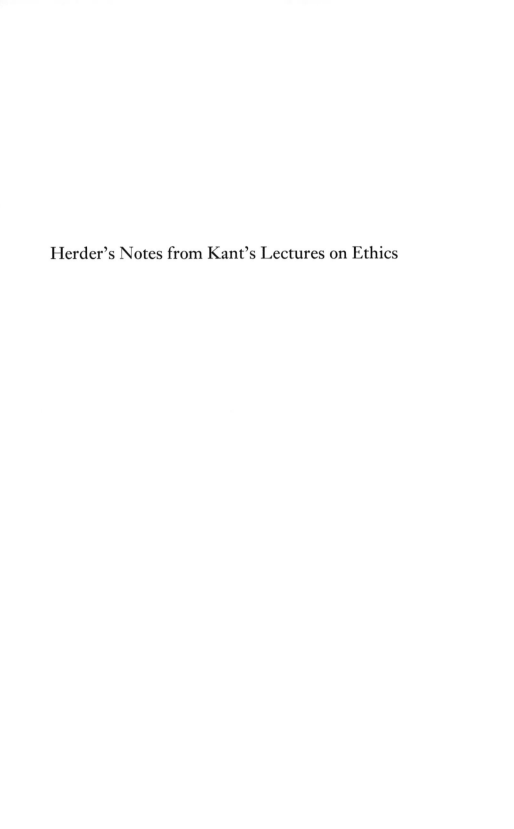

Herder's Notes from Kant's Lectures on Ethics

Herder's Notes from Kant's Lectures on Ethics

... Do I have, not merely a self-interested feeling, but also a disinterested [27:3] feeling of concern for others? Yes – the weal and woe of another touches us directly: the mere happiness of another pleases us in the telling: even that of fictional persons whose tale we know of, or in distant ages – this common concern is so great that it collides with the self-interested feeling. The sense of it is indeed a noble feeling, nobler than the self-interested one. Nobody despises it: everyone wishes for it, though not all have it in the same degree; in some it is great, and the greater it is, the more it is felt as a perfection. It is universal, though seldom so great that it inspires active exertions – in misers, for example, with whom self-interest has become very strong. As needy beings the creator gave us self-interest in our own perfection. As beings who have the power to be of service to our fellows, He gave us a disinterested concern for the perfection of others. The concern for others ranks high, since even the concern for self can be subordinated to it, but not vice versa. The more self-interested, the poorer (at least in thought), and hence the more to be despised. The disinterested feeling for the welfare, etc., of another has our own perfection, not as an end, but as a means.

Hobbes followed the plan of Lucretius and Epicurus, whose principles were of less nobility, by far, than those of the Stoics. And likewise the majority of Germans relate everything to self-interest, since it is fine to derive everything from a single *principium*, however little they may do this in metaphysics, etc. It was argued (1) that here we put ourselves in the other's shoes, and the deception of fancy creates this pleasure, which arises, not directly, but indirectly, from the other's pleasure. This false ordering of the matter comes about because, in the disinterested

263

feeling, we always envisage the other's joy, and such joy as we may have in his person. But if we had no disinterested feelings, this would not occur, because we do not *convince* ourselves that *we* are in his person – imagine yourself, too, in the shoes of a *wealthy* idler; you will not take any pleasure in him. This putting of oneself in the other's shoes is thus necessary, indeed, but is merely a means to vivacity, which presupposes the disinterested feeling. I have no pity for Damien's misfortune, though I do for that of Julius Caesar, since Brutus, his friend, murdered him. (2) It is said that the pleasure we have in [the welfare of others] is merely our own end, and a more refined self-interest. *Responsio*: the pleasure itself presupposes (1) a power of having it; (2) I cannot explain pleasure by means of pleasure. I *will* pleasure means, merely: I have pleasure in pleasure, and thus already presupposes a certain feeling. So there are merely lower grades of it. This feeling also constitutes a great beauty of our nature. A self-interested feeling presupposes our own imperfections, which can be acquired (so are not God-given), and imply neediness. A disinterested feeling presupposes our own perfections: the grounds for it may lie in the acquisition of other perfections, and it presupposes perfection. The disinterested feeling is like a force of attraction, and the self-interested feeling like a force of repulsion. The two of them, *in conflictu*,[1] constitute the world.

[27:4]

Free actions are good (1) in virtue of the consequences, and (to that extent) physically good; (2) in virtue of the intention, and (to that extent) morally good. The measuring-rod is very different in the two. Small will and great capacity is less morally good even in great benefactions. Great will and small capacity is morally better, even in benefactions that are small. We also esteem moral acts, not by their physical effects, but for their own sake, even when they are self-interested, and not always when disinterested (as Hutcheson mistakenly believes). Morally good actions must be directed to a physical good, but not measured by this. Physically good actions are always indifferent; they may be free effects, or necessary ones, for the good lies in the effect, and is measured by the consequences; the good is no greater than the effect. But morally free actions have a goodness which is assessed, not by the effect, but by the (free) intent; otherwise, the morally good would be less than the physically good. But this contradicts feeling and emotion. Free actions may be immediately

---

[1] Latin for "in conflict".

good (give pleasure), not as means to consequences, so that their value is not to be measured by the results, and they are not equivalent to the physical causes that produce the same effect.

Pleasure in free actions directly is called moral feeling. We have a moral feeling, which is (1) universal (2) unequivocal. At neglect of another I feel displeasure, hatred; not because he has to starve, but because of the neglect, for at privation through sickness I feel pity. A great disproportion, [27:5] which enhances self-interested feeling till the other feeling is outweighed, does not abolish the latter; for when we hear morally good things of another, we are touched with pleasure. A direct pleasure at the other's misfortune is devilish, and not to be thought of among us (though there can certainly be an indirect pleasure, and displeasure, and likewise direct displeasure). The moral feeling is unanalyzable, basic, the ground of conscience . . .

The feeling inspired by morality (without profit) is beautiful or sublime; my joy at the perfected in myself (feeling of self-esteem, of one's own worth) is noble; my joy at satisfaction (feeling of goodwill) is beautiful. Here the division of all actions according to these classes is completely reconstituted.

Sources of morality:

Morality as such. Moral beauty (not obligation, right and wrong) – In [27:6] morality perfection is never the transcendental; not what belongs merely to the essence, for the essence might be better still.

Solely from the fact that it is in accordance with *our* nature, it is not perfection merely, for I can have a better nature, e.g. angel; thus death is good. Hence the supreme law of morality is: act according to your moral nature. My reason can err; my moral feeling, only when I uphold custom before natural feeling; but in that case it is merely implicit reason; and my final yardstick still remains moral feeling, not true and false; just as the capacity for true and false is the final yardstick of the understanding, and both are universal.

In order not to err in logical matters, I must seek out the 1st *propositio* of the true.

In order not to err in moral matters, I must seek out the 1st *propositio* of the good.

The natural feeling is here opposed to the artificial; the feeling of modesty, for example, is almost artificial; Spartan children went naked up to 14 years old; Indian women never cover up the breasts, in Jamaica they go stark naked – and yet the feeling is very strong; Caesar, Livia, when dying would not uncover themselves.

Spartan women thrown naked on the street, worse than capital punishment.

Yet artificial, as with showing the fingers among the Chinese.

Thus marriage with a sister is artificially abhorred; but sacred with the Egyptians. To distinguish the artificial from the natural, we must therefore push back to the origin, as we do to distinguish prejudices (maxims) from certainty. One would have to investigate the feeling of the *natural* man, and this is far better than our artificial feeling; Rousseau has looked into it . . .

[27:9]   71. Can we, even without presupposing God's existence and His *arbitrium*, derive all obligations from within? *Responsio*: not merely in the affirmative, for this, rather, is *ex natura rei*,[2] and we conclude from this to God's choice.

1. From the *arbitrium divinum*[3] I cannot myself obtain the relevant concepts of the good, unless the concept of the morally good be assumed beforehand; apart from that, the sheer *arbitrium* of God is good merely in a physical sense. In short, the judgment as to the perfection of God's *arbitrium* presupposes the investigation of moral perfection.

2. Supposing the *arbitrium* of God to be known to me, where is the necessity that I should do it, if I have not already derived the obligation from the nature of the case? God wills it – why should I? He will punish me; in that case it is injurious, but not in itself wicked; that is how we obey a despot; in that case the act is no sin, in the strict sense, but politically imprudent; and why does God will it? Why does He punish it? Because I am obligated to do it, not because He has the power to punish. The very application of the *arbitrium divinum* to the *factum*, as a ground, presupposes the concept of obligation; and since this constitutes natural religion, the latter is a part, but not the basic principle, of morality. It is probable that, since God by His *arbitrium*, is the ground of all things, this is also the case here; He is indeed the ground of it, but not *per arbitrium*,

[27:10]   for since He is the ground of possibility, He is also the material ground (since in Him all things are given) of geometrical truths and morality. In Him there is already morality, therefore, and so His choice is not the ground.

---

[2] Latin for "from the nature of the case."   [3] Latin for "divine choice."

The quarrel between reformers and Lutherans over *arbitrium divinum* and *decretus absolutus*[4] is based on the fact that even in God, morality must exist; and every conception of the divine *arbitrium* itself vanishes, if morality is not presupposed; this cannot, however, be demonstrated from the world (where it is merely possible), since the good things of the world may merely be physical consequences. How dreadful, though, is a God without morality. The *jus naturae divinum*,[5] and even *positivum*, vanishes, if there be no morality as ground of the relation and conformity of my *arbitrium* and that of God. Without the prior assumption of obligation, punishments come to nothing; what God displays is merely ill-will; the physical consequences I can avoid, and thus the action is no longer a transgression. Morality is more general than the *arbitrium divinum*.

3. For one who has not wholly fulfilled his obligation, morality is incomplete, if all grounds of obligation are not included, and in that case, the *arbitrium divinum* is a ground of external obligation for our morality. So the *arbitrium divinum* should never be left out, as an external obligating ground; thus our moral perfection becomes incomplete, if it arises solely from inner morality, and is considered without reference to God's *arbitrium*. In the absence of the latter, my action is already still moral, indeed, but not so completely good, morally, as when it conforms to all grounds. Those who attend solely to the *arbitrium Dei* are considering merely their liability to the *jus naturae divinum*; but we should attend also to the inner morality, and consider obligation as well. *Ethica rationalis*:[6] the one without the other is not universal morality, and indeed far less than this; we are virtuous already from the nature of the case, pious only in having regard to the *arbitrium divinum*. To disregard the one is wicked; to disregard the other, godless; the former are moral errors, the latter, sins; the former concern the moral teacher, the latter, the preacher; the one wishes to have people morally good, the other wants their moral goodness to be complete. In education, we have first to awaken the moral feeling, and then must apply it to God's *arbitrium*; without that, religion is a prejudice, and hypocrisy. He who has a notion of the external obligation, without the inner, sees the motivating grounds as tasks, which do not make him moral at all, but merely politically crafty. If an immediate divine inspiration and influence are added to this, then (in that case only)

---

[4] Latin for "absolute decree."   [5] Latin for "divine/positive law of nature."
[6] Latin for "rational ethic."

[27:11]   the *arbitrium Dei* is sufficient. Thus cultivation of the moral feeling takes precedence over the cultivation of obedience.

Can an atheist be tolerated in society? There is the atheist *in sensu privationis*,[7] ignorant in the knowledge of God, who never thinks about the matter; and the atheist *in sensu contradictorie*, who errs in the knowledge of God, though well acquainted with the subject. The former are to be tolerated, because obligation remains – apart from the new motivating ground that is derived from God's *arbitrium*, and morality is still present. Such are many nations, who are, in a fashion, civilized folk; for example, the Hottentots, now informed by the Dutch that God is called a great commander – they possess moral feeling, nonetheless; their Hottentot ditties of ungrateful Holland are evidence of this. The *atheist* may be one who denies God from wantonness and lack of respect for the better conviction; or one who does so, not from wantonness, but because he thinks himself incapable of a better conviction. The former has a moral ground for his atheism, and is very dangerous to society. The latter has a logical ground for it, and is not so dangerous. Should the former have received the idea of the divine as a mere premise of his education, it is at least worthy already of respect and consideration. Since he has now been able to overcome this strong and weighty feeling, he may be presumed to have great moral wickedness in his principles. The majority of *wanton* atheists are in Rome, Paris, etc., where there is also the greatest hypocrisy; on them, too, theism has been imprinted, but because of certain errors, totally rejected – because of trifles, a feeling so worthy of veneration, and venerable even as a delusion, has been mocked; what wickedness, and what will that come to in regard to obligation towards other, lesser beings? Atheism may first occur with misgivings – without any show of proof, merely by imitation; but at once the misgivings are repressed, and people acquire an actual readiness to be atheists, for they think that others may have proved it, or could if they thought more about it. Atheists by reasoned conviction are dangerous simply because of the consequences, since others, from a desire to imitate, may follow their example. Because of their careful investigation, it is presumed that their morality is good. Hence they are not to be punished, and need, rather, to be persuaded, or their example removed, as with Spinoza, for example. He is not to be execrated, but deplored. He was honorable, with a very high degree

---

7 Latin for "in the privative/the contradictory sense."

of morality, but extremely speculative, and supposed that with the new Cartesian philosophy he might perhaps find out something altogether new; and as Descartes had destroyed everything, so he, Spinoza, also destroyed the concept of God, and thought he had demonstrated this . . . [27:12]

§1. *Ethics, the science of inner duties*, is ranked under general practical philosophy, and alongside law, the science of outer duties. [27:13]

The *jus naturae* and ethics are thus quite different, since the one demands liabilities, the other, obligations.

The topic of observation is in each case society, and for us, society in the *state of nature*, in so far as mankind does not impose on it the combination with others, and still less politics and economic laws.

Moral perfection is moral as end, and not as means; by that very fact it touches and satisfies us, not by relation to the effect, but immediately in itself. Nor is the action measured by the quality of the effect, but by the intention; for example, the death of a man, as effect, is of very small account, in regard to contingency and the whole; but the killing of a man is in itself of much importance, and is avenged.

Since the distinction between liability and obligation is very subtle, let us state it more clearly:

Ethics: the science of actions that are validly imputable before no other *forum* save the *internal* one. For example, even cases that partly belong before the *forum externum* (*jus*), fall into *ethics*, in so far as they belong before the *forum internum*. The principles of all that pertains to the *forum externum* are presented in natural law. The principles of all that pertains to the *forum internum* are presented in ethics.

Ethica est scientia imputabilitatis actionum liberarum coram foro interno.[8] We shall therefore not require to cast even a glance at any possible *forum externum*.

Ethics explained by a *doctrine of virtue* is good in as much as virtue belongs solely before the inner tribunal; but since virtue entails, not just *morally good* actions, but at the same time a great possibility of the opposite, and thus incorporates an inner struggle, this is therefore too narrow a concept, since we can also ascribe *ethics*, but not virtue (properly speaking) to the angels and to God; for in them there is assuredly holiness but not virtue.

---

[8] Latin for "ethics is the science of the imputability of free actions before the inner tribunal."

§2.   *Philosophical* ethics is ethics in so far as it is known *philosophically*, and thus not from the testimony of others, such as sages, for example, but on the basis of the matter itself.

[27.14]   §3.   *Utility*, and *perfection* are in themselves clear.

§4.   Morality is *laxa* or *rigida*, depending on whether it contains *pauca* or *multa motiva ad pauca* or *multa moleste apparentia*;[9] for example, if it impels men merely to kindness, sobriety, and moderation, it is too feeble; if it impels them also to self-sacrifice, to greater goods, it is serious; for the one coddles men, and presents them with easy duties, while the other represses the deceptive joys of the lower faculties of desire. The greater the moral perfection of the action is to be, the greater must be the obstacles, and the struggle, and hence the more needful, in that case, is the *strict* ethic. The other never constitutes true virtue, though it often produces moral *goods* as well; but the satisfaction of the strict ethic is serious, and is a *noble* morality.

§5.   The ethic of our author is *blandiens*,[10] since he always wrongly presupposes the broad concept of obligation, to which he attributes motivating grounds of utility, merely, in an improper sense of the term "ethics." For only he performs a morally good action, who does it from principles, not as a means, but as an end. By *sensitive jucunda*[11] I can certainly *motivate*, as by practical means, but cannot oblige, as by moral motivating grounds. Likewise by *sensitive molesta*; and so if it is to be *philosophia ethica*, it has to be *moral*, and the ethical motivating grounds should always be moral and not merely practical as physical means; even though the latter may become *mediately* motivating grounds, they would properly be a part of politics, which should, moreover, have been written down. All these subjectively motivating grounds are very good, and often preparatory to ethics, and hence, too, we have appended them; but they must always be distinguished from *ethical* grounds, since the latter must be drawn solely from noble, virtuous, and free choice. The tender-hearted ethic makes for a beautiful morality; the strict and serious ethic for a sublime one. Thus the charities of a rich man, *qua* consequence of kindliness, are morally beautiful; but as a consequence of principles and a sense of obligation, they are *sublime*.

---

9 Latin for "few or many motives to few or many irksome tasks."   10 Latin for "coaxing."
11 Latin for "pleasing/displeasing to the senses."

Everyone, to be sure, has need, in part, of *sensitive jucunda*, and in part of *sensitive molesta*, even for *moral* actions. For our moral feelings are so buried away under the sensuous, and the sensory motivating grounds thus make it easier for the soul subsequently to make its decisions on principle. By those principles which outweigh the sensory motives, we are brought nearer, as it were, to the domain of morality. This extends, [27:15] not merely to the teaching of ethics, but also to education and religion . . .

§8. Should the Christian ethic be given priority over philosophical ethics, or vice versa? One must certainly be explained from the other, as theoretical physics is explained from experimental physics; but the *natural* ethic must rightly be given priority, (1) since the other is related to it; (2) since the natural ethic contains also a ground of the other's truth; (3) since the natural ethic shows us many obligations which are impossible *secundum quid*,[12] and thus leads to the Christian ethic; the former creates the contradiction in man, that he *imputes* to himself something [27:16] which he cannot omit; it creates the collision between impotence and the moral ordinance, which the Christian ethic reconciles. (4) The revealed ethic, if it is to be practical, must ground itself upon the motives of the *natural* ethic. Like any revelation, it presupposes natural powers, e.g. capacities of the soul that are fit for the purpose. Otherwise, it would be at most a miraculously transforming book; but in fact it is a book that *lays obligations* upon us, and presupposes instruments and receptivity in the face of revealed religion.

§10. *Perfice te ut finem*, and *ut medium*,[13] are the two major rules of our author.

By this perfection is meant either moral perfection, and in that case the latter is already presupposed, so that this rule is not a basic one, for it presupposes a ground; or else by this perfection is meant something undetermined, e.g. health, etc., and again it is not a basic rule, on account of its instability. If I am to seek perfection as a rule, this amounts to saying: Desire all perfections, a proposition quite certain, indeed, subjectively speaking, whereby we always act; but objectively speaking an empty proposition, since it is wholly identical. The sole moral rule, therefore, is this: Act according to *your moral feeling*! In *philosophia practica prima*

---

[12] Latin for "by derivation."   [13] Latin for "perfect yourself as to the end/as to the means."

this feeling is defined merely negatively, viz., that it is not the physical, as means to an end; so merely as a relationship. This distinction is bungled by Baumgarten throughout his entire book, which is otherwise the *richest in content*, and perhaps his best book; though everything he says may make for great practical perfection, it does not constitute moral perfection. The latter he omits to define, according to the taste of the philosophy of Wolf, which continually based perfection on the relation between cause and effect, and thus treated it as a means to ends grounded in desire and aversion. With us, both moral and physical feeling are always combined. For God, in His goodness, has for the most part laid down the same rules for practical and moral perfections. So let us set forth, not only the difference, but also the consensus, between the two . . .

[27:17] All morally good actions are thus, in their highest stages, religious acts; but this is not the first stage from which we begin. On the contrary, moral beauty (weak morality) is made prior to the moral nobility of actions in terms of what is right, and this new and higher morality is only brought in afterwards. It contains a relationship to the greatest supreme rule, which is the ground of everything, and thus constitutes the greatest harmony. Meanwhile, I must first abstract my actions from the divine will, in order even to recognize the goodness of that will. But once I have perceived it with sufficient abundance, exactitude and vividness, it becomes the supreme basis, (1) because the knowledge is then noble, and (2) because it provides the highest degree of vividness. But if my knowledge of God does not yet have life enough, I must concern myself with other beings; otherwise, all this knowledge of God would remain merely dead, and fail of its purpose. We begin, then, with moral beauty, and with moral liability – these are grounds of morality that are sensuous and vivid. When a man then rises to the highest level, that shows him as God's supreme instrument; but if he begins at that point, there arises from it
[27:18] a hypocritical religion; our author's method is therefore incorrect, since it begins from religion, whereas it ought to have started from a morality, which would then be increasingly purified.

Obligation towards God (religion) is not merely a practical necessity of making use of God, as of a means to certain ends. Our author, however, puts the use of God as a means before His immediate goodness. Yet *obligatio* should merely have explained morally good actions in direct relation to God as an end; if I follow God's will, because he has coupled my best interests with those of others, then this is a borrowed God, and it is merely the *practical* attitude of a self-interested agent. The highest degree of connection with God as a means is when we utilize the divine will as a means to the betterment of our own morality. Julie says, for example:[14] Our good actions are noticed by witnesses: – she uses God's will to better her morality; but to use it merely as a means to happiness is ignoble, and no religion . . .

§14–22. The man who acts from motives of *welfare* is thereby subtly [27:19] self-interested, and is not acting from religion, since he does not act from morality, and the sole motivating grounds of religion are those of *blessedness*; to entice us to our duties, as physical goods, from *happiness*, and thus derive all motivating grounds from *pleasure*, but yet make blessedness the motive to morality, and happiness the motive to welfare. That is mere *misbinding*, but since *happiness* and *blessedness* require one way, they do not actually conflict, on the whole, though they have to be distinguished. Even self-interest prepares us for religion, though without constituting it.

§19. Perhaps the image of God consisted in the immediately clear sensation of the divine presence – not symbolic, but intuitive; not from inference but from sensation; and in that case, how vivid the effect upon morality and the ground of blessedness. With us, perhaps, the broadest and vaguest concept thereof still resides, even now, in conscience. If we directly improve our moral feeling, we approach the divine presence in sensation; so maybe such people again develop the image, although their spiritual utterances sound fanatical; and religion elevates us to the highest degree of such sensation.

§21. This is true morality; a part of it already precedes all religion, but a part is greatly enhanced by religion, and since religion enhances the whole *summa* of morality, this is a *truly* binding ground of motivation . . .

§44. All enthusiasm is hard to prevent, lest we fall at once into the [27.22] opposite vice of coldness. But in drawing conclusions from speculation it must be avoided, since passions do not confute or confirm opinions, but in regard to the *truth* are always blind; though in regard to the practically *good* they may be useful.

---

[14] Rousseau, *Julie*, Part III, Letter 18.

§45.   When pietists make the idea of religion dominant in all con- [2
versation and discourse, and it has to be inferred from their constant
behavior that this idea has lost the light of novelty, then they are mere
twaddlers. But were this state of mind *ours* in this world, it would be the
most blessed of all.

§46.   Try especially to always couple the idea of God with your morality; first with your *natural* moral feeling, so that your immediate liking
for the good becomes, in the light of God, religion. Try also to make the
idea of God *dominant* in the *depths* of the soul. This is difficult, but if
it always predominates in clear ideas, then it will also pass over into the
obscure ones . . .

[27:25]   §72.   Thou shalt love this or that, is not said apodeictically, since it is no
more of a duty than to *hold* something *to be true*; for it is not a *voluntary*
action, but a mere arousal of feeling. So the command is merely: Do
everything that can be a means to this. Nevertheless, though I perceive
the appropriateness of love, it cannot always be in my power, any more
than it often is when I would like to be rid of it. But when I perceive
myself in the *defective* state of *cold-heartedness*, whether towards God, or
my benefactor, or my brother who loves me, then I try to impress on
myself the moral qualities that arouse one to love. For example, consider
especially that God loves you (the very remark already inspires love), and
that men may be *moved* at receiving your love; so love them as objects of
one of the gentlest of impulses.

§73.   To feel the *concursus divinus*,[15] suppose yourself in possibly worse
circumstances, and you will then feel your own to be that much the
better.

§75.   In so far as we regard all acts of God as the best means, to the best
end, of happiness, we may be completely at ease. The great mutability
of things, and the storms of my passions, can best be comforted by the
thought that I am placed in the world, and placed there by supreme
goodness, not for my own benefit; and however uncertain the order of
nature may be, it is nevertheless under the supreme being; and in this way,
then, *religion* alone may be completely reassuring. For even a naturally
[27:26]   good and moral man must always tremble before *blind fate*.

---

[15] Latin for "divine reinforcement."

§77. Since all God's acts (1) cannot be self-interested, and (2) are aimed at happiness, and thus are real *benefactions*, they arouse, by that very fact, *thankfulness*; and anyone insusceptible to any disinterested beneficence, will also be insusceptible to gratitude, and *vice versa*; for if he does not feel the *nobility* of well-doing in his own actions, how will he do so in the case of another? And nobody will feel gratitude even for God's benefactions, who does not himself feel the *beauty* of well-doing; for example, the magnificence of a summer's evening will itself have an effect upon the benevolent.

That love is [not] tender, which seeks to please the object of love; the latter is in fact *amorous* love. *Amor* is, in fact, *tener, quo quis amatum laedere, admodum reformidat*;[16] amorousness does not presuppose esteem, but *tenderness* does. That which does not merely wish to make the other into an object of desire, as amorousness does, but presupposes, rather, something *noble* in the way of thinking, does not offend, of itself, by a want of love, since it merely takes away something *beautiful*. But he who regards tenderness as a *duty*[17] incumbent on him, and so fears to withdraw it, gives offence. Amorousness occurs also among the foolish, and is often very *pleasing*, but there is a want of esteem in it; the *tender* lover shows respect, and desires to preserve his own esteem, and is therefore not so laughing, not merely pleasing.

In love towards God, the amorous, and even the *tender* elements must disappear, since both are very anthropomorphic, and always presuppose a secret *grace* and *favor*. These are, however, simply the greatest of duties, and thus the highest degree of tender love, albeit without the name. Resignation to the divine will is necessary, in that we must trust God to have the utmost wisdom and benevolence. Thus Socrates told the praying Alcibiades: Cast your eyes down, and say, Give me, O God, what is best, whether I ask for it or not.

Love for the *creature* is always good, in so far as it is considered to be a creature; and idolatrous creature-love is merely the excessive degree of it.

If we walk upright in our inmost soul, then we shall not, perhaps, find love, but the esteem and reverence that arise from greatness, and bring   [27:27]

---

[16] Latin for "Love is tender when it shuns entirely anything harmful to the beloved."
[17] Reading *Pflicht* for *Recht*.

fear rather than love as their consequence. The *moral beauty* of God, and His benevolence, are far less vivid in us, (1) because we are accustomed, as grumblers, to attribute our ills to God; and (2) because we have a dim idea that God's benefactions may perhaps have cost Him very little love – for we take our *own virtue*, which always has obstacles to *overcome*, as a measure; and since that is not so with God, we also perhaps concede him little benevolence. The world cost Him but a word, etc., etc., and since the return of love always presupposes love, our *natural* love towards God is therefore so labored and small; nevertheless, through the agreeable feeling that, without our earning it, so much bounty streams upon us, we are seized by something akin to love. Only revealed religion discloses to us a love, on God's part, that cost Him an effort, and so, properly understood, can arouse love in return.

Mistrust in God: If I had no other evidences of God's benevolence beyond the course of nature, the judgment to that effect would inspire little confidence, since in human life I perceive a constant entanglement, and the opposite of good. It is not, therefore, from *individual* cases that I seek to determine the *general* concept of *benevolence as such*; for in that case I merely regard each action, in isolation, as a touchstone of benevolence, but cannot therefore conclude to the total happiness of my existence as a whole. And it is likewise possible to be without *mistrust* of God, if I do not attribute to Him the fulfillment of individual wishes. Despite my honesty, I can, for example, perhaps be unlucky for a long time. *Trust in God* is felt, therefore, merely in regard to the *whole* of our life, but not with respect to the *externals* of particular specific cases; otherwise, it can become a *tempting* of God. As the most benevolent of beings, God will, in total, at the end of it all, make everything good; without specifying the cases in which He is to evince benevolence, precisely in accordance with our own presumptions. In short, I shall one day be able to regard my whole existence with confidence; that is trust in God.

It is extravagant if, in individual cases, I rely upon God's goodness, as determined by my own intent; and it is for this reason a tempting of God, that I think myself able, by my own wish, to determine precisely the case where God's goodness is to display itself. A marriage with an uncertain [27:28] outcome cannot be settled by trusting to God, for He might be no less wise and benevolent, were He even to let me starve. I see this in such a case, because if my wish proves false, I could not stupidly declare that His goodness has been . . . [unfinished]

Awe presupposes reverence, and the latter, the feeling for the sublime in moral perfections, just as love presupposes the *intuitus*[18] of morally beautiful perfections. The sublime is a perfection that is distinguished from the beautiful, and in both, the perfections may move us either morally or *nonmorally*. To be moved by a morally perfect sublimity is reverence; it does not always presuppose *love*, for the grounds of the two are very different, and reverence, indeed, can actually suppress love, if the moral sublimity of the other seems greatly to collide with our own qualities, and we have not credited him with suitable goodwill in regard to ourselves. Thus a grave clergyman, who evokes our reverence, often arrives very inopportunely in a gathering where the beautiful predominates. Love wishes for closer union; sublimity frightens us away. Thus for the most part we have the greatest love for those we revere less, for example, the female sex, whose very weaknesses we forgive for the sake of their beauty, and are even delighted to win. So also there can be reverence for God, without loving Him, just as a miscreant may perhaps have great respect for his *upright* judge, but never loves him. Awe is a higher form of reverence, and thus in itself not mingled with love; but since reverence is commonly coupled with an anxiety not to offend its object, there arises from this the true concept of *awe*, which is also quite wholly distinct from *fear*, since we are guarding, not against the *evil* that he might visit upon us, but against that which we do ourselves. The *fear of God* is thus quite different from *fearfulness towards God*, the latter being a *servile* fear, which by no means increases reverence, but in fact diminishes love; for as soon as we see somebody against us, a degree of love is eliminated; who loves anyone, in so far as he punishes us? The *fear of God* (i.e. awe) is childlike, and that can coexist with love, because it is much on guard against the other's displeasure; and the *childlike fear* of God is thus an *awe coupled with love*. We guard against God's displeasure because of His beautiful and sublime qualities; but not, to that extent, from fear; it is ourselves we are in fear of, for we would in contrast be hateful in our own eyes.

[27:31]

[27:32]

---

[18] Latin for "intuition."

§89. Deficiency, here, may thus be either want of *fearfulness towards God*, or a lack of the fear *of God*; the two are very different and have to be separated. The former is much the worse; the *servile* fear recoils from actions because of punishment, and I would fear someone in servile fashion, were I to shun him because of an evil to be apprehended. This destroys love, and is to be guarded against, therefore, in tender minds, since the frightful always engraves itself far more deeply, and even afterwards is not wholly softened in the presence of *beautiful* qualities. *Human fear* is again either fearfulness *towards men*, or of them; the one fears the evil of men more than that of God, the other holds men more greatly in awe than God. For example, to prefer the displeasure of God to that of an awe-inspiring ruler, is the latter kind of human fear; and a reprobate who, as La Mettrie tells us, is frightened only of torture and authority, evinces *fearfulness towards men*. The latter is no *moral* defect, but a political one; just as the opposite fearfulness [towards God] presupposes, not morality, but mere calculation. The former kind of fear is moral, however, just as is the awe at moral qualities.

§90. Not everyone, who fulfills a command, *obeys* it on that account, if he does not fulfill it *just because* it has been commanded. Thus men fulfill

[27:33] many divine commands from their own impulses – through their own moral feeling – and yet with the *false luster* of one who obeys. Indeed, often the judgment concerning the divine command is superfluously added in this way, being entertained, *per subreptum*,[19] even prior to the true ground. Universal obedience seems to be impossible for us, so long as the knowledge of God is not the dominant idea in us; and in a future state, perhaps it will be like that, since everything else will then be very easily subordinated thereto . . .

[27:36] *Wisdom* and *prudence* are different. A man of much prudence may choose ends, for which he selects his means in the best way possible, without in fact being *wise*, i.e., having chosen a good end. Wisdom chooses ends, and the want of it makes men dolts; *prudence* chooses means, and without it, on the contrary, they are fools. Womenfolk have little wisdom, but much prudence, and more than men; for keeping their own secrets, finding out those of others, and conducting embassies, women would be better. But

---

[19] Latin for "surreptitiously."

men (if they have not, by laxity, become womanish) are able to choose better ends, and avoid doltishness. But feelings often make dolts of us, even though we may display the utmost prudence in the process. Passions, for the most part, run counter to wisdom, since they choose silly ends. *To seek honour* is not doltish; but to seek it overmuch is silly, because this end, though natural in itself, bulks too large in comparison with others. The *puffed-up person*, on the other hand, is a fool, because in this he has no proper end, though he may well choose good means for it. Any intention which, in regard to itself, is nothing, makes a man a dolt. An intention that is relatively of no importance makes him silly. An intention unattainable by any means makes him a fool.

So, too, in religion. A man shows himself a dolt, if he does not sufficiently subordinate the lesser intentions to the main one; for example, an old man, who instead of regulating his passions, wishes to provide for his children. *Prudence* is evinced in religion, if I select the appropriate means; he who errs in his ends, errs the more grossly; for a good end at least makes the morality good. The error of a dolt is morally the greater; that of a fool, logically the greater. The one is immediate, the other mediate, since the means are not well chosen. The nature of the end determines the morality . . .

Self-abasement is the opposite of self-esteem. He who so *grovels* that [27:39] he lowers himself, does not feel his own worth, though the other is distinguished only by an empty title, which depends merely on illusion.

Humility presupposes a *correct estimation* of self, and keeps it in bounds. We have more reason to observe imperfections than perfections, since they are more numerous, and the contemplation of perfections can very easily do harm. *Humility* is therefore not a *monkish virtue*, as Hume believes, but already needful even in natural morality. A vain science, such as geography or stargazing, can give us less distinction than moral worth. The latter will balance off imperfection with perfection; it is by rules of morality, not well-being, that I must be humble. Such humility will not be mingled with hypocrisy, but will be felt in that I perceive that I am not higher than others; and in fact, all men are not so far apart in that respect. The educator should implant self-esteem and humility, so that respect is evoked by achievements only, and not by illusion. The spoiling of the upper class is attributable to the middle class, and subjugation,[20] luxury and pomp are the result. Here I also begin to reform myself, and then Rousseau's ideas become attractive. If I compare myself with others, and form a lesser opinion of them, this should not arise from self-esteem. The latter compares itself with itself. In humility we compare ourselves with others to our disadvantage; otherwise the imperfections of others would give me occasion for rejoicing, and this is morally evil. To despise others is also in this respect a bad method, that it evokes hatred instead. To

[27:40] be sure, I may compare my imperfections with the better circumstances of others, if I perceive the possibility of a greater perfection; but I should not always be taking notice of this. I should not take note of relative imperfection – that doesn't matter; *whether I am inferior* to the other – the comparison is harmful, as it is in ranking perfection and imperfection; just so long as I go on, in addition, to frame my self-estimate as a whole, and also feel my imperfections, but not imperfection as calculated against the other. His worth remains the same, whether it be above mine or below it. From this comes hypocritical humility, which extenuates itself; and even an upright man despises such a person, not because of his imperfection, but because he declares it. That he feels it, is good for himself; but that he declares it – what is the good of that? It is useless. Humility is that honest self-esteem which is also aware of one's perfections, and must be sharply distinguished from self-abasement, which merely inspires contempt...

[27:41] §171. *Pride* is an inclination to think highly of oneself *in comparison with* others. It asks, not what one is worth, but how much more one is worth than another. It cannot well be *mistaken*, if it merely finds its own worth in the fact that others are imperfect. Thus this imperfection of theirs is the reason for its own joy, and that makes it a moral *defect*. It may be outwardly evinced, and is then called self-conceit.

The *vain man* seeks merely the *opinion* of others; he is wholly turned outward from himself, and does not judge by his own feeling: Frenchmen.

The *proud man* already believes in his own worth, but esteems it solely by the lesser stature of other people, and is thus at fault: Spaniards.

The *self-assured man* does not compare himself at all, and is inwardly good; but outwardly he must then be of sober mien.

---

[20] Reading *Unterwerfung* for *Unterweisung*.

The *man of pride*, who allows it to be very conspicuous, is also externally at fault, and is said to be *puffed-up*; disdain (Dutchmen).

Haughtiness is pride in display (since there is pride in the whole demeanor). Germans are vain and haughty.

Self-estimation is either *absolute* or relative; the latter is *inadequate*, since the other person may be very wicked, and so this does not determine that my own state is a good one; it is also *evil*, because it presupposes an inclination to take pleasure in the moral imperfection of another.

And thus humility, too, is strictly *absolute*, though the relative form can certainly help out the absolute one; it must never become ignoble, however, in that I become vexed at the virtues of others. Thus even the signs of humility are *absolute*, in that I should display them modestly, on the whole, and not *relatively* to others, since by the moral rules they are *needless*, and could be evil, in that they may make us self-abasing, and other people proud. As against this, the civil order demands outward marks of precedence, which emphasize relative merit; but this is absurd, since by such boasting absolute esteem is diminished. This relative worth is plainly false, since it changes with the circumstances. How does a prince figure among peasants? And how before his king? A man who dwells merely on that is *indoles abjecta*. I esteem a person of note hypocritically, on account of his rank; truly, on account of his inner worth, when he has risen (on his merits) into the middle class; and the more highly, because he has had [27:42] so many obstacles to overcome . . .

Conscience is *logica*,[21] in that I am aware of some property; and *moralis*, in that I couple this with my moral feeling. Defects are therefore *logical*, in the want of consciousness concerning one's actions, as with frivolous people, or young folk; and *moral*, in the want of moral feeling concerning one's actions, as with old scoundrels, who have been prevaricating for so long, that in time that feeling is stifled, and a sham version takes over; for example, a *shopkeeper's catechism*.

The falsified conscience *adultera*[22] is (1) *erronea*, when it is logically falsified; (2) *prave*, when it is morally so. The one goes astray, by intellectual error (*errores*); the other feels wrongly, by emotional defect (*depravitates*).[23]

---

[21] Latin for "cognitive/moral."   [22] Latin for "corrupted/errant/depraved."
[23] Latin for "viciousness."

[27:43] To distinguish the natural from the acquired conscience is often difficult. Much that is acquired is taken to be *natural*. The parental curse that we might incur through a marriage that we do not seek to contract in the proper way, is an *acquired* conscience. Since, by natural law, the father would retain parental control only until such time as the son is able to govern himself, all duty of obedience (other than gratitude) would have lapsed, and does so here, since it has been acquired only through custom. But when Voltaire holds *all* conscience to be *acquired*, and demonstrates it by various examples drawn from different nations, he goes too far; the Eskimos, who kill their parents as a loving service to them, are to some degree justified, since they foresee a more ignominious death for them in the hunting that is *necessary* for survival.

To what degree our conscientious feelings are acquired, in particular cases, is hard to say. Our relationships with friends are perhaps acquired – the feelings are too greatly enhanced; as they also are in moral concepts.

Of *bad* actions, conscience judges far more strongly and correctly *after* the deed than before, and *beforehand*, more strongly than in course of the act. This is exemplified in the *pangs of conscience* that are bound to result after a lustful act. The reason: any passion draws attention to the gracious side, and clouds the other – and once the passion is there no longer, then the cloud also falls away.

If we men here in the world are not always in a state of passion, we are nevertheless the prey of impulse; in a state of mind such that passion has to judge of things; and thus throughout life, our judgment is never wholly impartial. It is *itself* the judge in its own case. Debarred from passion after death, we are then impartial judges upon ourselves, and on our morality; the judgment upon our life will then be far more vivid and truthful, and we shall perceive the abhorrent aspects more clearly still. So long as passion remains, however, the judgment becomes even more partisan. The fiercer the passions, the more clouded the moral feeling, and even the physical one, so that physical evil is also left over. If *conscience* is silent before the deed, or if it *grumbles* ineffectually, it is a bad conscience, and in the latter case a pedant that fails to restrain, and yet plagues us. Yet there is one hope for a more lively impression: the conscience that speaks *long beforehand* is stronger than the one that immediately precedes, since the former, from a long perspective, presupposes a greater impression. Otherwise, however, the conscience that immediately precedes is the stronger. Hence one who is caught with dagger in hand is not punished with death. The *conscientia consequens*[24] is thus the strongest, but bad when the *conscientia antecedens* does not precede it; to be sorry afterwards is no reparation. [27:44]

Since our life is a whole in its existence, one part of it cannot be sacrificed to another; the pleasure of the one must also be the pleasure of the other, and happiness a whole. Foresight, a daughter of affluence, is the source of unhappiness; enjoyment of the present, with attention to our morality, is our happiness. We have to enjoy these things in *this world*, and the all-too-abundant talk of eternity must not tear us away *from time*; eternity should serve merely to diminish the evil of this world, but not to lessen its joy. Man engineers downright robberies of himself; robbing himself of youth, in order to secure enjoyment of old age, of which he then deprives himself, through getting set in his habits. A part of life should not be sacrificed to the whole.

I can employ the higher powers of mind for utility's sake, and that is good; or for the sake of appearances, and that is bad. The motive for enhancing my powers is largely the good *opinion* of other people. But this is either an actual lie, or if truthful, is nevertheless (if it serves no useful purpose) chimerical when regarded immediately in itself, since it does not promote the best in me. Apart from that, since all show is far easier than substance, honor is wholly false; and therefore is harmful to the human race. The philosopher throws a veil over his own weaknesses, just as the Chinese were unwilling to accept the calendar, so as not to run into mistakes. The teacher, who perceives the falsity of his views, is still happy to let himself be honored, and does not admit his errors. Should not Crusius, over so many years, have recognized the untruth of his insistent utterances? But he does not say so. The pursuit of honor is more harmful to morality than any other passion; all others have something real about them, but this one is a phantom of the brain. I depart entirely from my inner state of moral goodness, and try to improve it with something external; and what harm the sciences do then. The pursuit of honor will perhaps be totally suspended in beings somewhat higher than ourselves; with us, it is still useful as a counter to great immorality, and to stiffen our resolve against extreme laziness, and thus it is needed for the lesser morality of mankind. Self-esteem, however, is rooted in morality; not in

---

[24] Latin for "conscience after" and "before" the act ("pangs"/"qualms").

calculating on the opinion of other people. Thus people seldom marry on their own account; always with a view to others.

[27:45]   Suspension of judgment can occur from moral motives or logical ones. Prudential planning decides, up to a point, with certainty, yet indicates the uncertainties, the want of assurance, the uncompleted matters that are merely set aside. In social matters, the suspension of judgment is very necessary, and a sign of humility, that should be achieved still more in practical affairs than in writing. Of all people, however, the scholar is the most covetous of honor, and thinks of nothing else; works for it, apportions it himself, and is the trumpet of fame. Knowledge as such is splendid, and without the highest insight, the highest of beings would not be the most perfect; but man must learn to recognize his limitations, not merely in logic, but in morals as well. In themselves, mathematics or numismatics are well worth knowing; but not, perhaps, for us; such eagerness for knowledge can eventually throw us entirely out of our orbit. All these attractions cause us, thereafter, to become stuck in the mud, so to speak; the child hastens, in prospect, ahead of the man; the earth–dweller has his eyes on eternity; and thus he is unfit for either state.

Learn to shun the impulses that diminish morality; pursue the moral use of your powers of cognition. They may also be greatly cultivated in other things, but prematurely so; between the sublimest human spirit and the lowest man there is no true difference of merit, save in regard to morality.

At present, mere scientific acumen must serve to compensate the defects of the sciences; otherwise there would be no need of them, for the *analogon rationis*[25] is a surer guide in morality than reason is, and the good man's feeling more reliable than the reason that makes palpable errors in its inferences. Since the *analogon rationis* is actually given for our guidance, reason, equipped as it is with many needless adornments, must certainly not acquire many privileges. Confined by the law of necessity, and by human folly, we must therefore not be puffed up; to despise the useful guide, yet take the long way round to get home, is self-destroying.

A readiness in all circumstances to posit good ends for oneself, or to choose the best means, is *presence of mind*. Womenfolk are able to select

---

[25] Latin for "analogue of reason" (i.e. good sense).

good means, but not good ends. By long reflection we must accustom ourselves to presence of mind *in ancipiti*.[26] Young people should first accept counsel, therefore.

That man alone is blessedly happy, who has the highest enjoyment of [27:46] pleasure that he is capable of in the circumstances. So this life is to be distinguished from that to come. Blessed happiness consists:

1. of happiness; nonmoral good; physical well-being. Since this depends on external factors, it can be very defective, and very changeable.
2. of blessedness: the morally good.

The longing for mere well-being must therefore, by the law of mutability, already make for unhappiness, since all physical things relate to the whole, and cannot always affect us favorably. The morally good, in which we are the ground, is thus immutable, and fruitful in physical goodness, so that everything which comes about *through* me must come from moral goodness. If I am to make myself indifferent towards evil, am I also so towards the good?

If I am to make myself receptive to the good, am I also so towards evil?

Responsiveness to physical good often becomes a ground of aversion, and one must therefore try to make oneself impervious to certain things. This costs us deprivations, indeed; though they are not painful, since the feeling about them simultaneously *diminishes*, and a much finer moral feeling awakens for them instead. The savage, moreover, is in a state of *indifference* about many things. Virtue calls for *maxims* and principles, which are very different from instincts, and even from morality; and thus there can be forms of conduct that are abhorrent, without being *vices*, because they actually presuppose *maxims*, and are only *figuratively* called vices – just as actions from *good* instincts are only figuratively called *virtues*.

The motivating ground for acting according to principles is the constancy that remains ever the same, whereas *good instincts* depend on impression and variable circumstances. These latter, in fact, are provided by human society. *Maxims*, on the other hand, are actually universal *principles*, under which particular cases can be subsumed, plus the skill of subsuming such cases. Moreover, there are indeed maxims that are

---

[26] Latin for "in danger."

analogous to virtue, for example, maxims of honor; and how many have acquired great luster from these alone.

Self-conquest: No victory gives more evidence of personal activity than this, and hence it is the most satisfying . . .

[27:48] Of the sexual impulse we must judge, not merely in accordance with our civilized state, but according to the natural condition of man. And then, this impulse was very powerful, in order to sustain the species. Those who hold God's end to be always the principal one should consider here, whether the natural man has the providential intention to sustain the human race, or merely an inclination to immediate pleasure. The former is indeed the main end, but not the only one, and the remainder must certainly not conflict with it, but they can nevertheless be noninjurious to it; and it is thus altogether too scrupulous to forbid married couples those intimacies which are not immediately connected with propagation.

The sexual impulse would not have developed so early, but only once the powers of the body had matured, for it would not have been accelerated by instruction. The impulse satisfied itself merely by immediate pleasure, and there would probably not have been a permanent bond. But since, no doubt, the man will have felt that the impulse would recur, he would allow the woman to follow him into the forest; she became his companion, and both would have cared for the children. He would have had to help her [27:49] while she was suckling them, and thus arose monogamy, since there are as many women as men. The impulse would not have been so rampant then, since the fantasied pleasures of the civilized were lacking. Moreover, this impulse is covered with the veil of shame, which is also found among the majority of savages, and is quite unlike any other form of shame, and restrains the impulse. There is much truth in the objections of the cynic: we should be ashamed only of what is dishonorable; but for all that, there is a genuine shame-instinct, which has indeed no rational cause, and is strange, but whose aims are (1) to restrain the untamed sexual impulse; and (2) to maintain the attraction of it by secrecy. The male sex, which has more principles, possesses this shame in a lesser degree; for want of principles, the woman has a great deal of it, and it dominates her; and where this shame has already been uprooted in women, all virtue and respectability have lost their authority, and they go further in shamelessness than the most dissolute of men. Such shame, moreover, has an *analogon* with an act that is intrinsically dishonorable, and this has produced the stupid *shame of monkishness*. It is not, however, in itself the mark of an unpermitted act, but the veil of an honorable one, which *propagates* mankind. In addition to the sexual impulse, the female sex has many other qualities, which all focus on beauty, and are therefore charms and allurements. The male sex has friendship and devotion; the female, roguishness, kindness, etc.

The man has an acute judgment of beauty; coarse male kisses and matrimony are not so disgusting to womenfolk, and this is the wisest arrangement. This impulse is nowadays the source of so many vices, and plunged into such indecencies – so how, then, is it possible, amid such general corruption, where so many inhuman vices have sprung up, to effect an improvement? The Spartans let girls up to 9, and boys up to 13, go naked in the years before puberty. Our artificial virtues are chimeras, and become vices, if the hidden is regarded as vicious. As soon as chastity of speech, clothing, and demeanor increases, true chastity is thrust aside. Where one side of a thing is shown, the other side tempts us from out of the chimerical land of fantasy. Perhaps Rousseau has hit upon the best method. The precocious sexual urge must be confined, lest it hamper our growth and development, and enervate normal bonding, to our subsequent regret; yet this is to be accomplished, not by hiding [27:50] the impulse, but by holding up to the young man an image of the beauty that he is one day to make happy, and which will wish to have him pure. In that case, he will not throw himself away, but will travel with this image, and save it up for his happiness. The quite total removal of the concept never achieves this effect; it is rather by the following principles: As I summarize the duties of the man in the words: Be a man, so there is also a plan for womanly duties: Be a woman, etc. Unity and union are altogether different; the friendship between two men, from the concept of the sublime, can have unity, as can the friendship between women, from the concept of the beautiful. But in matrimony there must be not mere unity, but union, for a *single* purpose, the perfection of the marriage. Now to this end nature has endowed the pair with different gifts, whereby one has dominance over the other. The woman allures, the man arouses; the woman admires, the man loves; and so each prevails over the other, and there is union without tyranny on the husband's part, or servitude on that of the wife, but by way, rather, of mutual dominance. Thus the ultimate goal of the bond between the two sexes is marriage. But if the *husband* becomes *womanish*, or the *wife mannish*, the marriage is inverted and not perfect. Imagine a learned lady, bold and robust: she is then a competitor to my worth; I cannot prevail over her, and the marriage will not be perfect. Imagine a bejewelled man, a feeble, dressy fellow: he is then a competitor to the woman's beauty: she cannot prevail over him, and again the marriage is imperfect. On the contrary, she will be more pleased with a man of natural dignity and self-confidence, with a plain, unaffected style of dress. The two sexes should not be mixed up; *womanliness* is no reproach to a woman, but manliness is, and in our country, owing to their lesser education, the womenfolk are closer to nature than those amazons in France, for example. Thanks to their delicacy of feeling, they are still able to make the difference quite clear . . .

[27:53]   *Endeavoring to please others*: The motivating ground of utility is nonmoral; the inclination to please is moral – it does more to bring men together. Complaisance is a species of it, and the opposite of self-will, since I adjust myself to the will of another. It is a slippery quality – may be praiseworthy, but soon invites censure and contempt, since it shows that a man has no will of his own, and is without moral worth. It is a quality of weak souls. The noble prefer self-will, and the faults that result from it are not so grave as those due to complaisance, which in many people is often a cause of idleness. The young must still try to please, since as yet they have few principles. In trifles (and human life is so full of them that it almost seems to be a trifle itself, compared with the whole of what exists) self-will tends to separate us, etc.; but in morality it is worthy of praise.

Honorableness: Rousseau's conception of honor is purely internal, and such, also, is honorableness; a *true* self-esteem for one's inner worth. The judgment of others is merely an *accessorium*. It takes *personal* fortitude to overcome the constraints of conventional morality.

Egoismus moralis has two forms: that which breaches the limits in self-esteem, or in love of benevolence; since I am constantly promoting my own interest.

Self-abasement may be to oneself, or to others. The latter makes others puffed-up, and oneself into a worm. It proceeds from the former, and often makes our perfection useless, as when I do nothing for myself out of honor, but do it instead out of contempt.

Love towards others already indicates a lesser need in oneself for other things; self-love must take precedence, since the love for others simply rests upon it. That he, who thus loves others, enlarges his own happiness, is a property of dependents, and hence of created beings. He who enlarges the system of his love, also enlarges the well-being of his fellow men. How love is extended, is a practical question; I cannot say, as an absolute injunction, Thou shalt love! This love is that of wishing well, or of pleasing well. The latter is also nonmoral, but wishing well presupposes a morality of beauty: the idea of the *beautiful* in the action is the means thereto.

Affability is a sign of our love, and is not a real and efficient quality, i.e., readiness to be of service is symbolic, since we show the inclination to it, e.g. in our demeanor. Rules are very difficult – affable friendliness [27:54] requires greater equality.

Indifference, as a moral quality, is the opposite of human love; but even by this cold-bloodedness I may understand a very good trait, if it holds the love inspired by sympathy in check, and gives it due measure. If the sympathetic inclinations are blind and serve no purpose, the stoic must say: If you cannot be of help to others, then what business is it of yours, pray?

Friendship is very complex; it already presupposes the *alter ego*, and does not always exist where I love another and he loves me; for (1) I shall not, on that account, simply disclose my secrets to him; and (2) I am not convinced, either, that he will sacrifice something for my sake. We have to be able to assume that his efforts on his own behalf will be made also for us, and ours for his; but that is a great deal to expect, and so friends are few. If I multiply friends, I diminish friendship, and hence it is already much, to have but one true friend. Between different persons there can certainly be sincere human love, though not in the degree of friendship; for the latter is the highest form of that love, and presupposes an identity of personality. Yet some people come reasonably close to this, and are also said to be friends. Friendship proper is in part impossible (owing to the number of our own requirements), and in part needless (since my security is already manifestly looked after by many others) . . .

Compassion. The ability to put ourselves in the position of another, is not [27:58] moral only, but also logical, since I can project myself into the standpoint of another, e.g. of a follower of Crusius. So too in moral matters, when I project myself into another's feelings, to ask what he will be thinking about it. If I put myself, by a fiction, into another's shoes, this is a *heuristic* step, in order the better to get at certain things. It can be quite skillfully done, yet not moral, since I am not actually in his position; except in the case of true *sympathy*, where we really feel ourselves to be in his place. The *feeling of pity* would not be sufficient for morality. In the savage state, instincts are enough; everyone looks after himself; few are in need, and in that case pity is adequate. In civil society, where the needy have multiplied, it would often – however widespread – be futile to be merely sorry for them, and hence the feeling is much weakened, and evinced only to those in the *direst* necessity. In the common man, however, whose needs are fewer, and who can thus be the readier to share, the nearer he is to simplicity, these compassionate instincts will be greater. The civilized man is much constrained by self-serving artificial desires, so that pity is here replaced by the concept of what is *right*, what is *seemly*. This can never be futile, because I shall not be bound to the *impossible*; here virtue becomes calm and rational, and no longer remains a mere animal instinct, though such instincts certainly operate pretty regularly in the state of nature. In general, however, civil motives are insufficient . . .

[27:59] *Lying* is simply too restricted, as an injury to the other; as untruth, it already has an immediately abhorrent quality, for (a) this most *trenchantly* separates human society, of which truth is the bond; *truth* is simply lost, and with it, all the happiness of mankind; everything puts on a mask, and every indication of civility becomes a deceit; we make use of other men to *our own* best advantage. The lie is thus a higher degree of untruth. (b) So soon as the lust for honor becomes a prevailing principle, it already sets no bounds to the lie. Self-interest cannot be so strong a reason, for lying is not an *enduring* means of advantage, since others shun the liar. The greediest shopkeepers of all are the *most honorable* in their dealings, simply from self-interest, and this is thus often a reason for truthfulness, etc. The lust for honor makes *lying* easier, since here the inner content is not so apparent; religion and well-being, for example, can easily be [27:60] simulated, and not so readily exposed. (c) The longing for imaginary perfections, that perhaps were not thought suitable before; for example, a disinterested zeal to serve, is a *fantasy* too high for us. But since we can indeed be of service to a person in certain matters, there is the wish, in fantasy, to sacrifice ourselves; and since this cannot actually *be*, there is the *wish*, at least, for it to *seem* so. Second example: The fantasied desire for infinite knowledge, that is impossible to us, creates the *semblance* of this knowledge. In the indulgence in knowledge and enjoyment, do we therefore find the *lie* that is most abhorrent of all to the *natural man?*

Value of the love of truth: It is the basis of all virtue; the first law of nature, Be truthful!, is a ground (1) of virtue towards others, for if all are truthful, a man's untruth would be exposed as a *disgrace*; (2) of virtue to oneself, for a man cannot hide from himself, nor is he able to contain his abhorrence.

The *feeling of shame* (which is *later* made subject to delusion, and envelops even the best actions), seems to be a natural means (*pudor*,[27] not merely *pudicitium* in the pursuit of pleasure) of promoting truthfulness and betraying falsehood. If we wanted to use such shame, simply to betray the lie, it is very *practicable*. Providence would certainly not have furnished it to delude us, for it is the greatest of tortures; it is given, rather for betrayal – *involuntary* betrayal. It has never been there to cause us anxiety, but rather to betray *something* which nature did not want to hide. To thus make use of this shameful feeling as an antidote against lying, we must not employ it for any other purpose, e.g. to show up a child. Here I use merely the means for imitation; if he has behaved or spoken stupidly, I simply persuade, and *as a child* there is much that becomes him, which is not becoming to the *man*. But supposing that, regardless of his love of truth, he has *but once* told a lie, from self-interest, because the love of truth is not so lively as physical feeling; in that case I do not talk to him of *obedience* (of which no child has the *concept*, nor is of an age to do so), but simply of *untruth*. In the end he acquires as much abhorrence for it as he has for a spider. *Incest* with a sister is abhorrent, not because God has forbidden it, but because the wrongness of it has been imprinted since childhood. Such is the power of ideas of dreadfulness; and if a son were to see his father's abhorrence of lying, he would by moral sympathy [27:61] perceive the same himself. Suppose him now grown up, then everything would go better. I would openly declare my intention, for example, that I am working, not for the benefit of science, but from self-interest; I would yearn only for an official position that I am capable of filling. Nowadays, however, there is *untruth*, not merely in the world, but also before God, in solitude, since we cannot stand even before Him without pretence. To be truthful, we would now have to forfeit a great deal, and so each of us shies away from the truth, and most of all in a nightshirt. Untruth may end

---

[27] Latin for "shame/modesty."

by deceiving itself, and so self-examination becomes equally slippery; the good side of kindheartedness, for example, is put before its reprehensible aspect, and men eventually become deceivers even towards God: for example, Job's comforters. Certain untruths are not called lies, because the latter are *strictly untruths* that are contrary to *duty*; not, however, as our author thinks, merely to the duty *to myself*, but also to that *towards others*. The importance of the love of truth is so great that one can almost never make an exception to it.

Untruth, to the great *advantage of another*, still has something *sublime* in it, that is near allied to virtue. Yet to speak *truth*, to the *disadvantage of oneself*, is sublimer still, and to speak untruth to *one's own advantage* is doubtless always immoral. But since the *highest morality* is not on a par with the *moral level* of man, this is not, indeed, quite settled. Yet because the bounds of a man's strength and obligation are hard to determine, this *human ethic* of untruth will be as confused as the *logica probabilis*.[28] *Every coward* is a liar; Jews, for example, not only in business, but also in common life. It is hardest of all to judge Jews; they are cowards. Children, for example, that are brought up cowards, tell lies, since they are weak in conquering themselves, etc. But not every liar is a coward, for there are inveterate scoundrels as well.

With us, in many cases, a small untruth does not seem untoward, for weak persons; the case is often complicated; if another asks him something, a man cannot remain silent, for that would be to assent, etc., etc. In short, we should investigate the degree of morality that is suited to men. As with all fine inclinations, we can also enlarge the desire for holiness; but not all can be moral men, when they are weak or needy, since in few cases are we able to attain to holiness. If our untruth is in keeping [27:62] with our main intent, then it is bad; but if I can avert a truly great evil only by this means, then ... etc. Here goodness of heart takes the place of sincerity. To obtain a great good by untruthfulness is far less excusable than to ward off a great evil by that means; for (1) our inclination to our happiness is often fanciful, and morality should not be sacrificed on that account; (2) the taking away of what I have is a greater denial than a withdrawal of what I might have. A white lie is often a *contradictio in adjecto*;[29] like pretended tipsiness, it is *untruth* that breaches no *obligation*, and is thus properly no *lie*. *Joking* lies, if they are not taken to be *true*,

---

[28] Latin for "logic of the probable."   [29] Latin for "contradiction in terms."

are not immoral. But if it be that the other is *ever* meant to *believe* it, then, even though no harm is done, it is a lie, since at least there is always deception. If untruth presupposes cleverness and skill, we get *artful* lying and repute; courtiers and politicians, for example, have to achieve their aims by lying, and everyone should flee any position in which *untruth* is indispensable to him.

The inclinations of men in nature are to be distinguished from those that evolve from artificial motives; a primary piece of self-knowledge. An ethic for man, *determined* in his nature, by his knowledge, powers, and capacities, has yet to be written. For by reason we can also discern rational perfections that are suitable, indeed, for a higher being, but not for him. We here have to investigate his limitations; and to become acquainted with the *natural man*, let us adopt this as our rule, that we take those *parts* that are unalterable by any art; and what is contrary to them will be artificial. Such regular inclinations of nature are: (1) *self-preservation*, and (2) the inclination to preserve the species; these may be increased or diminished by reflection, but reflection does not produce the urge. We must also, reflection notwithstanding, eat and cover ourselves; the sexual impulse is purely a lustful thing. *The arrangements* of nature are ancient, original, irresistible *reflection*.

(a) *Freedom* is also an urge, because anyone wishes to follow his *own* *will*, and against physical hindrances he knows of means for this; but not against the will of another. This he considers to be the greatest misfortune, and so it is, since in part it is far more vexatious, and in part irremediable.   [27:63]
Hence all animals are *equally free*. From freedom there arises

(b) the desire for *equality*, especially in strength (or else by cunning), since this is the . . . [unfinished]

From the urge to *equality* there arises

(c) the urge to *honor*; if the other would take power over me, he must be made to think that I am equal to him. That is *honor*, and it takes two forms:

1. to preserve myself; to have *strength*, and to show it, in order not to become a serf.
2. to preserve one's kind; the man, being stronger, covets the trust of the woman, so that he may *preserve* and defend her. He will choose a wife, and must ensure that he is *pleasing to her*; and since she is *weak*, she

sets store by valor. This second urge to honor is more effective than the first. Hence Rousseau extols the sexual impulse. The first he can defy, but this one is strong in its effect.

The *urge to know* does not lie in *nature*; to us, indeed, it is now indispensable, but simply through long practice. The reason for it, in ourselves, is merely *tedium*. The scientific urge for purposes of *self-preservation* depends merely on the contingency of our condition; *immediate honor* is never the source, but always the end.

A thing cannot lie in nature, if (1) it can never be satisfied, and (2) it is out of proportion to the shortness of life, and to great desire.

In general, a thing is *unnatural* if it is contrary to the urges of nature; the scientific impulse is not merely somewhat at variance with the urge to self-preservation; it is particularly adverse to the sexual urge.

However, I am simply to know the *natural man*, not in the present connection, *to be one*. My heart may not yearn for that, indeed, but I must *nevertheless adapt* myself to it. So let *ambition* be no passion; since I despise it, it plagues me not; but I still need it as a goal, in order to be effective. Science, and the like, must not therefore be a blind thirst (so I must not be bored without it; not unsociable; not contemptuous of the unlearned, but gladly cherishing them); yet I still need it *externally*, as a goal. One can never attain to inner virtue in any other way. For the *moralist* or *cleric* already (1) presupposes comforts, honor, etc., though that is unnatural; (2) extends duties contrary to nature, e.g. by deriving [27:64] marriage, not from the sexual impulse, but from the command of God. People also fabricate false virtues; those that are *appropriate* to the *natural* man are too *elevated* and hyperbolical for the *artificial* one. The happy man is he who is good without virtue (by feeling, without concepts; the *man does*, the philosopher *knows it*). The happy man is he who is knowledgeable without science. Both of those things are mere glitter, etc.

Plan of judgments of the *common* judgment. Examination of nature and art; thence to judge projects. One should look first to the median; otherwise the *height* is never reached, since our life is commonly too short, and the project too fanciful.

§348. Relationship of men; towards a concept of the system of human love: the love of *well-wishing* (of the other's greater welfare) is either active or wishful. The merely *yearning* or *wishful* love comes *either* from the degree of weakness, or from the disposition, in that it is merely fanciful.

For a degree of love that is all-too-elevated for my practical capacity is just as ineffectual as a *want* of love. *Excessiveness* in the way of life also creates such wishes and yearnings, and is not good, since it is (1) *useless*; (2) *deceptive*, in that it squanders time and actually impedes practical love; for the love that is *too little practical* has the love that is all-too-greatly *fanciful* as its cause. So to enquire into them both, let us note (1) that a person does not actively *love* another *until he is himself in a state of well-being*; since he is the *principium* of the other's good, let him first better himself. He should be at ease with himself, and thus the more there is of excess, the less there is of practical human love. For by excess we multiply in fancy our own needs, and thus make practical love *difficult*, i.e., *eo ipso rare*. To make itself practical, it puts itself *at ease* with itself, making do with little; and from this comes practical love, etc. All other motives produce fanciful urges, and hence in a condition of simplicity there will be much practical love, and in a state of luxury, little; but more of the fanciful kind, and since this cannot be satisfied, for in that case the entire human race would be before me, *I merely wish*, and have simply thought up the fancy for myself, because practical love is wanting in me.

Transfer a man of nature (not a man of the woods, who is perhaps a chimera, but a simple man) into the midst of artificial society; a man whose heart is not set on anything. The man whose love is *real*, loves *in a more limited way*, and his love cannot be extended to *everyone*, without his [27:65] *forgetting*, for his own part, to take note of his *own position*. Thus a natural man has a care for himself, without informing himself much about the well-being of others. Our professions of sympathy, as compliments, seem foolish to him. Nevertheless, his love will be practical, e.g. for one who is suddenly in danger. Here this instinct cannot be eradicated by wickedness; it unites the whole human race, and is powerful, since it often does not wait upon reason. Yet this truly practical instinct is directed, not so much to the increase of good, as to the *prevention of great and sudden harms*; and as soon as they are too much for his powers, wishings and pityings strike him as too foolish; he would have to divert his attention *from himself*, and so he is perfectly ready to turn his thoughts elsewhere. In present-day civil society, since the needs multiply, the *objects of pity* mount up; the capacity of men itself declines, since in part *really*, and in part through illusion, they are weak and thus miserable; for the evils of illusion, which make me *in imagination*, and a thousand others *in reality* similar, are on the increase. What must *human love* be here? *A topsoil*, an imagined human love, a yearning of the fancy, is the natural consequence. So it now spreads abroad, and corrupts *the heart*. Since, through morality, the fanciful love of humanity is so widely diffused in people by instruction, it remains a matter of speculation everywhere in life, a topic of romances, such as Fielding's, etc., that has no effect, since (1) it is too exalted, and (2) does not get rid of the obstacles.

True love is (1) rectitude: It is the love we have by nature, the fundamental love, for it is founded upon a living feeling of *equality; otherwise, favor*, etc., will come of it, but here, *rectitude*; that I *owe* nothing. Equality means that the natural man is equal to all others, and they to him, and since *moral sympathy* is imprinted on all, he has to put himself in the other's place; and from this there follows *living rectitude*. From it there arises the *obligation* to alleviate the woes of others, which is equivalent to rectitude. Take, for example, one who fails to give me warning of a ditch; you would require this of others, so you must do it yourself. Without love of humanity this rectitude would be merely a semblance. Man in the civil state is called on to have *love of rectitude* only towards a few; yet truly the *whole human race* has an obligation to it for every single person; [27:66] not, however, *each* individual, because *his possibilities* are lessened. From *love of humanity, favor* will arise, since it *selects people*, without special compulsion or desert. The love due to *favor*, if it is not to be artificial, too extreme, too overpowering, has to be built upon love of humanity. Here we must examine how far the duties of society can be grafted on to *love of humanity* and the *obligation* towards it; on to *rectitude* – such is the indispensable goal of moral theory, and *rectitude* is based on the *exalted feeling of equality*. There exists in man a moral *sympathy*, to put oneself in the other's place; it is the basis of *righteous* love, and holds it to be an *obligation*, etc., and the opposite hateful. *Righteous* love differs from *kindly* love, in that absence of the former is hateful, while absence of kindly love means that one is not to be praised in a higher degree. Actions to which I am bound by the rule of rectitude are *obligations*. The boundaries between the two cases, where someone must hate the other, and simply does not love him, are very distinct, but hard to discriminate. Anyone who puts something before an *obligation* to himself, would find himself *hateful*. Nature has not framed us to be *generous*, but to be self-sustaining; sympathetic, indeed, to the woes of others, yet in such a way that the sum shall not be zero; that I not sacrifice as much as I redeem, but preserve myself and my kind.

In the state of nature, obligations are few, and the sense of them is great.

In the civil state, there are more obligations, and the sense of them is small.

In the one, men have little to do with one another, but the helpful actions they do encounter, have a bearing on their natural state: natural evils, and not the fabricated ills of delusion.

In the other, the commercium is greater. Many helpful actions are needed, even on account of the numerous invented evils, and hence there are many grounds for giving aid, but more obligations upon oneself. Many people live unjustly at the expense of others, and therefore incur so many debts that no room is left for kindness. They are a major reason for acts of violence towards others; and to such people their ill-fortune is not indifferent to them, as in the state of nature; rather, they have brought it on themselves. Hence there are many obligations; and here we have the first axiom: *All men are equal to one another*. To the savage, it is a principle; but to us, who have strayed so far from it, it is a thing to be proved, and the basis of *ethics*. *Every man* has an equal right to the soil. Thus *obligations* multiply, but the *sense* of them diminishes. For, (1) the sense of *equality* declines; I feel my superiority, though others yet rank above me, and I think myself willing to take after God. Yet I still am under *obligation*, for (2) there is a decline of *moral sympathy*; a cause of the harshness of superior folk, and of the misfortune of the poor. Their oppressions continue, since the others do not even claim responsibility for them. [27:67]

Acts of goodness. Man fancifully exaggerates his moral capacity, and sets before himself the most perfect goodness; the outcome is nonsense; but what is required of us? The Stoic's answer: I shall raise myself *above myself*, will become a *savage*, rise superior to my own afflictions and needs, and with all my might be *good*, be the *image of godhood*. But how so, for godhood has no obligations, yet you certainly do; anyone has a right upon me, on my work and help. Now the god departs, and we are left with *man*, a poor creature, loaded with obligations. *Seneca* was an impostor, *Epictetus* strange and fanciful. All *goodness* is not, in itself, *obligation*; from this it follows that our education, and mutual education, must be such that our sympathies do not become *fanciful*, but remain confined to the *practical*. I must be *upright*, and attend to my obligations; but the exalted pretension of wanting to love the whole of mankind is a fraud. He who loves the Tartar, loves not his neighbor. Loving *all*, we love *none*, and our love is therefore less. In place of rendering assistance to everyone, there should be simple *courtesy*, which is (1) not hatred, and (2) a mere *calm* willingness to assist in emergencies, according to *our powers*. Out of *rectitude* (but not *ardent desire*) there may be sacrifice; to that I am not obligated, though I am to courtesy, which has beauty because it springs from *equality*, and goes with self-esteem. To inferiors we owe, not *favor* merely, but a courteous attitude; to superiors, not hatred, but courtesies; for *they are simply equals. All favor* is offensive; here I shall neither cringe nor despise; with no *lofty ideas of virtue*, I shall be *honorable*, without wishing to be a great *saint* . . .

[27:73] §368.   The doctrine of *tolerance* is generally well known, and much invoked by the persecuted; its limits, however, are still very indefinite. It is (1) *moral tolerance*, as a duty that one person bears to another, without constituting them members of a state. Since all true religion is internal, and lies in the relationship of the human heart towards God, a man may judge of the signs thereof in another, but not of the religion itself. The external practice of religion can be imitated, without anything within. In Rome, the majority are atheists, including even popes. Now since the signs are so ambiguous, it is a *duty* not to deny somebody a religion, because in signs he differs from myself; for I *cannot* have insight into an inner religion. It is thus (1) possible with difficulty only, and (2) also unnecessary, according to the concerns of nature; because the judgment upon others, the presumptions of doing this, calls for great authority, if it is not to be an offense. Now in the state of nature there is no such authority, since religion is a relationship to God; to myself it can only represent a form of conduct, which religion admittedly elevates, but which can be sufficient for me even without religion. For example, the Talapoins of Pegu;[30] if they receive me, I *ought* not to trouble myself at all, for my own part, about their religion. I have a concern for what may be conformable to my welfare, but religion plays no part in that. Why should I not have a concern for it, out of a *general love of mankind*? *Responsio*: It is certainly worthy of note, but afterwards. In short, a moral code can exist without religion. But now if I detect in it a religion that may be very injurious to my own interests, for example, the vindictiveness that springs from

---

[30] Buddhist monks, in Burma.

religion, then it does concern me. A *persecuting* religion can be an object of suspicion, even in a state of nature, that I may guard myself against it, and keep out of its way. [27:74]

(2) *Civil Tolerance*. In the state of nature there is less occasion for religion, than there is for it as a means to civic well-being. Religion is for our eternal well-being, and for this and other reasons it is a major motivating ground to many human duties. But how if there be no religion? Is it always equally necessary, with regard to our welfare in the present? *Responsio*: No, and it is the less necessary in a state of nature, because there are fewer occasions for those departures from human duties, to which religion is held to be an antidote. Peoples that possess no other religion than some ancient traditional fancies, have much that is good among them, and little that is bad; warfare excepted, and that, too, is just a customary habit.

So since here there is little occasion for it, the other's religion is likewise of little concern to me. But as soon as the *interest* grows, and perfections have ascended to the fanciful level, moral feeling is no longer so sure a guide. In the end, that feeling becomes too weak to resist fervor; the love of humanity cools off; here the moral grounds of motivation are too feeble to provide defense against everything; higher grounds are called for, and thus religion becomes ever more needful (in the civil state; it can never be so in the natural one), and finally we get superstitious religion, in the degree to which extravagances increase. For things that I can do without, I shall not lie, and still less perjure myself; but, attracted by many things, to which I cleave, I have to be bound by oath against such major sources of temptation. There is an ever greater need for fantastical ceremonies, which in fact mean nothing, but are able to conquer rampant immorality. Here, religion is a police-force; morally, its boundaries are defined, but in civil society they become vague, because already we are at a loss to provide means sufficient to preserve us from ruin.

In regard to civil tolerance, religion is a matter of indifference to the natural man; there is already morality in his heart, before he has religion; so long as, in the state of simplicity, there are forces that impel him to be good, and no incentives are required for the avoidance of evil, he does not need religion. But when many of his comforts turn into necessities, his impulses gain the upper hand, so that morality becomes too weak, [27:75] and the religion of nature does not suffice. For this, more understanding and philosophical reflection are required, than can be expected of the whole human race. So it has to be complemented by a revelation, either pretended or true.

The Pulserro bridge of the Persians produces many noble deeds, so Chardin tells us. Pure morality asks for no rewards, etc., but this pure morality is nowadays not present in the human heart; nor can the religion of nature provide aid to morality. Without basing itself on reason, a revelation at least offers a pretence of doing so. All civilized nations have a revelation of their own, and the barbarous ones a myth. India has one of the most ancient. The dispute as to which is the true revelation, cannot be decided here. In religion of this kind, to be suitable to the most considerable portion of men, much must be symbolic, to make the duties of nature venerable by many solemnities; certain ceremonies must make the matter worthy of respect. A custom once adopted must not be impeached, for till now it has been the foundation of the state, and if it is changed (though only fractionally) and for the better, we finally come to think that, since something has been altered, it could all of it be false. Hence republics are at their strictest concerning the old religion.

Can a government protect a multiplicity of religions? *Responsio*: Yes; in so far as any one of them is already established, it is far better to protect it, instead of wishing to improve it; because eventually an indifference to all religion would result. The multiplicity of religions creates an attachment to your own, and the civic utility is very much the same; for, as experience shows, Holland, for example, is a well-governed state. To be sure, were the principles, if pursued, to be adverse to the state, as with the Jews, for example, who are permitted by the Talmud to practice deceit, then the natural feeling rectifies this false article of religion. Such evil freedoms are not followed; the principles of the Catholics, for example, would in practice be adverse to the state, but this does not actually occur. The improvements of religion relate, therefore, merely to the political, for example, monastic orders. If a customary traditional religion, that is not based on rational demonstration, is generally accepted, anybody ought to be prohibited, on the state's account, from impugning it, even when errors are perceived therein. Nor can anybody deprive me of my ability to *think for myself*, and that should not be permitted. But since I take the [27:76] greatest of pleasure in imparting my opinion to my fellow citizens, is it not injustice to forbid me from doing this? Yes indeed; however, the general welfare is not possible without these simple injustices, where luxury is concerned. In a state of perfect tolerance, a particular moral beauty must prevail; if everyone states his opinion, then every part will be put in a special light, and *truth* will be suppressed by coercion. Nor is any given error ever a moral transgression, even though it be an offense against the state. A universal tolerance is possible, but only if we again return to the first state of things; in that case, we are also morally good without God. Why should I not state my opinion of religion? In regard to this world, the decision concerning tolerance is solely a matter for authority; not for anyone else, and not for any clergyman. The latter is interested only in truth or falsity, not in what is useful or harmful; and the truth he is unable to decide. The cleric and his adversary are both citizens, about whom only authority has anything to say. But what degree of freedom do they have? To give no freedom at all is just as injurious as to give too much. Precisely because of a total lack of freedom, clever men become indifferentists. For this tolerance, the most subtle question is, whether there are errors worthy of respect.

So let us have *moral* tolerance, for it is in no way a form of doubt. Yet many religions foster a real hatred among men, when they set up their opponents as devils rather than men. Moral tolerance is called for in everything. Let us look upon the other with love; he *errs*, yet I do not hate him on that account, but have pity for him, that through error he should go astray. No individual who is morally intolerant is guilty of a crime, for the state has no concern with him. With luxury, religion proliferates in ceremonies; with profusion it declines; and one day complete tolerance may be possible.

Should authority, too, be concerned with the cure of souls? *Responsio*: This question must extend to all nations. Can the authority that is convinced of its religion forbid all others? *Responsio*: No, for if every nation, which also believes itself persuaded of its own religion, likewise totally denies entry to arguments from the other side, then all access to the truth would be closed off. Each thinks it has the truth, and if this *belief* is a reason for prohibition, then all nations possess such a right. Thus authority can certainly practice intolerance for political reasons, but not for the sake of salvation hereafter. However righteous a religion may be, and however great the conviction of it, there follows from this no right to deny entry to other opinions, for salvation's sake; for it is hard to dis- [27:77] tinguish between true and false conviction. Can an authority proselytize for a religion? *Responsio*: Yes, the propagation of a truth by argument is morally always useful (though it may often be politically harmful, since

301

it frequently promotes zealotry as well); but it is also man's prerogative to require arguments. This method is reasonable, and the compulsion to declare something true, that one did not hold before, is very unjust and offensive, extremely damaging and never useful, save perhaps to do away with certain other injustices.

Arguments for coercion. As soon as I regard a religion as the *sole* means of blessedness, then it is plainly a matter of humanity to snatch men from perdition, and here, assuredly, all means are good, for even small evils in this life are nothing to those that are eternal. So means of compulsion are not unjust if they are means; but physical coercion never produces conviction, as with the Saxons under Charlemagne. *Objectio*: But much consideration needs also to be given to the descendants, who, even if their ancestors were merely made hypocrites by coercion, will perhaps have good and true conviction, through a better education.

All this seems plausible; but in brief, (1) no means that is adverse to the supreme prerogatives of mankind, is a good one. Now men are all equal, and should mere inequality, coercion, be the means of eternal happiness, it is a means of injustice, which already presupposes force. (2) The whole of mankind rises up against *having* to maintain something. From all this it follows that, in regard to the hereafter, authority must avail itself merely of the prerogatives of mankind: the arguments, in which every man has a share.

The common man, who never uses or misuses reason, must admittedly be guided, and this, therefore, for the most part, in an historical way. The less noble portion, which uses and misuses arguments, should not be taught merely by authority, but supported by grounds of reason. If education has been *rightly* conducted, there is no injustice required in securing tolerance.

1. The subject will be brought up tolerant, with error distinguished from crime.

[27.78] 2. It will not be harmful to him, since he is being educated by means of reason.

To coerce other into *opinions*, or into *silence*, is in this way harmful as a moral intolerance, that one can thereupon never guard against the evil consequences of abhorrence:

1. Every man wants to have his own opinion as the general one; the *causes* of which are:
2. that he supposes all morality to be based on religion, and thus hates the other, for he sees in him wickedness rather than error. It is the clergyman's duty to expel this intolerance from the heart. Education should be made into the seedbed of moral tolerance.
3. a man's intolerance is often *founded upon great ignorance*. Since he cannot answer by reason, he thinks of it as an enemy that will expose his nakedness. He who has no arguments to offer is hostile to counterarguments. A clergyman, who has examined himself (we may suppose), will have no hatred, even for the ignorant theologian.

Moral intolerance, to be sure, is in itself already an absurdity, and if a proper education were to be universal, then political tolerance could be universal too. At present, however, authority must be vigilant *everywhere* . . .

Selected Notes and Fragments from the 1760s

Notes on anthropology prior to 1770

618. 1769? (1764–68?)   [15:265]
The strikingly natural or naïve (*later addition*: in the use of the under-   [15:266]
standing, if nature appears as art, is called naïvety), the unexpectedly
natural.

Poetic art is an artificial play of thoughts.

We play with thoughts if we do not labor with them, that is, are
[not] necessitated by an end. One merely seeks to entertain oneself with
thoughts.

For this it is necessary that all the powers of mind are set into an
harmonious play. Thus they must not be a hindrance to themselves and
to reason, although they must also not promote it. The play of images,
of ideas, of affects and inclinations, finally of mere impressions in the
division of time, of rhythm (versification) and unison (rhyme). The play
of the senses is for verse [*breaks off*]

(*Later addition:* Composition. 1. Poetry. 2. Oratory: harmony of
thoughts and of the imagination. B. 1. Painting and music: harmony
of intuitions and sentiments, both through relation to thoughts.)

It is no labor, thus also no servitude, yet is still the knowledge of
poesy. It must be counted as a merit of the poet that one learns nothing
through him; he must not himself make labor out of play. Poesy is the
most beautiful of all play, for it involves all of our powers of mind. It has
rhythm from music. Without the measure of syllables and rhymes it is
no regular play, no dance.

The sensible play of thoughts consists in the play of speech (versification) and of words (rhyme). It goes well with music. It awakens the
mind.

Poets are not liars, except in panegyrics. But they have abolished the doctrine of the gods through their fables.

[15:267]   The play of impressions is music.

The play of sentiments: the novel, theater.

The play of thoughts, sensations (images or forms (theater)) and impressions: poesy. The impressions are only through the language, since they are to accompany the thoughts.

Poesy has neither sensations nor intuitions nor insights as its end, but rather setting all the powers and springs in the mind into play; its images should not contribute more to the comprehensibility of the object, but should give lively motion to the imagination. It must have a content, because without understanding there is no order and its play arouses the greatest satisfaction.

Every action is either business (which has an end) or play which (*later addition*: serves for entertainment) certainly has a point, but not an end. In the latter the action has no end, but is itself the motivating ground.

In all products of nature there is something that is related merely to the end, and something that concerns merely the correspondence of the appearance with the state of mind, i.e., the manner, the vestiment. The latter, even if one does not understand any end, often counts for everything. E.g., figure and color in flowers, tone and harmony in music. Symmetry in buildings.

(*Addition: Suaviter in modo, fortiter in re.*[1])

[15:268] **619. 1769**

The primary elements of our cognitions are sensations. This is what one calls those representations in which the mind is regarded as merely passive, acted upon by the presence of an object. They comprise the matter, as it were, of all our cognition. For the form is given subsequently by the soul's own activity. This sensation, in so far as it signifies merely the state of the subject, is called feeling; but if it pertains (is in relation to) an outer object, then it is called appearance. From this we see that all of our representations are accompanied with a feeling, for they are affections of the state of the soul.

---

[1] Latin for "Agreeable in manner, strong in substance."

620. 1769. *M* 219, at the beginning of *M* § 606
The first faculty of the human soul and the condition of the rest is sensibility, by means of which the soul receives representations as effects of the presence of the object and does not produce them itself. As something belonging to the state of the subject, the representation of sensibility is called sensation; but as something that is related to an object, appearance. There are sensations without noticeable appearance, and appearances without noticeable sensation; yet both are always present.

621. 1769? (1764–68?)   [15:268]
All art is either that of instruction and precept or of genius; the former has its *a priori* rules and can be taught. Fine art is not grounded on any [15:269] science and is an art of genius.

(*Later addition*: Even an inference contains beauty: as a cognition it is related to the object, as a modification of the mind that is sensed, to the subject.)

622. 1769? (1764–68?)
The rational cognition of the beautiful is only criticism[2] and not science; it explains the *phaenomenon*, but its proof is *a posteriori*.

(*Later addition*: Science and art; the latter, of imitation or of genius.)

(*Later addition*: All appearance is of succession or simultaneity; the former is ——,[3] the latter the image.)

Good taste occurs only in the period of healthy but not merely subtle reason.

(*Later addition*: Taste for a thing (inclination) is not always taste for the same thing, e.g., music.)

(*Later addition*: The judgment of the amateur, of the connoisseur (the latter must know the rules), of the master.)

In the case of sensation I always judge only subjectively, hence my judgment is not also valid for others; in the case of experience, objectively.

---

[2] *Critik.* This is the word Kant uses in the title of his three main works, where it is translated "critique"; but here he is not referring to his special philosophical project of establishing the bases of our knowledge and practice, but to the ordinary practices of art criticism, literary criticism, and so on. Unless he is using the term in his special philosophical sense, it will be translated in this chapter as "criticism."
[3] Kant's blank.

Whether beauty and perfection, hence their causes as well as the rules for judging of them, do not stand in a secret connection. E.g., a beautiful person often has a good soul.

Tender sensitivity belongs to a judgment concerning that which can be agreeable etc. to everyone; receptivity to one's own state; the former pertains to the man, the latter to the woman. The power of choice must rule over this, and a limitation of it to the minimum is moderation, *apathia*.

[15:270]   (*Later addition*: Beauty in and for itself, if it is not accompanied, say, with vanity, arouses no desire, except only through charm.)

623. 1769? (1764–68?)
One has no *a priori* grounds for justifying a taste, but only the general consensus in an age of rational judging.

(*Later addition*: One's own or personal sentiments must be distinguished from substituted ones; the latter can be a disagreeable imitation, but still be personally agreeable. (The good is always agreeable in substituted sentiment.))

624. 1769? (1764–68?)
(*Later addition*: Sensible cognition is the most perfect among all those who intuit; confusion is only contingently attached to it.)

In the case of taste the representation must be sensible, i.e., synthetic and not through reason; second: intuitive; third: concerning the proportions of the sensations, immediate. Thus the judgment of taste is not objective, but subjective; not through reason, but *a posteriori* through pleasure and displeasure; further, it is not a mere sensation, but rather that which arises from sensations that are compared. It does not judge of the useful and the good, but of the contingently agreeable, bagatelles (*later addition*: so far as their appearance is consonant with the laws of the faculty of sensation.)

[15:271] **625.** 1769? (1764–68?)
In everything that is to be approved in accordance with taste there must be something that facilitates the differentiation of the manifold (singling out); something that promotes comprehensibility (relations, proportions); something that makes grasping it together possible (unity); and finally,

something that promotes its distinction from everything that is possible (precision).

Beauty has a subjective *principium*, namely the conformity with the laws of intuitive cognition; but this is not an obstacle to the universal validity of their judgments for human beings, if the cognitions are identical.

(*Later addition*: In objects of love one readily confuses charm with beauty.)

One cannot very well convince someone who has a false taste; one can convince others that he has a false taste, but can only bring him to abandon his opinion by examples.

626. 1769? (1765–68?) 1771?? 1775–77?? [15:271]

(*Later addition*: An idea is the basis of the intuition. Beautiful things, cognitions.)

What pleases in appearance, but without charm, is pretty, seemly, proper (harmonious, symmetrical). If the charm springs from the immediate sensation, then the beauty is sensible; but if it has sprung from associated thoughts, then it is called ideal. Almost all of the charm of beauty rests on associated thoughts.

That the grounds of the distinction of beauty are merely subjective can be seen from the fact that one cannot possibly conceive of a more beautiful shape for a rational being than the human shape.

All cognition of a product is either criticism (judging) or discipline (*later addition*: doctrine) (instruction) or science. If the relations that constitute the form of the beautiful are mathematical, i.e., those where [15:272] the same unit is always the basis, then the first principle of the cognition of the beautiful is experience and its criticism; second, a discipline is necessary that yields rules that are sufficiently determinate for practice (as in the case of the mathematics of probability), and this comes down to a science the principles of which are, however, empirical.

If the relations that constitute the ground of beauty are relations of quality (e.g., identity and difference, contrast, likeliness, etc.): then no discipline is possible, and even less science, but merely criticism. Architecture (in the general sense) (the art of horticulture, etc.) is a discipline, likewise music. For in the former it is a matter of pleasing relations in the division of space, in the latter with regard to time. Hence the scholastic term "aesthetics" must be avoided, because the object permits no scholastic instruction; one could just as well demonstrate amorous charms by a term of art.

There are immediate sentiments of the senses or hypothetical (and substituted) sentiments. The former arise from everything that pertains to our state and when we ourselves are the object of our consideration. The latter: when we as it were transform ourselves into an alien person and invent for ourselves a sensitivity that we approve or desire. The sensitivity always concerns our own state and its charm or disagreeableness. One can have such substituted sentiments with regard to such states or actions toward which one has no personal sentiment of one's own. E.g., an imagined normal life after an illness; magnanimity were one to win the big jackpot. Voltaire has the most excellent sentiments in the name of the Romans and of everyone in the tragedy. Such substituted sentiments [15:273] make [us] neither happy nor unhappy except when they are connected *indirecte* with our state. They are only *fictiones aestheticae* and are always agreeable.

[15:273] **627.** 1769? 1769–70? 1770–71? 1772? 1773–75?
Taste is the selection of that which is universally pleasing in accordance with rules of sensibility. It pertains preeminently to sensible form; for with respect to this there are rules that are valid for all.

[15:273] **628.** 1769
The inner perfection of a thing has a natural relation to beauty, for the subordination of the manifold under an end requires a coordination of it in accordance with common laws. Hence the same property through [15:274] which an edifice is beautiful is also compatible with its goodness, and a face would have to have no other shape for its end than for its beauty. Of many things in nature we cognize beauty, but not ends; it is to be believed that the satisfaction in their appearances is not the aim but the consequence of their aim.

[15:274] **630.** 1769
In everything beautiful, that the form of the object facilitates the actions of the understanding belongs to the gratification and is subjective; but it is objective that this form is universally valid.

638. 1769   [15:276]

The question is whether the play of sensations or the form and shape of intuitions is immediately agreeable or pleases only through providing the understanding with comprehensibility and facility in grasping a large manifold and at the same time with distinctness in the entire representation.

To shape[4] there belongs not merely the form of the object in accordance with spatial relations in appearance, but also the matter, i.e., sensation (color).

639. 1769   [15:276]

The sensible form (or the form of sensibility) of a cognition pleases either as a play of sensation or as a form of intuition (immediately) or as a means to the concept of the good. The former is charm, the second the sensibly beautiful, the third self-sufficient beauty. The charm is either immediate, as Rameau believes that it is in music, or mediate, as in laughing and [15:277] crying; the latter is ideal charm. Through neither of these does the object please in the intuition. The object pleases immediately in the intuition if [15:279] its form fits with the law of coordination among appearances and facilitates sensible clarity and magnitude. Like symmetry in buildings and harmony in music. The object pleases in the intuitive concept if its relation to the good can be expressed through a concept that pleases in sensible form.

(conventional or natural taste.)

640. 1769   [15:280]

Through feeling I do not judge about the object at all and hence do not judge objectively. Hence I do not believe myself to have erred if I choose other objects of sentiment and also not if I have a dispute with others. A poor building, a ridiculous book gratifies, but it does not please on that account, and the most beautiful building gives him who regards it a poor substitute for a missed meal unless through novelty and rarity, etc. By means of taste I judge of the object, whether my state is much or little affected by it. If I call it beautiful, I do not thereby declare merely my own satisfaction, but also that it should please others. We are ashamed when our taste does not correspond to that of others. In matters of taste one must distinguish charm from beauty; the former is often lost in this or that, but

---

[4] *Gestalt*

[15:281] the beauty remains. The decorated room always remains beautiful, but it has lost its charm with the death of the beloved, and the lover chooses other objects. This concept of beauty, says Winckelmann, is sensual, i.e., one does not distinguish the charm from the beauty; for in fact they were just as much connected (although not confused) among the ancients as among the moderns, although perhaps they were distinguished in the concepts of the artist who wanted to express them.

[15:282] The beautiful person pleases through her figure and charms through her sex. If you whisper into someone's ear that this admired beauty is a *castrato*, then the charm disappears in an instant, but the beauty remains. It is difficult to separate this charm from the beauty; but we need only to leave aside all our particular needs and private relations, in which we distinguish ourselves from others, and then the cool-headed judgment of taste remains. In the judgment of the connoisseur, who cannot view it without abhorrence, the debtor's prison nevertheless remains a beautiful building; but this judgment is without any charm; it pleases in taste, but displeases in sentiment.

[15:282] **641. 1769**
Just as judgments of taste are mixed up with sentiments, judgings of good and evil are likewise never completely pure, but have a strong supplement of other representations of beauty or charm mixed in. Benevolence receives strong recommendations from honor, from the love of others, through the flattering reckoning of the happiness of others to one's own account. If generosity is directed toward a woman who is young and beautiful then all these charms are elevated by the interest in sex.

[15:284] **646. 1769–70**
A representation is sensible if the form of space and time is in it; it is even more sensible if sensation is connected with it (color). It is maximally sensible if it is ascribed to the observer, and indeed as observed by others. Beautiful objects are those whose internal order[5] pleases in accordance with the laws of *intuitus*. Beautiful appearances of objects, e.g., pictures.

[5] *Zusammenordnung*

647. 1769–70. *M* 230 [15:284]

Taste is really [*crossed out* the capacity[6]] the faculty[7] for choosing that which sensibly pleases in unison with others. Now since unanimity is not so necessary in sensations as in appearance, taste pertains more to appearance than to sensation. If we blame someone for a lack of taste, we do not say that it does not have taste[8] for him but that it does not have taste for others. A perverted taste, moreover, is that which applies to what is evil or injurious.

648. 1769–70 [15:284]

Taste in appearance is grounded on the relations of space and time that are comprehensible to everyone, and on the rules of reflection.

Just because in taste it comes down to whether something also pleases others, it takes place only in society, that is, only in society does it have a charm.

650. 1769–70 [15:287]

All of our representations, when they are considered with regard to that which they represent, belong to two main species: sensibility and reason. The former consist in the relation of objects to the capacity of our nature to be stimulated or in a certain way altered by them. The latter, however, applies to all objects as such, in so far as they are considered apart from all relation to the sensitivity of the subject.

Sensible representations are sensations and require sense, or appearances and are grounded on the faculty of intuition; the former [*crossed out* consist] are represented alterations of the state of the subject through the presence of the object; the latter are representations of the object itself in so far as it is exposed to the senses.

There are two sorts of cognitions of reason: through reflection[9] (rational) and through concepts of reason. Geometry contains rational reflection[10] on objects, but only through sensible concepts. Rational reflection is common to all cognition.

---

⁶ *Fähigkeit*   ⁷ *Vermögen*   ⁸ *schmeke*
⁹ *Überlegung*   ¹⁰ *Die vernünftige Überlegung (reflexion)*

[15:289] **653.** 1769–70

That which pleases in taste is not actually the facilitation of one's own intuitions, but rather the universally valid in the appearance, thus that the universal intuition or the universal rules of feeling are accommodated by the merely private feeling. For in the relation of sensations there is also something that is universally valid, although each sensation may have only a private validity of agreeableness.

The facility of sensations makes for gratification, but not the faculty of cognition, except in so far as that which we cognize has a relation to our state. Hence in solitude the proportions of sensibility cannot provide any gratification, but those of what belongs to us can do so in society, for others thereby have something to thank us for.

[15:289] **654.** 1769–70

In the beautiful there is something that relates merely to others, namely the symmetry, and something that relates to the possessor, namely the comfortableness and usefulness; the latter is still to be distinguished from the immediate charm.

[15:289] **655.** 1769–70

The play of shapes and sensations is also present in fireworks. For in the appearance there is either an object, which is always placed in space, or merely a sensation, but in accordance with relations of time; the former is called the shape, the latter the play, both are often found together. One is sensitive either to one's state in action or in passivity, in so far as one feels oneself to be dependent or to be a ground of one's state. Hence sensation is either active or passive. The sensation is active in the case of the form of appearances on account of the comparison that one makes.

[15:290] The active sensation is in itself always agreeable as well as all passive ones that promote the active one. But it is not a sensation of the object, but is immanent. All sensation of personality, namely of oneself as an active principle, is active; but the sensation of oneself as an object of other forces is passive; and the more it is merely passive, the more disagreeable is it. The passive gratifications seem to be forceful only by means of the active springs that they set into motion.

316

669. 1769–71 [15:296]

Pleasure: *A*; indifference: *non A*; displeasure: −*A*. There is no indifference of sensation, except only relative to this or that sense; for with regard to all the senses together, i.e., one's state, something is always either agreeable or disagreeable. Likewise in the case of the beautiful or the good. But there is a counterbalance: *A* − *A* = 0. One says: Satisfaction, indifference, dissatisfaction. Gratification, indifference, abhorrence. Beautiful, ordinary, ugly. Good, worthless, evil. Respect, disdain, contempt. Hatred, coldness, love. For just as all simple sensations are agreeable and become disagreeable only through conflict, so all simple relations of sensibility or reason that are positive are good and become evil only through conflict.

670. 1769–71 [15:297]

With regard to the beautiful or to taste there is in addition to art criticism, observation, and comparison of objects with taste through analysis.[11] The science of the beautiful, however, is an attempt to explain the *phaenomena* of taste.

671. 1769–70 [15:297]

Taste is the basis of [*crossed out* criticism and] judging, genius however of execution. Criticism is judging in accordance with universal rules. But since these rules must be grounded on taste, a man of taste is better than a learned critic. But there is also a doctrine of judgings that rest on universal principles of reason, such as logic, metaphysics, and mathematics.

He can always be well satisfied with himself whose judging does not demand for perfection more than he is capable of doing. Taste without genius brings dissatisfaction with oneself; sharp criticism of oneself (it is peculiar that this is so difficult) with inadequate capacities makes one write not at all or with much anxiety; in contrast, much genius and little taste brings forth crude yet valuable products.

672. 1769–70 [15:298]

We have dealt with that which pleases in so far as it belongs to our state or affects that and concerns our well-being. Now we speak of that which

---

[11] *Zegliederung*

317

pleases in itself, whether our state is altered by it or not, thus with what pleases in so far as it is cognized rather than sensed. Since every object of sensibility has a relation to our state, even that which belongs to cognition and not to sensation, namely in the comparison of the manifold and the form (for this comparison itself affects our state, costing us effort or being easy, enlivening our entire cognitive activity or hemming it in): thus there is something in every cognition that belongs to agreeableness; but thus far the approval does not concern the object, and beauty is not something that can be cognized, but only sensed. That which pleases in the object and which we regard as a property of it must consist in that which is valid for everyone. Now the relations of space and time are valid for everyone, whatever sensations they may have. Thus in all appearances the form is universally valid; this form is also cognized in accordance with common rules of coordination; thus what fits the rules of coordination in space and time necessarily pleases everyone and is beautiful. That which is agreeable in the intuition of the beautiful comes down to the comprehensibility of a whole, but the beauty comes down to the universal validity of this fitting relation.

The good must please without relation to the condition of appearance.

[15:298]
673. 1769–70

[15:299] A clock is agreeable in so far as it measures time for someone; it is beautiful in so far as it pleases everyone in intuition; in so far as it may be connected with a possible willing in general, whether it is connected with agreeableness or not, and thus can serve everyone for the measurement of time, it is good, and thus without relation to the state of the person who is thereby to be affected with charm.

Freedom is necessarily agreeable to everyone, therefore good; likewise understanding.

To love one's own freedom comes from agreeableness; but to love freedom in general is because it is good. But this love itself is good; for whoever loves freedom in general, whoever loves well-being in general, demands it for everyone, thus his will also pleases everyone.

[15:299]
676. 1769–70. *M* 252c

[15:300] The perfection of a cognition with regard to the object is logical, with regard to the subject aesthetic. The latter, since it magnifies the

318

consciousness of one's state through the relation in which one's senses are placed toward the object and through appropriation, magnifies the consciousness of life and is therefore called lively. Abstract representation practically cancels the consciousness of life.

683. 1769–70   [15:304]

In order for sensibility to have a determinate form in our representation it is necessary that it have an order and not just be grasped together. This order is a connection of coordination, and not subordination of the sort that reason institutes. The basis of all coordination, hence the form of sensibility, is space and time. The representation of an object in accordance with the relations of space is shape, and the imitation of this is the image. The form of appearance without representation of an object consists merely in the order of sensations in accordance with temporal relation, and the appearance is called a sequence (or series or play). All objects can be sensibly or intuitively cognized only under a shape. Other appearances do not represent objects at all, but only alterations. Pantomime is an intuitive form of a series of human shapes, while dance is one of a succession of movements in accordance with time; both together are **mimetic dance**. Dance is to the eye what music is to the ear, only in the case of the latter there are finer divisions of time in more exact proportion. The arts are either formative or imitative.[12] The latter are painting and sculpture. They concern either merely the form or also the material. That which concerns merely form is landscape design; that which also concerns the material is architecture (even the art of furnishing); even tactics and maneuvers are a kind of the beautiful arrangement. To the formative arts there belongs in general the art of producing any beautiful form, such as the art of beautiful vessels, of the   [15:305] goldsmith, the jeweler, the furnisher, even the finery of a woman, just as much as architecture. Likewise all work of gallantry.

Dance loses its charm if one will no longer please the other sex. For that reason the inclination to the dance does not last long among married men; but among women it lasts until they are old because they continue to want to please.

---

[12] *Bildend oder Nachbildend*

Appearance is a representation of the senses so far as it pertains to an object; sensation, if it pertains merely to the subject. The reflected appearance is the shape, the reflected sensation [*breaks off*]

[15:305] **685. 1769–70**
The play of shapes and sensations requires, first, equal divisions of time (uniformity in the measure of time) or beat, 2. a comprehensible proportion that can be drawn from the relation of the alterations of the parts.

The charm in dance is either corporeal and rests on the seemly motion of the limbs, that in music on the proportionate movement of the vessels of the body through harmonious tones. Ideal charm rests on the relation that the alterable shapes have on the affects or that which the tones that accompany one another have on the human voice and the expression of sentiment.

[15:306] **686. 1769–70**
The contemplation of the beautiful is a judging and not an enjoyment. This appearance makes for some gratification, but nowhere near as much as in relation to the judgment of satisfaction in beauty; rather this consists merely in the judgment concerning the universality of the satisfaction in the object. From this it can be seen that, since this universal validity is useless as soon as society is lacking, then all the charm of beauty must also be lost; just as little would even any inclination to beauty arise *in statu solitario*.

[15:309] **696. 1769–70**
All perfection seems to consist in the agreement of a thing with freedom, hence in purposiveness, general usefulness, etc. Since all things in an empirical sense are properly only that which they are taken to be in relation to the law of sensibility, the perfection of objects of experience is a correspondence with the law of the senses, and this, as appearance, is called beauty; it is so to speak the outer side of perfection, and the object pleases merely in being contemplated. Satisfaction through taste and through *sentiment*[13] have in common that the object is approved

---

[13] Here Kant writes "sentiment" in a Latin hand rather than *Empfindung*.

without regard to the influence that it may have on the feeling of the subject through intuition or use. Only taste approves of something so far as it merely affects the senses; *sentiment* in so far as it is judged by reason. What is most fit for the entire play of the senses thereby indicates correspondence with the sensibility of the human being and through that perfection, since in the end this comes down to consensus with happiness.

697. 1769–70 [15:310]
There are three sorts of pleasure in an object through feeling: 1. Immediate pleasure through sensation. 2. Pleasure in our state concerning the possession of this object. 3. Pleasure in our person. If the first pleasure obtains without the second then it serves for judging.

698. 1769–70 [15:310]
In the beautiful it is not so much the thing as its appearance that pleases. In so far as we compose its representation from parts that are seen in themselves the human body yields a concept that contains nothing beautiful.

There is a beauty in the cognitions of reason. Even usefulness can be a sum of appearances.

Notes on moral philosophy prior to 1770

[19:77] **6560.** 1762–63? 1769?
The weakness of human nature consists in the weakness of the moral feeling relative to other inclinations. Hence providence has strengthened it with supporting drives as *analogis instinctorum moralium*,[14] e.g., honor, *storge*,[15] pity, sympathy, or also with rewards and punishments. When these are among the motives, then morality is not pure. The morality that excludes all these *motiva auxiliaria* is chimerical.

[19:93] **6581.** 1764–68
Of the *sensu morali*.[16] The rules of prudence presuppose no special inclination and feeling, but only a special relation of the understanding to them. The rules of morality proceed from a special, eponymous feeling, upon which the understanding is guided as in the former case.

According to the Stoics, active love has its maximum when it is equal to one's powers. There is no internal measure in space, but only arbitrary ones; but a circle is an absolute measure.

The doctrine of the mean is really that a greatest good [*breaks off*]

[19:96] **6586.** 1764–68? 1762–63?
There are different grades of the determination of our power of choice:

---

[14] Latin for "analogues of moral instincts." [15] Latin for "parental love."
[16] Latin for "moral sense."

1. In accordance with universal laws of the power of choice in general, right.
2. In accordance with universal rules of the good in general, goodness.
3. In accordance with universal rules of private good, rational self-love.
4. In accordance with particular rules of a private inclination, sensuous drive.

The *motiva moralia* are of different grades: [19:97]

1. The right of another.
2. My own right.
3. The need of another.
4. My own need.

Utility to myself is not the ground of a right.

Utility for many does not give them a right against one.

Right is not grounded on motives of goodness.

In moral matters, we see very sharply but not clearly through *sentiment*; e.g., a braggart is held in contempt for a *criminis publici*, since one will not entirely sacrifice private duties for public ones. One takes pity on a miscreant.

6589. 1764–68? 1769? [19:97]
Something is good in so far as it is in agreement with the will; agreeable, in so far as it agrees with sensation; now I can think of a will while abstracting from the charm[17] of the person who wills or of the subject to whom this charm is a response, thus I can think of something good without regard to charm. Yet without all charm nothing is good; but goodness consists in the relation to the will, until finally absolute goodness consists in the correspondence of happiness with the will.

6590. 1764–68? 1769? [19:98]
Whatever contributes to the happiness of human beings does not thereby belong to their perfection. If the righteous man is unhappy and the

---

[17] *Anmuth*

vicious man is happy, then not human beings but the order of nature is imperfect.

In duties toward oneself the worth of a person and not of the condition must comprise the motive. Soul and body and their perfection belong to one's person. Perfection does not consist in accidental goods, e.g. knowledge, elegance, etc., but in the essential. The perfection of one's body must be given preference over all pleasures. Only in view of great obligation to comply with the right of another, e.g. to preserve one's virginity, is the body no longer attributed to the person; accordingly death itself, although not voluntary death, is bound up with the worth of one's person.

6593. 1764–68
The order of reflection on human beings is as follows:
1. The natural indeterminacy in the type and proportion of his capacities and inclinations and his nature, which is capable of all sorts of configurations.

2. The determination of the human being. The actual state[18] of human beings; whether it consists in simplicity or in the highest cultivation of his capacities and the greatest enjoyment of his desires. Whether a natural final end is illuminated by the degree of ability would be very worthwhile to investigate. Whether the sciences belong to this necessarily.

(4. The wild or the raw human being [*crossed out* of nature]. Whether this condition would be a state of right and of satisfaction. Difference between the personal perfection of the raw human being and that which he has in the view of another. Whether the human being can remain in this condition.)

3. The human being of nature should be considered merely according to his personal properties without looking at his condition. Here the question is merely: what is natural and what is from external and contingent causes? The state of nature is an ideal of outer relationships of the merely natural, that is, of the raw human being. The social condition can also consist of persons of merely natural properties.

---

[18] *Stand.* Throughout **6593**, *Stand* is rendered as "state" and *Zustand* is rendered as "condition."

4. Émile[19] or the ethical human being. Art or cultivation of powers and inclinations which harmonize the most with nature. Through this the natural perfection is improved.

5. In the outer condition.[a] The social contract (civil union) or the ideal of the right of a state (according to the rule of equality) considered *in abstracto*, without looking at the special nature of human beings.

6. Leviathan:[20] the condition of society, which is in accordance with the nature of human beings. According to the rules of security. I can be either in a state of equality and have freedom to be unjust myself and suffer, or in a state of subjection without this freedom.

7. The union of nations: the ideal of the right of nations as the completion of society in view of outer relationships.

The social contract, or public right as a ground of the [*crossed out* public] supreme power. Leviathan or the supreme power as a ground of public right.

6596. 1764–68 [19:101]

All right action is a *maximum* of the free power of choice when it is taken reciprocally.

The human being is disposed to see the extreme in every quantity, the *maximum* and *minimum*, in part because he does not stop in addition and subtraction without this *terminum*, in part because he needs a measure: The greatest is thought either [as] undetermined, in so far as one thinks the mere extending, as (number) space, time (everything); or [as] determined: if the greatest depends on determined relations. The greatest of all beings can be thought to be determined in many ways according to relations which the many realities of things can have towards one another, in order to diminish or increase the quantity.

---

[a] The state of nature: Hobbes's ideal. Here the right in the state of nature and not the *factum* is [19:100]
considered. It is to be proved that it would not be arbitrary to leave the state of nature, but instead necessary according to the rules of right.
    With the right of war individual persons would lose all matter of right; however, in the case of nations, because they can be seen as at peace with each other, one only has a right to attack the whole and the goods which belong to it.

[19] Here Kant refers to the central character of Rousseau's *Émile, or on Education*, a book he is known to have read very shortly after it appeared in 1762.

[20] Here Kant refers to Thomas Hobbes's *Leviathan, or the Matter, Forme, & Power of a Commonwealth Ecclesiasticall and Civill*, first published in 1651.

This greatest is itself given either through certain determinations of a thing, which are in changing relations towards one another, or it consists merely in arbitrary increase. The latter is an ideal of fiction, the first is an ideal of reason, which is differentiated into the merely mathematical and the philosophical ideal. The smallest (of what is movable) can be called a moment.

There are no real *maximum* and *minimum* in an absolute sense in quantitative *continuis*, but there are in *discretis*.

[19:103] **6598. 1769–70? (1764–68?)**
The means are only the form of intention, or the method of execution, the end is the matter. Actions are rational with regard to the means or to the end; in the first case reason determines the form, in the second case reason also determines the matter of the intention.

The understanding is only mediately good, as a means to another good or to happiness. The immediate good can be found only in freedom. For, because freedom is a capacity for action, even if it does not please us, freedom is not dependent upon the condition of a private feeling; however, it always refers only to that which pleases, so it has a relation to feeling and can have a universally valid relation to feeling in general. Hence nothing has an absolute worth but persons, and this consists in the goodness of their free power of choice. Just as freedom contains the first ground of everything that begins, so is it also that which alone contains self-sufficient goodness.

The moral feeling is not an original feeling. It rests on a necessary inner law to consider and to sense oneself from an external standpoint. Likewise in the personality of reason: there one feels oneself in the universal and considers one's *individuum* as a contingent subject like an *accidens* of the universal.

[19:104] **6601. 1769–70? (1764–68?)**
Of the ethical ideal of the ancients, the highest good. It is either negative or positive, that is, the absence of vice and pain, innocence and modesty, or virtue and happiness. These last are either so subordinated that happiness is a necessary consequence of virtue or virtue is a necessary form of the

means to happiness. The first is Stoicism, the second is Epicureanism. Finally, the ground of the highest good is either in nature or in community with the highest being. The former *principium* is natural, the second mystic. This latter is the Platonic theory.

We highly respect everything that is good in itself; we love that which is good *respective* to us. Both are sentiments. The former is preeminent in the idea of approval, the latter is more a ground of inclination. Whatever we find worthy of the highest respect we really respect highly; whatever we find worthy of love we do not always love, namely if it is not especially connected to us.

Both sentiments are somewhat opposed to one another. Partiality towards us makes us love, but not highly respect, the one who is partial to us.

We have a greater drive to be respected than to be loved – but a greater drive to love others than to respect them. Because in love towards another one senses his own superiority, in respect for another he limits this superiority.

All real moving causes of action are either pathological (or subjective) and are called impulses or they are . . . [21] (objective) and are called *motiva*. The latter are pragmatic or moral. The universal pragmatic *imperativi* are also categorical; however, they are more like such sentences which say what everyone wills rather than what he should will. [19:105]

6603. 1769–70? (1764–68?) [19:105]

Whatever pleases only under the condition of a certain inclination or feeling is agreeable; whatever pleases under the condition of a certain nature of the power of cognition, through which all objects of feeling must be known, is beautiful; whatever has a universal and necessary relation to happiness in general without relation to a special feeling or a special cognitive ability, is good. E.g., nonexistence necessarily displeases, although this displeasure is outweighed by special aversions; illness, mutilation of a person require no special feeling in order to displease. Everything right has a general relation to happiness, in so far as each produces happiness through himself, but in such a way that the rules of private intention

---

[21] Kant's ellipses.

do not contradict one another according to universal laws. All duties of love consist in the desire to further universal happiness (not merely one's own) through one's own actions.

An arbitrarily fabricated intention without motivating grounds [*breaks off?*]

[19:105] **6605.** 1769–70? (1764–68?)

There is a free power of choice which does not have its own happiness
[19:106] as an aim but rather presupposes it. The essential perfection of a freely acting being depends on whether this freedom [*crossed out* of the power of choice] is not subject to inclination or in general would not be subject to any foreign cause at all. The chief rule of externally good actions is not that they conform with the happiness of others, but with their power of choice, and in the same way the **perfection** of a subject does not depend on whether he is happy but on whether his **condition** is **subordinated to freedom**: so also the universally valid perfection, that the actions must stand under universal laws of freedom.

[19:106] **6607.** 1769? 1770? 1772–73?

The ancients did not coordinate happiness and morality but subordinated them; because both amount to two different things whose means are distinct, they are often in conflict. The Stoic doctrine is the most genuine doctrine of true morals but the least suited to human nature. It is also the easiest to examine. The Epicurean is less true but [*crossed out* more] perfectly suited to the inclinations of humans. The Cynic is most in accord with human nature in idea but least natural in execution and is the ideal of the most artificial education as well as of civil society.

The Stoic ideal is the most correct pure ideal of morals, however incorrect [applied] *in concreto* to human nature; it is correct that one
[19:107] should so act but false that one will ever so act. The ideal of Epicurus is false according to the pure rule of morals and thus false in the theory of moral *principii*, although correct in moral doctrine; only it conforms most often with human volition. The Cynic ideal concerns **only the mean** and is correct in theory but very difficult in *praxi*, although the *norma*. The former ideals were merely theories of moral philosophy, the Cynic ideal merely a doctrine of the mean.

328

6610. 1769–70? 1764–68?? [19:107]

Morality is an objective [*crossed out* dependence] subordination of the will under the motivating grounds of reason. Sensibility (*practice*) is a *subordinatio* of the will under inclination.

Inclinations, united through reason, agree with happiness, i.e., with well-being from the enduring satisfaction of all our inclinations. Single inclinations, if they hinder attention to the satisfaction of the remaining ones, contradict happiness. [*Crossed out* Affects] Passions thus naturally contradict not just morality but also happiness. Happiness, however, only contingently agrees with morality (*actualiter sive subjective*[22]); but *objective* it agrees with morality necessarily, i.e., the worthiness to be happy.

6611. 1769–70? 1764–68?? [19:108]

(*Later addition*: Concept, idea, ideal. The concept is a universal ground of differentiation (mark). Only the *a priori* concept has true universality and is the *principium* of rules. Concerning virtue, only a judging in accordance with concepts, hence *a priori*, is possible. Empirical judging, in accordance with representations in pictures or in accordance with experience, gives no laws but only examples, which an *a priori* concept requires for judging. Many are not capable of deriving their principles from concepts.

An idea is the *a priori* cognition of the [*crossed out* pure] understanding, through which the object becomes possible. It refers to the objectively practical as a *principium*. It contains the greatest perfection for a certain purpose. A plant is possible only in accordance with an idea. That exists only in the understanding and, for humans, in concepts. The sensible is only the image, e.g., in the case of a house the idea contains all the ends. The sketch is only the sensible in conformity with the idea. All morality rests on ideas, and its image in the human being is always imperfect. In the divine understanding there are intuitions of itself, hence archetypes.

An ideal is the representation of an object of sense in conformity with an idea and the intellectual perfection in it. Ideals pertain only to objects of the understanding and occur only in human beings and are *fictiones* to them. It is a fiction used to posit an idea in intuition *in concreto*.

The three ideals of morality from concepts. The mystical ideal of Plato's intellectual intuition. Holiness is an ideal of supersensible influence.

---

[22] Latin for "actually or subjectively."

Concept of plants, but not idea.)

[19:109]   The ideal of innocence. Of prudence. Of [*crossed out* wisdom. virtue] Of wisdom and of holiness. (*Later addition*: ideals, etc. etc. The Cynic ideal was negative.)

In the 1ˢᵗ, simplicity in morals and moderation in well-being.

2. Morality is seen as the necessary consequence of the prudent aim at happiness, therefore well-being in amusements and virtue in the active cognition of the means.

3. Wisdom has as its sole end the good, perfection; and well-being depends not on things and sensations, but instead the wise person is happy in his virtue. To the Epicureans special laws of morality were dispensable, to the Stoics special laws of prudence were dispensable.

4. Holiness sees well-being as blessedness. Results from community with God.

(*Later addition*: Platonism: with God through nature; Christianity: through supernatural means. Philosophy or fantasy. Enthusiastic, fantastic, mystical.)

The Epicurean ideal consisted in the **satisfaction** of the whole union of inclinations, the Stoic ideal in power and dominion over all inclinations.[23] That of holiness, in moral peace with all inclinations, i.e., their harmony, or also release from them, the Cynic ideal in the extermination[24] of all inclinations.[25]

(*Later addition*: The Cyrenaic[26] philosophy. De la Mettrie[27] makes morality into mere adroitness in satisfying our desires. Helvetius.[28])

---

[23] See, for example, Seneca, *Letters*, 92.3.

[24] *Vertilgung*. A variant reading is *Verneinung*, "denial."

[25] The Cynic school, founded by Antisthenes and Diogenes of Sinope in the fourth century BC, was renowned for the moral ideal of self-sufficiency (*autarkeia*) achieved through both physical training (*askesis*) and freedom in thought.

[26] The Cyrenaic school, founded by Aristippus of Cyrene, a disciple of Socrates, described individual feelings of pleasure and pain (*pathē*), and considered such feelings the only things to be pursued for their own sake, and thus the moral end.

[27] Julien Offray de la Mettrie (1709–51), a French physician and philosopher, was renowned as both a materialist and an Epicurean hedonist. His main works include the *Histoire naturelle de l'âme* (1745), *L'Homme machine* (1747), *L'Système d'Epicure* (1750), and *Discours sur le bonheur* (1750). *L'Homme machine* (which was translated into English as soon as 1749) brought him instant fame as well as opprobrium.

[28] Claude-Adrien Helvetius (1715–71), a wealthy French patron of philosophers as well as a philosopher in his own right, was known for *De l'esprit* (1758) and *De l'homme, de ses facultés, et de son éducation*, published posthumously in 1772. He was a radical Lockean who considered all human faculties as well as ideas as derived entirely from education and environment, and an equally

(*Later addition*: 1. The natural human being (not the raw and animal [19:110] but the wise human being who is regulated according to the intentions of nature). 2. The man of the world. 3. The wise man. 4. The Christian and Platonist.)

(*Later addition*: The highest good. The grounds of the highest good lie either in nature, and the precepts are only negative, like moderation and innocence, namely not to corrupt nature, or in art, applied to happiness (prudence), or in morality (virtue, wisdom), or in a being above nature: holiness and blessedness.)

(*Later addition*: Morality, worthiness to be happy, lies in conduct. All worthiness lies in the use of freedom.)

6619. 1769–70? (1764–68?) [19:112]
Epicurus takes the subjective ground of execution, which moves us to action, for the objective ground of **adjudication**. Zeno reverses this.[29] That Epicurus reduces it all to bodily stimuli appears to be more an opinion, used to explain the decisions of human beings, than a prescription. The **greatest spiritual** joys find the ground of their own approbation in the intellectual concept, to be sure, but their *elateres* in the sensible.

It is noteworthy that the representations of utility and of honor are not able to produce any strong resolution to emulate virtue, unlike the pure picture of virtue in itself; and even if one is driven in secret by a view to [19:113] honor, one does it not for the sake of this honor alone but only in so far as we can imagine that the principles of virtue have produced it through a hidden conviction. We must hide the mechanism of our self-interested impulses from our own eyes.

The most powerful means to impel human beings toward the morally good is thus the representation of pure virtue, in order to esteem it highly and to see clearly that one can esteem oneself only in so far as one is in conformity with virtue, but also to show that this is the only means to become valued and loved by others, followed by the greatest security and ease; one does not do the good for the sake of these, but they accompany

radical utilitarian whose supreme criterion of morality was the maximum of possible pleasure combined with the minimum of possible pain throughout a society.
[29] Zeno of Citium (*c.* 336–265 BC), the founder of Stoicism.

331

the good. One must excite the inclinations that most closely agree with morality: love of honor, sociability, freedom.

The *praxis* of morality thus consists in that formation of the inclinations and of taste which makes us capable of uniting the actions that lead to our enjoyment with moral principles. This is the virtuous person, consequently the one who knows to conform his inclinations to moral principles.

(*Later addition*: The presently anticipated uses can also impel us, even without any morality, to the same action that ethics would command. Only from mere motives of self-love no one would ever undertake such actions universally and in accordance with a universal rule without any moral motive or conviction thereof.)

[19:114] **6621. 1769–70? (1764–68?)**
The doctrine of virtue does not so much restrict the gratifications of sensibility as teach how to chose among the various types of them those that have greatest agreement with the rules of universal approbation, which in turn is always the best universal rule of prudence. Because to rely upon one's directing oneself in every case not with a rule but according to the greatest gain is too anxiety-producing and always leaves the mind in unrest. (Moreover the conduct that one universally prescribes must also be assumed as if its intention were known and approved universally.) There are, however, various sources of satisfaction from which we can choose. If by following universally approved means I cannot acquire riches, still I will have the confidence of my friends; I will be restricted, but can live without worry over responsibility, or freely. (*Later addition*: Science, skill, prudence, wisdom, knowledge, skill, etc., etc. Because knowledge can exist without skill.)

In general, nature seems to us to have in the end subordinated sensible needs for the sake of all our actions. Only it was necessary that our understanding at the same time projected universal rules, in accordance with which we had to order, restrict, and make coherent the efforts at our happiness, so that our blind impulses will not push us now here, now there, just by chance. Since the latter commonly conflict with one another, a judgment was necessary, which with regard to all of these impulses projects rules impartially, and thus in abstraction from all inclination, through the pure will alone, which rules, valid for all actions and for all human beings, would produce the greatest harmony of a human [19:115] being with himself and with others. One must place in these rules the essential conditions under which one can give one's drives a hearing, and posit these rules as if their observation in itself could be an object of our volitions, and we must prosecute even with the sacrifice of our happiness, although to be sure they are only the constant and reliable form [thereof].

Epicurus placed the ends of all virtuous as well as vicious actions merely in the relationship of the objects to sensibility, i.e., to the satisfaction of inclinations, and he distinguished virtue only through the form of reason with regard to the means.

Zeno posited all ends of virtuous actions merely in the intellectual and the conquest of the whole of sensibility.

According to him, self-approval was the whole of true happiness. Yet the contingencies of conditions were not a person's own. The merely inner worth of the person.

6624. 1769–70? (1764–68?) [19:116]
The theories of the ancients appear to be aimed at bringing together the two elements or essential conditions of the highest good, happiness and morality. Diogenes brought happiness down to something negative, namely simplicity of nature.³⁰ Epicurus brought morality down to self-produced happiness. Zeno brought happiness down to self-sufficient morality. The systems of the moderns try to find the *principium* of moral judgment. Besides those that derive it from empirical sources (custom or authority), they divide themselves into the moral theorists of pure reason and those of moral sentiment. Among the former, _____,³¹ takes

---

³⁰ Diogenes of Sinope, fourth century BC, called the "Dog" (*kuon*), from which the term "Cynic" comes. He argued that happiness lies in freeing oneself from dependence on all but a bare minimum of natural needs.

³¹ Kant's manuscript contains a gap at this space, apparently for a name not then recalled. Berger, the editor of volume 19, suggests that Kant might have been thinking of William Wollaston, author of *The Religion of Nature Delineated* (1722), whose intellectualist view that morality depends simply upon the recognition of certain truths was mercilessly attacked by Hume in the *Treatise of Human Nature*, Book III, Part I, chapter 1. But Werner Stark, appealing to passages in Kant's lectures on ethics (*Moral Philosophy: Collins*, 27:277, and *Moral Mrongovius* II, 29:622), suggests that Kant had in mind Richard Cumberland, author of *De legibus naturae: disquisitio philosophica* (A philosophical disquisition on the laws of nature) of 1672. See Stark, *Nachforschungen zu Briefen und Handschriften Immanuel Kants*, Berlin: Akademie Verlag, 1993, p. 157.

the rule of truth to be the guiding rule of morality, Wolff assumes it to be the concept of perfection. But the general concept of perfection is not comprehensible through itself, and from it no practical judgments can be supplied; rather it is itself more a derived concept in which that which occurs in particular cases is given the general name "perfect." From this concept (from which one would certainly not judge what pain or pleasure is) all practical precepts are derived (although only tautological rules, namely that one should do the good), with regard to morality as well as to happiness, and this difference is not shown.

[19:116] **6625.** 1769–70? (1764–68?)
All systems derive morality either from reason or from feeling (from the coercion of authorities and from custom).

Those from reason: either from truth or from perfection (the middle road of inclination: Aristotle). Wolff turns the general name of "perfection" into a ground for determining morality and does not name the conditions under which actions and ends are good and deserve the name "perfection."

[19:116] **6626.** 1769–70? (1764–68?)
The doctrine of moral feeling is more a hypothesis to explain the
[19:117] *phaenomenon* of approbation that we give to certain actions than anything that should firmly establish maxims and first principles that are objectively valid concerning how one should approve or reject something, act or refrain from acting.

[19:117] **6627.** 1769–70? (1764–68?)
The conditions without which the **approval**[b] of an action cannot be **universal** (not stand under a universal principle of reason) are moral. The moral conditions of actions make the actions that agree with them permitted and restrict the pathological actions. The approbation of an action cannot be universal if it does not contain grounds of approbation that are without relation to the sensible impulses of the agent. Universal approbation accordingly pertains to the objective end of the matter or of a capacity, (e.g.,) of the freedom of speech, and this restricts all subjective

[b] (Either the negative approval of the permissive will or the positive approval of the desirous will.)

ends. Hence the ends that the human being has from inclination are to be distinguished from the end for which the human being has for this or that quality, limb, or inclination. The latter[32] is the primordial or original end, the former the properly subordinate end.

6628. 1769–70? (1764–68?)   [19:117]
The first investigation is: Which are the *principia prima dijudicationis moralis*[33] (*Later addition:* theoretical rules of dijudication), i.e., which are the highest maxims of morality and which is its highest law.

2. Which is the rule of application (*later addition*: for practical application of adjudicative rules) to an object of adjudication (sympathy for others and an impartial spectator). 3. Through what do the moral conditions become *motiva*, i.e. on what rests their *vis movens*[34] and thus their application to the subject? The latter are first the *motivum* essentially bound up with morality, namely the worthiness to be happy.

6629. 1769–70? (1764–68?) (1771–72?)   [19:117]
If it were certain that all good actions met with no advantage and that good   [19:118]
fortune were merely a prize for cunning or a gift of blind accident, then a well-thinking person would still follow the moral rule from sentiment, as long as it did not bring about his own greatest injury, on account of its greater beauty. If happiness could thereby be immediately attained, then the moral beauty would be entirely entwined with self-interest and would never earn the honor of merit. Now being virtuous brings a natural advantage in accordance with universal laws, although in exceptional cases vice can also be a means to gratification; but now since virtue does not carry with it a certain advantage; thus one must unite the motivating grounds with the utility that they produce.

6633. 1769–70? (1771–72?)   [19:120]
The supreme principles *diiudicationis moralis* are to be sure rational, but only *principia formalia*. They do not determine any end, but only the

---

[32] Following Berger in substituting *dieser* for *jener* here.
[33] Latin for "first principles of moral dijudication."   [34] Latin for "moving force."

moral form of every end; hence *in concreto* the *principia prima materialia*[35] are presented in accordance with this form.

[19:120] **6634.** 1769–70? (1764–68?)
Hutcheson's principle is unphilosophical, because it introduces a new feeling as a ground of explanation, and second because it sees objective grounds in the laws of sensibility.[36]

Wolff's principle is unphilosophical, because it makes empty propositions into principles and offers the *abstractum* in all *quaesitis* as if were the ground of cognition for the *quaesitii*,[37] just as if one were to seek the ground of hunger in the desire for happiness.[38]

The ideal of the Christians has the peculiarity that it makes the idea of moral purity not only into the [*crossed out* ground] *principio* of dijudication, but also into the unremitting guideline by which he should be **judged.** The incapacity that we would like to plead is not clear, and hence the greatest anxiety arises from the ideal of holiness. The Christian lifts this anxiety by saying that God would make good this lack of holiness, thereby doing away with the inner incapacity for following rules. Whoever believes that one must make himself worthy and capable of this supplementation through all natural efforts is the practical Christian. But whoever believes that one must merely be passive in regard to all those
[19:121] actions in order to produce them through the labor of his heart and to produce his dispositions, and that in place of these certain religious efforts can move the divinity to pour holiness into them [*breaks off*]

[19:122] **6639.** 1769–70? (1764–68?)
The categorical (objective) *necessitas* of free actions is necessity in accordance with laws of the pure will, the [*crossed out* hypothetical] conditional: in accordance with laws of the will affected (through inclinations).

---

[35] Latin for "first-order, material principles of actions; concrete maxims falling under the general formal principle of moral judgment" (the *principia formalia* of *diiudicationis moralis*).
[36] Kant refers to Hutcheson's view that all moral principles are based on our feelings of approbation and disapprobation; see Francis Hutcheson, *An Inquiry into the Original of our Ideas of Beauty and Virtue* (1725), Treatise II, *An Inquiry Concerning Moral Good and Evil*, particularly § 1, "Of the *Moral Sense* by which we perceive *Virtue* and *Vice*."
[37] That is, Wolff offers what is just an abstract restatement of a question as if it were an answer to the question.
[38] Christian Wolff argued for perfectionism in *Vernünfftige Gedancken von der Menschen Thun und Lassen*, Halle, 1720.

6648. 1769–1775 [19:124]

An action that is good in and of itself must necessarily be good for everyone, thus not related to feeling.

6659. 1769? 1770–71? (1773–75? 1776–78?) [19:126]

Lex moralis est vel absoluta (unconditional) *vel hypothetica. (Later addition*: The former obligates without any condition, the latter is restricted through conditions of its necessity.)

6674. 1769? 1764–68? 1776–78?? [19:130]

The moral laws are grounds of the divine will. The latter is a ground of our will by means of its goodness and justice, in accordance with which God connects happiness with good behavior.

If there were no God, then all our duties would vanish, because there would be an absurdity in the whole in which well-being would not agree with good behavior, and this absurdity would excuse the other.

I should be just toward others; but who protects my right for me?

Index

Cambridge texts in the history of philosophy

Titles published in the series thus far

Aquinas *Disputed Questions on the Virtues* (edited by E. M. Atkins and Thomas Williams)

Aquinas *Summa Theologiae, Questions on God* (edited by Brian Davies and Brian Leftow)

Aristotle *Nicomachean Ethics* (edited by Roger Crisp)

Arnauld and Nicole *Logic or the Art of Thinking* (edited by Jill Vance Buroker)

Augustine *On the Free Choice of the Will, On Grace and Free Choice, and Other Writings* (edited by Peter King)

Augustine *On the Trinity* (edited by Gareth Matthews)

Bacon *The New Organon* (edited by Lisa Jardine and Michael Silverthorne)

Berkeley *Philosophical Writings* (edited by Desmond M. Clarke)

Boyle *A Free Enquiry into the Vulgarly Received Notion of Nature* (edited by Edward B. Davis and Michael Hunter)

Bruno *Cause, Principle and Unity* and *Essays on Magic* (edited by Richard Blackwell and Robert de Lucca with an introduction by Alfonso Ingegno)

Cavendish *Observations upon Experimental Philosophy* (edited by Eileen O'Neill)

Cicero *On Moral Ends* (edited by Julia Annas, translated by Raphael Woolf)

Clarke *A Demonstration of the Being and Attributes of God and Other Writings* (edited by Ezio Vailati)

Classic and Romantic German Aesthetics (edited by J. M. Bernstein)

Condillac *Essay on the Origin of Human Knowledge* (edited by Hans Aarsleff)

Conway *The Principles of the Most Ancient and Modern Philosophy* (edited by Allison P. Coudert and Taylor Corse)

Cudworth *A Treatise Concerning Eternal and Immutable Morality* with *A Treatise of Freewill* (edited by Sarah Hutton)

Descartes *Meditations on First Philosophy*, with selections from the *Objections and Replies* (edited by John Cottingham)

Descartes *The World and Other Writings* (edited by Stephen Gaukroger)

Fichte *Attempt at a Critique of All Revelation* (edited by Allen Wood, translated by Garrett Green)

Fichte *Foundations of Natural Right* (edited by Frederick Neuhouser, translated by Michael Baur)

Fichte *The System of Ethics* (edited by Daniel Breazeale and Günter Zöller)

Greek and Roman Aesthetics (edited by Oleg V. Bychkov and Anne Sheppard)

Hamann *Philosophical Writings* (edited by Kenneth Haynes)

Heine *On the History of Religion and Philosophy in Germany and Other Writings* (edited by Terry Pinkard, translated by Howard Pollack-Milgate)

Herder *Philosophical Writings* (edited by Michael Forster)

Hobbes and Bramhall on Liberty and Necessity (edited by Vere Chappell)

Humboldt *On Language* (edited by Michael Losonsky, translated by Peter Heath)

Hume *Dialogues Concerning Natural Religion and Other Writings* (edited by Dorothy Coleman)

Hume *An Enquiry concerning Human Understanding* (edited by Stephen Buckle)

For EU product safety concerns, contact us at Calle de José Abascal, 56–1°,
28003 Madrid, Spain or eugpsr@cambridge.org.

www.ingramcontent.com/pod-product-compliance
Ingram Content Group UK Ltd.
Pitfield, Milton Keynes, MK11 3LW, UK
UKHW020343140625
459647UK00019B/2284